T0377254

NINETEENTH-CENTURY RELIGION, LITERATURE AND SOCIETY

NINETEENTH-CENTURY RELIGION, LITERATURE AND SOCIETY

General Editor:
Naomi Hetherington

Volume I

Traditions

Edited by Rebecca Styler

LONDON AND NEW YORK

First published 2020
by Routledge
2 Park Square, Milton Park, Abingdon, Oxon OX14 4RN

and by Routledge
52 Vanderbilt Avenue, New York, NY 10017

Routledge is an imprint of the Taylor & Francis Group, an informa business

© 2020 selection and editorial matter, Naomi Hetherington and Rebecca Styler; individual owners retain copyright in their own material.

The right of Naomi Hetherington and Rebecca Styler to be identified as the author[/s] of the editorial material, and of the authors for their individual chapters, has been asserted in accordance with sections 77 and 78 of the Copyright, Designs and Patents Act 1988.

All rights reserved. No part of this book may be reprinted or reproduced or utilised in any form or by any electronic, mechanical, or other means, now known or hereafter invented, including photocopying and recording, or in any information storage or retrieval system, without permission in writing from the publishers.

Trademark notice: Product or corporate names may be trademarks or registered trademarks, and are used only for identification and explanation without intent to infringe.

British Library Cataloguing-in-Publication Data
A catalogue record for this book is available from the British Library

Library of Congress Cataloging-in-Publication Data
A catalog record for this book has been requested

ISBN: 978-1-138-56315-5 (set)
eISBN: 978-1-351-27236-0 (set)
ISBN: 978-1-138-57280-5 (volume I)
eISBN: 978-1-351-27228-5 (volume I)

Typeset in Times New Roman
by Apex CoVantage, LLC

To Julie Melnyk (1964–2017)
whose work on nineteenth-century religion and literature was
an inspiration to all of us and with whom we had been
looking forward to working on this collection

CONTENTS

Dedication	v
Editor's acknowledgements	xii
Acknowledgements	xiii
General Introduction: Nineteenth-Century Religion, Literature and Society	1
Introduction to Volume I: Traditions	9

PART 1
Evangelical Religion — 19

1.1 'Vital' Religion — 21

1 Extracts from Emma Jane Worboise, *Married Life, or, The Story of Philip and Edith* (1863) — 25

1.2 The authority of the Bible — 35

2 Extracts from C. H. Spurgeon, 'How to Read the Bible: A Sermon' (1866) — 39

PART 2
Anglican Developments — 47

2.1 The High Church Movement — 49

3 Extracts from Frederick W. Faber, *The Church, a Safeguard against Modern Selfishness* (1840) — 53

4 Frederick W. Faber, 'Easter Communion' (1856) — 58

2.2 The Broad Church Movement — 61

   5 Extracts from A. I. Fitzroy, *Dogma and the Church of England* (1891) — 65

PART 3
Roman Catholicism — 75

3.1 Roman Catholicism in Britain — 77

   6 Extracts from M. E. Herbert, *Anglican Prejudices Against the Catholic Church* (1866) — 81

   7 Extracts from M. E. Herbert, *Impressions of Spain in 1866* (1866) — 87

3.2 Roman Catholicism in Ireland — 91

   8 Extracts from [Anon.], *Letters of an Irish Catholic Layman* (1883) — 95

PART 4
Scottish Presbyterianism — 105

4.1 The Church of Scotland — 107

   9 Extracts from Norman Macleod, *The Lord's Day* (1865) — 111

4.2 The Free Church in Scotland — 121

  10 Extracts from Thomas Guthrie, *The Principles of the Free Church of Scotland, and a Plea for the Ante-Disruption Ministers* (1859) — 125

PART 5
Forms of Dissent — 131

5.1 Wesleyan Methodism — 133

  11 Charles Wesley, selections from *Hymn Book of the United Methodist Free Churches* (1867) — 137

  12 Extracts from Mary Fletcher, *The Life of Mrs Mary Fletcher, Consort and Relict of the Rev. John Fletcher, Vicar of Madeley, Salop* (1817) — 139

CONTENTS

5.2	**Welsh Nonconformity**	**147**
13	Extracts from Henry Richard, 'The Established Church in Wales' (1871)	151
14	William Williams Pantycelyn, ''Rwy'n edrych dros y bryniau pell' ('I look across the distant hills') [n.d]	160
15	Ann Griffiths, 'Wele'n sefyll rhwng y myrtwydd' ('See him stand among the myrtles') [n.d.]	161
5.3	**Unitarianism**	**163**
16	Extracts from Lant Carpenter, *The Beneficial Tendency of Unitarianism* (1845)	167
17	Anna Laetitia Barbauld, 'The New Commandment' [n.d.]	177
5.4	**Quakers**	**179**
18	Extracts from Thomas Clarkson, *A Portraiture of Quakerism* (1806)	183

PART 6
New Nonconformist Movements   193

6.1	**Brethren**	**195**
19	Extract from J. N. Darby, *Reflections on the Ruined Condition of the Church* (1841)	199
20	A. N. Groves, 'On Departure from Catholic Christianity' (1836)	203
6.2	**The Church of Jesus Christ of Latter Day Saints**	**209**
21	John Jaques, 'Necessity of a Living Prophet. Part 1' (1853)	213
22	[Anon.], 'Gathering' (1853)	218
23	William G. Mills, 'Our Home at Great Salt Lake' (1853)	222

PART 7
Judaism   225

7.1	**Orthodox Judaism**	**227**

CONTENTS

24	Extracts from Nathan Marcus Adler, *The Jewish Faith* (1848)	231
25	Nina Davis, 'The Ark of the Covenant' (1895)	237

7.2 Reform Judaism — 243

26	Extract from D. W. Marks, *Discourse Delivered at the Consecration of the West London Synagogue of British Jews* (1842)	247

7.3 Liberal Judaism — 253

27	Extracts from Lily Montagu, 'Spiritual Possibilities of Judaism Today' (1899)	257

PART 8
Religious Traditions from Asia — 265

8.1 Hinduism — 267

28	Extracts from Rammohun Roy, *Translation of an Abridgement of the Vedant, or, a Resolution of All the Veds* (1816)	271
29	Miss Acland, 'The Rajah's Tomb' (1866)	277
30	Extract from Kissory Chand Mittra, 'The Last Days in England of Rajah Rammohun Roy' (1866)	279

8.2 Zoroastrianism — 281

31	Extracts from Dadabhai Naoroji, *The Parsee Religion* (1861)	285

8.3 Islam — 293

32	Extracts from Syed Ameer Ali, *The Life and Teachings of Mohammed* (1891)	297

PART 9
Interpretive Traditions — 305

9.1 Radical Christianity — 307

33	Extracts from Joseph Rayner Stephens, *The Political Preacher* (1839)	311

34	[Anon.], 'Hymn Thirteenth' (1835)	317
35	John Henry Bramwich, 'A Hymn' (1846)	318
36	Thomas Cooper, 'God of the Earth, And Sea, And Sky' (1842)	319

9.2 Feminist Religion — **321**

37	Extract from Frances Power Cobbe, *Italics* (1864)	325
38	Extract from Josephine E. Butler, 'Introduction' to *Woman's Work and Woman's Culture* (1869)	330

9.3 Poetic and Aesthetic Religion — **335**

39	Mary Howitt, 'The Spirit of Poetry' (1847)	339
40	Extract from Anna B. Jameson, 'Introduction' to *Sacred and Legendary Art* (1848)	342

9.4 Natural Religion — **347**

41	Extracts from Theodore Parker, 'The Relation of the Religious Sentiment to God' (1842)	351
42	Extract from J. R. Illingworth, *Divine Immanence* (1898)	356

EDITOR'S ACKNOWLEDGEMENTS

I would like to thank the University of Lincoln for financial support for library visits to the British Library, London, the Library of the Society of Friends, London, and the Gladstone Library in Hawarden, Flintshire. It is also my pleasure to thank the helpful staff at these and other institutions including in Special Collections at the University of Leicester, and in particular Karen Waddell of the British Library Newsroom for tracing a missing reference as well as Graham Johnson of Special Collections at the University Library of Manchester for locating and sending me copies of the Brethren sources.

I am grateful to Garmonn Gruffudd at Y Lolfa Press for arranging permission to reproduce Gwynfor Evans's translations of hymns by Williams Pantycelyn and Ann Griffiths.

I would like to thank Leon Charikar for his helpful explanations of Hebrew script and vocabulary. Finally, I would like to express my gratitude to Kimberley Smith, Simon Alexander and Sarahjayne Smith at Routledge for their oversight of this project from its early days to its successful completion in what has been an unprecedented global crisis.

Thanks are due also to the University of Pennsylvania Press for permission to reproduce Lily H. Montagu's article 'Spiritual Possibilities of Judaism Today' from *The Jewish Quarterly Review* 11:2 (Jan 1899).

I am grateful to Calderdale Council for kind permission to reproduce 'Hymn Thirteenth' from the *National Chartist Hymnbook* (Rochdale: [1845]) from the *National Chartist Hymn Book*: 'From Weaver to Web: Online Visual Archive of Calderdale History': https://www.calderdale.gov.uk/wtw/.

Rebecca Styler

ACKNOWLEDGEMENTS

The publishers would like to thank the following for permission to reprint their material:

Y Lolfa Press for permission to reprint William Williams Pantycelyn, ''Rwy'n edrych dros y bryniau pell' ('I look across the distant hills'), in Gwynfor Evans (ed.), *Land of My Fathers: 2000 Years of Welsh History* (Talybont: Y Lolfa Press, 1992), p. 338.

Y Lolfa Press for permission to reprint Ann Griffiths, 'Wele'n sefyll rhwng y myrtwydd' ('See him stand among the myrtles'), in Gwynfor Evans (ed.), *Land of My Fathers: 2000 Years of Welsh History* (Talybont: Y Lolfa Press, 1992), pp. 346–7.

Jewish Quarterly Review for permission to reprint Lily Montagu, extract from 'Spiritual Possibilities of Judaism Today', *Jewish Quarterly Review*, 11, 2 (January 1899), pp. 216–30.

Central Library & Archives, Calderdale Council, for permission to reprint Anon., 'Hymn Thirteenth', *National Chartist Hymnbook* (Rochdale: [1845]), p. 12. www.calderdale.gov.uk/wtw

Disclaimer

The publishers have made every effort to contact authors/copyright holders of works reprinted in *Nineteenth-Century Religion, Literature and Society*. This has not been possible in every case, however, and we would welcome correspondence from those individuals/companies whom we have been unable to trace.

GENERAL INTRODUCTION
Nineteenth-Century Religion, Literature and Society

The last twenty-five years have seen a 'religious turn' in nineteenth-century studies. Where previously religion has tended to be overlooked or dismissed as an oppressive force to be sloughed off as societies modernise, it is now taken seriously as a subject of study. This can be attributed, in large part, to the public re-emergence of religion following the events of the late twentieth and early twenty-first centuries. Post 9/11, predictions of a 'worldwide secular society' no longer appear plausible.[1] Although various revisionary accounts of the secularisation thesis have been put forward, it retains few supporters in its orthodox form, namely that religious decline is 'a prolonged unilinear and inevitable consequence of modernity'.[2] This has particular significance for scholars of the nineteenth century since it was traditionally taken as the turning-point in the history of secularisation. No longer perceived as the 'quaint anteroom to a secular present', the nineteenth century can be studied for the richness and complexity of its religious life.[3] However, what religion is understood to be in this period is far from self-evident.

Commonly applied to beliefs, practices, experiences, institutions, texts and traditions, the meaning of the term 'religion' may appear obvious. Yet, as the anthropologist Talal Asad has pointed out, the notion that religion has a set of generic features and functions has 'a specific Christian history'.[4] The first systematic attempts to produce a universal definition of religion occurred in the seventeenth century as a result of the threat posed to the unity and authority of the Roman Catholic Church by the Protestant Reformation in Europe.[5] Understood in terms of beliefs about a supernatural power, and related practices and ethics, that 'existed in all societies', religion 'could be conceived as a set of propositions, to which believers gave assent, and which could therefore be judged and compared as between different religions' that were encountered through trade and colonisation.[6] The rise of comparative religion as an academic discipline in the final decades of the nineteenth century created an evolutionary framework within which Protestantism became the measure of religious advancement. Tomoko Masuzawa has shown how this led to the invention of 'world religions' as a universal category which simultaneously represents religion in Western European terms.[7] Furthermore, in removing the material practices of religion from specific historical and political contexts, the discourse of world religions spiritualises and abstracts them by turning them 'into expressions of something timeless and suprahistorical'.[8]

Much recent work by both social historians and sociologists of religion has been concerned with the varied and complex ways in which religion is socially, culturally and materially embedded. This framework for conceptualising the everyday reality of religion has become known as 'lived religion', a term that 'recalls the phrase "lived experience"'.[9] As the historian Robert Orsi has outlined, it entails a fundamental redirection of scholarship away from 'great hypostatized constructs' and 'frozen "meanings"' to engage with the mutability and messiness of everyday religious practice.[10] It, therefore, necessitates a shift in focus from traditions and denominational difference 'toward a study of how particular people, in particular places and times, live in, with, through and against the religious idioms available to them in culture'.[11] Sarah Williams has argued for the centrality of 'participant criteria' in defining the parameters of what is considered to be religious so as not to impose distinctions on historical actors that they themselves would not recognise.[12] Williams' own work on popular belief in Southwark in the late nineteenth and early twentieth centuries has been highly significant in this respect. Considering participant accounts of belief alongside institutional descriptions, she has shown the 'multidimensional character of religious experience' in which orthodox elements of Christianity could co-exist with popular superstitions and folk customs.[13]

The shift of emphasis away from institutional religion to lived experience has led to a sustained scholarly debate as to what the term 'religion' can encompass. There have been a number of attempts by sociologists and historians to capture the pervasive influence and ambiguous role of Christianity within wider British culture. The sociologist Grace Davie has coined the phrases 'believing without belonging' and 'vicarious religion' to encapsulate the residual attachment to Christianity of many people in the late twentieth and twenty-first centuries together with a widespread experience of estrangement from religious institutions but not from religion itself.[14] Historian Jeffrey Cox has coined the term 'diffusive Christianity' to explain the influence of the philanthropic work of the churches in the late nineteenth- and early twentieth-centuries.[15] It describes a 'general belief in God' and respect for the Bible that he found to characterise the religion of the urban working class in this period.[16] Callum Brown has extended this notion of the cultural work performed by religion to argue for a 'discursive' base to Christianity which ensured its 'popular acceptance' and 'support' in Britain up until the 1960s.[17] This is characterised as a 'dominant discourse' which 'infused public culture and was adopted by individuals, whether churchgoers or not, in forming their own identities'.[18] Such expansive definitions of religion are not without their critics. Dominic Erdozain has argued that Brown's method amounts to a rejection of 'the theological concepts that made religion meaningful for the historical subjects' of his study.[19] Erdozain's critique highlights a tendency within historical scholarship to treat religion as an 'alibi' for other cultural categories such as class or gender.[20] However, as Joy Dixon has claimed, an overemphasis on the theological 'returns us to an essentialised religion and a bifurcated understanding of the relationship between belief and culture'.[21]

In unpicking what religion meant in the nineteenth century, we are up against the added difficulty that our conception of what it meant to be 'religious' or 'irreligious' was drawn up by society in this period.[22] Secularism, as an irreligious movement dedicated to ridding society of false or repressive belief systems, originated in the early nineteenth century. The term was coined in 1851 by George Jacob Holyoake in an attempt to abandon the negative and adversarial connotations of the older word 'infidel' and to present secularism as a more expansive and positive value system independent of religion.[23] However, the organisational structures and thought of the Secularist movement were influenced by the Christian climate within which it originated. Its tactics resembled those of the Evangelical revival in terms of 'reading groups, Sunday schools, tract circulation and itinerant preaching'.[24] The historical relationship between Christianity and secularism has important implications for how we understand the categories of the religious and the secular. In tracing the ways in which nineteenth-century Christians and Secularists responded to one another, Laura Schwartz has shown how the categories of the religious and the secular were both 'interdependent and mutually constitutive'.[25] The attempts of nineteenth-century Secularists to construct 'a secular public sphere' anticipate twentieth-century arguments about secularisation as a natural and inevitable result of modernisation, but it 'sits in tension with the historian's realisation that Secularist activities must be studied within the context of Christian thought and culture'.[26]

That nineteenth-century studies has found the secularisation paradigm so alluring is, at least in part, because it was 'a Victorian invention'.[27] The nineteenth century, and the Victorian period in particular, has long been characterised as a time of religious decline and crisis. This process was attributed to social and intellectual forces in the form of urbanisation, industrialisation and the rise of material science. It found intellectual expression in debates about the compatibility of new scientific discoveries and Higher Critical approaches to the Bible with traditional Christian truth claims. At the same time, there was perceived to be a decrease in church attendance based partly on the 1851 Census of Worship.[28] However, the reliability of this data has now been widely questioned together with the recognition that attendance at a place of worship is not the only measure of religiosity.[29] It is generally accepted that both church and chapel experienced significant growth until well into the twentieth century.[30] Moreover, 'the era's scholarly climate' tends to be discounted as 'more or less irrelevant to sociological change in religious belief and practice'.[31] Charles LaPorte has, therefore, cautioned against taking contemporary warnings of religious crisis and decline at face value since they attest to 'the Victorians' impressions of secularization rather than secularization per se'.[32]

The volumes

This resource provides new opportunities for investigating the relationship between religion, literature and society in Britain and its imperial territories in the nineteenth century. Aimed at researchers and students, it makes available a diverse selection of harder-to-find primary sources. Spanning the 'long nineteenth century' (c. 1789–1914), it resists the traditional periodisation of the Victorian and its association with crisis and doubt in order to redraw the religious landscape of the period. The resource does not attempt to provide a comprehensive overview of religious life in the nineteenth century. Rather, the intention is to offer new ways of conceptualising nineteenth-century religion by privileging previously neglected and marginalised voices. A key concern of the resource is to integrate non-Christian religions into our understanding and representations of religious life in this period. Whilst it may be true that 'most Britons' in the nineteenth century 'identified with some form of Christianity', the study of Christian institutions, forms and practices has disproportionately dominated literary and historical scholarship.[33]

Each of the four volumes is framed around a different conception of religion. Volume I is concerned with 'Traditions'. Offering an overview of the different religious traditions and denominations present in Britain in the long nineteenth century, it avoids imposing an 'official' version of these traditions by appealing to participant voices. Volume II on 'Mission and Reform' extends the scope of the first volume beyond Britain to its imperial territories. It considers the social and political importance of religious faith and practice as expressed through foreign and domestic mission and philanthropic and political movements at home and abroad. Volume III turns to 'Religious Feeling' as an important and distinct category for understanding the ways in which religion is embodied and expressed in culture. Organised by feeling, the volume groups together sources from diverse religious traditions and genres to show how the meaning and expression of different emotions was dependent on a specific faith context. Volume IV on 'Disbelief and New Beliefs' explores the transformation of the religious landscape of Britain and its imperial territories as a result of key cultural and intellectual forces during the nineteenth century. It brings alternative religious movements and convictions together with forms of irreligion that took hold in the period. Each volume can be studied independently, but they work together to elucidate the complex and multi-faceted nature of nineteenth-century religious life.

Volume editors were asked to choose from a broad range of different types of texts. Literary texts appear alongside non-literary texts in order to illuminate the various ways in which literature operated as a vehicle for theological debate and religious expression in the nineteenth century as well as the importance of religion as 'a generative place for literary work'.[34] Nineteenth-century literary studies 'has long been dominated by narratives detailing the period's "crisis of faith", its secularism and secularization'.[35] Indeed, the Arnoldian notion that literature, and more specifically poetry, is a substitute for religion has functioned as a founding narrative of the discipline.[36] Generations of undergraduate students have encountered the claim in Terry Eagleton's introduction to *Literary Theory* (1983) that 'the rise of English' is to be found in 'the failure of religion'.[37] This idea has been successfully challenged by a growing body of scholarship investigating the roles which religion has played in reading practices and the development of poetic and fictional forms.[38] Feminist scholars have shown the importance of these literary forms in enabling women to formulate and circulate religious ideas since they were 'denied any formal theological role in the church and academy'.[39] The literary texts included in this resource provide an important avenue for exploring the voices of women and working-class subjects outside of 'official' and institutional religion.

The selection of source material raised important questions about the impact of digitisation on how researchers search for and navigate primary sources. Besides the large number of nineteenth-century works that are publicly available through educational collaborations, such as archive.org, Project Gutenberg and the Haithi Trust Digital Library, many religious and ethical organisations have begun to digitise large parts of their archives. Much of this digitisation work has been done by groups of believers which influences how they select, present and interpret the material. In many cases, the decision about what to digitise has been made on the basis of what is available rather than what is most representative or of historical interest. This resource combines material which is readily available in digital form with material that is not and provides accurate transcriptions of digital sources. It also supplies an interpretative context for sources in the form of explanatory headnotes to each source or group of sources and an introduction to the overarching theme of each volume.

The resource orients researchers from different disciplinary backgrounds within the field of nineteenth-century religion through the organisation of and introduction to texts within discrete topics. In some cases, we have chosen to include extracts from longer texts in order to offer researchers and students a way into more challenging material or to contrast better-known texts and authors with rare or unpublished material. In reproducing sources, we have tried to maintain a balance between accessibility and preserving the integrity of the text. Texts have been reset and original footnotes and endnotes have been standardised for consistency. Long explanatory footnotes have been removed or condensed where they do not add to an understanding of the author's terminology or arguments. For those new to the field, a comprehensive bibliography of literary and historical works on nineteenth-century religion is located at the end of Volume IV. The range and volume of scholarship included in the bibliography is testimony to the vibrancy of the 'religious turn' in nineteenth-century studies that has taken place over the last two-and-a-half decades. We hope that the sources included here will facilitate new avenues of inquiry.

Notes

1. Peter Berger, quoted in 'A Bleak Outlook Is Seen for Religion', *New York Times*, 25 February 1968, p. 3.
2. Callum G. Brown, *The Death of Christian Britain: Understanding Secularisation 1800–2000*, 2nd edition (London: Routledge, 2009), p. 11. For a recent defence of the secularisation thesis, see, Steve Bruce, *Secularisation: In Defence of an Unfashionable Theory* (Oxford: Oxford University Press, 2013).
3. Dominic Erdozain, 'The Secularisation of Sin in the Nineteenth Century', *Journal of Ecclesiastical History* 62:1 (2011), pp. 59–88, on p. 62.
4. Talal Asad, *Genealogies of Religion: Disciplines and Reasons of Power in Christianity and Islam* (Baltimore: Johns Hopkins University Press, 1993), p. 42.
5. Asad, *Genealogies of Religion*, p. 40.
6. Asad, *Genealogies of Religion*, pp. 40–1.
7. Tomoko Masuzawa, *The Invention of World Religions; or, How European Universalism was Preserved in the Language of Pluralism* (Chicago: Chicago University Press, 2005), pp. 1–33.
8. Masuzawa, *The Invention of World Religions*, p. 20.
9. Robert Orsi, 'Everyday Miracles: the Study of Lived Religion', in David D. Hall (ed.) *Lived Religion in America: Toward a History of Practice* (Princeton: Princeton University Press, 1997), pp. 3–21 (p. 7). See also, Meredith B. McGuire, *Lived Religion: Faith and Practice in Everyday Life* (Oxford: Oxford University Press, 2008).
10. Orsi, 'Everyday Miracles', p. 10.
11. Orsi, 'Everyday Miracles', p. 7.
12. Sarah Williams, 'The Language of Belief: an Alternative Agenda for the Study of Working Class Religion', *Journal of Victorian Culture* 1:2 (1996), pp. 303–17 (p. 310).
13. Sarah Williams, *Religious Belief and Popular Culture in Southwark c.1880–1939* (Oxford: Oxford University Press, 1999), p. 10.
14. Grace Davie, *Believing Without Belonging: Religion in Britain Since 1945* (Oxford: Blackwell, 1994); *Religion in Britain: A Persistent Paradox* (Chichester: John Wiley, 2015), pp. 71–90.
15. Jeffrey Cox, *The English Churches in a Secular Society, Lambeth 1870–1930* (Oxford: Oxford University Press, 1982).
16. Cox, *English Churches*, p. 94.
17. Brown, *Death of Christian Britain*, p. 13.
18. Brown, *Death of Christian Britain*, p. 8.
19. Erdozain, 'Secularisation of Sin', p. 64.
20. Erdozain, 'Secularisation of Sin', p. 64.
21. Joy Dixon, '"Dark Ecstasies": Sex, Psychology and Mysticism in Early Twentieth-Century England', *Gender and History* 25:3 (2013), pp. 652–67, on p. 656.
22. Brown, *Death of Christian Britain*, p. 31.
23. Edward Royle, *Victorian Infidels: The Origins of the British Secularist Movement 1791–1866* (Manchester: Manchester University Press, 1974), pp. 150–5.
24. Laura Schwartz, *Infidel Feminism: Secularism, Religion and Women's Emancipation, England 1830–1914* (Manchester: Manchester University Press, 2013), p. 21.
25. Schwartz, *Infidel Feminism*, p. 22.
26. Schwartz, *Infidel Feminism*, p. 23.
27. William McKelvy, '"Children of the Sixties": Post-Secular Victorian Studies and Victorian Secularisation Theory', *Nineteenth-Century Prose* 39:1/2 (2012), pp. 1–37, on p. 20.
28. Horace Mann, *Census of Great Britain, 1851: Religious Worship, England and Wales. Reports and Tables. Presented to Both Houses of Parliament by Command of Her Majesty* (London: Eyre and Spottiswoode for Her Majesty's Stationery Office, 1853).

29 See, Robin Gill, 'Secularization and Census Data', in Steve Bruce (ed.), *Religion and Modernization: Sociologists and Historians Debate the Secularization Thesis* (Oxford: Clarendon Press, 2001), pp. 90–117; K. D. M. Snell and Paul S. Ell, *Rival Jerusalems: The Geography of Victorian Religion* (Cambridge: Cambridge University Press, 2000).
30 See, Alan D. Gilbert, *Religion and Society in Industrial England: Church, Chapel and Social Change, 1740–1914* (London: Longman, 1974), pp. 23–48; Hugh McLeod, *Religion and Society in England, 1850–1914* (London: St Martin's, 1996), pp. 169–220.
31 Charles LaPorte, 'Victorian Literature, Religion, and Secularization', *Literature Compass*, 10:3 (2013), pp. 277–87, on p. 278.
32 Charles LaPorte, *Victorian Poets and the Changing Bible* (Charlottesville: University of Virginia Press, 2011), p. 3.
33 Joshua King and Winter Jade Werner, 'Introduction' to *Constructing Nineteenth-Century Religion: Literary, Historical and Religious Studies in Dialogue*, edited by Joshua King and Winter Jade Werner (Columbus: Ohio State University Press, 2019), pp. 1–21, on p. 5.
34 Karen Dieleman, *Religious Imaginaries: The Liturgical and Poetic Practices of Elizabeth Barrett Browning, Christina Rossetti and Adelaide Proctor* (Athens, OH: Ohio University Press, 2012), p. 4.
35 King and Werner, 'Introduction', p. 8.
36 See, Michael W. Kaufman, 'The Religious, the Secular, and Literary Studies: Rethinking the Secularization Narrative in the Histories of the Profession', *New Literary History* 38:4 (2007), pp. 607–27.
37 Terry Eagleton, *Literary Theory: An Introduction*, Vol. 2 (Minneapolis: University of Minnesota Press, 1996), p. 20. Terry Eagleton has since shifted his position but this work continues to be widely set on undergraduate courses on literary theory.
38 See, for example, Kirstie Blair, *Form and Faith in Victorian Poetry and Religion* (Oxford: Oxford University Press, 2012); Miriam Burstein, *Victorian Reformations: Historical Fiction and Religious Controversy, 1820–1900* (Notre Dame, IN: University of Notre Dame Press, 2013); Michael D. Hurley, *Faith in Poetry: Verse Style as a Mode of Religious Belief* (London: Bloomsbury, 2017); Joshua King, *Imagined Spiritual Communities in Britain's Age of Print* (Columbus: Ohio State University Press, 2015); Andrew McCann, *Popular Literature, Authorship and the Occult in Late Victorian Britain* (Cambridge: Cambridge University Press, 2014); William McKelvy, *The English Cult of Literature: Devoted Readers 1770–1880* (Charlottesville: University of Virginia Press, 2007).
39 Rebecca Styler, *Literary Theology by Women Writers of the Nineteenth Century* (Aldershot: Ashgate, 2010), p. 1.

INTRODUCTION TO VOLUME I: TRADITIONS

This volume sketches a broad picture of the main varieties of religious opinion and practice within Britain during the nineteenth century. 'Tradition' is here understood to mean a collective body of thought and practice which refers to the authority of the past, is transmitted across at least several generations, and which has a public manifestation in the form of institutions and/or a recognised body of literature. The category is applied to different faiths, denominations and movements both within and transcending these structures. The volume seeks to bring to light new aspects of well known religious traditions, and new voices from within them, but also to broaden the range of what has typically been included in surveys of religion in this era: firstly, by including examples from different national contexts within the United Kingdom of Britain and Ireland; secondly, by including faith traditions beyond Christianity and Judaism which had an organised presence in Britain by the end of the century; and thirdly, by extending the idea of 'tradition' to include interpretive schools of thought defined by categories of social and cultural experience rather than purely by theological, ritual or institutional concerns. It is intended that the sources selected, all (with one exception) written by enthusiastic 'insiders', will convey the coherence and experiential validity of each tradition for those who practised it.

The elements used by the 1851 Religious Census to distinguish one sub-group of dissent from another are useful tools to begin with for distinguishing one tradition from another – distinctiveness of doctrine, ritual and organisational structure.[1] However, these criteria imply an understanding of religion as defined 'from above', by the theological and institutional concerns of ecclesiastical elites. This approach tends to present faith as 'socially decontextualised',[2] demarcated from social and cultural factors which have in fact been vital in shaping religious experience. Approaches to studying religion 'from below' deny that religion can be isolated from 'secular' conditions and contexts but is inevitably embedded in them, as the tripartite title of this four-volume series suggests. As Joseph Kitawaga puts it, 'there is no such thing as a purely religious phenomenon. A religious phenomenon is a human phenomenon and thus is not only religious but also social, cultural, psychological, biological, and so on.'[3] Therefore, as well as including traditions defined by scholarly and organisational concerns that were relevant to nineteenth-century believers as well as to many religious historians, categories are also included that emerge from particular social and cultural contexts such as gender, class, geopolitics and aesthetics.[4] This is most obvious in Part 9, 'Interpretive Traditions', where class, gender, poetry and nature are the experiential starting points from which inherited religious texts and tropes are explored and reinterpreted.

The geopolitical dimensions of nineteenth-century religion are recognised by the decision to include perspectives from England, Scotland, Ireland and Wales. While no claim is made that this volume represents anything like a full picture of faith's regional variations in all the component nations of the British Isles (each of which boasts its own historiography for this period), elements of this have been included in order to broaden the scope of the study in this respect, and to redress the common tendency to present as British what was essentially an English experience.[5] This approach allows room for religious traditions that are strongly inflected by geopolitical contexts, not least the colonial dynamics within the British Isles (especially following the Acts of Union in 1706, 1707 and 1801). In Wales and especially Ireland, the most populous religious traditions were increasingly shaped by a consciousness of Anglocentric hegemony, as shown in some of the sources presented here. Inclusion of the four nations complicates some of the familiar narratives of nineteenth-century religion, and ways of organising an account of it, that are most applicable in the English context. The distinction between the established church and nonconformity becomes less straightforward in Scotland where the established Church was not tied to the state in the same way as the Church of England, but the same distinction is much intensified in Wales and Ireland where for much of the century at least the established Church was bound up with colonial authority. The anxiety about working-class alienation from the churches that beset English commentators in the wake of the 1851 census, and was also a concern in Scotland, simply did not apply in Wales or Ireland for most of the century where religion flourished among working-class communities. Hence, some entries in this volume feature nationally specific religious formations (such as Irish Catholicism, Welsh Nonconformity, Scottish Presbyterianism and predominantly English Wesleyan Methodism) while others represent denominations and movements relevant to the whole of the British Isles.

This volume also aims to be more inclusive than has been usual in such surveys in its treatment of faiths beyond Christianity and Judaism which, while not populous, were nonetheless part of the picture of late-nineteenth-century religious life and signalled the beginnings of the religious diversity that developed more substantially in the twentieth century. It has been shown that natives of various faiths from India, the Middle East, Africa and China were living in Britain since at least as far back as the eighteenth century.[6] An organised Zoroastrian community can be dated from the foundation of the Zoroastrian Association in 1861, while Muslims had localised communities focused on mosques formed in the 1880s and 1890s. It is more debatable to speak of Hinduism as a nineteenth-century tradition in Britain, if this suggests an organised community of faith practitioners, but the movement of Brahmo Hinduism was developed by Indian intellectuals in the context of British-Indian political relations and religious dialogue, in Britain and India – so it is included here. (Buddhism was known and influential among a number of late-century believers both orthodox and otherwise, but was not represented in communities of practice at this point – see Vol. IV, section 4.1. The first Sikh societies and Gurdwara were not established until the early years of the twentieth century.) It is important to recognise that, while these groups may not have been numerous or geographically widespread, focused on London and its environs and a few other major cities, they were not marginal politically speaking: Britain had its first Zoroastrian (Parsi) Member of Parliament in 1892, Dadabhai Naoroji, with another, Mancherjee Bhownaggree, elected in 1895; and the Brahmo Rammohun Roy was for a few years the star of liberal hopes in Britain as the 1832 electoral reforms approached, and was mooted as a potential MP.[7]

This volume forms the foundation of this four-volume series, depicting the established bases of faith on which (as Volumes II–IV develop) were built structures of feeling, missionary endeavour, and from which sceptics dissented. But this should not imply that this volume represents static bodies of unquestioned thought, based on a simplistic binary of tradition versus innovation. Revision and development are intrinsic to religious traditions whose members are, as Simon Marsden argues, 'always involved in the active rereading and reinterpretation of [their] own sacred texts, language and theological concepts'.[8] Although a tradition by definition grants authority to the past (whether located in scripture, rite or clerical office) this does not exclude the possibility of reconfiguring inherited ideas and forms in the light of changing cultural contexts which generate newly felt personal and political needs and new bodies of knowledge. As is now widely accepted in nineteenth-century religious studies, the once popular simplistic linear narrative of the 'loss of faith' has been replaced by a more nuanced appreciation of the varied ways in which faith responded to modernity, often to reconfigure inherited belief in the light of new contexts and understandings.[9] Many of the sources featured in this volume register a desire to reanimate habitual forms, to push the tradition in a fresh direction, and to reinterpret its central topoi. Yet it is rare for these authors to wear innovation as a badge of virtue. More commonly they present their revisions as a return to lost origins, regaining a lost purity or fulfilling the spirit of their tradition more fully than recent aberrations. Even the more obviously progressive or liberalising movements typically claim to be recovering an original flexibility or balance that has been obscured by an anomalous phase of dogmatism. Volume IV addresses religious innovations that depart more radically from inherited religious traditions.

* * *

Given that Christianity was the religion of the majority, its various formations fill half the topics in this volume, which are organised into sections based on denominational categories, movements and national contexts. 'Evangelical Religion' (1) is taken as the starting point, to reflect the importance of this movement to defining the ethos of nineteenth-century religion, above all in its Protestant forms. In the first half of the century, Evangelicalism characterised orthodoxy and most forms of dissent although its ethos spread well beyond these. Proponents of non-Evangelical forms of faith (Christian and otherwise) often explained themselves in terms that responded to Evangelicalism's priorities, above all its revivalist tone and its purist scripturalism. These features are represented here in entries on ' "Vital" religion' and 'The authority of the Bible'.

There follows a group of entries focused on what might be broadly described as established churches and/or national churches, which as noted above are not straightforward categories given the complexities of religious structures and demographics within the British Isles. 'Anglican Developments' (2) demonstrates two substantial responses within the Church of England to revived Evangelicalism, in the High and Broad Church movements, both of which can be connected to much longer-standing ritualist and latitudinarian traditions, and which had parallel developments within the Church of Scotland. The section 'Roman Catholicism' (3) shows an older faith resurgent, represented here in English and Irish formations since the difference in national contexts for this tradition can hardly be overestimated. 'Roman Catholicism in Britain' shows a newly tolerated minority faith following legal emancipation in 1829, while in Ireland it was the faith of the majority emerging from an era of suppression under the Protestant Ascendancy. As the entry 'Roman Catholicism in Ireland' demonstrates, Irish Catholicism often interwove religious with socio-political concerns and found little fellowship with its English counterpart. The section 'Scottish Presbyterianism' (4) represents the prevalent form of Christianity in Scotland in both its established and free forms coming to terms with the new contexts of modernity while trying to hold fast to original principles of spiritual purity and independence.

Given the number of nonconformist Christian denominations recorded in the 1851 Religious Census, 'dissent' can only be represented in its most significant forms. The census names as native Protestant communities in England and Wales the Presbyterians, Independents (Congregationalists), Baptists, Quakers, Unitarians, Moravians and Methodists. Methodism boasted numerous breakaway groups, from the Bible Christians (populous in south-west England) to groups like the Stephenites who had just one congregation (see entry 9.1, 'Radical Christianity').[10] Many of these denominations had branches across Scotland and at least the Ulster counties of Ireland, while nations within the United Kingdom also had their own distinctive forms of nonconformity. The section called 'Forms of Dissent' (5) contains entries on 'Wesleyan Methodism', the prevalent form of Methodism in England, followed by an entry on 'Welsh Nonconformity' which demonstrates the distinctive tradition of Welsh Calvinist Methodism and the status of nonconformity more broadly as (for many) the true faith of Wales. The other dissenting groups included are 'Unitarianism' and 'Quakers' which while not large denominations were significant in the cultural consciousness due to their distinctiveness from Evangelical norms and their disproportionate presence in public life. The largest denominations not explicitly featured here – Independents

(Congregationalists) and Baptists – are given voice through the authors featured in 'Evangelical Religion'. The section entitled 'New Nonconformist Movements' (6) features the 'Brethren' and 'The Church of Jesus Christ of Latter Day Saints' as traditions emerging within the nineteenth century with strong international connections. (For another significant new denomination, the Salvation Army, see Vol. II, part 2.4.)

Moving beyond Christianity, this volume features Judaism (Part 7) as a longstanding tradition in Britain, but which diversified into various forms in the nineteenth century. While native British Jewish communities were constantly added to by immigration, the larger scale migration from Eastern Europe towards the end of the century presented new challenges to how Judaism defined itself, and who was in charge of that defining. 'Orthodox Judaism' is represented by clerical and lay voices seeking to consolidate and deepen faith, including through female visionary power. 'Reform Judaism' in Britain was a uniquely biblicist variant, more traditional in most ways than its European and North American counterparts. Lily Montagu's negotiation of contrasting modes of spirituality, in the wake of late-century diversification of the Jewish community, can retrospectively be recognised as the beginning of Liberal Judaism in Britain – the only tradition in this volume in which female leadership was utterly foundational.

The broadly titled section 'Religious Traditions from Asia' (8) includes faith traditions predominant in the Middle East and in India which were brought to Britain through the channels of trade and empire by migrants (both settled and transient) and converts. These entries on 'Hinduism', 'Zoroastrianism' and 'Islam' are each represented by a voice from one native to the faith who spent time in Britain and participated in cross-cultural dialogue within the context of British-Indian colonial dynamics. The writers representing 'Hinduism' and 'Zoroastrianism' demonstrate a reformist drive to revise popular belief and practice to better suit modern values and a transnational context, while the speaker for 'Islam' is particularly conscious of his faith's potential appeal to those disillusioned with Christianity. All speak with a dual audience in mind, consolidating or reinterpreting their tradition for its 'insiders', but with a keen sense of responsibility for shaping outsiders' perceptions. Whether implicitly or explicitly these accounts offer resistance to pejorative orientalist assumptions regarding the inevitable inferiority of the spiritual and ethical ideals of foreign religions.

The section 'Interpretive Traditions' (Part 9) demonstrates some of the key ways in which faith was redefined according to impulses that originated in social or cultural experience, some of which can be connected to longer transhistorical faith traditions. Two relate to categories of socio-political experience: 'Radical Christianity' and 'Feminist Religion' remind us of the limited place given to the perspectives of the working poor, and of women, in clerically led formulations of theology and practice. These entries effectively present 'contextual' theologies whereby praxis drives the reinterpretation of a tradition's texts and symbols. These political theologies are resonant with the modern-day schools of liberation theology and feminist theology, whose radical forebears in earlier centuries have now been recognised.[11] The final two topics in this section take what might be called 'secular' phenomena as starting points for exploring the divine – culture and nature – demonstrating aspects of the immanentist emphasis that grew increasingly prominent in the second half of the century. 'Poetic and Aesthetic' religion demonstrates a post-Romantic sensibility which regards literary and visual artefacts as scriptures of a sort, channels of divine truth, in a reversal of Evangelical logocentrism, while 'Natural Religion' finds revelatory qualities in the non-human organic environment and in the human personality. Each of these four sections features two or more writers from different denominational backgrounds in order to best demonstrate that these interpretive movements transcended such institutional categories.

* * *

In choosing sources to represent these traditions, the goal has been to identify relatively little known texts which capture a central facet of the faith, denomination or movement: a key principle, or debate, or moment of development. Texts have been chosen by writers who belong to the tradition they speak about: they are adherents and enthusiasts, not critics. The aim is to present an 'insider' perspective whereby the reader is invited into 'a kind of imaginative participation in the world of the actor', and to evoke the 'web of values and beliefs and feelings implicated in it for the participants'.[12] The one exception to this is for the Quakers where, for reasons explained in the related headnote, the viewpoint is that of a sympathetic outsider. Texts have been chosen that make their case with clarity and eloquence, and that are reasonably accessible, without heavy annotation or very specialist reference (some of this has been removed in the editing to increase readability), although a high level of scripture reference is inevitable.

Both clerical and lay voices are presented, to reflect the level to which religious debate in the nineteenth century was increasingly democratised and conducted through the literary marketplace by 'amateurs'. As journalist and cultural commentator Walter Bagehot observed around the mid-century, religious professionals not only had lost the monopoly on public religious discourse, but were often mistrusted:

> In religion the appeal now is not to the technicalities of scholars, or the fiction of recluse schoolmen, but to the deep feelings, the sure sentiments, the painful strivings of all who think and hope. . . . We must speak to the many so that they will listen – that they will like to listen – that they will understand. It is of no use addressing them with the forms of science, or the rigour of accuracy, or the tedium of exhaustive discussion. The multitude are impatient of system, desirous of brevity, puzzled by formality.[13]

While the communications of 'schoolmen' are dismissed here as alienatingly technical, 'we' – the community of authors appointed by consumer approval – are deemed to be in touch with modern readers' true spiritual needs and therefore to have earned the right to define religion for modern times. The literary market allowed new kinds of religious leaders to emerge, including women who had no formal voice in the congregations they belonged to but became influential expositors shaping public understandings of the faith traditions to which they belonged (e.g. Anna Barbauld and Nina Davis), as well as men who were first and foremost poets, essayists and social commentators rather than religious professionals, or who wrote in limited spare time alongside earning a living, such as the Chartist hymn writers. Nonetheless, there is also a substantial number of ministerial voices in this volume, several central to their tradition while not widely known beyond it; and where the authors are better known (such as Charles Wesley, Frederick W. Faber and Theodore Parker), less familiar texts have been chosen from their oeuvre.

A variety of genres and forms are drawn on for the sources, although there is inevitably a preponderance of persuasive non-fiction prose – the exhortative sermon or expository tract, the apologetic treatise aimed at critics or inquirers, the speech focused on a special occasion, letters and articles for periodicals reflecting on a contemporaneous issue that tests a spiritual principle, the religious history, as well as scripture translation and commentary. About a third of the sources are more experiential forms, including the prose forms of life writing, travel writing, art history, and the novel; and a selection of verse including devotional and tribute poems, and a number of hymns. While Volume III is dedicated to exploring religious feeling outside the boundaries of structured traditions, it was felt important to include some experiential writings in Volume I, partly for the sake of variety but also because these often best evoke the inner logic of the world view being characterised. A mixture of textual modes does justice to religion's intrinsic embeddedness in personal and communal life rather than suggesting it can be isolated in an autonomous 'religious' sphere, and shows a variety of the functions which religion serves in the lives of individuals and groups instead of focusing solely on its ideational content. For some traditions, such as Methodism, the mode of expression is more significant as a defining feature than any doctrinal point.

Formal and generic variety also allows new voices to be recognised in the work of (re)interpreting traditions and shaping public understandings of them. Studies in nineteenth-century women's theology and scriptural hermeneutics have been enabled by a recognition that, while lacking a formal role as preachers or theologians, women used 'secular' forms of literature to 'reinterpret the nature of God and of Christ, the relationships between God and humans, and the Scriptures'.[14] Until late in the century, women rarely deployed literary modes requiring highly specialised scholarship and a stance of rhetorical authority, but tended to use fiction, poetry, devotional writings, life writings and social and cultural commentary to contribute creatively to religious discussion. Formal variety is also important in giving room to working-class voices: for reasons of time, education, and publication opportunity, working-class writers tended to favour shorter contributions to radical journals, often speaking for a solidary working-class perspective.[15]

Chartist and Methodist hymn writers and preachers from labouring backgrounds drew on rhetorical forms familiar from oral culture, producing texts with a strong performative dimension. Inevitably this results in a different theology from writings forged in universities and clerical enclaves, even before politics are added to the mix. Anonymous writers have not been excluded, nor ones about whom very little could be discovered despite reasonable scholarly efforts.

In terms of presentation, ellipses within the sources are indicated by [...]. Lengthy explanatory footnotes have generally been omitted (as is noted in individual headnotes), and brief scripture references have been relocated to in-text parenthetic references, giving full names of scripture books. Where an original reference is unclear, or a reference to a quotation is missing but has been identified, or a word requires translation, additional information has been given in square brackets, as have missing scripture references. Minor typographical errors in the original have been silently corrected, while original spellings are unchanged.

The headnote introducing each source commences with an overview of the tradition concerned, summarising the current consensus of knowledge. The source (and where possible, the author) is then contextualised in relation to that, in terms of what aspect or debate or developmental moment is being captured. A brief analysis is offered of the text/s identifying key ideas, rhetorical and literary techniques, and explaining the significance of the publication context, as well as showing the source's reception and legacy when this can be traced. When more than one source is featured (which is the case when a pair or group of short texts has been identified that helpfully complement each other), their interrelationship is shown, and what they collectively reveal. It is hoped that these headnotes, as well as the sources themselves, convey something of the range, reflective depth and creativity of nineteenth-century writers' engagements with their religious traditions.

Notes

1 *Census of Great Britain, 1851: Religious Worship in England and Wales, abridged from the Official Report made by Horace Mann to George Graham, Registrar-General*, revised (London: George Routledge & Co., 1854), p. 15.
2 Rosalind Shaw, 'Feminist Anthropology and the Gendering of Religious Studies', in Russell T. McCutcheon (ed.), *The Insider/Outsider Problem in the Study of Religion: A Reader* (London: Continuum, 1999), pp. 104–13, on p. 106.
3 Quoted by Peter Donovan, 'Neutrality in Religious Studies', in McCutcheon (ed.), pp. 235–47, on p. 241.
4 Some of the earliest studies of nineteenth-century religion to explicitly take this viewpoint 'from below' are, for example, Hugh McLeod, *Religion and the Working Class in Nineteenth-Century Britain* (London: Macmillan, 1984), pp. 9–16, and Gail Malmgreen, 'Introduction', in Gail Malmgreen (ed.), *Religion in the Lives of English Women, 1760–1930* (London: Croom Helm, 1986), pp. 1–10.
5 Gerald Parsons also notes this problem in histories of nineteenth-century religion. See his 'Introduction' to Gerald Parsons (ed.), *Religion in Victorian Britain*, vol. 1: *Traditions* (Manchester: Manchester University Press, 1988), pp. 1–13, on p. 4.

6 See Rozina Visram, *Ayahs, Lascars and Princes: The Story of Indians in Britain, 1700–1947* (London: Pluto, 1986), pp. 1 and 9–10. G. Beckerlegge, 'Followers of "Mohammed, Kalee and Dada Nanuk": The Presence of Islam and South Asian Religions in Victorian Britain', in John Wolffe (ed.), *Religion in Victorian Britain*, vol. 5: *Culture and Empire* (Manchester: Manchester University Press, 1997), pp. 221–67, on pp. 224–30.
7 Lynn Zastoupil, 'Defining Christians, Making Britons: Rammohun Roy and the Unitarians', *Victorian Studies* (2002), pp. 215–43, on pp. 216–17.
8 Simon Marsden, *Emily Brontë and the Religious Imagination* (London: Bloomsbury, 2014), p. 3.
9 See for example Timothy Larsen, *Contested Christianity: The Political and Social Contexts of Victorian Christianity* (Waco, TX: Baylor University Press, 2004); and Linda Woodhead (ed.), *Reinventing Christianity: Nineteenth-Century Contexts* (Aldershot: Ashgate, 2001), esp. 'Introduction', pp. 1–21.
10 *Census of Great Britain, 1851*, pp. 2–3.
11 See e.g. Christopher Rowland, *Radical Christianity: A Reading of Recovery* (Oxford: Blackwell, 1988), and Ruth Y. Jenkins, *Reclaiming Myths of Power: Women Writers and the Victorian Spiritual Crisis* (Lewisberg: Bicknell University Press, 1995). While 'Liberation Theology' was forged in late-twentieth-century South America, the term has been applied to other emancipatory theologies emerging from contexts of oppression.
12 Ninian Smart, *The Science of Religion and the Sociology of Knowledge* (Princeton: Princeton University Press, 1973), p. 20.
13 From the *National Review*, 1855. Quoted in Walter E. Houghton, 'Periodical Literature and the Articulate Classes', in Joanne Shattock and Michael Wolff (eds), *The Victorian Periodical Press: Samplings and Soundings* (Leicester: Leicester University Press, 1982), pp. 3–27, on p. 5.
14 Julie Melnyk, 'Introduction', in Julie Melnyk (ed.), *Women's Theology in Nineteenth-Century Britain: Transfiguring the Faith of their Fathers* (New York: Garland, 1998), pp. xi–xviii, on p. xii.
15 Florence Boos, 'Introduction: The Literature of the Victorian Working Classes', *Philological Quarterly* 92:2 (Spring 2013), pp. 131–45.

Part 1

EVANGELICAL RELIGION

1.1

'Vital' Religion

1.1 'Vital' Religion

The Evangelical revival of the late eighteenth and early nineteenth centuries brought a new energy and intensity to Christian faith which was felt to have diminished to complacent formalism. Commonly described as 'vital' religion and 'the religion of the heart', it placed strong emphasis on a personal experience of God and a purist refusal to compromise with the world's values.[1] Conversion was central, and everyday words and actions became endowed with spiritual significance in the quest for holiness.[2] Evangelicalism's impact on early nineteenth-century Christianity was widespread and profound, forming the Low Church anti-ritualist party within the Church of England and infusing most branches of Dissent. The earnest Evangelical temper had significant social implications beyond the practice of religion itself, shaping what have come to be regarded as essentially Victorian values, and forging 'a powerful sense of self' that fed the meritocratic individualism central to middle-class identity.[3]

The first extract is taken from *Married Life* (chapters 12 and 36), by the popular Evangelical writer Emma Worboise (1825–87) who published fifty or so novels over the course of her lifetime. The extract stages an argument between wholehearted Evangelical conviction, and the commonplace religion of the unconverted. Emma Worboise was a prolific novelist whose fiction played a role in the church party warfare that was conducted through literature in the middle decades of the century. Although she worshipped at Carr Street Congregationalist Chapel in Birmingham for much of her life, her characters are not always dissenters – she spoke for a more general anti-clerical Evangelical ethos. Evangelical conviction often empowers her women protagonists to challenge male authorities in the church or home and to insist that ideal Evangelical values such as moral integrity and compassion should apply as much in the public as the private sphere.

Married Life presents Evangelical faith as a wholehearted spiritual commitment which must set the believer at odds with the materialistic spirit of the world. After marrying Philip, a shop owner with ambitious business plans, Edith experiences conversion, and especially after the birth of their daughter (Mary) finds Philip's commitment to material advancement an increasing strain on the quality of their family life. The first part of the extract shows their first confrontation, when Edith insists that fulfilment of religious and moral duty in a coolly rational spirit is not enough; she applies the language of the heart and affections to religious observance in ways that Philip clearly finds embarrassing, and takes a stance of judgement that offends him. The dialogic form allows Philip's viewpoint to come through, often seeming reasonable, and understandably defensive and jealous towards this rival in his wife's affections, as he sees her faith. His satirical portrait of the fanatical Evangelical wife immersed in committees and do-gooding is reminiscent of Dickens's caricature Mrs Jellerby in *Bleak House* ('dorcasing' refers to the groups who made clothes for the poor, named after the New Testament character Dorcas – see Acts 9:36–39). But through Edith's voice, Worboise uses marriage not just as a dramatic context, but as a metaphor for Evangelical faith: love for God, like love for a spouse, is only a vital relationship if 'cold duty' is transformed by 'the fervent impulse of devoted affection'.

It was something of a commonplace to align Evangelical values with womanly character, and worldly materialism with masculinity, a gendering that could narrow religion's influence to the domestic sphere but which in more radical interpretations impelled women, such as Josephine Butler, to embark on public roles in order to redeem the corrupt world. Worboise offers a modest challenge to convention in this respect, making Edith vocally bold in judgement of her acquisitive husband, but effective only through the traditional womanly channel of personal influence. The second part of the extract is taken from much later in the novel when Philip's ambitions and pride have resulted in bankruptcy (a punishment often meted out in fiction to overweening businessmen, e.g. in Dickens's *Nicholas Nickleby* and *Dombey and Son*, Gaskell's *North and South*, and Eliot's *Middlemarch*). His new sense of humility and dependence result in a dramatic conversion – Worboise's favourite plot resolution – along with a rather formulaic, tract-like confession of faith. Priorities are transformed and masculinity reconfigured through the Evangelical woman's bold witness.

Notes

1 Hannah More, *Practical Piety; or, the Influence of the Religion of the Heart on the Conduct of the Life* [1811], 2 vols, 8th edition (London: [n.p.], 1812), vol. 1, p. 11.
2 See David W. Bebbington, *The Dominance of Evangelicalism: The Age of Spurgeon and Moody* (Leicester: Intervarsity Press, 2005), pp. 21–36.
3 Leonore Davidoff and Catherine Hall, *Family Fortunes: Men and Women of the English Middle Class 1780–1850* (London: Hutchinson, 1987), p. 88.

1

EMMA JANE WORBOISE, *MARRIED LIFE, OR, THE STORY OF PHILIP AND EDITH*

(London: Christian World, 1863),
pp. 100–107 and pp. 322–224, 324–228

Though Edith never recovered her girlish bloom, she now began to regain strength steadily; and soon she was able to go in and out, and attend to all her duties, with her accustomed energy and cheerfulness.

And now that she was able to go to chapel once again, she began to consider how to carry into execution the plans upon which she had resolved in the long weary days of her tedious recovery. Privately, and in her own heart, she had given herself to Christ; she had been living now for many weeks the life of an earnest Christian; and deep and continual was the communion between God and her own soul. But this was not sufficient: having received pardon and peace, having taken the Lord Jesus Christ for her Saviour, her King, her Master, it behoved her to stand forth, and declare, in the sight of all men, what God had wrought in her behalf. She knew that she had passed from death unto life; she knew that old things had passed away, that all things had become new; that the pleasures of this world had lost their power to charm, while private prayer and praise and the services of the sanctuary were now her supreme delight: therefore must she publicly make profession of her faith, and join herself in communion to a Christian church.

And yet it cost her no small effort to decide upon her immediate profession; for she knew instinctively that Philip would be annoyed at the bond thus formed—a bond in which he could not and would not participate. The subject of religion was scarcely ever mentioned between them: in everything else there was perfect confidence and thorough unreserve; only on this momentous topic, was there silence and hesitation between the two, who in all else were one in heart. It was not Edith's fault; often she strove to speak of that which was now so near her heart; but Philip always replied in that tone that made her so sad, and as quickly as possible changed the theme of conversation. But now she must hesitate no longer; if she held back, for fear of displeasing her husband, she was loving him more than Christ; she was not taking up her cross; she was ashamed of her Master.

So one Sunday evening she plunged boldly into the subject. She could not attend the evening service while her baby was so young, and so delicate; and Philip, having a severe cold, was staying at home as a matter of prudence. Little Mary was undressed, and asleep in her berceaunette up-stairs, and Matty was keeping watch over her, so that the master and mistress of the house were likely to enjoy their Sabbath evening leisure undisturbed. Edith felt herself getting very nervous, when, the fire made up, and the hearth swept—Edith never forgot Miss Wilson's lesson—Philip drew up his own chair and gently placed her in the corner of the couch, clearly ready for a "comfortable talk," as he always called a quiet hour of conversation with his wife. It was of no use to beat about the bush; useless to think of leading the conversation into the channel she desired; her heart only beat more and more painfully as the moments sped by, and her confession was still to make. At length she said, with apparent calmness, and with a courage at which she was fairly surprised, "Philip, dearest, I have something to tell you: I am going to see Mr. Stanton this week; I wish to be proposed for church membership at the next church meeting."

"Indeed!" was all the answer she received; but that one cold, almost stern word of pretended surprise spoke volumes; it made her heart sink within her.

She went on. "I have too long, dear, deferred coming to this decision; and I feel that it is but a poor return for the mercies I have received, thus to linger in publicly dedicating myself to the service of Christ. I can wait no longer; I *must* obey the commands of my Master, who has said, 'Do this in remembrance of me;' and O, Philip love, if you knew how sweet a thing it is to yield implicit obedience to One who has loved you with such a love, One to whom you owe all joy, all blessing, you would not wonder at my earnest desire to participate in *all* the privileges of the Christian life. Indeed, love!" and she spoke quite imploringly now, his countenance wore so rigid and impassive an expression—"I cannot help it; I cannot even in outward semblance deny my Master; I *must* make this profession."

"Very well," was Philip's quiet answer; "you need not use that pleading tone, my dear; I am not thinking of preventing you doing that on which you have set your heart. By all means see Mr. Stanton, and propose yourself for church membership. The sooner the better, I should say, since you have made up your mind about it."

"But you do not quite like it, Philip?" she replied, timidly. If she had made any other proposition in the world, even if it were to do something which he thoroughly disapproved, she knew his tone would be softer, kinder, more cordial. "I am sure you are not altogether pleased with me; indeed, if it were anything else, I would not think of it; your wishes are law to me, I hope you know that, Philip?"

"Except in the present instance, my dear; however, let us say no more about it. As to *liking* the step you are about to take, I cannot honestly say I do. I think you are very well as you are: you are a thoroughly religious woman; I would not have married you had I believed you otherwise, for a woman without religion is as hateful, as revolting as a woman without modesty. Can you not be satisfied to go on as you have begun? Let your religion be between God and your own soul; why parade it in the eyes of the world? Besides, I tell you candidly, Edie, I cannot bear the idea of your engaging in work and entering upon engagements in which I am to have no share. Our interests will no longer be identical; you will be for ever trotting off to church meetings, and maternal meetings; you will be always dorcasing or district visiting, or taking the chair at some—some—tiresome"—Philip was going to say "infernal," only he restrained himself—"some tiresome Babel of a ladies' committee, and I shall half lose my bright little wife, who has made my home and hearth the pleasantest, dearest, sweetest spot in all the world. But do as you like, my dear."

"O, Philip!" said Edith, grieved at his words, and yet more grieved at the tone in which they were spoken, "how can you say such things? God helping me, I will never desert my home for any public call, unless you, dearest, counsel it; and I trust I shall never neglect any private duty, even to serve the church to which I belong. I think, dear, my right place is here, by your side; my great work in life now is ministering to your comfort, making you happy as far as I can, and being a good, wise, tender mother to the little darling God has sent us. No! do not fear; so far my religion has taught me to attend with greater strictness than ever to my home duties. Once I did many things right in themselves, because it pleased me to do them; now I feel more than ever, how imperatively I am called to the same actions, the same solicitudes, and from a motive far higher than any by which I have hitherto been actuated."

"What higher motive could you have than that of making your home happy? What higher ambition than that of being your husband's dearest treasure, his wise and gentle counsellor, his *help-meet*, as God Himself has willed it?"

Edith was silent. At length she summoned courage enough to say—"Nothing higher, either in motive or ambition, could I find; only my love for you, for our child, must be founded on a love still higher and purer. I do wish, above all things—it is the dearest wish of my heart—to be a good, true wife. But I know now I can never be that unless I love Christ. O Philip, do not look so hard and cold."

"Nonsense! I am only trying to catch your exact meaning; your words are rather enigmatical to a man of my simple understanding. I hear you say you cannot be true to me unless you love Christ. Well, it seems to me that that is a mere sentiment, the peculiar language of ultra-religionists, rather than a plain rational statement, alike logical and self-evident."

"I may, indeed, be true to you in the lower acceptation of the term," she replied, mournfully, "though I begin to think there is no safeguard even for that, where only a nominal Christianity exists; but in the highest, grandest sense of the word I cannot be true to you, nor true to any earthly vow or tie, if I am untrue to Him to whom I owe my first allegiance."

"I cannot see why you may not continue as you have been; of course, I wish you to perform every duty with scrupulous exactitude; I strive to do so myself; I do not think any man living can bring against me, Philip Proctor, any one charge of injustice, meanness, or ingratitude. I am true and just in all my dealings; I defraud no man; I am kind to my inferiors; I am charitable to the extent of my means—say, is it not so? Is not my life as blameless as that of any of those men in Laurel-street yonder, who are members of the church, and authorities in all spiritual matters? Tell me, dear, candidly and impartially, do I ever offend against the moral and social law?"

She was distressed beyond measure; she could not bear to vex him, to make him angry; and yet if indeed she would be a true wife in the highest acceptation of the term, now was the moment for the manifestation of her unwavering fidelity. Half tearfully she said—"Socially, I am sure you never offend, no, never; there is no better citizen anywhere than my husband. But morally, dearest—O! who can lay his hand on his heart, and say that, as regards the moral law, he is perfectly upright and pure from blame? For it is not only our words and our actions that are to be weighed in the balance, but our very thoughts, and whosoever offendeth in one point is guilty of all. It seems to me that the chain of our lives is like the chain we heard of the other day at Wigan—like it in many respects—that was in the main of good metal, well wrought and tempered; but one link, only one link, was faulty, and that one imperfection was the cause of a terrible calamity! And so if one link be wanting, or imperfect, in the whole chain of our moral being, it is worthless, and fit only to be condemned."

"You are too profound for me," returned Philip, coldly; "I cannot enter into such fine distinctions. I try to do my duty, and I know that is enough—can you think God requires more?"

"Yes, I am sure He does. He says, 'My son, give Me *thy heart.*' If I strove with all my might to do my duty towards you, obeying your slightest wish, treating you with all outward deference, and yet keep from you my heart, would you value my obedience, my reverence? Would you not say, 'All this docility, all this external respect, and pains-taking servitude, is nothing, seeing that my wife does not love me. She acts only from cold duty, perhaps from fear; but never is she prompted by that fervent impulse of a devoted affection, never constrained by that *loving* loyalty that a true wife ought to feel towards the husband in whom her every earthly desire and joy ought to be centred.' Would you not say this, Philip?"

"Of course I should, and much more too; but I do not see what your ingenious supposition has to do with me and my duty."

"O, Philip, you will not see! You will give to God all *but* your affections, and therefore the all is of no account."

"Edith, my dear, if we talk for seven years we shall never understand each other; henceforth let there be silence on this subject; let us agree to differ, since it must be so; but let us differ tacitly. If I am baited in this way I cannot answer for the consequences. I shall lose my temper, and say things I shall be very sorry to have said when the heat of altercation is over. You understand me; this subject is not to be renewed on any pretence whatever?"

"Yes," said Edith, meekly; "but you do not forbid my going to Mr. Stanton?"

"I have said that you are at liberty to act as you think proper," he replied, impatiently; "pray do not look so like a martyr: I should never dream of putting any restraint on your inclinations; so, once for all, there is my answer. Only do not expect from me any sympathy—any co-operation."

He spoke with so much heat that it was evident his threat of being seriously angry was fulfilled without loss of time.

And then Philip took up his book, and appeared absorbed in its contents: for an hour passed, and he spoke no word to Edith, who sat shading her face with her hand, and trying to keep back the rising tears that would fall over her *Sunday at Home;* and then, feeling that he had punished his offending wife quite sufficiently, he shut up the volume that had interested him so mightily, and began to talk volubly on indifferent subjects, and Edith tried to enter into the conversation; but in spite of all her endeavours, her voice would tremble, and her thoughts would wander, and her eyes would fill with tears when she met her husband's glance. Nothing provokes a man so thoroughly as crying, especially if he has been the actual source of the distress. So after a time the conversation flagged. Philip yawned, and pushed the coals about on the grate with the toe of his slipper, to its no small detriment; and Edith strove to find some meaning in the page before her, but in vain; and she looked very pale and weary, and felt sick at heart. She was really glad when the baby's piping little cry was heard above, for it gave her a fair excuse for going away; and she sprang up, saying "baby wanted her;" and ran up-stairs so quickly that her breath was almost gone when she reached the landing. Then she tried to recover herself, gasping and leaning on the baluster for support; but the tears that had been so long repressed, or only suffered to drop at rare intervals, burst forth in an irrepressible gush. In vain she tried to keep down the choking sobs; they would come loud and fast; and her limbs trembled so much, that, if she had not clung to the rail with desperate energy, she would have fallen. [...]

The long, sad day wore away—all the bustle and turmoil of life without, the shadow of death within! The hours glided by; that familiar voice from the cupola of St. Paul's tolled quarter after quarter, and stroke after stroke; the hot, close afternoon waned, and the narrow streets lay in cool shadow, and still there was no change. Sometimes Edith feared that there would be no change, save that which parts flesh and spirit. She feared lest there should be no awakening from that death-like trance on this side the grave, no revival of sense and memory, no recognition, no last looks, no last words. And the agony of this apprehension was almost beyond endurance; again and again she sank on her knees, praying that if it were possible this cup might pass from her—that at least it might be vouchsafed to her to hear from those dear lips, ere they closed for ever on earth, some words of peace, some assurance that the end of life was indeed gained, and the hope of eternal life, in and through Jesus Christ, steadfast and sure. She thought she could be almost content to be left alone, in an empty, dreary world, if only she were certain that the parting was but for a season—that they would meet again in their Father's house, to be for ever with the Lord. Yes, she felt that she could—bitter as it must be—forego the sight of those dear eyes, and the sound of that dear, familiar voice, and the clasp of that warm, strong hand, if only she were certified of the safety of that immortal soul. Almost had Philip been persuaded to be a Christian; but had not the cares of the world and the weary burden of his anxieties choked the good seed of the Blessed Word?

Then she thought of that miserable time, a year ago, when she had persuaded herself that Philip was no more the deeply-beloved of her heart. Justly estranged for awhile she might have been; but had she not nursed her proud resentment too long? She remembered her own dull, aching sense of sorrow, the void that had oppressed her through all those sad days of alienation; but more clearly she remembered Philip's shadowed brow and depressed mind. She felt now that she had been very cruel, that she had tortured him with her coldness, and tried him very sorely; especially the recollection of that night when he came to meet her on her return from chapel—the last Sunday evening in Liverpool—when she had repelled his affection, and hardened herself against his endeavours for reconciliation, came vividly before her mind. True it was, the shadow was not abiding; long since the coldness had melted away; injured pride had died out, and Philip was dearer to her than ever; but she could not forget the pain she had given him; with cruel pertinacity those hours came back again with ever-recurring force and minuteness.

And now it seemed too probable that Philip was dying: she would never be able to assure him again of her unchanged affection; and while life lasted the recollection of that sole, brief estrangement would haunt her memory—a spectre of the past, never to be laid, and never to be shunned! [...]

She ventured to whisper his name; and in strange, thick, low utterance came the answer, "Are you there, Edie, Edie?"

"Yes, dearest! Are you better?"

"I don't know: I am dying, Edie I am so glad you are come."

"No, dear, you will not die if we take care of you. But you must be quite quiet now: I have some medicine that Dr. Clinton left for you."

"It is better for me to die. I have ruined you, Edie I remember it now: I have done you no good, but harm."

"Hush! hush! my poor darling! Indeed, for my sake, you must say no more; only, dear, never mind about the ruin: I don't mind it! When you get well we will begin life over again. Dear me! we are not thirty, either of us, and we shall have learnt experience. You cannot think how brave I feel: indeed, the money trouble is nothing, if only you will get well and strong again."

"Do you know that you will lose your home?"

"Wherever my husband is will be my home."

"But the stock—the furniture—all we have must go!"

"I suppose so: it seems right and just for it to go. What then? we have each other and the dear children; and we have brains to think and plan, and hands to work: we will start afresh, Philip: I am not at all afraid Only do not think about it now: it will do you harm."

And Edith's brave words did their work, for they were not spoken for the nonce, but from the very depths of her heart: with God to bless her, and with her husband by her side, she was *not* afraid of cares, or poverty, or toil. Even a vision of Mr. Grabb, holding solitary Bacchanalian orgies in her drawing-room, did not greatly disquiet her; and from her tone and spirit her husband gathered calmness and strength.

When Mrs. Etherington returned, she thought Philip was certainly better. She had feared that returning consciousness might be only the harbinger of approaching dissolution; but there was an undefinable something in the expression of his face that told rather of renewed existence than of quickly-waning life. The deathly pallor was still there; one hand and arm lay nearly paralyzed on the counterpane, and articulation was difficult and indistinct; but there was a light in the eyes, dim and heavy as they were, that proclaimed unmistakeably the fresh impetus given to the life-springs, that had seemed a little while ago at their lowest ebb; the constitution, naturally vigorous and untampered with, was about to assert its sway; there would be still a season of suffering, and weakness, and intense anxiety for those who kept loving watch by his side, but there was every reason now to hope that this sickness of Philip Proctor's would not be unto death.

Such, at least, was Mrs. Etherington's impression; and it was confirmed when, later in the evening, Dr. Clinton came in, and congratulated Edith upon her good nursing.

But, though the worst was mercifully averted, Philip's progress to convalescence was slow and uncertain; sometimes he would seem better, and his anxious wife would begin to cherish bright hopes of what a few more days might effect, and again the bad symptoms would return, the numbness and nervelessness of the stricken members become more apparent, and the whole system appear sinking under the oppression of mind, and the long weariness of confinement. Sickness was to Philip Proctor an entirely new phase of existence; but he was very patient, and as Matty said, when she came back, as easy to manage as a baby.

And so the time went on, and Mr. Heathcote kept his word, and managed Philip's affairs with an ability and an address that surprised even his wife, who, of course, gave him credit for the profoundest sagacity, and for capabilities rarely, if ever, exceeded in the nineteenth century! He rather seemed to enjoy having to deal with day-books and ledgers once more. For old associations' sake, he affectionately regarded business matters; he only regretted that the task, which in itself was far from irksome, should have been imposed upon him through the painful necessities of his friend.

It was owing to him that the most favourable arrangements were concluded, so that Philip and Edith were permitted to remain unmolested for a far longer period than they had dared to anticipate, and it was not till the end of September that they found themselves called upon to leave the house where they had suffered so much, and that was endeared to them for many reasons, notwithstanding all the struggles and the anxieties that had been their lot ever since the very commencement of their London career.

It was the last evening of their stay, and the husband and wife sat alone together in the drawing-room, when all things were arranged for removal on the morrow, for convenience of sale. Susy and baby were again staying with Mrs. Heathcote, and Philip, and Edith, and Mary were going to spend a few days with Mrs. Etherington, till the humble domicile they had taken should be ready for their reception.

Philip still bore the traces of his severe illness; he was very thin, and he stooped, and his face showed many lines of anxiety, and pain of body and of mind; he looked quite forty years of age. Really, his thirtieth birthday had yet to arrive. The evening was wet and chilly, and they were glad to draw towards the fire, and enjoy, for the last time, the comfort of the hearth which, true to her principles, Edith had kept ever bright and cheery. They were rather silent, and, for some time, they listened sadly to the rain beating against the windows, and to the moaning and sighing of the wild autumnal wind in the long passages and empty rooms of the nearly deserted house.

At last Philip spoke:—"Edith, I have something to tell you: I want to say it here, before we go to another place, and now, before we begin what seems to me a new and untried career."

"Well, dearest?"

"Do you remember one Sunday evening in Myrtle-place, soon after little Mary was born—the Sunday evening when you told me you intended making full and public profession of your faith?"

"I remember it well, dear Philip."

"And you have never regretted that decision, my dear?"

"Never! How could I? It was only deferred too long."

"But I was so unkind to you—so unjust. I must have pained you exceedingly."

"Never mind that now, dear Philip. I, too, was very unkind to you before we left Castle-street."

"And I deserved it. Edith, it was your coldness and displeasure then, when contrasted with your natural gentleness and your previous warm affection, that first roused me from my egotistical complacency. I began to doubt myself: and from doubting my own wisdom in temporal matters, I fell to considering my long-cherished opinions on matters of faith; and there, too, I was led, or rather constrained—for it was spite of myself—to arrive at the conviction that I had been all my life little better than a fool."

"My dear husband! But is that all you wanted to tell me?"

"No, Edie; only a part of it. I want to make the same avowal to you, that you made to me so long ago, on that memorable Sunday evening in Myrtle-place. I want to tell you that I henceforth renounce the self-righteous creed I have so long professed; it is *not* enough to be upright, and strictly moral, and a rigid Nonconformist. I have found it so; and I desire now to cast in my lot with the people of God, with those whose only trust is in Jesus Christ our Lord; who strive to live to His glory, and who find in Him their strong salvation, their only and inalienable hope, their joy, and their earnest of the peace on earth and the bliss in heaven, which is their eternal inheritance."

"O, Philip!" and Edith could only hide her face, and weep in the fullness of her great joy. Presently she said, "O, how good God is! How happy we are! Philip, dear, will you not kneel down with me now, and thank God for me—for us both? I can bear anything now that you and I are travelling together on the same road. Never mind the poverty; it is good for us, or it would not have come; we are rich, though poor in worldly goods—rich in love, rich in friends, rich in content, and, above all, rich in the blessing that is more than all other blessings, now, or in the world to come! O, Philip! I shall always love this dingy city-home, where this last great blessing has come to me. Now let us thank our Father for all his mercies."

1.2

The Authority of the Bible

1.2 The Authority of the Bible

The Bible held a central place in Evangelical spirituality, upheld as the living revelation of God which contained all that was necessary for spiritual life. Evangelical preaching more often than not consisted of the exposition of a passage from the Bible, while private scripture reading and reflection were encouraged as a daily devotional practice. This was undertaken with faith that the Holy Spirit would speak through the text to apply the Bible as a living word directly to the believer's life. The Bible was held to be self-interpreting, needing no external scholarly key to make sense of its truths – a standpoint that had anti-elitist and anti-intellectual implications.

Charles Haddon Spurgeon (1834–92) epitomised this faith in the direct verbal inspiration of the Bible, which underpinned all his preaching. With no formal training in ministry, he became a hugely popular preacher, moving his ever-growing congregation to successively larger premises until he settled at the purpose-built Metropolitan Tabernacle in London, in 1861, which held almost 6,000 people and constituted the largest independent congregation in the world. Known for his colourful declamatory style as well as his experientially focused Bible exposition, he became something of a tourist attraction and published over 2,000 sermons which were translated into forty languages and sold in their millions worldwide.[1]

Spurgeon upheld his Bible literalism in the face of the 'Higher Criticism' emerging from Germany, which analysed the Bible as any other ancient text in terms of its multiple authorship and culturally contingent ideals. Spurgeon pugnaciously opposed such developments as 'the foolish affectation of intellectualism', defending simple faith in the power and efficacy of the divinely inspired Word of God, its sole author.[2] A number of Spurgeon's sermons, such as the one reproduced here, were themselves a defence and celebration of the Bible, delivered in a spirit of unwavering opposition to modern critical tendencies which were beginning to be absorbed even into the Evangelical mainstream by the 1880s and 1890s.[3] At the time Spurgeon delivered the sermon extracted here (21 June 1866), his views were on the conservative side but were still widely upheld.

Spurgeon takes the reader through the process of understanding and applying the Bible to life, using only the aid of prayer and the enlightenment provided by the Holy Spirit. He emphasises this is not an intellectual exercise – scripture is a guide to life, to be proven in experience, and finally shared in the spirit of mission. His prose is enlivened by a rich array of biblical allusions, homely idiom and rhetorical flourish. Meditation on scripture is compared to chewing the cud, quarrying for ore, gleaning for grain. The Word has a sensuous reality, often described through metaphors of food – it is manna and cinnamon; it is sweetness and fragrance, a stone to break, a bone to connect with other ligatures to build a body, a sealed letter broken only by prayer, gold to be tried in the acid test of experience, a kernel of a nut whose shell can only be broken by the faithful, a medicine to give to the sick in spirit. Its 'luscious sweetness' compares with the grapes first found in the Promised Land in the valley of Eshcol (Numbers 13:23–4). Such elemental vividness manifests the existential value of the Bible to nurture and sustain the non-critical spirit.

Notes

1 Patricia Stallings Kruppa, *Charles Haddon Spurgeon: A Preacher's Progress* (New York: Garland, 1982), pp. 4–5.
2 Quoted in David W. Bebbington, *The Dominance of Evangelicalism: The Age of Spurgeon and Moody* (Leicester: Intervarsity Press, 2005), p. 39.
3 John Rogerson, *Old Testament Criticism in the Nineteenth Century: England and Germany* (London: SPCK, 1984), p. 287.

2

C. H. SPURGEON, 'HOW TO READ THE BIBLE: A SERMON' [1866]

Metropolitan Tabernacle Pulpit, 58 (1912), pp. 422–430

"Till I come, give attendance to reading."
—I. Timothy iv. 13.

[...] I am not, however, going to keep so closely to my text as merely to exhort you to read. I want to ask you to read God's Word. That seems to me to be the Christian's book. You may read other books, and your mind may thereby be well-furnished with spiritual things, but if you keep to the Word of God, though you may be deficient in many points of a liberal education, you will not be deficient in the education that will fit you for blessed service here, for the service of skies, for communion with God on earth, and communion with Christ in glory.

My object this evening is to say a few things about how to read the Bible. Last Thursday night we spoke at length upon God's Word and as to its excellencies. To-night, I think it fitting that we should speak a little about how to read that Word with greatest profit to our souls. In doing so we shall hope to consider seven precepts all bearing powerfully upon this important matter. Our first precept shall be—I. READ AND DEPEND *on the Spirit of God*. How often do we open the sacred book and read a chapter through, perhaps at family-prayer, or perhaps in our own private devotions, and having read from the first verse to the last, we shut up the book, thinking we have done something very right and very proper, and in a vague way somehow profitable to us. Very right and very proper indeed, and yet, right and proper as the thing is, we may really have gained nothing thereby. We may, in fact, have only drilled ourselves in the merely external part of religion, and may not have enjoyed anything spiritual, or anything that can be beneficial to our souls, if we have forgotten the divine Spirit through whom the Word has come to us.

Ought we not even to remember that in order properly to understand the holy Word we need to have the Holy Spirit *to be his own expositor?* The hymn says concerning Providence—

"God is his own interpreter,
And he will make it plain;"

and certainly it is so with regard to the Scriptures. Commentators and expositors are very useful indeed, but the best expositor is always the author of a book himself. If I had a book which I did not quite understand, it would be a very great convenience to me to live next door to the author, for then I could run in, and ask him what he meant. This is just your position, Christian. The book will sometimes puzzle you, but the divine author, who must know his own meaning, is ever ready to lead you into its meaning. He dwelleth in you, and shall be with you, and saith Christ Jesus, "When he, the Spirit of truth is come, he shall lead you into all truth."

But to understand the Word is not enough. We need also that he *make us to feel its power*. How can we do this except through the Holy Ghost? "Thy Word hath quickened me," O God, but it is only as *thou* didst quicken me through it. The Word of God is to be read literally, but "it is the letter that killeth," only "the Spirit giveth life," and, excellent as are its statements, yet even they have no spiritual force in themselves. Unless the Holy Ghost shall fill them even they shall become as wells without water, and as clouds without rain. Have you not often found it so, yourselves? I appeal now to your own experience. You have sometimes read a portion of Scripture, and the page has seemed to glow, your heart has burned within you, and you have said that the Word came home to you with power.

Just so; but it was the Holy Spirit who was bringing it close home to your spirit in its true power and making it a sweet savour of life unto life to you. At other times, you may have read the very same passage, and missed painfully the sweetness which once you had tasted, and lost the lovely light that once flashed from it upon your mind's eye.

Everything must depend upon the Spirit speaking through it, for even the light of the Word of God is to a great extent but moonlight, that is to say, it is a reflection of the light which streams from God himself, who is the one, the true source of light. If God shineth not upon the Word when we read it, then the Word shineth not back upon us, but becomes a dark Word to us, or as one saith "rather an obscuration than a revelation, rather concealing God from us, than revealing him to us". Look up, reader the next time the book is in thy hands, look up before thou openest it, and while thine eye is running down the page, look up and pray that God would shine upon it; and when the chapter is finished and thou puttest the book away, afford a minute again to look up and ask his blessing. If by reading the Scriptures we were only always reminded of the Holy Spirit, if we got no other good from the Scripture itself except the turning of our souls to think upon that divine and blessed one, that would be in itself an inestimable boon. Do read, then, thoughtfully remembering the great author.

Our second precept is—II. READ AND MEDITATE.

There is no exercise more out of fashion nowadays than meditation; and yet, to use Brookes's expression, "it is a soul-fattening duty." The cattle crop the grass, but the nutriment comes from the chewing of the cud. Reading is the gathering together of our food, but meditation is the chewing of the cud, the digesting, the assimilating of the truth. I quarry out the truth when I read, but I smelt the ore and get the pure gold out of it when I meditate. Ruth gleaned, but afterwards she threshed. The reader is the gleaner, but he who meditates is the thresher, too. For lack of meditation the truth runneth by us, and we miss and lose it. Our treacherous memory is like a sieve, and what we hear and what we read runs through it and leaves but little behind, and that little is often unprofitable to us, by reason of our lack of diligence to get thoroughly at it. I often find it very profitable to get a text as a sweet morsel under my tongue in the morning and to keep the flavour of it, if I can, in my mouth all the day.

I like to turn it over and over again in my mind, for any one text of the Scriptures you will find to be like the kaleidoscope. Turn it one way, and you say, "What a fair truth is this!" Turn it another way and you see the same truth, but under how different an aspect! Turn it yet once more, and keep doing it all day, and you will be amazed and delighted to find in how many lights the same truth will appear, and what wonderful permutations and combinations you can find in it. When you have been all day doing this, you will be constrained to feel that there is an infinity about even one text, so that you can never completely comprehend it, but find it still is beyond you. If you get a passage of Scripture given you, do not give it up quickly, because you do not immediately seize its force and fulness. The manna which fell in the wilderness would not keep sweet beyond one day; if kept over unto the second it bred worms and stank. But there was one portion of manna which was put into a golden pot, and laid up in the ark of the covenant, which never lost its sweetness and heavenly nutriment. And there is a way of keeping the precious portions of God's word that are given you to-day, in such a manner that you may go in the strength of it for forty days, and continue to find fresh food in the same text day after day, and even month after month. But this is only to be done by meditating upon it. Our hymn has a fable in it when it says that the

"Spicy breezes
Blow soft o'er Ceylon's isle."

Voyagers who have been there tell us that they have never smelt "the spicy breezes," for the cinnamon yields no perfume till it is bruised and broken, and certainly God's Word is exceedingly full of perfume, but not till it has been graciously bruised by reverent and loving meditation. You cannot get the sweetness and fragrance therefrom till you have smitten it again and again in the mortar of thought with the pestle of recollection. Meditate, then, upon these things.

"But how can we meditate," says one, "when we have so many things to think of?" But "one thing is needful," and it is needful that the Christian should meditate upon the things of God. I know you must give your minds to many things, and I cannot ask you not to do so, but whenever you have time to rest, then let your minds come back to the old home. The birds of the air are all day long picking up their food, but they go straight away to the roosting-place at night, and so when the day's business is over, and the daily bread has been gained, do you fly to your nest, and rest your soul in some precious portion of God's Word. During the day too, whenever you are freed from anxiety, let your mind dart upwards, and it will help you so to do, if you take a text and make it as wings that enable you to fly to ponder heavenly things. Read and meditate.

The third rule for our guidance should be—III. READ AND APPLY. What I mean is just this. Do not read the Bible as a book for other people. Do not read it merely to say, "Yes, it is true; very true; I believe *its doctrines* to be the revelation of the infallible mind of God himself." But endeavour also in reading a passage of the Scriptures, always to see how much it belongs to you. For some of you there is very little in the Word of God except threatening. Pray God to help you to feel the solemnity even of the threatening, for if you feel deeply the threatening now, you may be delivered from the tragic fulfilment of it by-and-by. If you are made to tremble under God's Word, you may never be made to tremble under God's hand. If you feel the wrath to come now, you may never have to feel it in the next world. Ask God that his threatenings may drive you out of your sins, and drive you to seek pardon in Christ. Then when you read descriptions of the human heart, and the fall, the corruption, and the depravity of our nature, look, and see yourselves as in a looking glass, and say of each man as you hear of his sin, "I am such a man as this was, and if I do not fall into precisely the same sin, yet the possibility and peril of it is in my heart, and I should do so, but for God's restraining grace." Take the very histories home to your heart, and find a point in them, either of encouragement or of warning for yourselves. As for the doctrines, recollect that a doctrine killeth except as it is personally grasped and as you feel your interest in it. I have known some rejoice greatly in the doctrine of election who never were elected, and some who were very pleased with the doctrine of justification by faith, but who had no faith by which to be justified. I have known of some, too, who gloried in final perseverance, but who, if they had finally persevered would certainly have been in hell, for they were on the road there. It is one thing to know these truths, and even to fight for them with the zeal and bitterness of a controversialist, but it is quite another thing to enjoy them as our own heritage and our portion for ever. Ask the Lord to show you your interest in every truth, and do not be satisfied until you have an assured personal interest therein. Especially let this be so with *the promises*. "I will never leave thee, nor forsake thee." Well, it is a very fine promise, but if it is read to me thus: "I will never leave *thee*, nor forsake *thee*," what a transformed and glorified promise it then becomes! Stout old Martin Luther used to say, "All vital religion is in the personal and possessive pronouns." Is it not so? "When *thou* passest through the rivers I will be with *thee*, the floods shall not overflow *thee!*" Oh! truly, such a promise is as a cluster of Eshcol, but it is in Eshcol's valley and I cannot reach it there; but the promise applied is the cluster brought to me just where I am, and I can receive it, and delight myself in its luscious sweetness.

Take care, none the less, to seek for the application of *precepts*. Some are always looking out for other people's duty, and are great judges and critics of what others ought to do. "Who art thou that judgest another man?" To his own master he stands or falls. See what precepts are binding upon thyself, and then, as a child of God, be thy feet swift to run in the way of his commandments. Read the Bible as a man reads his relation's will, to find what legacy there is in it for himself. Do with the Bible as the sick man does with the doctor's prescription. Follow it by personally doing what it bids thee. Ask God not to let thy Bible be another man's Bible, but thine own Bible, God's own mouth speaking to thy soul of the things which make for thy peace.

Fourthly—and this is very hard work—IV. READ AND PRACTISE.

If you do not this, you are reading to your own condemnation. If you read, "He that believeth on him is not condemned," if you believe not then you are "condemned already," because you have not believed in the Son of God. The gospel is a very solemn thing to every man, because if it be not a savour of life unto life, since it must always be a savour of some sort, it therefore becomes a savour of death unto death. Some seem as if they read the Bible in order to know how *not* to do, and the more God commands the more they will not obey. Though he draw them they will not come to him, and when he calls them they will give him no answer. A sorry, sorry heart is that which so useth God's Word as to make it an aggravation of its sin. Our life ought to be—and if God's grace be much in it, it will be—a new translation of the Bible. Speak of bringing the Bible down into the vernacular! Well, this is it. The worldling's Bible is the Christian. He never reads the book, but he reads the disciple of Christ, and he judges the Christian religion, by the lives of its professors. The world will learn better, and will more likely be brought to know Christ when the lives of Christians are better, and when the Bible of the Christian life shall be more in accordance with the Bible of Christian doctrine. God make us holy; sanctify us, spirit, soul, and body, and then we shall be made finely serviceable both to the Church and to the world. Read and practise; but we shall only be able to do this, as God the Holy Spirit shall help us. Then let us—

V. READ AND PRAY. This is, perhaps, coming back almost to the first point, viz., read with dependence on the Holy Spirit; but I desire to impress a rather different thought upon your souls. Martin Luther says he learned more by prayer than he ever learned in any other way. A stone-breaker was one day on his knees breaking flints, when a minister came by and said, "I see you are doing what I often do, breaking up hard things." "Yes, sir," was the answer, and I am doing it in the way in which you must do it, on my knees."

A passage of Scripture will often open up when you pray over it, which will defy mere criticism or looking to expositors. You put the text into action, and them you comprehend it. I suppose if a man were studying anatomy, and had never seen the body in life, he might not be able to know what a certain ligature was for, or such a bone, but if he could set that body moving then might he understand the use of all the different parts, supposing he were able to see them. So when a text of Scripture lies, as it were, dead before us we may not be able to understand it, but when by prayer the text grows into life, and we set it in motion, we comprehend it at once. We may hammer away at a text sometimes in meditation, and strike it again and again, and yet it may not yield to us, but we cry to God, and straightway the text opens, and we see concealed in it wondrous treasures of wisdom and of grace.

But the prayer should not be merely that we may understand the text. I think we should pray over every passage in order that we may be enabled to get out of it what God would impart to us. A text is like a casket which is locked, and prayer is the key to open it, and then we get God's treasure. The text is God's letter, full of loving words, but prayer must break the seal. When reading goes with praying and praying goes with reading, then a man goes on both his feet, the bird flies with both his wings. To read only is unprofitable: to pray without reading is not so soul-enriching; but when the two run together, they are like the horses in the chariot, and they speed along right merrily.

Read and pray Christian! but take care thou dost not read without watering thy reading with thy prayer. Paul may plant, and Apollos may water, but God gives the increase, and even in this blessed Book Moses may plant and David may water, but prayer must cry to God or else the increase will not come. Now in the sixth place,

VI. READ AND TRY. Try what you hear; try what you profess; try what you read. Goldsmiths keep bottles of acid by which they test everything that is offered them for sale, whether it is gold or merely tinsel, and the Christian should keep God's word near at hand and treasured in the soul, to test thereby all that he hears. "Prove all things; hold fast that which is good." Many hearers believe all that is said because of the person who declares it to them. This is not according to Christ's mind. We ought to receive nothing as vital religious truth except it be sent us from above; and however much we may respect the pastor or the teacher, we must not so give up our judgment to any man as to receive his teaching merely because he chooses to utter it. Bring every form of truth that is delivered to you, though it may glitter with oratory and seem reasonable and proper, to the test of Scripture. It is very difficult, however, to get men to do this. They seem to fancy that you have sinister motives the moment you tell them so. There is a conservatism in the nature of us all with regard to our religious faith, which is right enough if it were balanced by another principle. To hold fast what I do know is right, but to be willing to receive or to do anything that God would teach me to receive or do is more right still. I must know what it is to which I do hold fast, or else I may be injuring myself by the fixedness by which I stand to what I have learned. The woman of Samaria said, "Our fathers worshipped God in this mountain." That is the argument of numbers of persons. "Our fathers did so-and-so." This would be a capital argument supposing that our fathers were always right, but a very absurd argument supposing that they were wrong. I hope we are not like that early Saxon who asked where his father and all his ancestors had gone, and when he was told they were no doubt lost, replied to the missionary that he would rather go where they were than become a Christian and be separated from them.

There are some who seem to be of this blood, and boast in it. Their ancestors believed this or that, and they desire to follow them. Many there are who profess doctrines they have never learned, and which they do not really know and grasp. They have the shell but they never reach the kernel. Is not this the case with many of us here to-night? If thou even hast a doctrine in thy mind, find out the text or texts which prove it. If there should happen to be other texts which seem to point the other way, do not cut and pare any of them down, but accept all, and wait until the Spirit reveals wherein they really agree. Scripture is not to fit your opinions, but your opinions to conform to the blessed Word. There is a fable of a foolish gardener who had a tree that would persist in growing oddly. He did not like to restrain it, and therefore had a wall built for it to grow upon. I think the man was wiser far who left the wall alone, and changed the tree. There are people who are very apt to alter Scripture to suit their views, pulling out one word until it is never so long, dropping another, or completely changing the meaning of it, though every-body knows that it is the forced and unnatural one, or else tinkering up a text till it will fit some crank or peculiarity of theirs. This is not reverence; it is not treating God's Word as it ought to be treated. God's Word is no nose of wax to be shapen according to our fancies—or anybody else's. Though nobody else should say what he means God always does. He would not have us talk in language that is capable of half-a-dozen meanings; and he does not talk so himself. He speaks so plainly that if we are candid and desire to know what he means it is not difficult to do so, especially if we go to him for it. Let us, then, take this advice, and try the spirits whether they be of God, and, like the noble Bereans, search the Scriptures whether these things be so, and so read the Scriptures and try what we read.

And, lastly, the text is significantly followed by, "Give attendance to reading, to exhortation." I will, therefore, say, in the seventh place.

VII. READ AND TELL OUT *what you read.*

This will be an effectual way of imprinting it upon your own memory. When thou readest a passage of Scripture, and hast any enjoyment therein, go to thy sick neighbour and tell what God hath said to thee. If thou meetest an ignorant one when thou knowest somewhat of the things of God, tell them to him. Nations are enriched by the interchanges of commerce, and so are Christians. We each have something that another has not, and he has something that we need. Let us trade together. "Then they that feared the Lord spake often one to another," and it is very good that they should do so. Our talk is alas! too often very frivolous; there is much chaff but little wheat. If we would but talk more of Scripture, and establish it as a fashion among Christians, we should grow much faster and stronger, and be wiser in the things of the kingdom.

I know one who, when he was a young man, read all day until evening came, and then went every evening and preached. The preaching in the evening what he had read during the day stamped and fastened the truths upon his own mind, and made them unspeakably profitable to him. When you have read for an hour or so, spend another half-hour in communicating to a child, or a servant, or a seeker, or to some bed-ridden saint, the thing that has enriched and helped you.

How I would press this upon you every one, my dear brethren and sisters, who are members of this church. We owe very many of the conversions that have been wrought here to the personal exertions of our church-members. God owns *our* ministry, but he also owns *yours*. It is our delight at church-meetings that when converts come they often have to say that the word preached from the pulpit was blessed to them, and yet I think that almost as often they say it was the word spoken in some of the classes, or in the pews; for not a few of you have been spiritual parents to strangers who have dropped in. Do this still. Let our congregation be full of these spiritual sharpshooters, who shall pick out, each man his man, and who shall fire with the gun of the gospel directly at each individual.

Of course, if you know nothing, you can tell nothing. If you have never read anything which by the blessing of God has been brought powerfully home to your own soul, do not attempt to speak to others. There must be something begun in your own soul first, but if you have been brought into personal contact with divine truth, let it be the first impulse of your soul to

"Tell to the sinners round
What a dear Saviour you have found."

The woman of Samaria left her water-pot and went into the city, and said, "Come, see a man that told me all things that ever I did; is not this the Christ?" My beloved, let us do the same. I do not know a living thing, even a wild flower in the hedge, but seeks to prolong the existence of its species. The foxglove sheds its seeds all adown the banks; no matter how tiny the flower may be it seeks to produce its like. So you, Christian! who are the noblest work of God, should not be satisfied unless your life is a continual spreading around of the truth which has been made vital to you, and will be new life to others.

Part 2

ANGLICAN DEVELOPMENTS

2.1

The High Church Movement

2.1 The High Church Movement

The High Church movement in the nineteenth century reasserted the longstanding Anglican tradition that cherished ritual as a site for encountering the divine, and revered the spiritual authority of the institutional Church. The Oxford Movement emerged in response to the anti-ritualistic and anti-clerical emphases of the Evangelical revival, led by a group of clerics at Oxford University who gave the movement its name. While this movement technically lasted only from 1833 to 1845, it stimulated a revival of High Church practice which formed the basis of modern Anglo-Catholicism. Clerics with High Church leanings revived a number of Roman Catholic practices such as the use of incense, the rite of confession, the veneration of saints, and often rich church decoration. Rather than exercising individual judgement to determine matters of faith, believers were encouraged to 'rest in the church' (a phrase used as the title for an 1848 High Church novel by Elizabeth Harris), respecting priests as arbiters of doctrine about which some sense of mystery was preserved. The movement can be seen as a reaction against modernity, 'a sort of romantic medievalism' which refused to rationalise faith and which yearned for a sense of continuity with a less utilitarian past.[1]

Frederick William Faber (1814–63) is better known for his Roman Catholic writings – as for a number of Anglican luminaries, his journey through Oxford led him finally to Rome. Before his conversion in 1845, he served as rector at a church in Huntingdonshire where he introduced practices such as confession and the celebration of feast days. A renowned poet, hymn writer and theologian, his early work *The Church, a Safeguard against Modern Selfishness* is imbued with faith in the institution as a spiritual framework for the modern believer. While not one of the Oxford Movement's 'Tracts for the Times', the series of ninety pamphlets that gave the movement its alternative name of Tractarianism, it shares with several of these an insistence on the Church's centrality to healthy spiritual life.

However, Faber's argument is less about the location of spiritual authority and more about the recovery of inter-relationality and a charitable spirit in the face of rampant modern individualism. Faber presents the church as a transhistorical, transnational community through which the worshipper can escape the bounds of self and became part of a sacramental collective: the whole practice of High Church faith 'is a looking out of ourselves'. Collective worship, eucharistic celebration, liturgical prayers for rulers and neighbours, and remembrance of the dead all serve to rekindle our connectedness with others, past and present. The universal catholic church (Faber regrets the separation brought about by the Reformation) transcends national boundaries, its 'capacious' spirit countering political and religious tribalism. Anglo-Catholicism's incarnational emphasis is shown – Christ corporeally present in the sacraments and rites of the Church. The church as a collective body of self-offering worshippers is no less than 'the abiding, continuing, and going on of the Incarnation of the Son of God' of which the believer is a vital element. Faber's allusion to the description of God's tabernacle in Ecclesiasticus

24:18–19 and 35 demonstrates the High Anglican acceptance of some apocryphal as well as canonical scripture texts.

Several of Faber's poems demonstrate at an experiential level this participation in a transhistorical and transgeographical communion of the saints, achieved through ecclesiastical ritual. In 'Easter Communion' the worshipper engages in the rite with high emotion, achieving a felt unity with saints elsewhere and gone before, and senses a piercing of the veil between temporal and eternal realms; the vision of angels with wings and wheels alludes to the prophet's vision in Ezekiel 1:4–18. The worshipper feels transported before the heavenly throne, of which the church's altar is transformed into an earthly type, but there is no allusion to the fully Roman Catholic belief in transubstantiation of the bread and wine. Imagery of music, pulse, and vibration predominates to suggest a sensuous epiphany in which the believer is absorbed into the collective 'Body Mystical'.

Note

1 Nigel Yates, *The Oxford Movement and Anglican Ritualism* (London: Historical Association, 1983), p. 8.

3

FREDERICK W. FABER, *THE CHURCH, A SAFEGUARD AGAINST MODERN SELFISHNESS*

(London: [n.p.], 1840),
pp. 10–18, 20–1, 23–4, 25–7

[...] There is nothing we dislike so much in other people as selfishness; and, if we are honest with ourselves, there is nothing to which we ourselves are more liable. Every body will acknowledge this; so I will not waste time in proving it, nor in showing, what must be obvious, how it keeps us back in our way to Heaven, and does us all manner of harm here as well as hereafter, on earth as well as elsewhere. Let us rather look at what God has done for us, and how He has placed us, so as to protect us from this miserable sin.

We are not set down in the world by ourselves. We cannot move about independent of our neighbour. We cannot live alone. We cannot love ourselves, except as we are reflected in the love of others. We do not like to think of dying alone. Our peace and health and happiness, all depend upon our neighbour. They are more in his power than they are in our own. We see this in many ways. Our neighbour can vex and annoy us every day: he can stand in the way of our getting on: he can say illnatured things of us; and, in a word, if he chooses to act wickedly and maliciously towards us, he can make the world very wretched and miserable to us. Nay more than this, we cannot even keep our souls safe from the harm which our neighbour may do them. Our very souls are put in one another's power. He may do harm to us by not praying for us, by setting an evil example to our children, by frightening us from confessing Christ bravely and openly before men, and the like. His sin may hinder many a blessing which would otherwise have fallen on the city or parish where he dwells. Thus do all we can to keep to ourselves and by ourselves, and to get to Heaven of ourselves and alone, it is impossible. God has so mixed us up with our neighbours., He has so entangled our concerns with their concerns, that we cannot act and live and feel alone. Thus selfishness is made difficult by the law of the world, and by God's arrangement of it. He has so ordered the world that our natural conscience might tell us how unnatural selfishness was; and not the world only, for this is the point I have been all along bringing you to, but He has put down among us the Church of Christ to help us in this very thing, to be a refuge to us from our own selfishness, to be a protection to us against the selfishness of others, to destroy selfishness from one end of the world to the other.

This is a most wonderful blessing if we only thought about it seriously, and like earnest men. Now look at the Prayer Book and the common service of the Church, how little there is in it about ourselves. It is like the Lord's Prayer, the only prayer which Christ Himself taught us to use, and which is in the plural number throughout. For example: what matter, so we might say, does it make to us at this distance and in our humble stations, whether the Queen is religious or not? It is not likely, so we think when we think selfishly, it is not likely she could do us much harm, or interfere with *our* being religious. Yet the Church makes us pray for her twice in the Morning Prayer, once in the Litany, once in the Communion Service, twice when there is the Holy Communion; and twice in the evening prayer. So at the least the Church makes us pray four times a day for the Queen, which we should never have thought of doing ourselves. This is one way in which the Church prevents our being selfish in our prayers; because to the Church at large it is a matter of immense importance that the Lord's anointed should be religious, and have religious people about her. So in our private prayers we should never have thought of praying for the nobility and the magistrates, perhaps not even for our fathers the Bishops. We should often have neglected the sick and afflicted, in far off countries as well as at home: prisoners, captives, travellers, young children and the like. We should not have given up so much of our time to praising God in psalms, as we do in Church. Thus the Church is continually leading our thoughts to any body rather than ourselves. She is continually trying to make us unselfish. Indeed the whole of religion is a looking out of ourselves unto Christ, whether as He is ascended to the Right Hand of the Father, or as He is reflected in the feeble shinings of His saints, or represented to us by the poor and desolate. Still it is a looking out of ourselves.

So for the same great end, among others, we have festivals in honour of the Dead: the blessed Virgin, the holy Apostles and other saints, yea, all the saints of God. The thought of the dead makes us gentle and childlike, and leads us to forget ourselves, as well it may. For we know that, according to St. Paul's teaching, the spirits of just men made perfect are not far from us. We are come to them and they are come to us. They can touch us and we can touch them: perchance do touch them when we know it not; they are gliding by every hour. The spirit has but ceased to act upon and through the body, and so we do not see them in their places. They keep threading in and out among us, going up and down, and moving round about us: especially, so we believe from St. John, in holy Churches where their bodies rest in hope (Revelation vi.). They are the first ranks of the Church who have gone before us in the Lord, so far as to be out of sight. They are beyond our view. They may see us: we cannot see them. This should make us speak very little and surely very cautiously of the Dead, and not without the warrant of the Church: whether they be our own kindred, or saints of old, or holy men of later times. All the dead are our kindred now; for there is no marrying or giving in marriage in the Church invisible. We cannot feel selfish among the Dead; and in the Church of Christ we are among the Dead.

Then again the blessed Sacrament of the Body and Blood of Christ kills selfishness within us, because it keeps drawing us further and further into the communion of saints. It is a hand put forth, and taking us back into the ark from time to time continually. It makes us every one members one of another in the mystical body; for we, St. Paul teaches us, "We being many are one bread and one body: for we are all partakers of that one bread" (1 Corinthians 10:17). Thus the Church sets herself against all selfish views, all narrow opinions, all vanity, conceit, childishness, self-praise, uncharitableness, little-mindedness; it gives us great thoughts; it opens out views of heaven; it promises glorious and magnificent things which shall be hereafter; it leads us to the throne of God; it joins with Angels and Archangels and all the company of Heaven about the Altar; it feeds us with the Body of our Lord: and what have they to do with selfishness who feed thereon?

In like manner the holy doctrines on which the Church is founded, and the history of the heresies by which those doctrines have been assailed, warn us very fearfully against selfishness and selfish times. The great and foremost doctrine of Church teaching is the Incarnation of our Lord and Saviour Jesus Christ. This comes uppermost in her Creeds; this comes uppermost in her best and soundest doctors. The Church does, as it were, in all her gifts and offices set forth and embody after a living way the Incarnation of the Lord. It is in the Church, says one, that Jesus Christ is re-appearing always, and is living eternally. The Church is, as it were, the abiding, continuing, and going on of the Incarnation of the Son of God. Christ is one and the same and always unchanging; and so He has made His Church one. He is made flesh, and has taken an outward form; and so He has made His Church visible. He, as our Mediator, is God; and so He has made His Church indefectible. He is an eternal Priest; and so He has made His Church to have no end. But, if we look at some of the schools of theology which sprung up abroad in the sixteenth century, we find quite other doctrines coming uppermost; not that the doctrine of the Incarnation of the Lord is denied (God forbid!), only it does not occupy the place it did in the harmonious teaching of ancient times. Original sin, grace, free-will, election, assurance, come in Lutheran and Zwinglian writers, where in the Fathers we should find references to the Incarnation, and Sacraments by which it is conveyed to us and given us, as St. Leo expresses it, "as a step for us to tread upon, that we by It may ascend to Him." The effect of this difference, of this distortion of the analogy of faith, is, that by putting over-prominently and exclusively forward questions concerning our own soul, and the effects wrought in it, it leads to excessive self-contemplation, and so lowers the standard of holiness by weakening the temper of faith. [...]

Selfishness too, is effectually warred against and cast out by the temper, which it is the Church's office to give birth to and bring about within us,—the Catholic temper. It is by this temper which God has given her, and which she would fain communicate to her sons, that the Church Universal has been "exalted like a palm tree in Engaddi, and as a rose plant in Jericho, as a fair olive tree in a pleasant field, and as a plane tree by the water," and filled with God's wisdom, "as Phison and as Tigris in the time of the new fruits." (Ecclesiasticus ch. 14). This is the temper by which partition walls are broken down, and the earth made one and of one speech, and the curse of Babel turned aside, and the miracle of Pentecost made abiding. The narrow views of politicians, and their still narrower jealousies, literary theories of national characters, and attempts after union, such as conquerors or men of science weakly strive to gain, are all broken through and swept away, and set at nought by this temper, of which we speak. The world at times has seen this temper living and working, and it has feared it and obeyed it. But now the Body of Christ is torn asunder, and the members war against each other, and endeavour to be by themselves; and thereof has come weakness, disease, slumbering, and fearful dejection in men's souls. Time was in Europe when the Church was free to have the same rites, and pray the same prayers all over. It may not be so now. Time was when foreigners, travellers, and merchants went here and there, and found in every place his own Church, priest, Altar, home. It is not so now. [...]

Now this is what we have lost; this is what all good men are sickening for the want of, what all good men must in their measure strive to bring back again, by cultivating in his own heart, and carrying out in his own modest practice, the Catholic temper. He must not look at his particular Church, as if, like his country, it were an island. He must not let his sympathy, or love, or admiration be confined within any bounds short of the Church Universal. He must feel as the Church Universal feels. He must teach as the Church Universal teaches, and ever has taught. He must pray God for the time when he may worship as the Church Universal worshipped. He must guard the faith jealously, as the salutary deposit handed on to him; but he must shun the close, bitter, schismatical spirit of controversy, that spirit which is nothing but "the disquieting of good men, and the forgetfulness of good turns." He must throw himself out of systems, sects, schools, parties, into the free, capacious teaching and temper of the Church Universal. Thus by God's grace may the sundered members of His Church begin to stir, and move, and come one to another, and join themselves, and live anew; and the shape and outline and attitude, which long past centuries had known, shall gradually grow clearer, more forcible, and more distinct before men's eyes, lovely and venerable. [...]

Lastly the Church itself, the way it is left with us and trusted to us, teaches us very forcibly how hateful selfishness is in God's sight. Christ gave His Name, the only one under heaven whereby men can be saved. But He did not leave it to every man's judgment what to think of His great Name, how to believe in Him, with what rites He was to be worshipped, and the like. He did not leave the faith with this man or that man, or any set of men. He left it with the Church, with the Church only, the Church Catholic, one and entire; and made it impossible it should be pure and whole anywhere out of the Church, or any where short of the Church. In Scripture language the Church was to be the pillar and ground of the truth: the *pillar*, as bearing it up and witnessing to it and keeping it safe and not letting the world reach it to lower it or do it violence; the *ground*, as being the authority on which the truth rests, the lawful and very sufficient evidence upon which men are to receive it. Now in this view it is clear the Church is of immense importance; the salvation of all generations depends upon it. What means then did our Saviour ordain for handing the Church on from one generation to another, for preserving it amid storms and persecutions, for enabling it by its own inward purity to overcome the world and to save alive the souls of those within its gates? Visible miracles gradually ceased, that is to say, they were not put forward in the same way they were before. God did not visibly interfere; heretics and blasphemers were not always struck dead as by a miracle, though here and there God did interpose, and the world wondered. Still as a general rule, it was left to men, to our fathers, to us, to hand on the Church, to leave the old faith as we received it. This was the law: "Tell ye your children of it; and let your children tell their children, and their children another generation." Thus the Church was made to depend on us, the salvation of all generations was made to depend on us. This is a fearful thought, almost too fearful to bear. The salvation of all after generations depends on us. And yet we are careless about it, ungenerous, little-minded, sparing, selfish in saving souls.

Yet still we have among us the Church, which is a refuge from our selfishness: and she is from time to time calling upon us to exercise this privilege of taking refuge with her by our alms. We are for ever being called upon to aid in handing on the Gospel, the one sound faith, the wisdom hidden from of old, to our posterity. We are invited to be fellow workmen with Apostles, primitive confessors, martyrs, bishops, saints, men who raised dead bodies, workers of miracles, lords over evil spirits, mighty teachers, masters in Israel.

4

FREDERICK W. FABER, 'EASTER COMMUNION'

In *Poems* (London: Burns and Oates, 1856), pp. 148–149

The mystery of mysteries!
Now let the pure in heart draw nigh,
While every pulse is beating high
    With love and holy fear;
For Christ hath risen at break of day,
And bids us from the world away
    And haste to meet Him here.

The mystery of mysteries!
The Angels and Archangels come
On wings of light from out their home
    In ranks of glory wheeling;
Our souls shall mix and blend with theirs,
In loud thank-offerings and prayers,
    Before the Altar kneeling.

The mystery of mysteries!
The souls that still in dimness dwell
Deep in the Church invisible,
    From doubt and care remote, –
They too shall keep the feast today,
And to their cells, though far away,
    The hymn of joy shall float.

The mystery of mysteries!
Oh! far and wide through all the earth
Emotions of unwonted mirth
    And feeling strange shall be;
And secret sounds shall come and go

Harmonious as the throbbing flow
    Of the mysterious sea.

    The mystery of mysteries!
The dead and living shall be one,
And thrills of fiery transport run
    With sweetest power through all;
For one in heart and faith are we,
And moulded one, our Head! through Thee,
    The Body Mystical!

    The mystery of mysteries!
From east to west the earth shall turn,
And stay its busy feet to learn
    The musical vibration;
While Saints and Angels high shall raise
In one vast choir the hymn to praise
    The Feast of our Salvation.

2.2

The Broad Church Movement

2.2 The Broad Church Movement

Broad Church Anglicans, along with Unitarians, led the development of liberal religious thought in the nineteenth century, adapting traditional belief in the light of modern knowledge. Its adherents applied historical critical perspectives to the Bible, recognising the human element in the composition of the scripture's component texts and the metaphorical nature of much religious language. They liberalised doctrines such as the atonement, everlasting punishment, and the divinity of Christ in the light of moral reason. As important as these progressive intellectual trends was the desire for a national church that was inclusive, as summarised by Broad Church pioneer Thomas Arnold: 'a church thoroughly national, thoroughly united, thoroughly Christian, which should allow great varieties of opinion, and of ceremonies and forms of worship, according to the various knowledge, and habits, and tempers of its members' enough even to accommodate most Dissenters.[1] While the term 'Broad Church' seems to have been coined in 1853 by W. J. Conybeare writing for the *Edinburgh Review*, its forebears were the Latitudinarians of earlier centuries. As A. I. Fitzroy claims in the extract below, the Broad Church idea was not a nineteenth-century innovation but a revival of a tolerant, inclusive branch of Anglicanism that pleaded for freedom of clerical conscience, and interpreted 'conformity' to the Thirty-Nine Articles with a degree of flexibility and vagueness.

Fitzroy, about whom little is known, writes a late-century retrospect of the movement from the viewpoint that Broad Church ideas, while radical in the century's middle decades, had been normalised by its end. The body of his book traces in some detail the contributions of the movement's leading divines, but their summative achievement occupies the preface and conclusion, from which these extracts are taken. While noting the importance of debates on scripture and doctrine, Fitzroy is keen to emphasise the reduction of emphasis on dogma per se, so that theological assertion was replaced by a creed that was 'very simple, very flexible and very rational'. Fitzroy makes much of the idea of a *national* church which is intrinsically anti-dogmatic, arguing that doctrinal narrowness and enforced conformity are 'contrary to the real character of the Church of England', as well as to 'Christ's Christianity'. Interestingly, Fitzroy de-emphasises the influence of German Higher Criticism on the general liberalisation of religious thought beyond the academy, which he rather attributes to the popular libertarian and rational spirit engendered during the era of the French Revolution. Broad Anglicanism is reclaimed from being the preserve of a scholarly elite and is instead presented as a kind of national religious common sense.

However, Fitzroy's history does little to dispel the impression that the Broad Church's concerns were primarily intellectual, speaking to 'educated doubt' while neglecting to address urgent social needs and working-class alienation from the established Church.[2] He quotes Matthew Arnold's famous description of the divine as 'simply the stream of tendency ... the eternal, not ourselves, that makes for righteousness'.[3] Nonetheless, he goes as far as suggesting that the erosion of dogma was a prerequisite for the Church's late-century turn to social Christianity. The underlying aim of the anti-dogmatists, he argues, was always 'to restore conduct to its rightful place in religion' and to reduce the importance of doctrinal correctness. While confident that liberal doctrine has won the day, Fitzroy ends by prescribing further adjustments needed to Anglican practice in order to complete the (never realised) vision of a truly inclusive broad national church.

Notes

1 Thomas Arnold, *Principles of Church Reform* (1833), quoted in D. G. Wigmore-Beddoes, *Yesterday's Radicals: A Study of the Affinity between Unitarianism and Broad Church Anglicanism in the Nineteenth Century* (Cambridge: James Clarke & Co., 1971), p. 111.
2 M. A. Crowther, *Church Embattled: Religious Controversy in Mid-Victorian England* (Newton Abbott: David & Charles, 1970), p. 7.
3 Matthew Arnold, *Literature and Dogma: Towards a Better Apprehension of the Bible* (New York: Macmillan 1903 [1873]), pp. 37 and 39.

5

A. I. FITZROY, *DOGMA AND THE CHURCH OF ENGLAND*

(Edinburgh: William Blackwood and Sons, 1891), pp. ix–xviii, 269–271, 272–277

CHRISTIANITY is commonly supposed to be a dogmatic religion. Dogmatism in theology may be defined as the authoritative statement of opinions claiming to be supernaturally revealed, and not otherwise obtainable, on the acceptance of which salvation is said to depend.

There are two large classes of dogmatists in Christendom, each including several varieties, which, nevertheless, are agreed upon the dogmatic principle. These are the biblical and the traditional schools. The former asserts that "Holy Scripture containeth all things necessary to salvation; so that whatsoever is not read therein, nor may be proved thereby, is not to be required of any man that it should be received as an article of faith, or be thought requisite or necessary to salvation."[1] The latter holds that there are "Truths contained in the Word of God, written or unwritten, . . . and proposed by the Church for the belief of the faithful."[2] "That truth and falsehood are set before us for the trial of our hearts; that our choice is an awful giving forth of lots on which salvation or rejection is inscribed; that before all things it is necessary to hold the Catholic faith," and that "he that would be saved must thus think, and not otherwise."[3] That is to say, this school believes in the inspiration of the majorities in Church Councils, by whom the hints and indistinct foreshadowings of doctrine in Holy Writ are developed into creeds and formulæ.

Both schools of dogmatists believe that on the acceptance of these metaphysical subtleties depends our everlasting welfare. Most of them regard moral conduct as the result of creed, and of secondary importance thereto. The extreme members—Calvinists, Antinomians, Mystics—attach no importance whatever to practice, even considering good works a stumbling-block and an occasion of falling. By far the greater part, however, are more moderate; and though they will not admit that a man's deeds can be good if his creed be not sound, they yet refuse to credit the sincerity of his faith if it be not shown in right living.

The change from primitive Christianity to a metaphysical system began early. Mankind speedily erected a standard of belief, first by the side of, then above and finally in some cases instead of, that of conduct. Before long the exhortations of the Master to love peace and forbearance were drowned in a hubbub of angry quarrels about His nature, His past and future existence, or, still worse, about the proper time, mode and place for celebrating His death, or for making the simple pledge of membership He required of His followers.

But during these nineteen centuries of doctrinal extension, there have always been certain opponents of dogmatism. Even in the darkest ages of the Church, when paltry quarrels and bitter hatreds threatened her very life, there were at least a few seers of righteousness—hated, despised, and often rejected, doubtless—who by their protests against what they regarded as a lamentable fall from grace in the Church of Christ, showed that they belonged to that goodly fellowship of prophets whose message to their generation has always been that conduct is more important than creed and ritual, and loving-kindness more honouring to God than persecution and anathema.

These anti-dogmatists or liberals deny that there are any truths necessary to salvation. They maintain that the Founder of their religion proposed no doctrinal tests for admission into His kingdom, insisted on no ceremonial observances, and taught no articles of belief, but simply required of His followers to live as He lived, and if need be to die as He died, in a spirit of brotherly love and self-devotion; that His entire teaching—so much, that is, as we can know of it from the witness of His immediate followers—was of the beauty of holiness and the obligations to righteousness, without any metaphysical or theoretical propositions whatever; in short, that Christ preached little theology and much religion. They acknowledge no development of doctrine in Christianity, for they say there are, properly speaking, no doctrines to develop; they simply apply and reapply, under all the changing circumstances of the individual and of the race, the fundamental moral principle of Christ, seeking ever to widen, deepen, and strengthen the power of the Golden Rule.

Corresponding to the extreme dogmatists who attach an ultra-importance to belief, there are some anti-dogmatists who seem to attach an almost equal importance to disbelief. The latter denounce metaphysics for being useless and harmful, as the former repudiate good works for being superfluous and misleading. This school has a few followers in the Church of England, but more among Agnostics, Positivists, &c. With neither of these extreme parties, however, have we here anything to do.

Metaphysical speculations are allowed, even encouraged, by the greater part of the anti-dogmatic school, but not as being essential to the Christian religion. "The best creed in the world," says one of the leading members of this party, "will never save a single soul."[4] But it is natural to man to reason and to speculate. It is instinctive with him to question "What God and man is." To seek and to love truth, according to his ability, is, indeed, required of every Christian, inasmuch as it is his duty to aim at perfection in mind as in spirit. Still to arrogate to one's self the complete possession of truth, is not the same thing as to seek it; nor is to hate and despise those who differ from as about it, the same thing as to love it. Some belief may indeed be helpful to good conduct. Confidence in the wise government of the world; hope that good will at last triumph over evil, and that there is indeed "a stream of tendency which makes for righteousness;" faith in a Supreme Being, good, powerful and loving; trust that all our strivings, our yearnings, our aspirations are but the earnest of a glorious achievement hereafter: all this may be helpful to some of us; but that it is not indispensable is shown by the lives of those who, with a noble irrationality, love righteousness and pursue holiness, even though, as it seems to them, in a world all out of joint, and for the brief span of a single life. If only the righteousness has been loved and the holiness pursued, such men may be as spiritually developed, as Christ-like, as much "saved," as those who, happily for themselves, can believe that they live under the rule of a God who doeth all things well, and that an eternity of progress awaits both the individual and the race.

It is, then, the aim of the anti-dogmatists, first, to restore conduct to its rightful place in religion; and, second, to substitute a sound and reasonable philosophy for mere theological assertion. If the Christianity of the future have any creed at all, it will be one that is very simple, very flexible and very rational.

It is not my purpose to trace this real Apostolic succession through the whole history of Christianity back to Christ. Nor, after the works of Réville, Renan, Stanley, Edwin Hatch, and others, does it seem necessary for any one else to show the gradual process whereby poetical, metaphorical and legendary speculation have been petrified into dogmas, and simple Eastern habits and customs expanded into elaborate ceremonials and unnatural practices.

My aim is merely to show that dogmatic teaching, however general it may be among individual clergy, is contrary to the real character of the Church of England; that the Church of England has since she broke with Rome ever recognised righteousness rather than doctrine or ceremony to be the essence of Christianity; that its members by right of membership should enjoy full freedom of thought and speech on doctrinal subjects; that the spirit of rationalism, tolerance and charity should be naturally active within it, so that it is entitled to be called a Broad Church, and may—after a few minor reforms and a clearer understanding of its own character—justly claim to be representative of Christ's Christianity.

The breadth of a Church is shown in three ways: first, by the nature of its constitution; second, by the number of its liberal divines; third, by its comprehension of all parties.

As to the first mark of a Broad Church, I hope to prove that it is not merely by occasional quibbles or by accidental omissions in its charters, that liberal views have effected an entrance into the Church of England. But that, on the contrary, by almost every act of the legislature on Church matters, freedom of thought has been confirmed and extended. That the evident, and often the avowed, object of the ecclesiastical reformers, from the sixteenth to the nineteenth century, has been to increase its comprehensiveness, to ensure its freedom from theological bondage, and to maintain the superiority of conduct over creed. From the compilation of the Liturgy under Elizabeth to the passing of the Clerical Subscription Amendment Act under Victoria, the ideal of comprehension, of liberty, of non-dogmatism has been pretty steadily pursued. As to the second mark, I hope to trace in the Church of England a steadily increasing school of true Protestants, always maintaining the rights and duties of English Churchmen to free thought and free speech; to show how dogma has decayed directly, in that the heresy of one age is received as orthodox, or as at least tolerable in the next; and indirectly, in that doctrines are ever less dwelt upon in the sermons of our divines, and moral lessons more often enforced. I venture to believe that there cannot be found as large a body or as unbroken a continuity of able High Church or Low Church teachers as can be produced of liberal or undogmatic Churchmen. With regard to the third characteristic, I hope to show that the Church of England, as the national Establishment, demands agreement only upon axiomatic moral truths, and not upon subjects of argument and dispute. In accordance with this principle the Church of England, besides starting with scanty doctrinal tests, has grown more and more lax about even these. It has shown its indifference to doctrinal matters by permitting within its borders both the extreme parties—the Ritualistic and Evangelical—only checking their inclination to persecute each other, or to arrogate to themselves alone the title of the National Church.

In confirmation of this estimate of the character of the English Church let me quote three entirely independent opinions:—

Dr. Döllinger taunts the English Church with a lack of authoritative utterance on doctrinal matters. "The Established Church," he says, "has not so much as the semblance of the unity of doctrine or character. This," he continues, "has the effect that, even to the religious-minded Englishman, doctrine appears as something relatively unimportant and subordinate, which one need not be too exact about."[5]

Bishop Ryle says:—"A strong dislike to all 'dogma' in religion is a most conspicuous and growing sign of the times."[6]

Mr. Wilfrid Ward, in his study of "the Oxford Movement," points out that the High Church party is not in accordance with the tone of the Establishment, but is merely suffered within its pale because of its total indifference to dogma. "Never could one-tenth of the views of the present High Church party have been tolerated on the ground that the English Church teaches them, and that dogma is, in its view, a sacred and important thing. A ruling power, whose spirit is that of indifferentism, declares all dogma to be unimportant, and High Churchmen may hold what they like, not in virtue of any special approval on the part of the Established Church, but because that Church does not either enforce or condemn *any* doctrinal system."[7]

Two factors are supposed to have largely contributed to the development of free-thought in England during the present century. These are the French Revolution and the introduction of German criticism. Neither of these has, however, been productive of any radical alteration in the English character. The love of freedom and the appreciation of practical Christianity have been distinctive traits in English religious thought from the first. With these tendencies the influences of the French Revolution and of German erudition have but amalgamated. We shall find in the writings of the sixteenth, seventeenth, and eighteenth century divines unmistakable evidence of that desire to return to primitive Christianity so openly advocated by many in the nineteenth century. With these characteristics of the English nation the influence of the French Revolution has combined far more effectively and immediately than has that of German criticism. The shock of the political events of the later years of 1700 and the early years of 1800 seem to have aroused the rather torpid tendencies of the English into great activity. Since then our religion has been ever increasingly practical. Doctrines have been but little combated or rationalised; they have rather been neglected for the more pressing claims of mankind. Men are learning to love, instead of to dispute with, one another. German philosophy, since about the middle of the nineteenth century, has had some little effect upon our theology, but it has hardly taken any immediate or popular hold, and is scarcely suited to the general tone of the English people. The wider character of the religion of England at the end of the nineteenth century is due to the original bias of the nation towards freedom, kindliness and common sense, prompted, doubtless, somewhat by the example of France, and to a far less degree by the teaching of Germany.

In following the movement of reform in the English Church it must not be supposed that the friends of progress venture to claim the day as already theirs. The battle of freedom is not yet won, but the enemy's ranks are in many places broken through. The citadel is not yet taken, but several outposts have surrendered. The recent judgment pronounced by the Archbishop of Canterbury upon the case of the Bishop of Lincoln, the failure of a veteran persecutor to obtain the censure of Convocation on "Lux Mundi," illustrate the growth of liberty in the English Church during the last fifty or even thirty years. The tone of "Lux Mundi," and of the writings of many modern High Churchmen, notably of the late Canon Aubrey Moore, show the influence of liberalism even in the dogmatic party. The doctrines for which the dogmatists of the last generation fought so stubbornly against the Essayists, Maurice, Colenso and Stanley, are now either adopted, abandoned, or so transformed as to be practically repudiated. The Moderate Churchmen of these last years of the nineteenth century would have been called Erastians, Unitarians, Latitudinarians, even Atheists at its beginning. For one liberal Churchman in the early years of 1800 we now have fifty; for one Broad Churchman we now have ten. The battle not yet won, but the enemy's ranks are wavering from end to end. The citadel is not yet taken, but by their desperate valour and fierce denunciation its defenders show that their hearts grow faint within them. One after another crosses over from the dogmatic to the anti-dogmatic party; one after another of the onlookers joins the side of peace, of love, of toleration. May we not hope that ere long there will be no parties to divide the Church of God in England, but that all will be united in one common work of love, with the one common aim of following Christ? Then will be fulfilled in our midst that ancient prophecy of the seer at Patmos, "And there shall be no more curse; but the throne of God and of the Lamb shall be in it, and His servants shall serve Him." Then indeed may our Church be defined as "THE NATION LOVING RIGHTEOUSNESS." [...]

Assent to the "general doctrine" of the National Church is all that is now required of the English clergy. What then is this "general doctrine?" What is the general belief expressed by the prayers and psalms, the readings from Scripture, and the rites and ceremonies of the Church? Is it dry dogma, or is it a belief in an ideal of goodness, of love, of justice, of mercy, and of truth; in a capacity within us to rise to that ideal, and in a power not of ourselves, but in ourselves, by which we may hope to attain thereto? And is not this a confession of faith in God the Father, God the Son, and God the Holy Ghost? Does not such a faith as this, taken in its largest, least defined and particularised sense, include all parties, all sects and churches and all schools of thought? Do not Theists, Unitarians, Trinitarians, Agnostics, and Positivists alike hold this catholic faith, in that they reverence goodness, hope to increase in goodness, and welcome all helps to goodness? What is this but to believe in thought, if not in form, in the three aspects of the one God of orthodoxy?

It is impossible to overrate the importance of this measure to the English Church. General agreement with the doctrine of the Articles being all that is required of the clergy, it is difficult to see how any one wishing to be a minister of God, acknowledging Christ as his Master, and believing in the inspiration of the Holy Ghost, need scruple to seek holy orders. Neither would it now be possible to obtain a legal verdict of heresy. The manner of administering the law of the Church of England has never been to compare the general tendency of the writings of the accused with the general tendency of the Articles and Formularies, but to compare given passages from the one with specified portions of the other. As therefore no one particular Article can be held binding on the clergy, no one particular Article can ever be said to be violated. So that unless a man distinctly denies the truth of the whole tenour of the doctrine of the English Church he cannot be cited for heresy. This no one is likely to do, for it would be an avowal of disbelief in goodness and in the possibility of becoming better, in truth and the possibility of acquiring truth, in love and the possibility of growing in love. No sane man would deny these things and yet wish to remain a professed servant of the God of love, of truth and of goodness. [...]

Turning now to the internal history of religious thought in the Church of England of the nineteenth century, there are two or three doctrines on which it may be safely said to have become less dogmatic:—

1st. *The infallibility of Scripture.* [...]

A glance through the preceding pages will show with what an increasing clearness the difference between inspiration and infallibility has been recognised. A comparison between the treatment of the Scriptures by Arnold and Maurice with some volumes and articles by living Churchmen will show a very remarkable change. Fifty years ago Bible history was believed to have been specially planned by God as an object lesson to the human race; now the events recorded are believed to have happened without the direct intervention of the Almighty, but to be illustrative of the evolution of the spiritual nature of man, of his ascent from very low depths of cruelty and ignorance towards purity and knowledge. Fifty years ago, to have parts of the Bible treated as common history was distressing to pious-minded men, while to-day to have parts of the Bible treated as other than myth and poetry is equally distressing to equally pious-minded men. Whether we regard this change of tone with hope or with fear depends a good deal on whether we love the spirit better than the letter, and can dare, in the strength of God, to face all truth.

2nd. *The question of Christian Evidences.* Here too a great change has taken place. We now set little or no store by the testimony of miracles. Some effort is still made to retain a semblance of faith in these events. Miracles are generally now defined as adaptations and not violations of the laws of nature, and consequently cease to be miraculous in the real sense of the word. To reduce the legends in the Old and New Testaments as far as possible to the level of ordinary occurrences is the endeavour of those conscientious but poor-spirited divines who cannot fully accept the conclusions of criticism and philosophy and yet dare not altogether deny their teaching. Miracles fifty years ago were accepted as simple marvels, on the word of Scripture. Then, as the voice of Science made itself better heard, it was found that the moral truths of Christian doctrine were more readily believed than was the miraculous element. Finally, when men began to perceive the fallibility of the Bible, the invariability of law, and the self-sufficiency of the Christian religion, they discovered, at the same time, that miracles may be only the result of ignorant and enthusiastic hero-worship, which turned metaphor into fact, parable into history, and magnified kindly deeds into vulgar conjuring tricks. The change of tone in this matter has been very slow, and is even yet barely admitted. The clergy, however, though they may for the most part still think they believe theoretically in miracles, seldom make any explicit mention of them except in order to illustrate a point of conduct or of doctrine. It will be remembered that Thirlwall owned that the Christian religion is dependent on no single miracle, except that of the resurrection, that Milman acknowledged that more conversions to Christianity were wrought by its doctrines than by the mighty works of its Founder, and that Stanley confessed his pleasure that the progress of science should have shown that "the limits of the natural and supernatural are less definite than was once imagined." There are clergymen of the Church of England to-day who have ventured to explain the growth of these illusions, and to deny the occurrence of any supernatural event at any time or in any place from the speaking of Balaam's ass to the bodily resurrection of Christ. They have shown us that an unbroken adherence to law and order is more in keeping with our highest conception of God than any conjuring tricks and jugglery.

The Christian faith now stands on much firmer ground:—not on the authority of a book or of a Church, but on reason and experience; not on the witness of this man or that, but on the testimony of our conscience; not on miracles or fulfilment of prophecy, or Church councils, or supposed judgments of God, but on the witness in ourselves and in the world around us of a God who is "not far from any one of us," "in Whom we live and move and have our being." Even if the traditional account of the birth, death and rising again of the Founder of Christianity fade before the light of reason and knowledge, the essence of the religion of Christ is too deeply rooted in the moral nature of man, has won its way too steadily in all countries, under all circumstances, among all varieties of men, to be ever overthrown. The Being of God, the divinity of man, the universality of the Spirit are increasingly recognised as facts of philosophy, and will continue to be believed even when it has been acknowledged that the story of the Deity walking in a garden is but an Eastern poem, that the theory of a unique incarnation is but a crude expression of a great truth, and that the notions of the Spirit of the universe appearing in the form of a dove or speaking with the voice of a man, are but Oriental metaphors materialised by our dull Western minds.

3rd. *The doctrine of the Trinity.* From Maurice to Hatch may be perceived the steadily increasing influences of a philosophy at once subtler and sounder than any of its predecessors, not excepting those of Plato and Aristotle,—I mean the metaphysic of modern Germany recast and interpreted by Professor T. H. Green, Principal Caird, and others. The difference between the philosophical creed commonly called the Athanasian and that of our modern Broad Churchmen is one of degree, not of kind. But the difference is as great as that between the Copernican and the Aristotelian theory of the heavens, between the astronomy of the author of Genesis and that of the author of the "Principia." The Trinity is seldom now taught as a sort of charm against perdition; but is presented to us, by those who are capable of looking at the subject philosophically, as a rational and sublime theory of the universe—God in nature, God in history, God in the individual.

Some minor alterations in our Church are still, no doubt, desirable. It would, for one thing, be well if the creeds were altogether withdrawn from our services. The prayers and hymns, the psalms and lessons, the preaching of the clergy should be a sufficient profession and exposition of our faith. True, the creeds do not occur as a setting forth of dogma, and are not accompanied by any corresponding denunciation of error. But their place in our services is liable to be misunderstood; they have too much the appearance of being there for offensive and defensive purposes. Even more desirable is it that the Scriptural form of baptism be recognised as alone essential in the public service, the promises of the sponsors and the assent to the creed being made perfectly optional. For those who might still object to this retention of the *duo necessaria*—i.e., the invocation and the sprinkling with water—the repeal of that infamous canon against Christian burial for those who die unbaptized would be but consistent with the charity and liberality of our Church, such a cruel and useless visiting of the sin, if sin it be, of the parents on the children being utterly at variance with the Christian religion. Another desirable point is the free admission to our pulpits and communion of members of all existing denominations. Arnold's suggestion that services other than those of the Church of England might sometimes be held in the national churches is indeed worthy of consideration. These measures would perhaps result, in the course of time, in an amalgamation of all sects with the Established Church. It would also be well if it were understood that sermons are intended chiefly for moral exhortation, and that instruction in metaphysics or theology, like lessons in geology or biology, bear only indirectly on religion. Lastly, there should be much greater freedom in the selection and rejection of portions of Scripture for reading in our churches than is afforded by the present lectionary.

Notes

1 VI. Article of Religion.
2 Catholic Dictionary of Theology.
3 Newman's *Essay on the Development of Doct[rine]*, p. 357.
4 Church and Creed, by Rev. A. W. Momerie, LLD., D.Sc [1890], p. 79.
5 [Johann von Dollinger], The Church and the Churches [1861], pp. 168–9.
6 [J. C. Ryle], *Principles for Churchmen* [1884].
7 *W[illiam] G[eorge] Ward and the Oxford Movement* [1889], pp. 379–80

Part 3

ROMAN CATHOLICISM

3.1

Roman Catholicism in Britain

31

Roman Catholicism in Britain

3.1 Roman Catholicism in Britain

Following Emancipation in 1829, the Roman Catholic Church expanded in numbers and confidence through Britain, attracting converts and being added to by steady immigration from Ireland. The Roman Catholic Church hierarchy was re-established in England and Wales (1850) and in Scotland (1878), ending at least formally the longstanding prejudice that Catholic faith was somehow incompatible with Britishness. Anti-Catholic feeling, a feature of British popular culture since the Reformation, was still rife in the first half of the century, but gradually more tolerant views spread. The High Church movement increased Anglican sympathy for Catholic rites and iconography, as did a resurgent taste among many religious liberals 'for a symbolism of the spirit' felt to be lacking in aesthetically barren Protestant orthodoxy.[1] These changes took place against the backdrop of a Europe-wide Catholicism that was becoming insistently anti-modern, intensifying its Marian devotion and reverence for Papal Infallibility.

While in many parts of the country Catholicism was the religion of the urban poor, its vocal proponents were often aristocratic converts. One such was Mary Elizabeth Herbert (1822–1911, known as Lady Elizabeth Herbert of Lea), who corresponded with many leading Catholics and whose apologetic work *Anglican Prejudices Against the Catholic Church* (first published in 1866) defends her new-found faith above all against Protestant accusations of idolatry. One strategy is simply to correct misunderstandings of Catholic rite: venerated images are not worshipped per se but work by association – like a picture of a loved one, 'the representation brings the substance more clearly before you'. Confession, rightly conducted, is not an empty rite that cheapens divine forgiveness but an expression of 'heartfelt penitence'. But she also declares her sacramental belief in objects as symbols that corporeally partake of spiritual reality, hence incarnating the divine within the temporal sphere. With reference to Jesus's real presence in the eucharistic elements, and the reserved sacrament, she celebrates the 'intense comfort' brought by these material divine embodiments amid dry secular life. She reveals her elite social experience by exemplifying this in terms of escaping the pressures of the London season.

Marian devotion is negotiated carefully given the many vitriolic Protestant responses that had greeted the declaration of Mary's Immaculate Conception in 1850, an event interpreted by some as a near-pagan deification of a mere earthly woman.[2] Herbert insists that the doctrine makes Mary not divine, but a perfect woman such as Eve was before the fall. She makes love of Mary a family matter, a natural extension of devotion towards the son to include his mother. At times Herbert calls upon the Bible to support her case, beating Protestants at their own game, but more often she cites the teachings of the early Church fathers which are presented as the earliest and most authentic Christianity; there are also quotations from, and paraphrases of, Joseph Hall's *No Peace with Rome* (1852), Martin Luther's *Commentary on the Magnificat* (1521) and works by John Henry Newman,

Victorian England's most famous Catholic convert and theologian including his *Lectures on the Present Position of Catholics in England* (1851).

Herbert's second piece pays tribute to a feature of Roman Catholic tradition often admired, even envied, by Protestants (e.g. Florence Nightingale, Anna Jameson and Mary Howitt) i.e. its charitable institutions. European travel afforded Herbert the opportunity to see Catholicism as a society-wide ethos, not just a minority devotional practice, and to experience a sense of international fellowship. In her tour of the hospitals in Seville, Herbert admires the homely care given by the religious orders to the poor and sick and contrasts this with the parsimony and coldness of state care, at times making critical comparisons with provision in her own nation. Her retelling of the gothic legend of Don Miguel de Manara shows her enjoyment of immersion in a culture still connected to its Catholic past, and emphasises humility and charity as the heart of her faith.

Notes

1 Sheridan Gilley, 'Roman Catholicism', in D. G. Paz (ed.), *Nineteenth-Century English Religious Traditions: Retrospect and Prospect* (London: Greenwood Press, 1995), pp. 33–56, on p. 44. See also Andrew L. Drummond and James Bulloch, *The Church in Victorian Scotland 1843–1874* (Edinburgh: St Andrew Press, 1975), pp. 58–78.
2 Carol Engelhardt Herringer, *Victorians and the Virgin Mary: Religion and Gender in England 1830–85* (Manchester: Manchester University Press, 2014), pp. 116–143.

6

M. E. HERBERT, *ANGLICAN PREJUDICES AGAINST THE CATHOLIC CHURCH* [1866]

2nd edition (London: Catholic Truth Society, 1899), pp. 8–11, 13–16, 19–21

The Ten Commandments

I believed for years that Catholics either omitted altogether, or garbled, or altered, the Second Commandment, which was a standing protest against the "worship of images." The simple fact is, that Catholics regard the second commandment as an extension of the first, and print it as such; and divide the tenth. But as to this very "worship" of images, as the Protestants call it, it is no more "worship" than my feeling towards my husband is worship. I have his picture in my room; I wear it on my breast; I love to keep up the remembrance of his presence in every way. And in the same manner, and with the same feeling, I wear a crucifix, hidden from all eyes like his picture. I love to have one in my room to help me to realize the wonderful mystery of His suffering and His love; to have before me the representation and image of Him "who bore our griefs and carried our sorrows," [Isaiah 5:4] and who has been ever since my widowhood the only one who could fill up the aching void in my heart.

The difference in my feelings since I became a Catholic is this: formerly I believed in Jesus and loved Him as an abstraction of faith; now I seem to have a more intimate personal love of Him; a something tangible, the worship and adoration of which, whether in the Blessed Sacrament on the altar, or kneeling before the crucifix in my own room, gives me inexpressible comfort and peace. It is only that the representation brings the substance more clearly before you, and that one loves to have such a representation of the object loved. This, it appears to me, is the real and only reason of pictures and crucifixes in churches, and is clearly so understood by those who use them. St. Jerome says: "As, therefore, the Jews venerated the Ark of the Covenant, and the two images of gold of the Cherubim, though it was nowhere permitted of God that these things should be worshipped, so neither do we Christians *worship the crucifix as God,* but as showing the sincere affection of our souls towards Him that was crucified." I will conclude this subject with the words of Dr. Arnold, in a letter to Mr. Hull, quoted in Dean Stanley's; *Life*, and giving, therefore, the views of even Protestants on this head: "The Second Commandment is, in the letter, utterly done away with by the fact of the Incarnation. To refuse, then, the benefit which we might derive from the frequent use of the crucifix, under pretence of the Second Commandment, is a folly; because God has sanctioned one conceivable similitude of Himself when He declared Himself in the person of Christ."[1]

The Eucharist

Regarding the Holy Communion, I think there is little difference between the Catholic belief and that held by most High Church Anglicans of the present day. No one amongst them now denies a *real Presence* in this Sacrament. But I have found in the writings of the early Fathers the clearest possible evidence of this mystery. I find that in the very first century St Ignatius, speaking of certain heretics, writes: "They abstain from the Eucharist because they will not believe that the Eucharist is the actual Flesh of our Saviour Jesus Christ, that Flesh which suffered for our sins, and which the Father raised again. *They, therefore, who deny this gift of God perish in their disputing.*" All the subsequent Fathers hold the same doctrine. But skipping over what is too long for my purpose, I will quote two passages from St. Ambrose and St. Augustine.

"The Jews exclaimed: 'How can this man give us His Flesh to eat?' Human understanding rejects as false what exceeds its comprehension. You ask: 'How can you prove to me that I shall receive the Body of Christ?' I will prove that the force of benediction is greater than the force of nature. Moses held a rod: he cast it down, and it became a serpent. Again, he took hold of the tail of the serpent, and it returned to the nature of the rod. See, then, that by grace the nature both of serpent and rod was twice changed." After quoting the waters of Marah, the Jordon, and the miracles of Elisha, he goes on: "Now if the word of Elias so availed, *shall not the word of Christ be of avail to change the nature and species of the elements?* He spoke, and they were made; He commanded, and they were created. . . . But let us establish the verity of the mystery by the Incarnation. Did not the Virgin conceive contrary to nature? Why seekest thou, then, the order of nature in the Body of Christ, when the Lord Jesus Himself was, contrary to nature, born of a Virgin? Real, in truth, was Christ's Flesh that was crucified." So far St. Ambrose. Now St. Augustine: "The Lord Jesus Himself says, 'This is My Body.' *Before* the benediction another species is named; *after,* His Body is signified. It is the same with His Blood, and thou sayest, 'Amen.' What the mouth speaks, let the inward man confess." And again: "We also are fed from the Cross of Christ, because we eat His Body." St. Cyril says: "Our Lord omits to tell the Jews in what way He will give them His Flesh to eat, *declaring that they must believe before inquiring.*"

The result of all I have read, therefore, is to convince me that in the Holy Communion there is truly and actually contained the Body and Blood of Christ; the *substance* being changed, though the *species* remains, by the power and will of God. [...]

I come now to the reservation of the Blessed Sacrament. One day this subject was discussed among several clergy, some of whom lamented the discontinuance of the practice in the Anglican Church; but they were met by the usual answer, that it was an "innovation," "Roman," and "new." Now I find proofs of it in the second century, in Tertullian; in the third, in St. Cyprian; in the fourth, in St. Chrysostom and St. Paulinus; and so on. It used to be reserved in private houses in the time of persecution; but when the Church had peace, the reservation was restricted to the churches, as the common home of Christians. St. Paulinus mentions that there were often two tabernacles side by side: "One for the Blessed Sacrament, the Word Incarnate"; the other for the Holy Scriptures, the "Word written." The whole Greek Church has practised it from a high antiquity; so, I think, have the Nestorians, Copts, and all Oriental Churches. It is a curious fact, that the Churches which "reserve" believe in and worship Jesus in the Blessed Sacrament; while the Church which has rejected it has lost both the adoration and the faith in the Blessed Eucharist. Who can deny the effect on the human mind of the "little light" telling of the perpetual presence? Who does not feel chilled in entering the finest of our Anglican cathedrals where it is absent? I have elsewhere spoken of the intense comfort that the Benediction service has all along been to me. *It made me a Catholic* long before I knew it. "It is one of the most beautiful, soothing, and natural actions of the Church. It is our Lord's solemn benediction to His people, as when He lifted up His hands over the children, or when He blessed His chosen ones when He ascended up from Mount Olivet. As sons might come before a parent before going to bed at night, so the great Catholic family comes before the Eternal Father, after the bustle or toil of the day, and He smiles upon them and sheds upon them the light of His countenance".[2] How often have I felt in London, coming, in "the season," out of the crowd and turmoil of Regent and Oxford Streets, the blessing and calm of that service in Harley House, "whilst outside the anger of the strong is like a whirlwind beating against the wall"! I say nothing of what the habitual nearness of the Blessed Sacrament does for us, or of the mystical connection which it bears to His sacred infancy and His descent from the cross. The love of the Blessed Sacrament is ever increasing, is daily and life-long. In stillness, in reverence, in heartfelt awe and worship, we kneel before the tabernacle; we pour out before Him our hopes, our wishes, our fears; and it is rarely, if ever, that we do not return home comforted, strengthened, and refreshed by the benediction which He is ever ready to pour out on those who thus seek Him daily in faith and hope and love.

With heart and soul, then, do I daily repeat the words in the "divine praises" said after the Mass: "Blessed be Jesus in the most holy Sacrament of the Altar!"

Confession. Indulgences

I do not think it is necessary for me to say much on the subject of confession. It is recognized as a necessary means of grace among most High Church Anglicans. St. Ambrose, speaking to a penitent as in God's name, exclaims: "Wilt thou plead shame that thou didst not confess to my priest? *I gave a remedy; why didst thou refuse it?*" Again, St. Athanasius: "He who confesses with penitence receives *through the priest,* by the grace of Christ, the remission of his sins." St. Augustine, in the fifth century, exclaims: "Believe and confess. Let no one say to himself: 'I do it in secret. I do it before God. God (may He pardon me!) knows I do it to Him in my heart.' Was it then said *without cause,* 'What ye shall loose on earth shall be loosed in heaven'? *Without cause* do ye imagine are the keys given to the Church of God? Will ye make void the words of Christ?" and so on, in an indignant protest. Again, speaking of the words of Christ, "Receive ye the Holy Ghost, . . . whosesoever sins ye remit," &c., he says: "For to what purpose was this power given if it imposed not on men the obligation of making known their sins? or how could this power be exercised if no sins were communicated?"

I do not dwell on the absurd allegations of certain Protestants, that absolution is given "beforehand," that you may thus obtain a licence to sin, and that there is a kind of tariff for big and little sins—the latter, *moyennant* a few "aves," being allowed to be committed with impunity; that on the church-doors are fixed a catalogue of sins, with a specification of the prices at which remission of each might severally be obtained. If I had not heard members of my own family make such assertions, I should be ashamed to write them down. As it is, I will only say that it is *utterly false* to assert that the Catholic Church has ever held the doctrine that the perpetration of crime could be "indulged" for any sum of money; and that absolution could not be bought without horrible sacrilege. Every Catholic child knows that without heartfelt penitence towards God, and a firm resolution to amend, absolution is never given, and, if given, would be invalid. I do not for a moment imagine that this Sacrament has never been abused or used for bad and vile purposes. But so have the holiest rites. The *abuse* of a good thing does not make the thing itself bad. But take confession *as it is in fact*—as those can bear witness who know it by experience, and, as Dr. Newman says, "No other ordinance of the Church is so helpful, so soothing, or so full of blessing." [...]

The Devotion to the Blessed Virgin

And now to come to a point which is, and ever must be, the great difficulty with all Anglicans. Talk to an Englishman about Popery, and in five minutes he will come to the "blasphemous new doctrine of the Immaculate Conception," and wonder what the Church of Rome will "develop next." But here, again, I found that the ideas I had previously conceived as to the Catholic belief in the matter were entirely erroneous. That any soul in the Catholic Church worships the Virgin as *God,* I simply and invincibly disbelieve. They put her in the exact position of Eve before the fall. They argue that our Saviour could not have been born of one less pure than was the first mother of our race; and with this view agree all the early Fathers. Even the Protestant Bishop Hall, in his work entitled *No Peace with Rome,* exclaimed: "O blessed Mary! he cannot honour thee too much who defies thee not." Martin Luther says of her, in his famous sermon on her conception:

"The Virgin Mary holds as it were a middle position between Christ and man; for in the first moment she began to live she was exempt from all sin." "For it could not be said to her by the angel Gabriel, '*Blessed* art thou among women,' if at any time she had been obnoxious to the curse."

But let us return to the first days of Christianity. I find in some Acts, which are very early, if not, as some have thought, so early as to contain the profession of faith of St. Andrew before his martyrdom, these words: "Because the first man was created of immaculate earth, it was necessary that the perfect man should be born of an *immaculate* virgin." The celebrated comparison between Eve while yet immaculate and incorrupt, and the Blessed Virgin, is drawn out and enlarged upon by St. Irenæus, Tertullian, St. Justin, St. Cyril, St. Epiphanius, St. Hippolytus, Origen, St. Ephrem, St. Anselm, St. Ambrose, St. Augustine, and a mass of other Fathers from the first to the fifth centuries. No controversy on the point seems, in fact, to have arisen till the twelfth century. The festival of the Immaculate Conception had been established in the East from the earliest times, and in the West in the seventh century, but not authoritatively from Rome. Then came discussions on the question of whether her innocence began at the moment of her conception or at that of her birth; and St. Bernard, St. Thomas Aquinas, St. Bonaventure, and others hotly contested the point. They believed that she was, as it were, the firstfruits of the redemption; and that, by a new kind of sanctification, the Holy Spirit had preserved her immaculate, to be a fitting temple for her Divine Son. In 1497 the University of Paris proclaimed the doctrine by statute, and their example was followed by most of the other European Universities. For many years, I fancied that this doctrine of the "Immaculate Conception" was a new dogma, invented by Pius IX.; whereas thirty-three Popes before him had sanctioned and encouraged the devotion, which was first decreed by Sixtus IV. in 1476. All that Pius IX did was to define and proclaim that doctrine which the Catholic Church had for so many centuries believed. Dr. Newman on this point, in his *Apologia*, says: "Be large-minded enough to believe that men may reason and feel very differently from yourselves; that we have no intellectual difficulty in that in particular which you call a 'novelty' of this day.... Indeed, it is a simple fact to say that Catholics have not come to believe it because it is defined, but *it was defined because they believed it*."

But now as to the "cultus" of the Blessed Virgin. Dr. Newman says it was "his great crux as regards Catholicism"; and I confess it has been one of my greatest difficulties. The intervention of the Blessed Virgin is looked upon by Catholics as a part of the doctrine of the Communion of Saints, as it is revealed through the Incarnation, and recognised also in Scripture. They ask for her intercession with her Divine Son, as we should plead for the prayers of those whom we love when we are in trouble. But I do not think it rests with them on logic or development, but on the order of divine facts. Next after the love and veneration which the Apostles paid to their divine Lord was the love and veneration they paid to His Mother; and this domestic affection, as I may call it, in the family of God, has descended, by a living tradition of heart and mind, to this day. The Incarnation, which made the Son of God our Brother, made His Father our Father, and His Mother our Mother. True, though supernatural, relations exist between us and her; and relations impose *duties* and elicit *affections*. It is, however, a great and difficult mystery still. St. Eucherius exclaims: "If you would try to realize how great is the Mother, think how great is the Son"; and St. Anselm: "To proclaim this alone of the Blessed Virgin, that she is the *Mother of God,* exceeds every height and name which, after that of God, it is possible to conceive."

Notes

1 [Arthur Penrhyn Stanley, *The Life and Correspondence of Thomas Arnold*, D.D., 2 vols (London: B. Fellowes, 1844), vol. 1. p. 244.]
2 (Newman) ['Prejudice the Life of the Protestant View', in *Lectures on the Present Position of Catholics in England* (1851), pp. 244–245.]

7

M. E. HERBERT, 'THE CHARITABLE INSTITUTIONS AND CONVENTS OF SEVILLE'

In *Impressions of Spain in 1866*
(London: Richard Bentley, 1866), pp. 152–161

A few days after the Holy Week, our travellers decided on visiting some of the far-famed charitable institutions of Seville; and taking the kind and benevolent Padre B—as their interpreter, they went first to the Hospital del Sangre, or of the 'five Wounds,' a magnificent building of the sixteenth century, with a Doric façade 600 feet long, a beautiful portal, and a 'patio,' in the centre of which is the church, a fine building, built in the shape of a Latin cross, and containing one or two good Zurbarans. There are between 300 and 400 patients; and in addition to the large wards, there are—what is so much needed in our great London hospitals, and which we have before alluded to at Madrid—a number of nicely-furnished little separate rooms for a higher class of patients, who pay about two shillings a day, and have both the skill of the doctors and the tender care of the sisters of charity, instead of being neglected in their own homes. There was a poor priest in one of these apartments, in another a painter, and in a third a naval captain, a Swede, and so on. The hospital is abundantly supplied with everything ordered by the doctors, including wine, brandy, chickens, or the like; and in this respect is a great contrast to that at Malaga, where the patients literally die for want of the necessary extra diets and stimulants which the parsimony of the administration denies them. In each quadrangle is a nice garden, with seats and fountains, and full of sweet flowers, where the patients, when well enough, can sit out and enjoy the sunshine. There is not the slightest *hospital smell* in any one of the wards. The whole is under the administration of the Spanish sisters of charity of St. Vincent de Paul; and knowing that, no surprise was felt at the perfection of the 'lingerie,' or the admirable arrangement and order of the hospital. They have a touching custom when one of the patients is dying, and has received the viaticum, to place above his head a special cross, so that he may be left undisturbed by casual visitors. The sisters have a little oratory upstairs, near the women's ward, beautifully fitted up. An air of refinement, of comfort, and of *home*, pervades the whole establishment.

Close to this hospital is the old tower where St. Hermengilde was put to death, on Easter eve, by order of his unnatural father, because he would not join the Arian heresy, or receive his paschal communion from the hands of an Arian bishop. This was in the sixth century: and is not the same persecution, and for the same cause, going on in Poland in the nineteenth? The old Gothic tower still remains, and in it his close dungeon. A church has been built adjoining, but the actual prison remains intact. There are some good pictures in the church, especially a Madonna, by Murillo; and a clever picture of St. Ignatius in his room, meditating on his conversion. There is also a fine statue of St. Hermengilde himself, by Mountanés, over the high altar. The good old priest who had the care of this church lived in a little room adjoining, like a hermit in his cell, entirely devoted to painting and to the 'culte' of his patron saint. St. Gregory the Great attributes to the merits of this martyr the conversion of his brother, afterwards King Recared, the penitence of his father, and the Christianising of the whole kingdom of the Visigoths in Spain.

From thence our travellers went on to the orphanage managed by the 'Trinitarian sisters.' The house was built in the last century, by a charitable lady, who richly endowed it, and placed 200 children there; now, the government, without a shadow of right, has taken the whole of the funds of the institution, and allows them barely enough to purchase bread. The superior is in despair, and has scarcely the heart to go on with the work. She has diminished the number of the children, and has been obliged to curtail their food, giving them neither milk nor meat except on great festivals. But for the intervention of the Duc de Montpensier, and other charitable persons, the whole establishment must long since have been given up. There are twenty-four sisters. The children work and embroider beautifully, and are trained to every kind of industrial occupation. From this orphanage our party went to the Hospital for Women, managed by the sisters of the third order of St. Francis. It is one of the best hospitals in Seville. There are about 100 women, admirably kept and cared for, and a ward of old and incurable patients besides. The superior, a most motherly, loving soul, to whom everyone seemed much attached, took them over every part of the building. She has a passion for cats, and beautiful 'Angoras' were seen basking in the sun in every window-sill.

This hospital, like the orphanage, is a private foundation; but the government has given notice that they mean to appropriate its funds, and the poor sisters are in terror lest their supplies should cease for their sick. It is a positive satisfaction to think that the government which has dealt in this wholesale robbery of the widow and orphan is not a bit the better for it. One feels inclined to exclaim twenty times a day: 'Thy money perish with thee!'

But of all the charitable institutions of Seville, the finest is the Caridad, a magnificent hospital, or rather 'asilo,' for poor and incurable patients, nursed and tended by the Spanish sisters of St. Vincent de Paul. It was founded in the seventeenth century, by Don Miguel de Mañara, a man eminent for his high birth and large fortune, and one of the knights of Calatrava, an order only given to people whose quarterings showed nobility for several generations. He was in his youth the Don Juan of Seville, abandoning himself to every kind of luxury and excess, although many strange warnings were sent to him, from time to time, to arrest him in his headlong, downward course. On one occasion especially, he had followed a young and apparently beautiful figure through the streets and into the cathedral, where, regardless of the sanctity of the place, he insisted on her listening to his addresses. What was his horror, on her turning round, in answer to his repeated solicitations, when the face behind the mask proved to be that of a skeleton! So strongly was this circumstance impressed on his mind, that he caused it afterwards to be painted by Valdés, and hung in the council-room of the hospital. Another time, when returning from one of his nocturnal orgies, he lost his way, and, passing by the Church of Santiago, saw, to his surprise, that the doors were open, the church lit, and a number of priests were kneeling with lighted tapers round a bier in perfect silence. He went in and asked 'whose was the funeral?' The answer of one after the other was: 'Don Miguel de Mañara.' Thinking this a bad joke, be approached the coffin, and hastily lifted up the black pall which covered the features of the dead. To his horror, he recognised himself. This event produced a complete change in his life. He resolved to abandon his vicious course, and marry, choosing the only daughter of a noble house, as much noted for her piety as for her beauty. But God had higher designs in store for him, and after a few years spent in the enjoyment of the purest happiness, his young wife died suddenly. In the first violence of his grief, Don Miguel thought but of escaping from the world altogether, and burying himself in a monastery. But God willed it otherwise. There was at that time, on the right bank of the Guadalquiver, a little hermitage dedicated to St. George, which was the resort of a confraternity of young men who had formed themselves into brothers of charity, and devoted themselves to the care of the sick and dying poor. Don Diego Mirafuentes was their 'hermano mayor,' or chief brother, and being an old friend of Don Miguel's, invited him to stay with him, and, by degrees, enlisted all his sympathies in their labours of love. He desired to be enrolled in their confraternity, but his reputation was so bad, that the brotherhood hesitated to admit him; and when at last they yielded, determined to put his sincerity and humility to the test by ordering him to go at once from door to door throughout Seville (where he was so well known) with the bodies of certain paupers, and to crave alms for their interment. Grace triumphed over all natural repugnance to such a task; and with his penitence had come that natural thirst for penance which made all things appear easy and light to bear, so that very soon he became the leader in all noble and charitable works.

Finding that an asylum or home was sadly needed in winter for the reception of the houseless poor, he purchased a large warehouse, which he converted into rooms for this purpose; and by dint of begging, got together a few beds and necessaries, so that by the Christmas following more than 200 sick or destitute persons were here boarded and lodged. From this humble beginning arose one of the most magnificent charitable institutions in Spain. The example of Don Miguel, his burning charity, his austere self-denial, his simple faith, won all hearts. Money poured in on every side; every day fresh candidates from the highest classes pleaded for admission into the confraternity. It was necessary to draw up certain rules for their guidance, and this work was entrusted to Don Miguel, who had been unanimously elected as their superior. Nowhere did his wisdom, prudence, and zeal appear more strongly than in these regulations, which still form the constitutions of this noble foundation. Defining, first, the nature of their work—the seeking out and succouring the miserable, nursing the sick, burying the dead, and attending criminals to their execution—he goes on to insist on the value of personal service, both private and public; on the humility and self-abnegation required of each brother; that each, on entering the hospital, should forget his rank, and style himself simply 'servant of the poor,' kissing the hand of the oldest among the sufferers, and serving them as seeing Jesus Christ in the persons of each. The notices of certain monthly meetings and church services which formed part of the rule of the community were couched in the following terms:—'This notice is sent you lest you should neglect these holy exercises, which may be the last at which God will allow you to assist.' Sermons and meditations on the Passion of our Lord, and on the nearness of death and of eternity, formed the principal religious exercises of the confraternity; in fact, the Passion is the abiding devotion of the order.

3.2

Roman Catholicism in Ireland

3.2 Roman Catholicism in Ireland

A nineteenth-century historian of Roman Catholicism stated: 'To give any adequate account of the Catholic Church in Ireland . . . would be to write the history of a nation; for no people in the world have ever been more identified with their faith and with the Church.'[1] The first reliable religious census in Ireland (1861) reported 77.7 per cent of the population as Roman Catholics, a dispossessed majority in the context of the Protestant Ascendancy.[2] By the late nineteenth century, Catholicism was becoming aligned with a new popular politics which explicitly connected religious, political and economic grievances. The extract assumes such a connection, written at a crucial time for Irish national consciousness: the Home Rule movement was gaining pace, the National Land League was working to undo the oppressions of landlordism, and Protestant privilege was being dismantled, not least through the disestablishment of the Anglican Church of Ireland in 1871: Roman Catholicism was emerging from an era of suppression.

The series of letters from which the extract is taken were published from May to November 1883 in the *Nation*, a Catholic nationalist journal, then issued in volume form in 1884 and again, expanded, in 1888. The whole work is an extended critique of the Church for failing to align itself coherently with the Irish people's interests and to act as their moral leader and champion of their rights. Even though the colonial establishment no longer had its own church, the author accuses church leaders, 'Castle Bishops', of being allied ideologically with it.

For this unidentified author, Roman Catholicism is the native as well as the true religion, intrinsically bound up with Irish spiritual interests and cultural survival. Dating the start of Ireland's liberation to Daniel O'Connell's entry to the British Parliament in 1828, the 'layman' considers the people to have been failed in their journey to full political and cultural nationhood, first by the Catholic aristocracy who placed class interests before patriotism, but more egregiously by the Church whom he accuses of 'paralysis'. Convinced that in its ideal form '[t]he spirit of the Catholic Church . . . is the spirit of justice', he attacks the Church for failing to support land rights for the rack-rented majority, or to fight for a distinctly Catholic education which might produce a non-anglicised intelligentsia as well as preserving souls. He alludes to the policy of non-denominational education in schools and colleges, which he interprets as effectively a strategy to dilute Catholicism. Reserving praise for John McHale, the late Archbishop of Tuam who strove for the Irish nationalist cause as a matter of religious justice, he condemns Archbishop Cullen, the first Irish Cardinal and an Ultramontane extremist – having high regard for the Pope's authority in secular as well as spiritual affairs – who whilst leading a devotional revival was vigorously opposed to nationalist organisations. The author's tone is impassioned, sometimes bitter, in his disappointment at the Catholic Church's wasted opportunity, arguing that in the crisis context of the battle for Home Rule 'polite euphemisms would be wholly out of place'. Some choice words are reserved for Catholics in Britain who have unanimously failed to support their Irish brethren, such as the English ecclesiastic who poured forth a 'tirade' against Charles Stewart Parnell and Michael Davitt, key activists in the Irish National Land League: 'The average British Catholic is, in Irish affairs, an Englishman first, and a Catholic after'.

The extract entitled 'The Roman letter' alludes to an event which tested the loyalty of Irish nationalists to the Church of Rome, since it set the two causes in explicit conflict. In 1883 the Church of Rome had issued a circular to condemn the Parnell Testimonial Fund which was set up to support the leader of the National Land League, fearing that this kind of activity would 'inflame popular passions . . . leading men into rebellion against the laws'.[3] This political intervention exasperated nationalist Irish clergy, while testing the faithful's submission to Papal Infallibility (declared doctrine in 1870). The author's indignant protest against the circular negotiates this conflict of loyalties by recognising the Pope's absolute authority in *spiritual* affairs (citing Comte Joseph-Marie de Maistre's 1819 theologically conservative work 'Du Pape'), but not in *temporal* matters, and he correctly assumes that the Pope had little to do with this high-handed pronouncement.[4] Throughout the *Letters*, the writer maintains that loyalty to the true Catholic Church is not only compatible with, but inseparable from, full nationalist commitment. (Note that a lengthy explanatory footnote has been omitted from the extract).

Notes

1 Anon., 'The Church of Rome', in *Christianity in Great Britain: An Outline of its Rise, Progress and Present Condition* (London: Hodder & Stoughton, 1874), p. 44.
2 Sean Connolly, *Religion and Society in Nineteenth-Century Ireland* (Dundalk: Dundalgan Press Ltd, 1994 [1985]), p. 4.
3 Quoted by Emmet Larkin, *The Roman Catholic Church and the Creation of the Modern Irish State 1878–1886* (Dublin: Gill and Macmillan, 1975), p. 186.
4 According to Larkin, *The Roman Catholic Church*, pp. 193–194.

8

[ANON.], *LETTERS OF AN IRISH CATHOLIC LAYMAN; BEING AN EXAMINATION OF THE PRESENT STATE OF IRISH AFFAIRS IN RELATION TO THE IRISH CHURCH AND THE HOLY SEE* [1883]

(Dublin: Nation Office, 1884),
pp. 12–20 (abridged), 97–98, 2–5 (abridged)

The Irish Church and Irish Politics

When O'Connell wrung from an unwilling Legislature the Act which made him one of the most beneficent as he was himself one of the greatest of men, he emancipated a people who were in many ways as unfit for as they were unused to freedom. Their slavish submission to their former masters was continued long after it ceased to be imperative. The habit of association for the conduct of affairs, the noble and disinterested public spirit developed in free communities, were almost wholly wanting. The various orders of the social hierarchy had either no cohesion or were at deadly enmity with each other. Emancipation itself was mainly theoretical. It gave the Irish a nominal freedom—permission to follow their own destiny on their own soil, the governing classes taking care to retain the shaping of that destiny and the ownership of that soil. "Catholics," said Sir Robert Peel to the old Tory who reproached him with raising Papists to the magistracy, "will be eligible, but they won't be appointed;" and they are not appointed to this day, save on condition of attorning to the English interest and doing their master's work.

Two classes there were who were capable of completing the social, industrial, and political emancipation of Ireland, the Catholic aristocracy and the Catholic Church. The people were always ready. The strength and courage, the virtue and self-sacrifice of the Irish race are in the masses, and they grow stronger as the lowest stratum (in rank) is approached. There is no possible height of patriotism, of religion, of devotion to every great and noble end, to which they are not willing and ready to be led, if leading there be, but unhappily "light and leading" have long been wanting in the quarters from which they might have been expected.

Taking first the Catholic aristocracy, the natural leaders of the people in the public order, it may well be doubted if the world's history shows anything more thoroughly contemptible than the character and conduct of this class. Instead of using their newly-found liberty to raise their fellow-Catholics from poverty and ignorance, they rushed to seize the fruits of a victory in the gaining of which they had no part. O'Connell's action was paralysed and thwarted by the selfishness and corruption of his surroundings. The nobles voted him "vulgar" and "violent." They went with their class and order, and so far from concerning themselves with the welfare of the people, they would not acknowledge the man who gave them the freedom of which they were unworthy. The Catholic landowners were so much engaged in following, and often surpassing the rack-renting and evicting practices of their Protestant fellows that they had neither time nor inclination to attempt the foundation of a better order of things. And so the unhappy country struggled on from famine to famine, from convulsion to convulsion, till Davitt and Parnell and the Land League came to raise it to renewed hope and a higher aim and life. This contemptible and emasculate Catholic landocracy had their opportunity. They might have led the people in the paths of justice and right, of peace and progress: they preferred to go over to the enemy; they also preferred to stand by their class and order, though the majority of these were descendants of Cromwell's troopers, who despised them while they accepted their aid to trample on the people. Their profound selfishness and meanness, their want of self-respect and Catholic spirit, were in nothing so well seen as in their joining in numbers the Orange Emergency Eviction Committee, which had for its avowed object the extermination of Catholics and the replanting of the country with "loyal" Protestants! [...]

There remained that great institution, the Church of God, set by Divine Wisdom to repair the defects of human society and restore it, as far as the loss of man's integrity permits, to its original condition. The spirit of the Catholic Church, however it may be occasionally deflected by human weakness, is the spirit of justice. It emancipated the slave, and made the poor in all times and countries the object of its tenderest concern. It stood for legitimate freedom against German emperor and Tudor king, defending human liberty as the surest foundation of religion. The history of the Middle Ages, from the eighth to the fourteenth century, is mainly composed of the struggles of the Popes to preserve it from the attacks of tyrants. In various times and places it is true that ecclesiastics have been found on the wrong side, but this was when the State had intruded its baneful influence. The nomination to benefices on the part of the Sovereign led to the gradual decay of Catholic spirit among the clergy. The Church in France is now suffering martyrdom because a section of its members allied itself with a corrupt court and a worthless aristocracy; and whenever she loses her influence and fails in her Divine work, it is because of this unnatural connection with her and our enemies. To her it might be held to fall, with special suitability, to reform and refound society in Ireland. For to her it is due that the Irish nation exists as it is, or exists at all in any condition above savage life. To the strict morality she imposes are due the wonderful vitality and recuperative power of the Irish race; to her humanising influence the amenity and courtesy of manner which distinguish the Irish peasant above all his fellows. To the Church, which sustained him in a struggle of unrivalled intensity and duration, he might naturally have looked to complete his triumph; and in happier circumstances he would not have looked in vain.

But while nation and Church emerged victorious from the conflict, they bore, and long must continue to bear, the scars and wounds of that mortal strife. It would be preposterous to expect the arts of peace to flourish in times of war. It would be still more absurd to expect that the Irish Church should display, when the time of combat was over, the beauteous developments which adorn her in times of peace—the flowers and fruit of the counsels of perfection which, where the fulness of her power prevails, make the earth itself a paradise and give her children a foretaste of heaven.

Frankly, the Church was unequal to the task before her when Emancipation struck the fetters from her limbs. A later "discipline of the secret" had tied, as it still ties, her tongue. Though she has at her command the pulpit, the press, and the platform, though of a race one of whose gifts is oratory, she is rarely heard, and her eminent speakers may be numbered by units instead of hundreds. This is one of the results of the repression of her natural life and the paralysis which falls on the noblest faculties when unused.

These who form their opinion of the Church's power from her action in this country, thwarted on all sides and depressed as she has been, have little notion of the effect she produces when her Divine powers have free play. The least acquaintance with the centuries succeeding the fall of the Roman Empire suffices to show that she everywhere displayed an amazing vigour and resource in laying the foundations of the Christian order of society, from whence has come to us everything of value in modern civilisation. The action of the secular power in the social and moral orders was little more than a disturbance or perversion of the beneficent work of the Church. In the religious orders, pre-eminently in the Benedictine, were contained the most fruitful and active principles of true civilisation; while their government gave the best example of the union of freedom with authority. To impute to the Church then the power to reform society and place it on a sound and progressive basis is simply to declare what she has done before, and may at any time do again. Her canon law embraces the principles of natural equity and the higher law revealed by the Gospel; and on these must all just secular legislation proceed.

We are contemplating what the Irish Hierarchy might have done. What it did do was unhappily very different. And this makes it necessary in the present exigency, to declare that, while the Irish Church has succeeded magnificently in the spiritual order, she has failed signally, if not utterly, in the temporal. Not without a grave sense of responsibility is this charge made; and some distinctions and reservations should properly precede it. When using the word Hierarchy then, I do so only collectively, and as regards the Church's corporate action. The Providence of God has always provided that the Hierarchy in this country should include prelates as truly and ardently Irish, as they are Catholic. It is clear that, whatever may be said of the failure of the Church to use its enormous power for the public good, no blame can attach to the bishops who would have done their duty if permitted. Neither do I presume to impute to the policy followed by any bishop the slightest shade of moral wrong. Such an imputation would be as abhorrent to my sense of duty and of fitness, as it is wholly unnecessary for the effect of the argument. It is no just reproach to a good and zealous bishop that he is not also a wise politician or a sagacious statesman. It is my happiness and advantage to know some of the prelates whose public conduct will be most severely arraigned. They are one and all men of simple and most edifying lives, exemplary in the discharge of the essential duties of their great office, and of such personal holiness that we may well believe they would not shrink from the striking of

——"A deeper, darker dye,
In purple of their dignity,"

did country or faith require the sacrifice of their lives. Again, in estimating the public action of our prelates, it cannot be overlooked that they have to view questions from all sides; that they are charged with the salvation of every baptised Christian within the bounds of their jurisdiction; and that prudence, one of the first of episcopal virtues, is from its very nature exceedingly apt to degenerate into timidity, and to ally itself with the selfishness from which the human heart is seldom entirely free. In reviewing their political action, as I intend doing with the utmost freedom consistent with due respect, I again declare that I am Catholic before all and beyond all. As, with God's help, I am ready to sacrifice everything, even life itself, rather than yield one jot or tittle of the inestimable treasure of the faith—supposing that the indivisible could be divided—so for Ireland I can desire no less than the good I claim for myself, and would rather see her remain a martyr till the crack of doom than she should lose the glorious distinction of being the most Catholic of nations.

But martyrdom is not the normal condition of a nation's life; nor is it desirable save when inevitable.

Ireland has had a long spell of it, and her children may now hope that in the councils of Divine Wisdom a brighter and happier day is approaching. It is to hasten that day that I dare point out the gravest obstacles to its advent, and to declare that these exist not in the machinations of our enemies so much as in the errors of our friends. [...]

It is surely an evil day for Ireland when it has become necessary to arraign at the bar of public opinion the action of a considerable portion of her hierarchy. The creation of this necessity is not the work of the Irish people, but of their enemies; and on them be the blame, if such there be. Assuming it to exist, as we are amply justified in doing, the gravity of the facts, and the importance of the principles involved, require that the indictment should be drawn with the utmost frankness. In the crisis which exists at this moment in Irish affairs, polite euphemisms would be wholly out of place.

Again declaring that I do not presume to judge the moral nature of the action in question, I have nevertheless to charge that portion of the hierarchy which has made and makes common cause with the English Government in Ireland with the violation of several of the gravest obligations belonging to the episcopal office. Their action has been in many respects a practical abandonment of their duty as guardians of faith and morals. As publicists they have failed to vindicate the principles of the Christian order, as patriots they sided with the open and avowed enemies of their country.

Short of the charge of heresy no weightier could be brought. It is not done without reflection, nor without the sanction and approval of many whose characters, training, and sacred office satisfy the writer that the task he has undertaken is not only justifiable but meritorious. Individual examples and detailed proofs of the truth of the indictment will be forthcoming. Meanwhile, it will be useful to point out that as on Irish soil two hostile and mutually destructive principles have combated for centuries, so within the circle of the Irish hierarchy the two have always found advocates and defenders. In old times we have had bishops of the Pale; now we have bishops of the Castle; formerly the statute of Kilkenny, now the "suppression" in many dioceses of any priest brave enough to show any feeling of patriotism. It is clear that if the policy with which the late Dr. McHale was identified represented every Irish and Catholic interest, that identified with the late Cardinal Cullen was subversive and destructive of all embraced by these words. If Dr. McHale truly represented, as we know he did, the Irish people and the Church of God, the Cardinal on every point where the two prelates were in opposition represented the enemies of both. [...]

"Pontius Pilate," wrote the Bishop of Orleans to Napoleon III., when charging him with betraying the Pope, "has been placed in the pillory of our creed, not for commanding, or even desiring, the commission of the greatest crime of all history, but for not preventing it when in his power." In like manner, by no straining of argument, but by direct consequence of his action or inaction, the Castle Bishop is in a great degree answerable for the suffering and crime, the untold misery and sin, arising from our condition for the past fifty years; for he it was who broke the unity of the Irish Church and paralysed its action—he it was who, abandoning the straight and noble paths of Irish nationality and Catholic principle, allied himself with the basest forms of heretical pravity, and imperilled the very faith of Ireland in return for places for corrupt Whig lawyers. When prompt and decided action was needed, he temporised; when strict adherence to principle was necessary, he compromised; and in these two words, "temporise" and "compromise," are found the unhappy source of all our more recent sufferings. The proof unhappily is on the face of our history. At one of the first meetings of the hierarchy after emancipation, Dr. McHale proposed, as the Church's first duty in the public order, to formulate, with aid of jurist and canonist, the claim of the Irish people. 1st, to the most elementary of all rights, the right of existence by their labour on the soil of their country. 2nd, to the just and impartial administration of the law—such as it was; and 3rd, the right of the Irish Catholic people to Irish and

Catholic education. He was withstood in this as in many another proposal, the carrying of which would have begun, if not wrought out, our real emancipation. His sagacity, courage, and patriotism was brought to nought by the inconsistent, the timid, and time serving. Some provision for Irish Catholic education was the necessary complement of emancipation. Some consistency, courage, and adherence to principle were all that were wanting to provide that the Irish Catholic people should have Irish Catholic schools. The hierarchy were wanting in all three, and, with a blindness which amazes us yet, consented to a compromise condemned by Catholic principles, and issuing in a system neither Irish nor Catholic—save by accident. From this compromise have issued, in congruous and monstrous series, the Model Schools, the Godless Colleges, and the Queen's (and now the Royal) University. From this has also arisen the destruction of thousands of young men whom a Catholic education would have saved, and the absence of a truly educated class of Irish gentry, who would have long ere this led the country to freedom and peace. John of Tuam, indeed, strove like a hero, as he was, for freedom and purity in education; but he strove almost alone, and the most powerful external agency of the Church—the Christian School—was given up to our enemies by the sworn defenders of the Christian order. [...]

If I were writing a history of Ireland, many chapters could be given to the action of ecclesiastics from 1830 to 1850. As it is, I can only point out that our Churchmen were incapable, or at all events did not attempt, to undertake the work of which the Catholic aristocracy was not worthy. The first necessity after political emancipation was industrial. The first duty was to bring the law of the land into conformity with justice and the law of God. Three fourths of the people of Ireland dwelt on its soil strangers in their own country, subject to be deprived of land and life at the will of an alien and too often hostile proprietary. That they were so deprived in hundreds of thousands, we know too well. To this evil condition may be traced two of the principal defects in the national character. The serf deceives his master to escape the lash, and drinks to drown the feeling of degradation. Our later history, that of a people declining in numbers and wealth, acquiring little by little, by force of *quasi* insurrection, the commonest rights of citizens, is proof of the absurdity of endeavouring to found a new order on such conditions as were present in Ireland fifty years ago. Now, all the bishops had mastered the tract "of justice." They knew the labourer was worthy of his hire; they knew that what a man made was justly his; and they looked on and saw their people rack-rented and evicted, scourged and decimated, and they made no combined or effective effort for their protection. [...]

In the organisation of the Church of Ireland exists a power never yet used for Ireland. It is a power co-extensive with the island, touching and controlling all within it, Catholic and non-Catholic. Did the Irish bishops unite at any time on the attainment of any Irish or Catholic measure, their organisation would make them irresistible. The land question could have been settled half a century ago, and the strife of classes prevented by the stoppage of landgrabbing, the erection in every parish of a tenants' defence association, with the parish priest for president, and the assertion of the principle, now happily in force, that no man should take a farm evicted for non-payment of an unjust rent. This would have been a land law making the inequitable and, as events have too well proved, inefficient operation of the present Land Courts unnecessary. The first duty incumbent on the leaders of the Irish people, either in the lay or ecclesiastical orders, was the protection by law of their lives and properties. Neither one nor other was equal to the task.

The Castle Bishop and the English Catholic Faction

... The average British Catholic is, in Irish affairs, an Englishman first, and a Catholic after. He never reads an Irish Catholic or national paper. I met lately a friend, an English ecclesiastic of high position, and almost before the ordinary greeting was over, he literally burst into a tirade of abuse against Parnell and Davitt, and the Irish movement generally. While he was exhausting himself, I thought: is it any use trying to enlighten this good man? and concluding it was not, replied never a word, and talked of the weather. Another priest on the London mission made, in the hearing of the writer, an extraordinary statement respecting an event which had just occurred. On being challenged for his authority, he replied: "Oh, I saw it in the *Times* and the speech of the Attorney-General." This gentleman would resent being called unfair and unjust, yet he goes for his facts to a hired slanderer, and to the most notorious and inveterate enemy of everything Irish.

This is the ordinary state of mind of the average Englishman—Catholic and Protestant, lay and cleric. It is created and supported by a thousand influences. It is upheld by a feeling of his own superiority, and of consequent contempt for the people who trouble his peace and rather damage him in the world's opinion. Not always consciously, there is yet at the bottom of his mind the notion that the Irish are an inferior people, and therefore defends the whole course of English rule in Ireland by "the right of conquest," which is pure paganism, and that their domination by the imperial race is part of the "eternal fitness of things."

Those who have had opportunities of comparing the two peoples in every one particular honourable to men may smile at this feeling, but it is a very real misfortune for us, since it is that which most constantly operates against the formation in England of a just public opinion. Whatever excuse or palliation there may be for the layman who yields willingly to the anti-Irish influence, there is none, it seems to me, for the cleric. For he is bound to weigh facts in the scale of the sanctuary. He is doubly bound as a teacher to know the truth. He should remember that English society is essentially pagan; that its beginning was in an impious lie—the assertion that Henry VIII and not the Pope was the Vicar of Christ; that it is the outcome of a blasphemous rebellion against God and the Church of which he is a minister; and that in its every development it shows daily clearer and clearer the evidence of its origin, and the doom to which it hastens. When he "comes to terms with modern civilisation," when he makes himself one with English society as it exists around him, he acts as the early Christians would have done had they entered into the society of pagan Rome and accepted its toleration, which is another way of saying that Christianity would have perished ere it arose.

In the whole controversy between the two countries the English view is worldly, corrupt, and pagan; the Irish spiritual, just, Christian, Catholic. In adopting the former the English ecclesiastic makes himself, unconsciously though it be, one with the enemies of the Cross of Christ, and impedes with all his power the salvation of his country. [...]

The Roman Letter

SIR,—In the letter to which you gave the unlooked for honour of a place in your leading columns, I proposed to examine the nature and scope of the Papal authority, and, in the light of this inquiry, the value of the document presented for our acceptance by Propaganda.

No man can so well defend his own rights as he who is ready to yield prompt and full obedience to lawful authority. I declare myself, then, an Ultramontane of extremest type—if "extreme" can be correctly predicated of anything relating to the absolute. To the Holy Father I willingly grant all the power he claims, and this not more as a matter of faith than a conclusion of reason. For to him was given the command to "go and teach all nations," the power of Christ Himself to enforce and defend that teaching, and the inerrancy of which the Holy Spirit is the source and guard. Now, our Lord did not come on earth to form a school of philosophy or a sect among sects, but a spiritual kingdom, of which He is the real though unseen Sovereign.

The Church, in claiming such rights and franchises as are necessary for her action in the world, has not only the support of eighteen centuries of beneficence, but the right and authority of Christ dwelling within her, and whose practical providence she is.

In constitution and essence the Church is a Divine and perfect society, sole remaining example in the world of the perfection with which its Creator originally endowed it. By this society God reveals Himself and his law to men; and of this revelation she is the depositary, guardian, and expounder. Her infallibility is a necessary corollary of these offices, since it would be contrary to the wisdom of God to reveal Himself for man's salvation without providing a means by which that knowledge could be certainly gained, and contrary to His justice to impose a law binding under the weightiest sanction without making that law patent to all who desired to live by it.

Of this perfect and Divine society the Pope is chief: not merely her executive, but in a special manner her head. For Christ being one Person, his Vicar must also be one. He must be entitled to present himself to the world as inheriting the princedom of Peter. Assembling the councils of the Church, he dictates the matters of discussion, closes the debates, and gives authority and force to their decrees. All this goes to show that the plenitude of apostolic power is in the Papacy, and demonstrates, as De Maistre long ago pointed out, that it would be utterly irrational and preposterous to predicate a fallible head of an infallible body.

Not only do I gladly and thankfully embrace the doctrine of Papal infallibility in respect of the *matter* defined, but I assert for the Pope the right of declaring the range of subjects within the scope of definition. That is to say, the Pope, in imposing on us the duty of implicit obedience, is prevented by the Holy Spirit from transcending his own powers. [...]

But this perfect and grateful obedience is rendered to the Pontiff in the spiritual order only. In this he, like his Master, has the word of Eternal Life, and to whom should we go but to him? As Doctor of the Universal Church and Vicar of Christ, we listen with profound veneration, and accept *ex animo* all he teaches. But just in proportion to our prompt docility, when he has right to command, we claim the fuller liberty without the boundary of that right. [...] Finally, this absolute and unconditional authority is confined to the definition of matters of faith and morals alone, and to such matters of order and discipline as necessarily issue from them.

Besides the matters of moment in which the Pope personally intervenes, a vast amount of business is transacted by the various Congregations and by Propaganda; and this naturally brings us to the present circular, which, I am deeply thankful to say, does not seem to be, in any true sense, a Papal utterance at all. Probably the Pope knew of some disciplinary circular being in preparation; more probably he was not aware of its terms; and most certainly he was not cognisant of its true nature. It is clear that a vast mass of business must pass through the courts which cannot possibly come under the personal observation of his Holiness. And we will best consult for his dignity by assuming that this document, as it has reached us, was never seen by him. Surely never before did anything so injurious and unfounded issue from the Roman Chancery. The style, so rash and violent, is unwholly unlike that of a Roman circular, and is much more nearly allied to what we are used to from the London *Times* or from Dublin Castle. Putting aside "Mr. Parnell and his objects" (as if these did not include the cause of Ireland and all that that implies), we are told that "some of his followers adopted a line of conduct different from instructions sent to the Irish bishops." We would like to know, first, in what sense the persons alluded to were "Mr. Parnell's followers," and what was "the line of conduct" they adopted. In a document of this gravity we want not vague assertions nor railing accusations, but the *ipsissima verba* of the peccant matter condemned. Further, we would like to be informed how instructions to the Irish bishops for their own guidance could be held to bind Mr. Parnell and his followers, to whom these instructions were not conveyed; and why he or they were to be stigmatised and punished for not obeying instructions they never saw, and which were not meant for them.

It is difficult to analyse fully this extraordinary paper and preserve the respect due to Propaganda. Even now it is hard to believe it ever came from Rome. The most offensive and injurious thing about it is the implication underlying it all, that "Mr. Parnell and his followers" (the nine bishops and hundreds of priests who go to make up his committee included) are answerable for the crimes which are the natural and almost necessary outcome of English rule in Ireland!

Part 4

SCOTTISH PRESBYTERIANISM

4.1

The Church of Scotland

4.1 The Church of Scotland

The Church of Scotland was not a state church in the same sense as was the Church of England, enjoying a higher degree of autonomy over clerical appointments through its Presbyterian structure of government compared to the Anglican Church's deference to the crown. Following the Great Disruption of 1843, when over a third of the Church's more Evangelical ministers seceded to form the Free Church, the Church of Scotland's size and status was considerably diminished; 752 out of 1,206 ministers remained. The Church of Scotland, now 'the Auld Kirk', could no longer claim to speak for the nation, having an attendance of only 32.2 per cent of the population according to the 1861 census.[1] Through the nineteenth century, Scottish Presbyterianism of established and non-established varieties went through something of a 'religious revolution' in terms of doctrine, worship and social attitudes.[2] The early nineteenth-century Presbyterian ethos was strictly ascetic in its worship and morality: by its critics, Scottish Calvinism was easily caricatured as gloomy, oppressive and dry. However, in the second half of the century this severity softened to accommodate more liberal social and theological perspectives, and the Church of Scotland, with its larger contingent of Moderates, adapted a little more easily than its Free Church counterpart.

Nowhere is the struggle between puritanical values and adaptation to the world better demonstrated than in debates about Sabbath observance, the subject of the following extract. The Evangelical ascendancy stood for a rigid Sabbatarianism which criminalised (and indeed prosecuted) Sunday labour that was not 'a work of necessity or of mercy' as was permitted according to Matthew Henry's popular Bible commentary on Luke 6:1–11 when Jesus feeds his disciples and heals a man on the Sabbath, to the indignation of the legalistic Pharisees.[3] The Sabbatarian stance commanded enough popular support in Scotland to prevent the running of Sunday trains in the 1840s, and to stop the Sunday opening of leisure venues such as the Edinburgh Botanic Gardens in 1863. The test case for changing attitudes came in September 1865 when the newly launched Sunday train service between Edinburgh and Glasgow evoked a disapproving letter from the Glasgow Presbytery. This objection was vigorously countered by Reverend Dr Norman MacLeod (1812–72), minister at Barony Church, Glasgow, and known for his moderate tendencies as well as his key role in Scottish Presbyterianism's development of a social theology.

In his speech to the Glasgow Presbytery, from which the extract is taken, MacLeod makes a firm distinction between the Sabbath, an Old Testament ordinance particular to ancient Jewish culture, and 'the Lord's Day' established in the era of Christ. Showing what the Sabbath meant in its original context, he demonstrates that perfect imitation is not achievable even if desirable, also noting hypocrisies in rigid modern Sabbatarian practice: he targets the middle classes for making their servants work on a Sunday. Painting a grim image of the ascetic Scottish Sunday (where, like many Protestant polemicists of the era, he pejoratively describes pedantic legalism as 'Judaism'), he then argues for keeping the

Lord's Day in the spirit of Jesus's announcement that the Sabbath was made for man, not man for the Sabbath (Mark 2:27).

In what he calls 'the socialism of Christianity', MacLeod then presents a range of physical, intellectual, social and spiritual benefits that the Lord's Day can serve, not least the rare opportunity of leisure for the working classes, which renders closure of parks and the banning of trains on Sunday a form of oppression. Above all, he has in mind the needs of the working man for rest and sociability, placing religious duties last in what is in fact a powerful defence *for* Sabbatarianism of a more human-centred kind. MacLeod's speech reveals a modernising Church in its application of cultural relativism to Old Testament legislation, and in his (anti-Calvinistic) humanist interpretation of the function of religious ordinances: 'It is not that the day *itself* is holy, but the great ends and objects which are secured by the day are so.'

MacLeod's speech and publication provoked a brief but intense pamphlet war, and some personal obloquy, but four years later he was appointed Moderator of the Church of Scotland, a sign that the Church was coming to terms with the altered conditions of modern society.[4] More permissive attitudes towards a limited use of recreational facilities on a Sunday emerged, so that the Church raised little protest in the 1870s against Sunday pleasure steamers, museum and park openings, concerts, lectures and tram services, leaving it to the consciences of individual ministers to judge how to guide their flock in Sabbath practice. (Footnotes referencing expansive appendices have been omitted from the extract).

Notes

1 Callum G. Brown, *Religion and Society in Scotland since 1707* (Edinburgh: Edinburgh University Press, 1997), p. 22.
2 A. C. Cheyne, *Transforming of the Kirk: Victorian Scotland's Religious Revolution* (Edinburgh: St Andrew Press, 1983), pp. 1–3.
3 https://www.biblegateway.com/resources/matthew-henry/Luke.6.1-Luke.6.11
4 See R. D. Brackenbridge, 'The "Sabbath War" of 1865–66: the Shaking of the Foundations', *Records of the Scottish Church History Society*, 16 (1966), pp. 23–34.

9

NORMAN MACLEOD, *THE LORD'S DAY: SUBSTANCE OF A SPEECH DELIVERED AT A MEETING OF THE PRESBYTERY OF GLASGOW ON THURSDAY 16TH NOVEMBER 1865*

(Glasgow: James MacLehose, 1865), pp. 11–16 [abridged] and 29–35 [abridged]

Let us, then, briefly inquire as to the nature of the Fourth Commandment. What is it? Under what obligations does it really place us, for the discharge of which we are responsible to God? As to its letter, it is clear, for example, that it authoritatively binds us to keep *the* seventh day holy. It is not *a* seventh—that is, in my opinion, not fair criticism. Indeed, I am not aware that this has ever been seriously questioned, except perhaps by those who, judging from their line of argument, fear that the elasticity of "*a* day" is required to make the commandment applicable to the whole world, while *"the* day" would seem to favour the conclusion to which they object, that it was for a limited portion of the globe only. Further, the Sabbath of the Fourth Commandment was from evening to evening. It began upon—what we should call—the Friday evening, and ended upon the Saturday evening. This fact is of some importance as telling on social habits. You remember, doubtless, what Michaelis makes of this, shewing the much more favourable position in which the Jew was placed in the fine climate of Palestine, as compared with the Christian, especially the poor Christian, in the cold, damp climate of Northern Europe. The Jew, he reminds us, might, for example, have his hot dinner on the Friday afternoon before the Sabbath began. In the delicious climate of Palestine he might have on the Sabbath his milk, his grapes,—all, in fact, that he could desire in hot weather; and then, when the evening of Saturday closed, he might have his hot dinner again. This, as a fact, bears very materially upon the question of breaking the Fourth Commandment, as it has been hitherto explained in Scotland, where men seriously talk of the sin of cooking a hot dinner on Sunday!

Then, consider further, the *objects* of the Fourth Commandment. The Sabbath was, no doubt, a grand witness for Jehovah as the Creator of the world, but especially for that Creator as being the very same God who had brought the children of Israel out of Egypt. It was also a blessed day of rest, and I doubt not, to the spiritually seeing Jew, was a shadow of better things to come. It is a fair question, indeed, how far the blessed rest secured by the Jewish Sabbath was at all connected with *public* worship. I certainly am very much inclined to think that it was more of an end in itself than a means of attaining anything higher, beyond that of individual worship and social instruction—not necessarily by Levites—on Divine things. For let us recollect the circumstances of the country. How, for example, could there have been any *united* worship upon that day? You may force the word "sanctify" to mean that, though it may also mean simply "separate," or "set apart." But if you mean *public* worship—where could that worship have been performed, according to the Mosaic law? Synagogues did not exist for a long time after the giving of the law. The question of their origin is a difficult one. They were not Mosaic, but began probably about the time of Ezra. The convocations that are spoken of up to that time were connected with the sacrifice at the Tabernacle or Temple, for social worship was then connected so much with a place, either at Gilgal, or Gibeon, or Shiloh, or in the Temple, or wherever the Ark was, that to enjoy it in Palestine every "Sabbath," as we do now in Scotland, was for ages physically and "ecclesiastically" impossible. There was of course on that, as on every other day, individual worship; but when you are running a parallel between the Sabbath of the Fourth Commandment as observed by the Jews in Palestine, and the Lord's-day as enjoyed by Christians, you cannot prove that there was anything among the former corresponding to our worship in our churches. [...]

We do not keep the day; and in a hundred things we do on Sunday what it would have been unlawful for the pious Jew to have done on his Sabbath. Our servants do servile work,—light fires, make beds, clean out our rooms, cook our dinners, &c., and probably drive those to church who have carriages. This is too notorious to be insisted upon; and so, many men feel themselves to be in an inconsistent position, and try to get out of it, just like my excellent friend Dr. Macduff, who, while he holds so firmly to this Fourth Commandment, would allow to be done upon his Sabbath what would have horrified any pious Israelite of any age or time. Dr. Macduff does it because he cannot see any ill in it. He uses his own good Christian common sense, walks in the spirit—but yet, unfortunately, as I think, for my friend's consistency. I maintain that, whatever we clergy may say to the contrary, unprejudiced laymen see in our conduct a manifest inconsistency. I was very often inconsistent on this point, I admit, when I believed as you did. But should any man try to be consistent, and to keep the commandment as it has been described from the pulpit and in tracts by those who lay burdens on men's shoulders which they, perhaps, do not carry themselves—then what follows? Asceticism does. Not, however, that I am one who would despise an ascetic for conscience-sake. It is often a grand visible triumph of spirit over sense, from conviction, however erroneous. And this asceticism, or Judaism, I cannot help seeing in the old Covenanters—noble men, who, if they did not fight for the liberty of others, fought at least for their own, and have preserved the independence of our country. [...]

But there have been other results than mere asceticism from the views I am comparing and combating. I think that the *tone* of teaching, in general, throughout Scotland, which has logically sprung from this view regarding the Sabbath law of the Fourth Commandment, has produced in our country a Judaical spirit, which I think is to be deplored, and ought to be kindly, but firmly exposed, in order to be changed into the true freedom of the Christian life of faith and love through God's Spirit. Look, for example, at the state of most districts in the North of Scotland where this teaching has had full and uncontrolled sway. I might, without any unkindly feeling, challenge any Free Church Minister,—and perhaps I might extend the challenge to those who, in my opinion, are still freer—to some of the Established clergy also in those districts,—whether he would dare to shave on Sunday morning, and let his people know it? Would not his influence be weakened, and his piety suspected? Take another illustration of what I mean. A friend of mine, a deacon of my church, went with a party to fish, the other summer, in one of the outer Hebrides. He was living with a good man, but an out-and-out Jew. My friend had a nice ham, a few slices of which he wished to cook for breakfast on Sunday morning. His host did not refuse to cook the ham, for a Highland Jew, as well as a Palestine one, likes his food. So John began to slice the ham until he came to the bone, when he put down the knife and said, "I would rather not!" "Why, John?" "Because it is the Sabbath." So my deacon had to saw the bone, when John continued the cutting of the ham. I don't "despise" John at all for his scruples. He acted according to his light. I state the fact only as it illustrates the feelings and practices of thousands in the North regarding the Lord's-day; and only by such facts, however trifling they appear to some, can the state of feeling in a country be understood. I could give innumerable illustrations of the same sort, to shew how *hide-bound* people are by the letter. And, alas! many of the clergy themselves have become slaves, and have conscientiously forged the very chains from which they cannot now escape, even while feeling their bondage. [...]

But is this Judaism confined to one part of the country only? I grant that our freedom has been immensely increased. Sentiments to-day even have been uttered that no minister would have dared to have spoken a few years ago. I think we owe much of this liberty, not to the clergy, but to Christian laymen, who have not been so much bound by their position as we have been, and also to the leaders of opinion beyond our country who have unconsciously fought for us. But there is even now in Glasgow a vast deal of Judaism; while things have been done, within our memories, by clergy, magistrates, and police, in the way of interfering with others, which, thanks to public opinion, would not be tolerated now. Yet even now, for example, some will worship with an instrument in Church, and yet will not do so in their own houses. They will train up little children to keep the Lord's-day as if they were old apostles. And in regard to walking on Sunday by those who need it for health, or for recreation,—about which I rejoice to hear the sentiments of my friend, Dr. Macduff,—I ask you, sir, whether Christian men—whether from the effects of long teaching or mere prejudice, I do not know—would not have been, a few years or even months ago, very much shocked at his sentiments? I myself having incidentally mentioned, in a speech about a North-End Park, that I thought on the Sunday evening working-men might enjoy God's fair world with their families, was publicly spoken against, and of course impeached as *exhorting* men to spend the evening in that way only, when I had an extra service in Church for them! There was a howl got up immediately for my daring to say this. [...] Only think of it! We get parks for those working-men—men who rise at five o'clock in the morning, and drudge through life during the day, and come home weary at night—and we have, hitherto, practically said to these men, in the name of the Sabbath of the Lord, "Kennel up into your wretched abodes!" Who dares deny it? For what else was I blamed, I should like to know? Against what else was the cry raised? And let Dr. Macduff beware, or he will have the cry against him too. And to put our Judaism beyond a doubt in this respect, let me remind writers of kind and sensible Pastorals, that our own General Assembly, as late as 1834—I quote second-hand—in a Pastoral addressed to our churches, declared walking on Sunday to be "an impious encroachment on one of the inalienable prerogatives of the Lord's-day." That is what I call clerical Judaism. The same thing comes constantly into play. It comes in contact with the merest trifles as "an everlasting No." Wet or dry, can we take a cab?—No. Why?—The Fourth Commandment. Dare we have a hot joint for dinner on Sunday?—No. Why?—The Fourth Commandment. Can we walk out with our children on Sunday?—No. Why?—The Fourth Commandment. Can we let young children amuse themselves in any way on Sunday?—No. Why?—The Fourth Commandment! [...] What more remarkable proof could I give of the presence and influence of this spirit with which our habits of mind are imbued, than what was said at the recent public meeting in our City Hall about Sabbath trains? A clergyman from England, of our own city,—for whose Christian character I have the highest respect,—stood up, without one single person to dissent from him, not even my friend Dr. Jamieson, who was present, and said, as a proof of how strictly he had been accustomed to keep the Sabbath, that he had never seen a hot joint of meat on Sunday till he came to Scotland; and never had been in a carriage on Sunday; and then, speaking of Sunday travelling, pronounced the judgment, that any man who travelled on a railway on the Lord's-day could not have in him the love of Christ! What Sabbath-breaking could be so bad as the utterance of such a sentiment? And this is just one of the dangers of enslaving people to the letter, instead of leading them up to a spirit and life in Christ; that we get a style of religion which strains at gnats, and swallows camels; which tithes mint, anise, and cummin, and omits the weightier matters of the law—judgment, mercy, and faith; and which has a constant tendency to substitute outward forms, shibboleths, phrases, even tones of voice and peculiarities of manner, for the genuine life which is in and by Jesus Christ,—yea, alas! in many cases, the hate of the old Pharisees at the alleged breaking of an outward rule, for that Christian love which is the fulfilling of the law. With unfeigned sorrow, God knows, I utter this; and greater sorrow must I, or any man, endure, who will dare expose it, though with no other wish than to lead brethren to a truer and nobler position. [...]

Let me, then, endeavour to shew you the grounds on which I think the Lord's-day may be established as an ordinance, which cannot but command the approval of every Christian man, or of any man, indeed, who has any respect for God, or any sense of his own responsibility.

In doing so, let me, in the first place, remind you, that there is a fact essential to Christianity, and that is, the existence of a Church. There is an absolute necessity, as a part of our Christianity, for Christians to meet together for worship, and to remember Christ at the Lord's Supper,—an ordinance given us as a symbol of our fellowship, not only with Christ, but with one another, expressed and strengthened by our eating the one bread and drinking the one cup. [...] The whole social system of the Gospel is a protest against the individual man shrinking up within himself, or remaining alone, saying, "I believe in Christ, that is enough." The Christian, by his very faith and obedience to Christ, dare not do this if he would; and I am sure he would not if he had that love to his brethren which necessarily springs out of love to the Father and Elder Brother. The brotherhood of the Church is rooted in its relationship to the Eternal Son. I maintain, therefore, that if a Christian went to a distant part of the world,—to India, or anywhere else,—he ought to find out other believers, if no Church already existed in the place, and to worship along with them on Sunday, remembering the promise, "Where two or three are met together in my name, there am I in the midst of them." Nay, more, they would meet together to remember Christ at the Lord's Supper, even where there was no ordained minister of the Gospel to dispense it. For am I to be told that Christians, thus meeting in the distant wilderness, are never to remember Jesus Christ till some clergyman comes amongst them; that they have no liberty to constitute themselves into a church for a time; and that if, *in such peculiar circumstances,* they said, in the presence of God, "We recognize this bread and wine no longer as ordinary food, but partake of it in remembrance of Christ,"—this would not be recognized as a holy sacrament? I cannot deny this without going into the Popish idea of the Eucharist, as *necessarily* requiring the consecration of the priest. But for the sake of order,—believing, as I heartily do, in a Christian ministry as the *rule,* and in government of some kind as necessary for every society as distinct from a mob,—such cases are exceptional. But I allude to them as bearing out the great idea of what I might call—if you will pardon the expression—the socialism of Christianity. And I have illustrated, by an extreme case, the importance which I humbly think is attached to the social Christian fellowship of the Church. But if what I have alleged regarding our duty on the Lord's-day, would hold true, even where there was no organized branch of Christ's Catholic Church, how much more binding is the duty in a Christian country!

But supposing that this first duty is granted,—which, remember, I base on *the revealed will of Christ,* and the very existence and necessity of a Christian Church,—I further affirm, that the duty and privilege of such Christian fellowship in holy worship, necessarily involves the appointment of *some fixed day* for the performance of such Christian duties, and for the enjoyment of such Christian privileges. This does not require any proof.

Now I find such a day, as a matter of fact, in existence. I am born into it. I never made it; but I awake and find myself, as a baptized man and a Christian, in the light and glory of a day of rest and worship. I do not at present speak of this or that day of the week, or of *the* day, whether it be the seventh or the first, but of *a* day in each week, which, as a fact, is set apart, in the providence of God, for the social worship of the Christian Church. Now, the fact is a most marvellous one, and one the importance of which can hardly be exaggerated, that *a* day is consecrated wherever the name of Christ is known and Christianity professed, for the worship of God, Father, Son, and Holy Ghost. Once a-week the sun, during twenty-four hours, sheds its light on Christian congregations in prayer throughout the whole earth. And let me here ask, in passing, whether any Christian objects to such a holy day as this? Can he, dare he, do so? Is it possible for him to allege that the Christian Church either need not, or ought not thus to consecrate *any* day of the week? And if one professing Christian were found capable of saying this, is it conceivable that the Christian Church will ever agree with him, and alter the usage of eighteen centuries?

But that we may more fully appreciate the singular blessings of *a* day such as that which, whatever be its origin, we now, as a fact, possess; let me, for the sake of others—because I speak to and for others without, more than to or for those within this house—glance at some of the benefits of this day.

It is, first of all, adapted to our whole wants as men and as Christians,—adapted to our wants physically. The great mass of men require rest from labour. I do not allege that any physical law makes one day in seven necessary, but I am quite sure that this proportion of rest to hard-wrought men is a felt blessing, and is adapted to their wants. I will give an illustration of this. Some years ago, for certain reasons, I went upon a private expedition to Paris, furnished with letters not easily got, to investigate into the state of the working-classes, and some of those cooperative societies which had begun in the time of the Republic. In the course of my inquiry it was necessary to come in contact with many of the Socialists in Paris. I met them in their workshops, and I found a body of men the most intellectual and most intelligent I almost ever met in my life,—men who had utterly broken away from Romanism, but who were more religious in their feelings than most in that city. They believed in a God, in a right and wrong, and in a future state, and led comparatively moral lives. To these men I said, "Well, what is your rule in regard to Sunday work?" The reply was, "We once worked upon it as on other days." "How did you find that succeed?" I asked. "Not at all; very badly: we found at the end of the month that we had not turned out more work; and that it was best to rest on Sunday." I said to my friend, a Protestant clergyman, who was with me,

"I had rather have that testimony from these men, than whole tons of pamphlets by Sabbath Alliances; those might be written with an unconscious bias, but with these men it is not so." And you all know that infidel France, after having banished the day of rest, restored it as a necessity.

Consider, further, this day in *its social aspect*. What a fearful breaking up this busy commercial life is of social ties! Think of the separation among members of the same family: the merchant going off in the morning, working all day, and returning in the evening to dinner, hardly meeting with his family at all. No person blames him for this: it is a necessity—a duty; yet it is socially a loss. He is hardly able to meet his friends in a quiet way, or—so busy is he—to visit that old lonely gentleman or gentlewoman, or even sick relation; or to cultivate much intimacy with his dear children, far less to visit the poor and needy. But this day enables him to do this. He can cultivate all those sweet, tender, affections round the fireside, with wife, children, and friend, and keep up a delightful intercourse with Christian acquaintances. The importance of such a day in this respect to the working-classes it is hardly possible to exaggerate. Here is the father of a family, who, in the morning, in pitch darkness, leaves his house at five or six o'clock,—leaves all his little children in bed, takes a hurried meal, has hardly time to speak to any one at home, and trudges, amidst the clanging of bells, or long before they begin to sound, to a distant part of the town. There you see him in the afternoon, sitting, perhaps on a cold stone, taking his meal that is carried to him in a tin can by some little child. He does not see his family at his meals. He may, indeed, be supplied at one of those noble refreshment rooms of Mr. Corbet's,—and what a blessing they are to the town!—but there is no family life there! At night he returns home, but the children he left in bed he finds in bed. He sits at his fireside; but there is no sweet and pleasant intercourse between the wearied man and wife or child. He hardly knows them. The children, even if not in bed, have probably been out working, and have come back wearied and sleepy. The wife has been toiling all day, and is now busy getting a little supper for her husband. And then the night and oblivion come, and in the morning they rise to pursue again the same routine of labour. Unless these men meet their families on the Lord's-day, and cultivate family affection, I know not what will become of our population. [...]

I might dwell also upon its *intellectual* advantages, as affording opportunity of culture to the mind; and I have no hesitation in saying that, while much has been rightly attributed to the power of our schools, in giving an educational training to our working-classes, far too little has been said about the training of our pulpits. I hold that this has been, perhaps, the most powerful training of all. Some critics, who do not know us, affect to ridicule the argumentative and logical sermons that are preached to the people of Scotland by the Presbyterian clergy; but our people, in former days, at least, understood these sermons, and grappled with their arguments. This was at once a religious and an intellectual training. It may be so now, and often is, as much as in any former age. And, besides, this is almost the only day which men working hard during six days can command for reading. And when we remember the stores of rich intellectual thought and varied information which are placed within the reach of the working-classes, and which even the most scrupulous on the point of "Sunday reading" would not forbid them upon this day, we are more and more impressed with its adaptation to the intellectual wants of man.

But there is another end attained by this day, and that is, the scope which it affords for our active powers in a moral direction. There are an immense number of duties which Christian people ought to discharge to the poor, the needy, and ignorant, that we have no time for during the week. And this activity in the "doing good unto all men as we have opportunity, especially unto them who are of the household of faith," is a true rest for the affections. Rest is thus often but a change of labour; and the Sunday affords a noble opportunity for such activity. Yet, how selfishly is it neglected! How poorly is the noble privilege enjoyed!

But I have hardly alluded to the highest of all ends of this day—its *spiritual* advantages. Nothing has been said by any of my respected brethren on this point with which I do not sympathize most deeply. I pray God for the time when I shall see our wishes more realized. What would become of us if we had not its worship and teaching? All men have to be reminded, that "Man doth not live by bread alone;" but needs the Bread of Life; and must be dealt with as an immortal being; and be led into the peace and blessedness of his Father's home. How is it possible to estimate the moral value, to man, of such a day as we now possess in each week!—a day when all that can quicken the conscience, purify the affections, and elevate the spirit of immortal man, is brought before him in the word read and preached;—when he is taught all that can guide, strengthen, and comfort him in duty, in temptation, and in sorrow;—when true light is cast on this life, and on that which is to come;—when, in one word, *Jesus Christ* as the light, revealing God and man and all things, as the very eternal life of the soul, the all in all, is preached to sinful men, and is remembered by all who know and love Him, while united worship from glad hearts ascends by Him to the throne of God. The very silence of the day is a sermon of rest, in Jesus, for all who are weary and heavy laden. [...]

But not only have we such *a* day as I have described, but we have emphatically *the first day of the week,* being the day of our Lord's resurrection, consecrated as *the* day for all those noble ends. Let us glance at the evidence for this. It is a fact, that the first day of the week has been set apart by the whole Christian Church, up to the days of the Apostles, as a day of worship,—a holy day unto the Lord. Moreover, for three or four centuries before we reach apostolic times, a constant and uniform testimony is borne by all the Fathers, and corroborated by heathen testimony, that Christians met for worship, and for partaking of the sacraments, on the first day of the week, *because* on that day Jesus rose from the dead; while *not one* of the Fathers, in a single instance, connects this sacred day with the Sabbath of the Fourth Commandment; and others protest against the Sabbath, while vindicating "the Lord's-day." But when we examine the teaching of the Apostles themselves, and read the history of the early Church, its institutions and practices, what do we find? We find the first day of the week greatly honoured by Jesus Christ after He rose from the dead, but never the Sabbath in which He lay in the grave.

We find the early Christians everywhere meeting for worship, mutual instruction, and Christian intercourse, on the first day of the week, but never, if Gentile Christians, on the Sabbath. We find St. Paul assuming, everywhere, the existence of social worship on the Lord's-day, but never mentioning the Sabbath, except to protest against its being imposed on Gentiles. And when all this is taken in connection with the glorious objects which are gained by *a* day, I can come to no other conclusion than that *this* day is sanctioned by the Apostles, inspired by the Spirit of God, and under the authority of Jesus Christ. It is not that the day *itself* is holy, but the great ends and objects which are secured by the day are so. These sanctify the day. And what other day could be selected by our Lord with more will and wisdom for the good of His Church than the day of His resurrection?

4.2

The Free Church in Scotland

4.2 The Free Church in Scotland

The Scottish Free Church, the second largest denomination in nineteenth-century Scotland, was formed in the 1843 Disruption when over a third of the ministers, and nearly half the congregation, broke away from the Church of Scotland. Their goal was to preserve the Church's freedom from state interference, a freedom which in theory the Church of Scotland enjoyed, but which in practice was under threat from the government's habit of influencing appointments. Departing ministers also objected to 'broad' tendencies in the established Church, and its failure to reach the urban middle and working classes. Hence the Free Church claimed to be 'not a sect, but the national Church set free', true inheritors of the pure Presbyterian spirit.[1] While not the first or by any means only group to secede from the established Church on these grounds, the Free Church was unique in its size, influence and authority during the Evangelical ascendancy. In 1900 it merged with another secessionist denomination, the United Presbyterian Church, and in 1929 reunited with the established Church to form the National Church of Scotland.

The extract is from Thomas Guthrie's speech commemorating the sixteenth anniversary of the formation of the Free Church, taking stock of its achievements to date and issuing a call for much-needed donations to support its work. Thomas Guthrie (1803–73), minister of a Free Church congregation in Edinburgh, was one of the most popular preachers of his day and became Moderator of the Free Church in 1862. His best-known legacy was his provision for street orphans in Edinburgh in the Ragged Schools, and his advocacy for young criminals.

Money was a constant problem for the Free Church, whose clergy had lost their livings and accommodation, but whose ambitions in mission and social reform placed a heavy burden on voluntary contributions from congregation members; there was also the cost of funding chapels in areas of low population. Guthrie performed the service of raising £116,370 for the Manse fund in 1845–6.[2] This continuing financial need forms the immediate context of Guthrie's speech which reminds listeners of what they owe their ministers who had maintained the purity of the Presbyterian tradition at considerable personal cost.

Subtitled 'A Sermon on Esther ix. 28', the speech associates the Disruption with Purim, which recalls the preservation of God's people from brutal persecution through the bravery of Esther, evoking a theme of crisis and self-sacrifice. After paralleling the Free Church with the people led by Moses away from 'the fleshpots of Egypt' (i.e. the worldly system of secular patronage), Guthrie reminds his audience of the central principle at stake – a congregation's right to choose its own pastor. He likens the Free Church to the Pilgrim Fathers who left Europe to set up a Puritan colony in North America, and presents it as the true inheritor of the spirit of the Covenanters who refused compromise with Episcopalians through the Scottish Reformation (and whose anti-Catholicism Guthrie evidently shares). This is exemplified by mention of the Presbyterian martyr James Guthrie who was arraigned for High Treason and executed in 1661 for opposing state authority over the church. Thomas Guthrie alludes to Jesus's instruction to 'render unto Caesar the things that are Caesar's, and unto God the things that are God's' (Matthew 22:21) as a mandate for the separation of secular and spiritual powers. He also alludes to William Hamilton's critical view on the Disruption, *Be Not Schismatics, Be Not Martyrs by Mistake* (1843).

Guthrie is not shy of listing financial details as illustration of clerical self-sacrifice consequent of the Disruption, and calls for generous support in the subsequent Sunday collection. The history of institutional division is revisited, not to rekindle divisive feeling or self-righteousness (as he is keen to emphasise in his introductory comments preceding this extract), but to press home his audience's responsibilities in the newly contractual relationship between the Free Church minister and his congregation.

Notes

1 Andrew L. Drummond and James Bulloch, *The Church in Victorian Scotland 1843–1874* (Edinburgh: St Andrew Press, 1975), p. 91.
2 See Lionel Alexander Dixie, 'Guthrie, Thomas', 2004, *Oxford Dictionary of National Biography*, https://doi.org/10.1093/ref:odnb/11790

10

THOMAS GUTHRIE, *THE PRINCIPLES OF THE FREE CHURCH OF SCOTLAND, AND A PLEA FOR THE ANTE-DISRUPTION MINISTERS*

(Edinburgh: [n.p.], 1859),
pp. 11, 12–14, 15–19, 20–23, 24

II. The Principles of the Disruption

These are very plain, and may be summed up under the two following heads:—

(1.) The rights of the people. By "the people" we do not understand all and sundry, as many, especially in England, supposed, and thereby misunderstood our cause and question. "The people," in this case, are those who are members of the Church, and in full communion with her. [...]

The right of the people which we insisted on is a very plain one—a constitutional one—one as old as the Church of Scotland—one as old as the New Testament—and one involving the most precious interests of souls. So far from being exorbitant in our demands, many of us consented to put that right in the very lowest shape which could at all satisfy our consciences. I hold, and have ever held, that the members of a Christian congregation should have the uncontrolled power of choosing their own pastor. All, however, that we asked was, that no pastor should be intruded by a patron, or a church court, on an unwilling and reclaiming congregation. This right the Church of Scotland has ever claimed as one belonging to the people; and the great day of judgment will reveal the irreparable loss that souls have suffered from the intrusion of unspiritual and unacceptable pastors—ungodly and careless men—unconverted men—men who, insensible to the value of their own souls, cared nothing for the souls of others—dumb dogs that could not bark—false and faithless shepherds, who prized the flock for nothing but the fleece.

In Popish churches, where empty ceremonies are substituted for gospel preaching, and even in those other churches where a fixed and rigid ritual has stereotyped the language of prayer, it is a matter, I grant, of less importance that the congregation should have a voice in the choice of their pastor. Any man can read a prayer; and if free of bodily infirmities, as the Popish church requires her priests to be, any man who is not blind, and is not lame, can bend to a crucifix, or kiss a wafer, or make the sign of the cross, or go through any of the other mummeries of Roman Catholic worship. But where souls are to be fed or starved on Sabbath days; where the people come hungering for bread and may be put off with a stone—seeking fish, but may be presented and poisoned with a serpent; where, instead of the pulpit being thrust into a corner, the exposition and the application of God's Word form a prominent part of religious services—can any man deny that it is of the highest importance that congregations should be protected against the intrusion of incompetent pastors; and that that should not be attempted within the church which all men would repudiate with one voice out of it?

Where is the political constituency that would allow an alien, not to say an enemy of our country, to dictate to them who should be their representative in Parliament? With all our loyalty to our beloved Sovereign—for the purity of whose court and the benignity of whose rule we give thanks to God—what family among us would allow even her, or her ministers, or her Parliament, to thrust a physician on us when sickness was in our homes, and the shadow of death was creeping over them? In a cause that concerned his character, his property, or his life, is there a man among us who would yield up his right to choose what counsel he liked from the roll of advocates? I have seen a man stand in the dock, at the bar, a felon with the jail mark on his brow, and on his head a hundred crimes, claiming that liberty of choice; nor claiming it in vain. These are precious rights. Yet which of them involves such momentous consequences, touches such eternal interests as the right of Christ's members to choose the man who shall care for their souls; stand by their dying beds; smooth death's thorny pillow; guide the sinner's faltering feet to Jesus, and from Sabbath to Sabbath break to hungry congregations the bread of life? I do not wonder that the Church of Scotland claimed for her people a right at once so consonant with the dictates of reason, and the Word of God. I only wonder that she delayed so long to claim it. Nothing but custom, which reconciles men as well as beasts to chains and collars, can account for the tameness with which Christian churches wear their bonds. [...]

In God's good providence, and with growing grace and light, the Church of Scotland came at length, as we pray God all true churches soon may do, to see it to be her duty to assert the liberties of her people. For these she perilled her existence—at least her existence as an Established Church. She claimed that, agreeably to the faith of ancient treaties, the oaths of kingdoms, and the Word of God, her people should go free. That claim was as sternly as unwisely refused. Sagacious statesmen, whom God seemed to have smitten with judicial blindness, and whom low-minded men had perhaps persuaded that we would sell the birthright for a mess of pottage, refused all redress—the very lowest demand that we felt justified in making. What then remained for us? We could not continue the painful and unseemly spectacle of remaining in the Establishment and resisting the orders of the State. Much as we loved the walls of our old church—unwilling as we were to leave them—we felt compelled to go. And as the Pilgrim Fathers, the old Puritans of England, the founders of the great American Republic, crossed the seas, and sought in the untrodden forests of the New World, the liberty they were denied at home, we went forth under the old banner to enjoy that freedom without the Establishment which we were denied within its pale. And here we are this day, with no regrets for the past, nor fears for the future—forming a body of citizens, I am bold to say, as loyal to the Queen, as attached to the Constitution, as ready to obey the laws, and on these shores, in the event of an invasion, to meet the enemies of our country, as any subjects in her Majesty's dominions. Our motto is: "Fear God and honour the king."

(2.) The right of Christ, by his Word, and through its Courts, to rule in his own Church.

It has ever been the doctrine of this, as of all other reformed and enlightened churches, that Jesus Christ has set up a kingdom of his own upon earth. Indeed Popery herself maintains this doctrine; and while we here have been called to resist those that would sink the Church in the State, she goes to the opposite extreme, and sinks the State in the Church. Assigning to the Church a spiritual province, and to the State one cognisant of temporal interests, we avoid both extremes; holding that neither should encroach upon the territories of the other.

Christ's kingdom has a region of its own, where kings, with their crowns, swords of state, and iron mace, are barred from entering. This kingdom is in other kingdoms, yet different from them; higher than all other kingdoms, it yet claims no right to interfere with their jurisdiction. It owns no throne but Christ's, recognises no acts but the Acts of the Apostles, and yields no obedience to any laws but those that are written in the statute-book of heaven. Its subjects are Christ's people; and its office-bearers are not lords of God's heritage, but servants of the Church. Within the precincts of this kingdom kings are not sovereigns, but subjects; as was beautifully set forth by George III when, kneeling at the communion-table on the day of his coronation, he uncrowned his head, as one that had no more power or rank or state there than the poorest believer—one who uncovers his head beneath a roof of thatch, and kneels to the God of heaven on a bare clay floor. Of this kingdom the armies are saints, the weapons are truth, and the boundaries shall one day be the shores of the world. A kingdom this within which no act of parliament, no mandate of the sovereign, no orders of council, no decision of civil courts, carry any more authority than an act of the French Chambers, or the will of the Austrian despot, on the free soil of Britain. Notwithstanding this, Cæsar, so to speak, intruded on Christ's province. In matters entirely spiritual and most sacred, the civil courts commanded us to do what they had no right to order; and our duty to Christ clearly forbade. In temporal matters we rendered all obedience to the State; in spiritual matters we would yield none. We might lay our own heads at Cæsar's feet; we dare not lay Christ's crown there. On such conditions we could not hold our livings. Better not live at all than live traitors to the cause of Christ and so, whatever other men might think, we felt in our consciences that no choice was left us but, with slow and sorrowful steps, to leave an Establishment that we had loved and defended; and, taking up our cross, go without the camp, bearing our Lord's reproach.

An eminent philosopher, greater perhaps in the realms of metaphysics than divinity, declared that we were "martyrs by mistake." I know not that we were worthy of the name of martyrs; but certainly we were not open to the reproach of "dying as a fool dieth." There was no mistake about the matter. Indeed that could hardly be. This controversy was neither new to us nor new in Scotland. For one long and weary century, from the days of Popish Mary, down to the blessed Revolution, our stout fathers had fought the very same battle. The whole blood of the Covenant had been shed on this field. We had nought else to do but to pluck the old weapons from the dead men's hands; and, when the State came down on us in its pride and power, man once more the moss-grown ramparts where our fathers had bled and died. The rust was rubbed from the old swords; the self-same arguments which James Guthrie used 200 years ago at the bar, when on trial for his life, were pled over again; nor was there a bit of ground on all the field but was dyed with our fathers' blood, and indented with their footmarks.

The only difference between the struggle of the seventeenth, and that of the nineteenth century, lay in the results. The Covenanters fell on moor and mountain; while such of our ministers as sank beneath their trials, died calmly in their beds; leaving what our own ears heard, their dying testimony to the cause, and expressions of devout thankfulness to God that their pillow was not that of the recreant or apostate—though a lowly, was not a thorny one. The men of the seventeenth century bore testimony to our principles on the reeking scaffold, and sang their last psalm to listening thousands, gathered in that Grassmarket to see how bravely a good man could die; we, living in happier times, under the sceptre of a beloved sovereign, and, thanks to our fathers, in a free country, had only to leave a church within which a good conscience would allow us no longer to remain. We cast ourselves on what has never failed us—the providence of God; the confidence and affection of a sympathizing people. [...]

Yet I must ask, faithful to my trust and to your souls—I feel constrained to ask, of what avail all that will be, unless He for whose royal rights we have contended has a throne erected within our hearts? The highest honour we can confer on Jesus Christ is to crown him, King of our affections; nor, unless he reigns over us, will it be anything to us, though all the kings of the world should lay their sceptres at his feet, and queens in royal palaces become nursing mothers to his church. People may belong to the Free Church; yet not be free. [...]

III. Attend to the present and practical application of this subject

Along with that brief and plain exposition which I have now given of the Principles and Facts of the Disruption, our General Assembly has required its ministers to direct the attention of their people to another subject. It is a very pressing and a most important one. What we wish you to take, I shall not say into your generous, but into your just consideration, is the claims of those ministers, who,—those brethren who are in some good measure provided for being set aside—have, for the last sixteen years been great, though patient, sufferers in consequence of the Disruption. That event threw many of them into circumstances of peculiar hardship. Impressed with the duty of making a special provision for those who went out at the Disruption, and not located in large towns, nor settled over large congregations, left full endowments for a very inadequate provision, I urged their claims on the very first General Assembly of our Church. I urged them in vain. The appeal was not attended to; although I believe that a different fate would have awaited it had the appeal, made to a Court of the Church, been made to a free assembly of the people. But passing that matter, the claims which these brethren have on our sympathy are now revived; and I have the greatest pleasure in addressing you on this topic. Yet they have not been revived, let me say, at their request. The courage with which they stood the day of trial, and, leaving for ever their lovely and happy homes, submitted, with their uncomplaining wives and children, to be, all of a sudden, reduced to narrow and straitened circumstances, is, in point of moral grandeur, only equalled by the silent, unmurmuring, and dignified patience with which they have struggled with the difficulties, and borne the privations of their lot. No man has heard them complaining. We regret to think that many of them have been allowed to pass away without any due acknowledgment of their sacrifices, and their services. And though one hour of heaven has more than made up for all, yet, as sometimes happens at a father or mother's death, we have the pain of thinking that they may have deeply felt our culpable neglect—wrongs which it is now too late to remedy. Justice to these worthy men was one of those things which, to be well done, should have been quickly done. Yet better late than never. And let us now turn from the quiet graves of the dead and our own unavailing regrets, to discharge a long outstanding debt, and bless with unaccustomed comforts the homes of survivors.

I take from the paper which the Committee have issued, a few examples of the pecuniary sacrifices made by some of them since 1843. "One country minister had, prior to that period, a stipend of £284, besides a manse and a glebe; and since then, he has not drawn more, including supplement, than £164 a year. Another was in the receipt of £233, besides manse and glebe; and since the Disruption, he has not received more than £142 a year. Another has received, during the last 16 years, such a diminished income, as, compared with his former stipend, leaves him a sufferer, in a pecuniary point of view, of not less than £2,000. The total sacrifices made by these noble-minded Christian ministers, who came out in 1843, cannot be less than £300,000." Those sacrifices were self-denying. They made them for the honour of Christ, and for the rights of his people. And in the judgment of every generous and right-minded man, it surely does not abate from their claim on our sympathy, that what they did, they did nobly, did cheerfully, did unhesitatingly. Since the Disruption, they have extended the church at their own expense; and have been ever ready to plant new charges, and supply the wants of the people, although every increase in the number of ministers diminished the amount of their own livings.

I am not here to depreciate, but rather to extol the pecuniary sacrifices which our people have made; the abundance and unparalleled liberality of their gifts. Year by year this congregation contributes some £2,500; year by year the whole Church raises, from the free-will offerings of her congregations, some £300,000;

and the sum total of the gifts towards the maintenance of the Gospel at home, and its extension abroad, has, in the last sixteen years, reached a sum of more than FOUR, and nearly FIVE MILLIONS sterling. We have much cause to be thankful; but no cause to be proud. How much larger, how enormous, are the sums which the world spends in the devil's service, or offers at the shrine of pleasure! Think of Great Britain spending, according to calculations which I have seen, and blushed to see, a sum of EIGHT MILLIONS annually, in dens of iniquity—on the grossest forms of licentiousness! Think of SIXTY MILLIONS wasted year by year on intoxicating liquors, and indulgences as useless, if not so dangerous. Reading these things, we hang down our heads. We feel that Christ's people have done comparatively little for Him.

Besides, while ascribing all glory to God, and awarding to our people the meed of praise that is their due, I must remind you that some of those I plead for are in truth the largest contributors to the funds of our Church. [...] Theirs, though a blessed, has been a bitter sacrifice. And I loathe the religion which can put aside their claim; and, closing its hands, turns up its hypocritical eyes, to say, "Good men! they will have their reward in heaven." Brethren! I cast this cause with confidence, I cannot say on your generosity, and I shall not say on your justice. I cast it on your love. These men are worthy of our affections. If we honour the King, we will not fail to honour those who saved His Crown from being rolled in the dust; and so I hope that next Lord's day we will put forth our utmost efforts; and that a collection will be made in Scotland which shall once more astonish a drowsy world, and shall prove both the gratitude of our people, and the vitality of a church which, though it has parted with the endowments and the countenance of the State, still claims and still carries the old ensign of "a Bush burning, but not consumed."

Part 5

FORMS OF DISSENT

5.1 Wesleyan Methodism

5.1 Wesleyan Methodism

In England, Methodism originated as an Anglican revivalist movement, forming a new denomination just before the start of the nineteenth century. It involved a commitment less to a new body of belief and more to a new mode of spirituality – an intense emotionalism, a deep sense of assured salvation, and a quest for holiness. English Methodism was mostly Wesleyan, and Armenian in its offer of salvation to all who sought it, while Welsh Methodism, a separate movement, was Calvinist (see 5.2 Welsh Nonconformity). The number of Methodists grew exponentially in Britain and Ireland between 1770 and 1840, but slowed significantly thereafter, and in Ireland declined.[1] While it first appealed to the unlearned and socially powerless, it increasingly conformed to the values of middle-class respectability.

Methodist spirituality was 'inexorably bound up with the medium of oral culture' including preaching, exhorting, confessing, singing, public prayer and testimony, classes and revival meetings.[2] In his preface, John Wesley described his *Collection of Hymns*, first published in 1780 and reissued in expanded form throughout the nineteenth century, as 'a little body of experimental and practical divinity' for private and public use to aid the believer in various stages of the spiritual life journey (p. viii). In fact Charles Wesley (1707–88) wrote most of the hymns, and the 1867 edition names him as author of the examples below, although they are taken as representative of the thought and feeling of both the Wesleys.[3] The examples demonstrate Methodism's characteristic combination of liberty and discipline. The first celebrates salvation achieved, the believer progressing from a statement of faith to an increasingly intense intimacy with God, finally achieving a personal epiphany in which the boundaries between self and other are dissolved. Heaven is not a destination so much as a quality of life attainable in the here and now – 'paradise' means dwelling in God's presence. The second demonstrates the ongoing quest for holiness and the battle of the believer to overcome the 'old Adam' within (Romans 6:4). The writer internalises the paradigm of crucifixion and resurrection, with language reminiscent of the metaphysical poets in its use of paradox and imagery of muscular violence: he asks to be killed to come alive, buried to rise. The self is effaced, not expanded, God experienced more as conqueror than lover.

Second only to hymns in importance for articulating experiential religion was life writing, which provided an opportunity for self-analysis as well as an encouraging example for others. As Mary Fletcher's autobiography demonstrates, Methodism gave a new significance to women's spiritual experience and voice. Fletcher (née Bosanquet, 1739–1815) was prominent among a number of Methodist women who took to preaching, with Wesley's approval of some women's 'extraordinary' call, until the practice was banned in 1803 (although it continued in breakaway groups). Honoured as a 'Mother in Israel', her story continued to be in the public eye through the nineteenth century, her *Life* going through at least twenty editions following its first publication in 1817. The extract shows Fletcher's childhood discovery of 'inward religion' in place of mere outward conformity, helped by the family servant and her grandparents; the convert's conflict with parental expectations was a common feature of Methodist women's memoirs, as was mentoring by other women converts. Birth into a wealthy Anglican family, and confirmation at St Paul's Cathedral in London, contextualise her rejection of the world. The second part narrates her call to preach (in 1775), and her careful negotiation of societal disapproval that she has herself internalised but which she construes as contrary to the will of God. Scripture and hymn quotations, mostly from Wesley collections, are woven into her self-justification, including Charles Wesley's 'Come Lord, from above' and 'Here from afar the finished height', and John Wesley's translations of Johann Andreas Rothe's 'Now I have found the grace wherein' and 'Jesus, I know, hath died for me'. Fletcher's other textual allusions include Foxe's 1563 *Book of Martyrs* (a history of the persecution of Protestants), and John Bunyan's 1678 *The Pilgrim's Progress*, both popular reading well into the nineteenth century. To 'blaspheme against the Holy Spirit' is considered the one unforgivable sin in Matthew 12:31, and William Brammagh who lends her support was a fellow Methodist minister. Henry Moore, a Wesleyan Methodist minister who wrote a number of biographical accounts of women preachers, frames her narrative with comments to emphasise the importance of fellowship in spiritual development, and to remind the reader of another Methodist woman's writings, Mrs LeFevre's *Extracts of Letters, Chiefly on Religious Subjects* (1800). Bosanquet went on to speak in the open air to as many as two thousand people on occasions, and after marriage to the Methodist preacher John Fletcher served with him as co-pastor of a congregation in Madeley, Shropshire.[4]

Notes

1 See figures in David Hempton, *Methodism: Empire of the Spirit* (New Haven: Yale University Press, 2005), pp. 214–215.
2 Hempton, *Methodism: Empire of the Spirit*, p. 56.
3 See 'Introduction' to *The Works of John Wesley*, vol. 7: *A Collection of Hymns for the Use of the People called Methodists*, edited by Franz Hilderbrandt, Oliver A. Beckerlegge and James Dale (Oxford: Clarendon Press, 1983), pp. 1–69, on pp. 1–2.
4 Jennifer Lloyd, *Women and the Shaping of British Methodism: Persistent Preachers 1807–1907* (Manchester: Manchester University Press, 2009), p. 35.

11

CHARLES WESLEY, 'JESUS HATH DIED THAT I MIGHT LIVE' (NO. 415) AND 'JESUS, MY LIFE!' (NO. 347)

In J. Everett and M. Baxter (eds), *Hymn Book of the United Methodist Free Churches, comprising the Collection of Hymns by the Rev. J. Wesley with Miscellaneous Hymns Suited for Occasional Services* (London: William Reed, 1867), n.p.

Jesus hath died that I might live,
    Might live to God alone;
In him eternal life receive,
    And be in spirit one.

Saviour, I thank thee for the grace,
    The gift unspeakable!
And wait with arms of faith to'embrace,
    And all thy love to feel.

My soul breaks out in strong desire
    The perfect bliss to prove;
My longing heart is all on fire
    To be dissolved in love.

Give me thyself; from every boast,
    From every wish set free:
Let all I am in thee be lost;
    But give thyself to me.

Thy gifts, alas, cannot suffice,
    Unless thyself be given;

Thy presence makes my paradise,
> And where thou art is heaven.

* * *

Jesus, my life! thyself apply,
> Conform me to thy death.
My vile affections crucify,
> Thy Holy Spirit breathe;

Conq'ror of hell, and earth, and sin,
> Still with thy rebel strive;
Enter my soul, and work within,
> And kill, and make alive!

More of thy life, and more, I have,
> As the old Adam dies:
Bury me, Saviour, in thy grave,
> That I with thee may rise.

Reign in me, Lord, they foes control,
> Who would not own thy sway;
Diffuse thine image through my soul,
> Shine to the perfect day.

Scatter the last remains of sin,
> And seal me thine abode;
O make me glorious all within,
> A temple built by God!

12

MARY FLETCHER, *THE LIFE OF MRS MARY FLETCHER, CONSORT AND RELICT OF THE REV. JOHN FLETCHER, VICAR OF MADELEY, SALOP: COMPILED FROM HER JOURNAL AND OTHER AUTHENTIC DOCUMENTS*

Ed. Henry Moore [1817]
(London: J. Kershaw, 1824), pp. 15–23, 107–108

About this time [when I was five years old] there came a servant maid to live with my father, who had heard of, and felt some little of the power of inward religion. It was among the people called Methodists she had received her instructions. Seeing the uneasiness my sister was under, she took some opportunities of conversing with her. I was at this season with my grandmother. On my return home my sister repeated the substance of these conversations to me. I well remember the very spot we stood on, and the words she spake, which, though we were but a few minutes together, sunk so deeply into my heart, that they were never afterward erased. My reflections were suited to a child not seven years old. I thought if I became a Methodist I should be sure of salvation; and determined, if ever I could get to that people, whatever it cost, I would be one of them. But after a few conversations, and hearing my sister read some little books which this servant had given to her, I found out, it was not the being joined to any people that would save me, but I must be converted, and have faith in Christ; that I was to be saved by believing; and that believing would make me holy, and give me a power to love and serve God.

    The servant had now left our family, and we continued like blind persons groping our way in the dark; yet though we had so far discerned the truth as to express it in the above manner, I could not comprehend it. My heart rose against the idea of being saved by faith which I could not understand. One day, looking over the pictures in the Book of Martyrs, I thought it would be easier to burn than to believe, and heartily did I wish that the Papists would come and burn me, and then I thought I should be quite safe. Yet these troubled thoughts were mixed with a degree of hope. I thought, God does love me, I believe, after all; and perhaps, he will show me what it is to believe, and be converted.

When I was between seven and eight years old, musing one day on that thought, What can it be to know my sins forgiven, and to have faith in Jesus? I felt my heart rise against God, for having appointed a way of salvation so hard to be understood; and with anguish of soul I said, If it were to die a martyr, I could do it: or to give away all I have; or when grown up, to become a servant, that would be easy; but I shall never know how to believe. In that moment these words were applied with mighty power to my soul,

> "Who on Jesus relies, without money or price,
> The pearl of forgiveness and holiness buys."

They were accompanied with a light and power I had never known before; and with joy I cried out, I do, I do rely on Jesus; yes, I do rely on Jesus, and God counts me righteous for what he has done and suffered, and hath forgiven all my sins! I was surprised that I could not find out this before. I had thought every thing easier than to believe; but now I thought the way of believing more easy than any other. A ray of light into the Gospel-plan shone upon my soul, and I began to adore the wonders of redeeming love. But, alas! it was but as the drops before a shower; in a few days I lost the power in a great measure,[1] though not the light of this blessing. I can remember many promises, after this, being at times brought to my mind. Something also of a confidence in the Lord Jesus I ever retained, and when fears would spring up concerning the day of judgment, I used to comfort myself with this thought, Jesus is to be the Judge, and I cannot be afraid of Jesus. But I had not yet learned that lesson,

> "Man, for the simple life divine,
>   What will it cost to break?
> Ere pleasure soft, and wily pride,
>   No more within him speak?"

Some time after I had thus by faith "tasted of the powers of the world to come" [Hebrews 6:5], I fell into an uncommon lowness, and weakness of nerves, which was accompanied with grievous temptations. I was oppressed beyond measure with the fear of sin, and accused in almost every thing I said or did, so that I was altogether a heap of inconsistency. This was followed by temptations unspeakably afflicting: it was continually suggested to my mind, I had blasphemed against the Holy Ghost. The consequent effect of these temptations on my temper, drew on me very grievous burdens, and exposed me to so much anger and reproach from my parents, as made me weary of life. It appeared to them that I was obstinate and disobedient; and my flesh has seemed ready to move on my bones, when I have heard my dear mother say, "That girl is the most perverse creature that ever lived; I cannot think what is come to her:" and my heart used to sink like a stone, for I knew not what to do, and the grief of my mind quite destroyed my health. My grandfather and grandmother, who were to me the tenderest of parents, seeing me in such a poor way, as to my body, (though they knew not the cause,) desired to have me with them. I grew something better while I was there, but on my return home, I became as bad as ever.

This heavy season lasted, I think, nine weeks; when one day, opening my mind to my sister, (as indeed I had often before attempted to do, but could not explain myself,) she providentially used these words in her answer, "Why, you do not *mean* to blaspheme, do you?" A light immediately struck into my mind; I weighed the thought, over and over, and could truly say, 'Lord, thou knowest I do not mean to blaspheme.' I then recollected that I had heard something about temptation, and often wondered what it was. I thought, it may be Satan whispers this into my mind, like what we read about Christian in the Pilgrim's Progress, going through the valley of the shadow of death. I then determined never to regard it more, but always answer with these words, 'I do not *mean* to blaspheme, I will acknowledge Christ for ever:' and in a few days I was perfectly delivered. I am the more full on this head, because it has been a warning to me ever since, not to be too severe in passing a judgment on the actions of children, whose reflections are far deeper, and their feelings much keener, than we are apt to imagine.

I was now, 1 believe, about ten years old, and can recollect many comfortable moments in reading the word of God. The promises in Isaiah were in a particular manner applied to my soul, and I hardly ever opened the Bible, but there was something for me: till one day I heard a person make this remark, that 'many people took promises to themselves which did not belong to them.' Of some, she observed, 'they belonged to the Church; others to the Jews; such and such to the Gentiles, &c.,' and then began to blame the presumption of those who applied them to their own souls! Such a thought had never entered my heart before. I knew the words were primarily spoken on particular occasions; but the Lord had led me to believe that his word was written to every soul, so far as they were willing to receive it by faith. But, from the above conversation, I was unhinged:[2] I knew not what to choose, or what to refuse, so that being cast into reasonings, I lost all my love for reading the Scriptures, and sunk into a very cold and lifeless state. When I was twelve years old, we went to Bath for three months. Here I met with many dissipations, and had, I may truly say, no enjoyment of religion; only when in the midst of the ball-room I used to think, if I knew where to find the Methodists, or any who would show me how to please God, I would tear off all my fine things, and run through the fire to them: and sometimes I thought, if ever I am my own mistress, I will spend half the day in working for the poor, and the other half in prayer.

When I was about thirteen, the things of God began to return with more power on my mind. One day my sister visiting Mrs. Lefevre,[3] found her truly awakened, and in earnest to save her soul. She told me this news with great delight; for as our parents hail no suspicion of her bring a Methodist, we saw the Lord had opened us a door into that Christian liberty we so much longed after. At her house we got opportunities of conversation with religious persons, which a good deal strengthened our hands; though we often said to each other, these Methodists do not quite answer our expectations; though our time is short with them, they lose much of it before they begin to converse with us about our souls: the Apostles would not have done so. But we must not form our judgment by the rich, let us wait till we get acquainted with some of the poor among them; perhaps they will be right Methodists, and more like the first Christians.

Sometimes that promise was brought powerfully to my mind, "Whatsoever ye shall ask believing, ye shall receive" [Matthew 21:22]: then, thought I, 'I may ask all the grace I will; I may ask power never to offend my God again.' Faith sprung up in my soul, and I was much drawn out in prayer for holiness; till one day, speaking of it to a particular person, she raised many objections to the thought of all sin being removed from the heart. I felt as if cold water were thrown on a newly-kindled fire, and the wings of my faith seemed clipt. Fearing lest I was wrong, I prayed the Lord to answer for himself by his word. So taking up the Bible, with much prayer I opened it, and immediately cast my eyes on these words, "Behold, I am the Lord, the God of all flesh; is any thing too hard for me?" [Jeremiah 32:27] It came with power; my heart, as it were, leaped for joy; and I cried out, 'Now I will wrestle, and I shall prevail" [Genesis 32:25].

Towards the end of the following winter, there was a confirmation at St. Paul's; and my father desired I should be confirmed. This was a very rousing ordinance to me; for some time before, I had felt how unworthy I was of it; how unfit thus solemnly to devote myself to God, by renewing that covenant I had so often broken. I read the Order of Confirmation, with the Ministration of Baptism, over and over, and besought my God to give me power to keep the charge of the Lord faithfully. For some months after, every time I approached the Lord's table, I had a very peculiar sense of his presence, and sometimes I felt as if the Lord Jesus did from his own hand give me the sacred emblems of his body and blood.

But the next year my mind again wandered after many things, and though I tasted now and then a little of the loving-kindness of the Lord, yet in the general I was greatly under the power of my own will. Pride and perverseness got many times the upper hand, and there was nothing in my life or conversation which could adorn the Gospel: but I did not then see my conduct in that light. While our love is small, our perceptions in spiritual things are very dark. Alas! I thought I walked as a Christian; but now that I see so much more of the holiness of God, I also discern more fully the depth of my fall, and am astonished that either God or man bore with me. While the carnal mind retained this power, I do not wonder my dear mother should not love me as the rest of her children; for I was not only more dull and indolent in every thing I had to learn, but I gave way to an insolent and disobedient spirit in such a degree towards the whole family, that the recollection has often seemed to draw blood from my heart. How perfectly do I feel these words my own,

> "Sink down my soul, sink lower still,
>   Lie level with the dust."

But the Lord did not forsake me. One night, after spending some time in prayer, I cast my eyes on a book Mrs. Lefevre had given me, and read these words:—

> "I'll look into my Saviour's breast;
> Away sad doubt and anxious care,
> Mercy is all that's written there."

> "—Jesu's blood through earth and skies,
> Mercy, free, boundless mercy, cries."

I saw as it were the Father of Mercy opening his arms to receive me, and on that boundless love I had liberty to cast my whole soul. I was more and more thankful for my union with Mrs. Lefevre, and experienced in her the greatest comfort of my life.

About this season my ever-honoured grandfather and grandmother were taken from us. He was one of the excellent of the earth: his life, in many respects, was remarkable and singular. In his last illness he delighted much in these words, "My sheep hear my voice; I know them, and they follow me," &c [John 10: 27]. He was aged seventy-nine, and had lived with my grandmother forty-five years in a union not usually to be met with. He was a pattern in many respects; plain in his dress, mortified in his food, and strictly conscientious in all his expenses. When many dishes were on his table, he scarcely ate of any thing but mutton, and that for many years, because he believed it most conducive to his health. His love and charity to the poor were uncommon. He esteemed it a reproach to any man to say, 'he died very rich;' adding, it is too plain a mark he has not made a good use of his income.

One day, upon the Exchange, a gentleman who was by him said to another, "Sir John, I give you joy; they tell me you have completed your hundred thousand pounds." The other replied, "I hope to double it before I die." My grandfather, turning short, said, "Then, Sir John, you are not worthy of it." Once, being at the table of a nobleman, he observed the guests drinking to excess, and conversing in a very unchristian manner. At first he tried to turn the conversation, but the torrent being too strong, he rose up, and leaning over the back of his chair, he gave them a solemn reproof, joined to an affectionate warning, and then left the company. I have been with him in his chariot when he has suddenly stopped to reprove profane swearing on the road.

My grandmother was a woman of an uncommonly sweet temper; and having acquired a good deal of skill in physic, she so helped the poor, that they looked on her as a mother, a nurse, and a counsellor. When my grandfather had been dead three months, she dreamed one night, he came to her, and standing by the bed-side, said, she "should come to him shortly, till then his happiness was not so complete as it would be; and added, *Study the Scriptures, study the Scriptures,* 'in them ye think ye have eternal life'" [John 5:39]. From this time she applied to them daily, in a manner superior to what she had done before; though she had always a high veneration for the word of God. About three weeks after, she said to us one day, "Air that room; I will go into it, that I may die in the bed Mr. Dunster died in." From the night she went into it, she come out no more; for she died within the week. As she did not appear any worse than usual, she was at first thought to be in no danger. She said herself two or three times, "What a blessing! I am dying without pain! I have no more than I can very well bear!"

From this time we began to get rather more liberty; and one day as my sister was on a visit at Mrs. Lefevre's, Mr. Romaine came in, and began to speak of the sinfulness of attending the playhouse. She listened with great earnestness to all he said; which repeating to me on her return, it was as "a nail in a sure place," and I began to cry for power to stand to the light which I had then received.

A few months after this my sister married, by which I was left alone. I must observe, to this time, my parents had very little suspicion of our having any intercourse with the Methodists, but thought, (when the before-mentioned servant was put away, and our books taken from us,) that our religious impressions had worn off. I now saw the time was come, when I must "confess Christ before men," if I would wish him to confess me "before his Father and the holy angels." [John 1:20, Mark 8:38] I consulted some of my serious friends about the playhouse; but they said, "Were you older, we should know what to advise, but as you are but sixteen, if your parents insist on your going, we do not see how you can avoid it." This answer did not fully satisfy me; and I was much distressed both ways. I saw the duty I owed to an absolute command from my parents in a very strong light; and, on the other hand, I remembered that my obedience to them was to be—*in the Lord*. I sought direction in prayer, and endeavoured to examine the question on both sides; but the more I searched, the clearer it appeared to me, I must not comply. I considered the playhouse had a tendency to weaken every Christian temper, and to strengthen all that was contrary; to represent vice under the false colour of virtue, and to lead in every respect into the spirit of the world, of which the Apostle declares, "The friendship of the world is enmity with God" [James 4:4]. When the time came, and my obedient compliance was required, I begged to be left at home. On a refusal, I laid open my whole heart to my father; apprising him, I would not willingly be disobedient in any thing, unless where conscience made it appear to be my duty. We conversed on the subject with great freedom; for my dear father was a man of deep reason, calmness, and condescension. He replied, "Child, your arguments prove too much; and, therefore, are not conclusive. If what you say be true, then all places of diversion, all dress and company, nay, all agreeable liveliness, and the whole spirit of the world, is sinful." I embraced the opportunity and said, "Sir, *I* see it as such, and, therefore, am determined no more to be conformed to its customs, fashions, or maxims." This was a season of great trial, but the Lord stood by me: glory be to his holy name!

I daily discerned a great difference between my manner of life, and that which the Bible described, as the life of a Christian. I had often strong desires to be wholly given to the Lord. Much opposition I met with for having declared my sentiments; and what was very cutting to me, I was often debarred from the pleasure of seeing my friend Mrs. Lefevre. This was the consequence I much feared, if I should openly declare my mind; but I was thoroughly convinced, if I loved my friend more than God's law, I should never know the power of true religion. It is my natural temper to be very anxious about any one I love, and to fix too much of my confidence in them. This was the case with respect to Mrs. Lefevre. I saw and lamented it, beseeching the Lord to take away all *idolatry* out of my affections, and give me to love her as I ought.

I dreamed one night I was in a church, and saw written on the wall, in letters of gold, these words: "Thou shalt have no other Gods but me" [Exodus 20:3]. While I was looking on it, I saw the name of Mrs. Lefevre wrote under it. I was surprised, and presently beheld the following line, 'If this is your God, then what am I?' I awakened with a deep conviction, that I had placed too much confidence on an arm of flesh. I knew it was the voice of God by this mark, a great sweetness accompanied the reproof. This was the method the Lord has always used towards me; he held me up with one hand, while he smote me with the other. [...]

May 28—This day I set apart for prayer, to inquire of the Lord, why I am so held in bondage about speaking in public. It cannot be expressed what I suffer:—it is only known to God what trials I go through in that respect. Lord, give me more humility, and then I shall not care for any thing but thee! There are a variety of reasons why it is such a cross. The other day one told me, "He was sure I must be an impudent woman; no modest woman, he was sure, could proceed thus." Ah! how glad would nature be to find out,—Thou, Lord, dost not require it!—Mr. William Brammah observed to-day, "The reason why your witness is not more clear, is, because you do not glorify God by believing, and more freely declaring what he hath done for your soul." He spake much on these words, "What things soever ye ask in prayer, believe that ye receive them, and ye shall have them" [Matthew 21:22]. His words came with power, and my soul got a further hold on Jesus. I do see that by his death he hath purchased perfect salvation for "all who believe" [Romans 3:22]; and that we receive it in proportion as we thus believe. "Be it unto you according to your faith," is the word of the Lord [Matthew 9:29]; Then I will, I do cast my whole soul on thee! O let me find "salvation as walls and bulwarks!" [Isaiah 26:1]

Sept. 10, Sunday.—I rose this morning with a sore weight on my mind. It was given out for me to be at D——. There was much wind and rain, and the roads were very bad. I feared the journey. I feared also I should have nothing to say when I came there:—I feared all manner of things. Those words however came to my mind, "Take no thought what ye shall say" [Luke 12:11]. I then felt myself led to consider those words, "Repent, for the kingdom of heaven is at hand" [Matthew 4:17]. I found some liberty in speaking from them, and the people were affected. As I was riding back, I clearly saw I was called to stand still; to live the present moment, and always to praise the Lord that His will was done, though I might have much to suffer. I had a clear conviction, God brought me to Yorkshire, and that I had a message to this people; and that, notwithstanding the darkness which hung over my situation, I was at present where God would have me. Well, then, answered my heart, if I am but in His will I am safe; for where the Lord leads me, there He will be my light.

Notes

1 She was not favoured at this time with Christian fellowship. She had none to help her in the way of faith. EDITOR.
2 Here again she felt the want of Christian fellowship. ED.
3 Well known in the Methodist Connexion by her admirable letters, published many years ago. ED.

5.2

Welsh Nonconformity

5.2 Welsh Nonconformity

By the mid-nineteenth century, two salient truths were known about the state of faith in Wales: firstly, that Wales was a far more religious country than England or Scotland, and secondly that its religion was primarily nonconformist. The 1851 census showed only 9 per cent of worshippers attending the Church of Wales, while a remarkable 87 per cent attended other denominations.[1] Working-class alienation of the kind that troubled English religious leaders did not occur in Wales, where nonconformity thrived in newly industrialised urban communities as a source of identity, community and the preservation of the Welsh language. Welsh nonconformity consisted mostly of Evangelical moderate Calvinism, its largest denomination being the Welsh Calvinistic Methodists, followed by older forms of dissent such as Independents and Baptists.

Nonconformity in Wales became increasingly identified with a national culture, language and politics through the nineteenth century. Colonial aggressions like 'The Treason of the Blue Books' (an 1847 report that blamed the lamentable state of Welsh society on the survival of the native language and the spread of nonconformity), and the later suppression of Welsh in schools, produced a situation where '[t]he Anglicans were now identified with Toryism and Englishness, the nonconformists with Liberal radicals and Welshness'.[2] Nonconformity developed into the driving force of cultural and political nationalist movements in the last third of the nineteenth century, most of whose leaders were also chapel ministers.

One of these was Henry Richard (1812–88), a congregational minister and Liberal MP for Merthyr Tydfil for twenty years. His essay 'The Established Church in Wales' was first published in the *British Quarterly Review*, 1871, two years after disestablishment in Ireland, an event which gave hope to Dissenters across Britain seeking to end Anglican privilege. Richard was a leading figure in the movement for disestablishment of the Anglican Church in Wales (achieved 1914). He responds particularly to British Prime Minister Gladstone's reservations about full disestablishment despite sympathising with many of the criticisms levelled at the Church. Richard presents the Church as essentially an instrument of the English state, a collective of foreign prelates and anglicised gentry who were at best negligent of their pastoral duties, and at worst a tool for the oppression of the Welsh people. The established Church is shown as a colonial imposition on an original British or Celtic Christianity, successively by the Anglo-Saxons, Normans, and the medieval and Tudor monarchs who subjected Wales entirely to English rule. Richard imbues his account of popular revivals since the Reformation with nationalist sentiment, although in truth he was frustrated by the political lethargy of many nonconformists. He argues that in nonconformity the enthralled Welsh spirit re-emerges, invigorating not only the nation's spiritual life, but also its language, culture and political identity.

As Richard's account shows, Welsh Methodism arose as an eighteenth-century native movement entirely independent of English Methodism (led by Howell Harris and Daniel Rowlands), but it was likewise characterised by a warm emotionalism that produced a rich hymnody. Two outstanding writers of early Welsh Methodist hymns that were cherished through numerous nineteenth-century revivals were preacher and writer William Williams of Pantycelyn (1717–91), 'Father of the Welsh hymn',[3] and Ann Griffiths (1776–1805), a farmer's daughter credited with being a mystic. The two hymns given below share a theme of the sheer goodness and loveliness of God, whose presence evokes romantic devotion and sensory delight.

Pantycelyn voices an adventist hope, the oncoming 'sunset' suggestive of approaching death or simply a loss of spiritual fervour. Heaven is pictured as a renewed earth, of which the Welsh landscape is itself a foretaste or type. Griffiths inhabits the voice of the speaker in Song of Songs who sings desirously to her lover. For her, heaven is an all-absorbing exclusive intimacy with God. Both writers transcend their gendered subject positions, Pantycelyn occupying the more typically feminine passive role of the waiting lover, and Griffiths briefly feminising her beloved Rose of Sharon (Song of Songs 2:1) as 'white and blushing'. The hymn translations are by the eminent twentieth-century Welsh nationalist politician and nonconformist Gwynfor Evans whose 1974 *Land of My Fathers* is a vivid history of Wales intertwining politics, religion and nationhood.

Notes

1 Ieuan Gwynned Jones, *Explorations and Explanations: Essays in the Social History of Victorian Wales* (1981), p. 227.
2 Prys Morgan and David Thomas, *Wales: The Shaping of a Nation* (London: David and Charles, 1984), p. 163.
3 E. Wyn James, 'The Evolution of the Welsh Hymn', in Isabel Rivers and David L. Wykes (eds), *Dissenting Praise: Religious Dissent and the Hymn in England and Wales* (Oxford: Oxford University Press, 2011), pp. 229–268, on p. 244.

13

HENRY RICHARD, 'THE ESTABLISHED CHURCH IN WALES' (1871)

In *Letters and Essays on Wales* (London: James Clarke, 1884), pp. 129–135, 135–137, 146–147, 150–151, 159-160, 170–171, 179–183

The Act for the Disestablishment and Disendowment of the Irish Church was one of great importance for what it did, but of still greater importance for what it implied; for in that measure there was distinct legislative recognition of certain general principles, which are susceptible of far wider application than to the particular case they were invoked to sustain. It disposed, once for all, of the fond fantasy that the State is bound in its collective capacity to have a conscience, and in obedience to the dictates of that conscience, to impose its own creed upon the community, as the established faith of the country, to be supported by the authority, and enforced by the sanction of law. It acknowledged the principle that where an established Church never has been, or has ceased to be the Church of the nation, and fails, therefore, in its professed function as the religious instructor of the people, it has no longer any *raison d'être*, and ought to be swept away as an anomaly and incumbrance. It recognised the fact, if not for the first time, at least with more distinctness and emphasis than was ever done before, that ecclesiastical property is national property, which the nation has a perfect right through its legitimate organ, the legislature, to apply to any purpose it may think fit, whether sacred or secular.

We need not wonder that when the Irish Establishment was abolished, men's minds should turn almost instinctively to the sister institution in Wales, as furnishing a case in many respects parallel, but in other respects still less admitting of justification. The discussion of this subject in Parliament last session, on the motion of Mr. Watkin Williams, did not take place, perhaps, under the most favourable auspices. But it was, at least, attended with this advantage, that it obliged those who oppose the Disestablishment of the Welsh Church to show their hand. As Mr. Gladstone, in addition to his many other merits as an orator, is the most accomplished debater in the House of Commons, we may safely assume that whatever could be said in defence of the Church in Wales, and in deprecation of its proposed severance from the State, was said by him with the utmost degree of plausibility and point. But certainly, on a calm review of the arguments he used on that occasion, they do not appear to be very formidable.

It may be said, indeed, that the Prime Minister made no attempt to defend the Welsh Church. He abandoned it to the strongest condemnation pronounced upon it by its adversaries, for the "gross neglect, corruption, nepotism, plunder," to use his own words, by which it has been marked; and only tried to account for these evils by laying them all to the charge of "Anglicising prelates." He admitted that, even granting what Churchmen claimed, namely, about one-fourth of the population as belonging to the Establishment—a claim, let us say, in passing, which in the face of notorious facts is wholly untenable—"the disproportion is very remarkable in the case of a Church purporting to be the Church of the nation." He admitted, moreover, as a circumstance seriously militating against the Welsh Church, that "so large a proportion of her members belong to the upper classes of the community, the classes who are most able to provide themselves with the ministrations of religion, and, therefore, in whose special and peculiar interest it is most difficult to make any effectual appeal for public resources and support." But while acknowledging all this, he resists the proposal for its disestablishment. On what grounds? First, on this ground—that there is no hostility in Wales to the Church Establishment, and that its existence does not, as in Ireland, produce alienation or bitterness of feeling between different classes of the community. But this argument, if it were well founded in fact, which, unhappily, it is as far as possible from being, does not address itself in the least to the reason or justice of the case. Even if the Welsh people were so devoid of spirit and self-respect as to feel it no grievance to have a costly Church Establishment, which exists almost exclusively for the benefit of the rich, saddled upon their necks, surely that is no proof that it is right to perpetuate the privileges of a body, whose history for generations has been marked by "gross neglect, corruption, and nepotism," and which, purporting to be the Church of a nation, does not pretend, even according to the claims of its most audacious advocates, to number among its adherents more than one-fourth of the nation. But Mr. Gladstone is wholly misinformed as to the fact. Because the Nonconformists of Wales are an eminently peaceable, loyal, and orderly people, and do not proclaim their grievances with clamour and menace, it is imagined that they do not feel the gross injustice and indignity of the position they occupy. They do feel it deeply, and they are made to feel it, by events continually occurring in their social and political life, which all spring from this one root of bitterness. We need only refer in illustration of what we mean to the circumstances which attended and followed the last general election. Every form of unfair pressure was brought to bear upon the people to induce them to vote against their convictions, and many of those who had the courage to resist were mercilessly evicted from their holdings, or otherwise injured and persecuted. All this sprang from the existence of the Established Church, as is evidenced by the fact that in every instance—we believe without a single exception—the oppressors were Churchmen and the sufferers Nonconformists.

The other, and the only other, argument of Mr. Gladstone is this—that, except for conventional purposes, there is really no Church in Wales, that the Welsh Church is only a part of the Church of England, and cannot therefore be dealt with separately. We confess we are not very much dismayed by this difficulty; for we can remember the time when the same reason was urged to show the impossibility of touching the Irish Church. Properly speaking, we were told, there was no Church of Ireland, but only the United Church of England and Ireland—the two Churches having, at the time of the Union, been joined together by a compact so solemn and binding that Her Majesty the Queen could not give her consent to any measure for dissolving that compact without incurring the danger of committing perjury, and bringing her crown into jeopardy. And as for providing legislation for Ireland distinct from that of England, the suggestion was scouted as an absurdity. Ireland was as much a part of the United Kingdom as Yorkshire or Lancashire, and must be governed by the same laws. The sense of justice, however, and the urgent necessities of the case, triumphed over those foregone conclusions.

There is one fact that gives a sort of sinister unity to the religious history of Wales through all its vicissitudes. It is this: that the influence of its relations with England, whether they were hostile or friendly, whether under Saxon or Norman rule, whether in Catholic or Protestant times, has been, in this respect, uniformly disastrous. We can only glance very briefly at the proofs of this allegation. Without raising again the controversial dust which envelopes the discussion as to the time and manner of the first introduction of Christianity into this island, we may at least assume it as an admitted historical fact that early in the second century the Gospel had been planted here, and that long before the Saxon invasion there was a flourishing Christian Church in Britain. In the records of the first three or four hundred years of its existence, we find that many large collegiate establishments were formed and dedicated to religion and literature. From these institutions went forth men thoroughly instructed in the learning of their times, some of them bearing the fame of their country's piety and erudition to the uttermost parts of Europe. In the œcumenical councils summoned under Constantine the Great and his sons, in the third and fourth centuries, at Arles, at Nice, and at Sardica, to decide the great Donatist and Arian controversies that disturbed the unity of the Catholic faith, we are told that the British Churches were represented by men who bore an honourable part in the defence of sound doctrine; for Athanasius himself testifies that bishops from Britain joined in condemnation of the heresy of Arius, and in vindication of himself. But when, in the sixth century, the Pope sent the celebrated Augustin, as a missionary, to convert the pagan Anglo-Saxon inhabitants of this island to Christianity, there came on the British Church a time of terrible persecution. Having resolutely refused to recognise the papal authority, Augustin and his successors, in accordance with the policy of that persecuting Church which they represented, incited their Saxon converts to make war upon the British recusants, exasperating the national animosities, already sufficiently bitter between the two races, by adding to it the fanatical frenzy of religious bigotry. For many ages, therefore, the Britons were liable to frequent incursions from their

Saxon neighbours, who, instigated by the counsels of Rome, invaded their country, destroying their churches, burning their monasteries, and putting to death the pious and learned monks, who, in the seclusion of those establishments, were pursuing the peaceable occupations of literature and religion.[1] The struggle between the ancient British Church, on the one side, and that of Rome, backed by the Saxon sword, on the other, continued for centuries. And when the Saxon conquerors had in their turn to succumb to the Norman invaders, that struggle was renewed with greater fierceness than ever. Religion was again unscrupulously used as an instrument of State, the Norman princes forcing ecclesiastics of their own race into all the higher offices of the Church in Wales, not from any regard for the spiritual interests of the people, but that they might aid in extinguishing the national spirit of the Cymri, and in subjugating the country to the Norman yoke. This policy, of course, failed, as it richly deserved to fail. The bishops and other dignitaries thus intruded upon the country were only safe when surrounded by bodies of armed retainers, and whenever the Cymric arms won a victory in the field, the interlopers had to flee to England to save themselves from popular indignation, About the end of the twelfth century, the Welsh princes appealed to the Pope for a redress of these intolerable wrongs. A petition couched in eloquent language was presented to his Holiness from Llywelyn, Prince of Gwynedd; Gwenwynwyn and Madoc, Princes of Powys; Gruffydd, Maelgwn, Rhys, and Meredith, sons of Rhys, Prince of South Wales. It is curious, in reading this document, to observe that some of the ecclesiastical grievances of which the British princes complain are precisely those which the friends of the Church in Wales are still reiterating in our own day. [...]

When the Reformation came, the influence of the connection with England was, if possible, still more disastrous on the religious interests of Wales. "The robbery in times of peace," says Mr. Johnes, "proved worse than the spoliation in the times of war, and the rapacity of the Reformation was added to the rapacity of Popery." He then describes, in language of eloquent indignation, how the ecclesiastical endowments of the Principality were pitilessly plundered by being bestowed upon laymen, the descendants of the Norman invaders, or by being alienated from the Church of Wales to endow English bishoprics and colleges! For the last century and a half, again, the policy of the civil and ecclesiastical authorities in dealing with the Welsh Church has, it would seem, been steadily directed to the extinction of the Welsh language and nationality by the appointment of Englishmen to bishoprics, canonries, deaneries, and most of the richest livings in Wales, in utter contempt of all decency. And now when, by the legitimate operation of a State Establishment of religion, nearly the whole nation has been alienated from the Church, so that it has become a mere encumbrance in the land, we are told that Wales is so inseparably united with England that it cannot expect to be rid of the incubus until England has made up its mind to deal with its own Church Establishment.

But what we have to do with most especially at present is the Protestant Church Establishment in Wales, and our indictment against it is this, that at no period of its history has it fulfilled, in anything approaching to a satisfactory manner, its proper function as the religious instructor of the Welsh people. We have a chain of testimonies in support of this allegation that are unimpeachable as to their quality, and of overwhelming force in their concurrence and cumulation of evidence. We are anxious to make this point clear, because the line of defence that has been lately taken by the friends of the Church of England in Wales is to this effect. It is true, they say, that towards the middle of the last century the Church had fallen into a deep sleep, and so afforded occasion, and to some degree excuse, for the rise of Nonconformity, which was previously almost unknown in Wales. And then they point, in vague and sounding phrases, to a golden age that preceded that period of spiritual torpor, when the Church, alive to her high mission, ruled by native bishops, who understood the language and commanded the confidence and veneration of the country, comprehended and cared for within her ample fold the whole population of the Principality. Dissent, we are assured, is in Wales an exotic of quite modern growth, which, it is further implied, will prove to have a very ephemeral life, like Jonah's gourd, which came up in a night and perished in a night. Now all this is pure fiction. Dissent is not a thing of modern growth in Wales. It has existed more or less for more than 200 years, and whatever of vital religion has prevailed there during the whole of that period, has been owing far more to its influence than to that of the Established Church. It is not correct to say that the Church "fell asleep" in the last century, simply because it had never been awake. [...]

To aggravate the evils of all kinds already sufficiently rife in the Welsh Church, the English Government, about the beginning of the eighteenth century, adopted the practice, which it has continued ever since, of appointing Englishmen utterly ignorant of the Welsh language to Welsh bishoprics.[2] And the bishops, following the example thus set by those acting for the head of the Church, inundated the Principality with English clergymen, their own relatives and connections, to whom all the highest dignities and the richest livings were, almost without exception, assigned. A more monstrous abuse than this it is difficult to conceive, and yet it has been persevered in for 150 years in the face of all complaint and remonstrance, and in the teeth of the express judgment of the Church itself, which declares in its 26th Article that "it is a thing plainly repugnant to the Word of God, and to the custom of the primitive Church, to have public prayer in the church, or to minister the sacraments in a tongue not understanded of the people." We need not wonder, therefore, that great prominence should be henceforth given by the friends of the Church to this, as one of the causes, if not, indeed, the sole cause, of its inefficiency and decay. [...]

It is well known that the man who may be called the father of Welsh Methodism was Mr. Howell Harris. He was, and continued to the day of his death, a dutiful son of the Church. He applied for ordination but was refused. He pressed his request for six years, but to no purpose. "Wherever he went," we quote again the language of a Welsh clergyman, "as a simple and unoffending preacher of the Gospel, either in the South or the North, he was denounced by the clergy from their pulpits, he was arrested by the magistrates, and persecuted by the rabble."[3] [...]

The second great name in connection with the rise of Methodism in Wales, was the Rev. Daniel Rowlands, of Llangeitho, a man whose powers as a preacher are described by those who knew both, to have surpassed even those of Whitfield. The effect of his eloquence among his countrymen was extraordinary. It ran like a stream of electricity through the nation, kindling into life thousands who had been previously wrapped in spiritual torpor. Like Howell Harris, he was not merely content, but anxious, to continue his ministrations in the Church. "But he was cast out of the Church of England," says one of his biographers—the Rev. J. C. Ryle[4]—"for no other fault than excess of zeal." And what was the condition of the Church from which this over-zealous man was expelled by episcopal judgment? Mr. Ryle shall answer. "This ejection took place at a time when scores of Welsh clergymen were shamefully neglecting their duties, and too often were drunkards, gamblers, and sportsmen, if not worse."[5]

The simple truth is, that the history of the Welsh Church is only a crucial illustration of the invariable and inevitable evils that attend State establishments of religion. It is true that in its case these evils appear in a somewhat aggravated form, from the attempt made by the English Government to treat Wales as a conquered country, and to employ the Church as an agent in the extinction of its language and nationality. But when the life of a Christian Church is made to depend not on the faith, love, and liberality of its own members, and the presence and blessing of its Divine Master, but upon the protection and patronage of the civil government, and when, as a necessary consequence, the administration of its affairs falls into the hands of worldly politicians, who use it as an instrument of State, what can be expected but what always has ensued, that its spiritual life should wither, until those who seek real religious nourishment from its breasts are driven in sheer desperation to seek it elsewhere? [...]

But these facts, sufficiently remarkable as they are in themselves, give really but an imperfect impression of the real magnitude of the anomaly which exists in Wales. An Established Church is presumably a *national* Church, and rests its claim to being established on the ground of its being national. Above all, it ought to be *par excellence* the poor man's Church, as some of the friends of the English Establishment are wont to allege, with what truth we pause not now to inquire, that theirs is. But in Wales the Church is not only not national, but it is antinational; and the whole policy of its rulers for at least a hundred and fifty years has been inspired by a prejudice as stupid as it was mean, against the Welsh nationality and language. At present, of the small remnant of the population which still remains within its pale, by far the larger part are either English immigrants into Wales, or that portion of the Welsh people which have become Anglicised in their feelings and tastes; and instead of being the poor man's Church, that of Wales is emphatically and almost exclusively the rich man's Church. There are scores, we might safely say hundreds of churches, in which, if the clergyman's family and the squire's family, and their few dependents and parasites were removed, there would be absolutely no congregation at all. [...]

With regard to the whole of Wales, our information as respects what the Church has done during the last twenty years, is not so perfect as we could wish. The number of new churches built in the four dioceses appears, as nearly as we can calculate from the data within our reach, to be about 110. But there is more difficulty in getting at those rebuilt and enlarged, as in one of the returns (that of St. Asaph) we find churches "restored" and "improved"—words implying merely repairs of existing fabrics without any additional accommodation—mixed up with those which have been "rebuilt and enlarged." We have the precise number rebuilt, and we are willing to presume somewhat enlarged, in Llandaff, which is thirty-six, and in Bangor, which is thirty-one. We think it would be a liberal allowance from the statistical report before us to assign thirty-five "enlarged" churches to St. Asaph, and, judging by the number of new churches built in St. David's, we presume that thirty "enlarged" churches would cover all that has been done in that diocese, making a total rebuilt and enlarged of 132. Let us now turn to the Nonconformists. The following are facts on the substantial accuracy of which our readers may rely. Since 1850, the Calvinistic Methodists have built 321 new chapels, and have rebuilt and enlarged 435 more, providing additional accommodation in all for 123,881 worshippers, at a cost of £366,000. The Independents, during the same period, have built 118 new chapels, and have rebuilt and enlarged 200 more, furnishing additional accommodation for 130,000 at a cost of £294,000. The Baptists have built 142 new chapels, and rebuilt and enlarged ninety-nine more, furnishing additional accommodation for 81,800, at a cost of £163,000. Thus, those three denominations alone have in twenty years built 581 new chapels, and rebuilt and enlarged 734 more, providing accommodation for 308,681 persons, at a cost of £823,000.

But it must be further observed, that it is not merely in the matter of religious instruction that the Nonconformists have become almost exclusively the leaders of the Welsh people. As respects literature and science, and all important social and political movements, it is the same. The literature of Wales, and not its religious literature merely, is almost wholly Nonconformist. There are about thirty periodicals, quarterly, monthly, and weekly, at present published in the Welsh language. Of these all but three are owned and edited by Dissenters. There are nine commentaries on the whole Bible, and nine besides on the New Testament alone, some original and some translated from English, and only two of these were done by Churchmen, and even they were Dissenters when they began their work. There are eight Biblical and Theological Dictionaries, and as many bodies of divinity or systems of theology, and no Churchman, we believe, has had a hand in the production of any one of them. There is a History of the World, a History of Great Britain, a History of Christianity, a History of the Church, a History of the Welsh Nation, a History of Religion in Wales, all by Dissenters, besides elaborate denominational Histories of the Calvinistic Methodists, the Independents, the Baptists, &c. Indeed, all the ecclesiastical histories in the language are Nonconformist, and all the general histories except the History of Wales, by the Rev. Thomas Price, and a small work called the "Mirror of the Principal Ages." There is a valuable work, illustrated by many excellent maps and diagrams, entitled "The History of Heaven and Earth," treating of geography and astronomy, by the Rev. J. T. Jones, of Aberdare, formerly a Nonconformist minister. There is another large geographical dictionary in course of publication by a Dissenting minister. There are two copious Biographical Dictionaries edited and principally written by Dissenters. There is now, and has been for several years, in course of publication an Encyclopædia in the Welsh language (Encyclopædia Cambrensis), dealing, as such works do, with the entire circle of human knowledge. It was described by the late Archdeacon Williams, who had seen the earlier volumes, as "a work of great promise, as sound in doctrine as it is unsectarian in principle." It is studiously free from denominational taint, and was intended to be a great national undertaking, the contributors being indiscriminately selected from the ablest writers of all denominations, the combined learning and talent of Wales being thus engaged in its preparation. The enterprising publisher at the outset addressed a letter to all those among his countrymen, of whatever Church or creed, who had distinguished themselves in any way by their literary acquirements and productions, inviting their co-operation. We have now before us a list of the contributors, amounting to ninety names, and out of these ninety, there are certainly not more than nine Churchmen.

The English public has of late years become partially acquainted with a remarkable institution existing in Wales, which has come down from very ancient times, called Yr Eisteddfod, or the Session, meaning in its primitive signification the Session of the Bards. Its object is to encourage the cultivation of literature, poetry, and music. Prizes ranging from £1 to £100 are offered for the best compositions in poetry, prose, and music. The highest honour bestowed by the Eisteddfod is the Bardic chair, and the productions entitling the successful candidates to this distinction are supposed to possess rare merit. There are now living nine chaired bards, of whom one is a clergyman, seven are Nonconformist ministers, and one a Nonconformist layman. In musical compositions the proportion would be about the same. And certainly the Welsh clergy of the present day have not, any more than their predecessors, distinguished themselves as authors. A catalogue of Welsh books published within the last twenty years would show a very "beggarly account" standing to the credit of the official instructors of the Welsh people.

Such are the past history and the present condition of the Established Church in Wales. Surely no legislature with any sense of justice can long refuse to deal with so anomalous an institution as that we have described. A Church which has wholly failed, and is still failing, to accomplish the only object for which it pretends to exist, from which—and that entirely owing to its own criminal neglect—the great body of the people are hopelessly alienated, and which has no vital relation with the religious, political, social, or literary life of the nation, is not merely a theoretical anomaly. It is an intolerable practical grievance, and is becoming more and more so every day. For its friends, numbering as they do nearly all the landowners and wealthy classes, galvanised, of late years, into a sort of spasmodic zeal, which is far more political than religious, are making frantic efforts to regain for their

Church the ascendancy it has so righteously lost, by a very unscrupulous use of their wealth, their social position, and their control over the land. The advocates of the Church, especially in the English Press, are trying to wreak their vengeance on a nation of Dissenters, by traducing the character of the people and ridiculing their language, their literature, and their religious institutions; and this they are not deterred from doing by their utter ignorance of all three.

Notes

1 Thierry's "History of the Norman Conquest" [Augustin Thierry, *History of the Conquest of England by the Normans* (1825)], Book 1.
2 Mr. Gladstone, to his great honour, had the courage to break through this practice, by his appointment of a thorough Welshman to the diocese of St. Asaph.
3 "Justice to Wales: Report of the Association of Welsh Clergy in the West Riding of the County of York", p. 8.
4 Now bishop of Liverpool.
5 "The Christian Leader[s] of the Last Century," by the Rev. J. C. Ryle [1869], p. 192.

14

WILLIAM WILLIAMS PANTYCELYN, ''RWY'N EDRYCH DROS Y BRYNIAU PELL' ('I LOOK ACROSS THE DISTANT HILLS')

In Gwynfor Evans (ed.), *Land of My Fathers: 2000 Years of Welsh History* (Talybont: Y Lolfa Press, 1992), p. 338

'Rwy'n edrych dros y bryniau pell
    Amdanat bob yr awr;
Tyrd, fy anwylyd, mae'n hwyrhau,
    A'm haul bron mynd i lawr.

Melysach nag yw'r diliau mêl
    Yw munud o'th fwynhau,
Ac nid oes gennyf bleser sydd
    Ond hynny yn parhau.

A phan y syrthio sêr y nen
    Fel ffigys îr i'r llawr,
Bydd fy niddanwch heb ddim trai
    Oll yn fy Arglwydd mawr.

I look across the distant hills
    each hour for thy coming:
come, my loved one, for it's late
    and my sun's near to setting.

Sweeter than the honey drops
    a minute's joy in thee,
and I've no other pleasure that
    lasts everlastingly.

And when the stars of heaven fall
    like ripe figs to the sward,
there'll be no ebb to the delight
    that's all in my great Lord.

15

ANN GRIFFITHS, 'WELE'N SEFYLL RHWNG Y MYRTWYDD' ('SEE HIM STAND AMONG THE MYRTLES')

In Gwynfor Evans (ed.), *Land of My Fathers: 2000 Years of Welsh History* (Talybont: Y Lolfa Press, 1992), pp. 346–347

Wele'n sefyll rhwng y myrtwydd
    Wrthych teilwng o fy mryd:
Er mai o ran, yr wy'n adnabod
    Ei fod uwchlaw gwrthrychau'r byd:
        Henffych fore
    Y caf ei weled fel y mae.

Rhosyn Saron yw ei enw,
    Gwyn a gwridog, teg o bryd;
Ar ddeng mil y mae'n rhagori
    O wrthrychau penna'r byd:
        Ffrind pechadur,
    Dyma ei Beilat ar y mor.

Beth sydd imi mwy a wnelwyf
    Ag eilunod gwael y llawr?
Tystio'r wyf nad yw eu cwmni
    I'w gystadlu â Iesu mawr:
        O! am aros
    Yn ei gariad ddyddiau f'oes.

See him stand among the myrtles,
    worthy object of my love,
though as yet I barely know

    that he's all earthly things above:
        come, the morning
    he'll be hidden by no veil.

He is called the Rose of Sharon,
    white and blushing, featured fair:
he excels above ten thousand
    earthly things that men count fair:
        friend of sinners,
    he's our pilot on the sea.

What have I to do in future
    with vain idols of this earth?
All their company, I swear it,
    by my Christ is nothing worth.
        O! to linger
    my whole lifetime in his love.

5.3

Unitarianism

5.3 Unitarianism

Radically unorthodox in doctrine, Unitarians were widely viewed with suspicion and hostility by most branches of Dissent as well as the Established Church, at least in the early nineteenth century. Their beliefs derived from a mixture of Enlightenment Deism, which emphasised the primacy of natural law, and the ancient Socinian and Aryan heresies which denied the divinity of Christ. Unitarians rejected many of the apparently 'magical' elements in orthodox doctrine and were among the first to proclaim that post-mortal punishment was not everlasting, but reformative. In the early nineteenth century Unitarians boasted no shortage of apologetic literature, mostly defensive in nature and focused on detailed corrections of orthodox doctrine to make the case for rational religion. The extract below derives from a lengthy work of this kind,[1] more specifically from the final chapter which was republished as a stand-alone pamphlet in 1845. This commends Unitarianism to the intellectual and social sensibilities of the modern era. Its author, Lant Carpenter (1780–1840), was minister of a Bristol congregation and a leading figure in early-nineteenth-century Unitarianism who worked to broaden his denomination's outlook. The republication in 1845 of just the 'application' section of the 1820 work speaks to the changed condition of Unitarianism mid-century. The spirit of 'New' Unitarianism placed less emphasis on doctrinal specifics and more on the experiential and practical dimensions of faith, for now that Unitarians had lost many of their civil disabilities they were gaining public prominence as leaders of progressive causes.

Carpenter promotes Unitarianism as ethical theism which rejects doctrines that complicate simple biblical truth and contradict moral reason. It is therefore more doubt-proof, he suggests, than orthodoxy. Criticising orthodoxy for maligning the divine character, he argues that God consistently inspires love not fear, consigns no one to eternal damnation, and is not split into separate persons with confliction temperaments such as the judgmental Father and merciful son of Trinitarian Christianity. Unitarianism emphasises works, personal moral responsibility, and a spirit of ecumenism which accepts people of all creeds and nations as children of 'the common Parent of all'. Carpenter scatters scripture quotation throughout his work, and refers to dissenting forebear Philip Doddridge, a nonconformist minister, educator and hymn writer whose *The Rise and Progress of Religion in the Soul* (1745) was widely influential. While the work's main emphasis is on the rational and practical, it makes some concessions to the pressure for rational religionists to show theirs was not a coldly intellectual faith. 'Unitarian Christianity goes to the heart' says Carpenter, making much of the warm image of God as father who appeals to the 'affections' of the worshipper. This continues the Romantic thread in early as well as New Unitarianism which poet Anna Barbauld promoted in her 1775 essay 'Thoughts on the Devotional Taste', arguing that even the most philosophical faith required 'warm and pathetic imagery . . . that strikes upon the heart and senses'.[2] Carpenter extols an enlightened spiritual and social ethos that balances devotion, reason and charity.

Hymnody is more readily associated with feelings-oriented denominations such as Methodism, but a number of Unitarian hymnals appeared through the century which encouraged error-free veneration. Several of these (including the hymn given below) were by Anna Barbauld (1743–1825), showing her continued influence on the denomination. Barbauld takes the worshipper to the foot of the cross in a meditation that accorded with James Martineau's mid-century emphasis 'on a new personal spirituality, [and] on the importance of Jesus'.[3] The hymn makes Jesus's message of compassionate social concern the heart of the gospel, alluding to his 'new commandment' to 'love one another, as I have loved you' (John 13:34). Barbauld adopts Jesus's first-person voice with authority to instruct generosity, mercy and inclusion, especially of the weak and suffering. She employs the language of sensibility in images of the 'softening heart', 'melting eye' and 'trembling soul'. The dying Jesus is presented not as divine incarnation or atoning saviour but as a model of pathos in this emotively social gospel.

Notes

1 Lant Carpenter, *An Examination of the Charges Made Against Unitarians, and Unitarianism, by Right Rev Dr Magee, Bishop of Raphoe* (Bristol, 1820).
2 *Anna Barbauld: Selected Poetry and Prose*, edited by William McCarthy and Elizabeth Kraft (Ormskirk: Broadview Press, 2002), p. 217.
3 Alan Ruston, 'James Martineau and the Evolution of Unitarian Hymnody', in Isabel Rivers and David L. Wykes (eds), *Dissenting Praise: Religious Dissent and the Hymn in England and Wales* (Oxford: Oxford University Press, 2011), pp. 173–196, on p. 183.

16

EXTRACTS FROM LANT CARPENTER, *THE BENEFICIAL TENDENCY OF UNITARIANISM*

(London: [n.p.], 1845), pp. 5–11, 11–13, 13–15, 16–20

I see that Unitarianism embraces all the great motives of Christianity; that it impedes the operation of none; and that it frees the practical principles of the Gospel from the influence of doctrines, which, in their natural efficacy, impede or pervert them.

1. I consider it as a great excellence of *Unitarianism* that it *encourages and rewards the sound exercise of the understanding in matters of religion.*

Unitarianism peculiarly falls in with the liberal and intellectual character of the Gospel and of the instructions of Christ and his Apostles. The religion of Christ is a religion of the heart, but it is also a religion of the understanding. Truth is the food, and divine truth the best food of the understanding; 'to bear witness to the truth,' was the object (our Saviour himself says) 'for which he was born, for which he came forth into the world, and he prays that by the truth, God would sanctify his disciples [John 18:37].

The spirit of the Gospel dispensation is admirably expressed in the words of the Apostle Paul. 'I will pray with the spirit, I will pray with the understanding also; I will sing with the spirit, I will sing with the understanding also,' [1 Corinthians 14:15]—The Christian religion was designed, not as a temporary dispensation, but to last through every period of the world. It was of great importance, for its future acceptance and usefulness, that it should approve itself to the sound understanding; that it should appear to all, who will seriously examine, to be indeed the *wisdom* of God unto salvation; that it should be obvious to all who 'desire to do the will of God,' not only that grace, but that truth also came by Jesus Christ.

Some there are who value a doctrine in proportion to its obscurity; and those who make religion a matter of the imagination and of strong feeling, rather than of solid conviction and of steady though lively Christian affection and principle, might wish for more than 'the simplicity which is in Christ' [2 Corinthians 11:3]. But where the judgment is duly exercised, and the imagination properly placed under its regulation, the disciple of Jesus must rejoice when he sees the complete accordance of the truths of the Gospel with the dictates of the soundest understanding; and must feel grateful to the Father of lights, that the bright display of himself and his dispensations, which the Gospel affords, is not obscured by the impenetrable cloud of incomprehensibility.—Is it possible that the clear understanding of important truth can make it less interesting or less valuable?

Now if the Unitarian views of Christian truth are correct, there is nothing in the scheme of the Gospel which it is difficult to understand. Those principles, which were most inconsistent with the prejudices of the Jews, and therefore to them most mysterious, are not so to us. On the contrary—though they may excite our admiration, and our adoration of the unsearchable wisdom of him, who seeth the end from the beginning, and often chooseth means to execute his purposes which baffle human wisdom and presumption—they contribute to bind the Gospel to the heart. That the blessings of the Gospel should be free to all, without distinction of Jew and Gentile—free as the air we breathe—and that they should be conveyed to us, not by the temporal prince and triumphant conqueror, but by the 'man of sorrows,' who through suffering and death became the author of eternal salvation to all who obey him, present to our minds nothing mysterious; but, on the contrary, more clearly display to our eyes the wisdom of him, who is called 'the only wise God.'

I do not say, that Unitarianism entirely removes all difficulties from religion; I believe that difficulties will exist, as long as human excellence must include humility, trust, and resignation: and such is the admirable adaptation of revelation to the wants of man, that these very difficulties are one cause of the attention which the mind pays to it, and which, where humbly and piously directed, is constantly rewarded by clearer and clearer perceptions of divine truth. But I do say that Unitarianism removes the greatest and most oppressive difficulties, which have tended to prejudice the minds of thinking men against the Gospel. And though I would never relinquish a doctrine, proved by adequate evidence, merely because it is obscure, yet surely it is a presumption in favour of the divine origin of a doctrine, that it is clear and intelligible.— To many it may not be of any consequence whether they understand a thing or not. They may feel at perfect ease in receiving as true, from the authority of their parents and spiritual guides, that which they in no way profess to understand. But the more the mind is exercised, and the more knowledge on other subjects it acquires, the more it seeks to understand that which it is taught to believe; and the more extensively intellectual culture is diffused, the more generally will this want be experienced. In periods of spiritual darkness and spiritual slavery, the most absurd dogmas may be implicitly received; but where the light of knowledge beams on other subjects, and the rights of religious liberty and free inquiry are understood and exercised, the mind cannot rest in religious ignorance. And I do gratefully rejoice in the conviction, that, in the search after divine truth in the records and dictates of revelation, the understanding may not only find its noblest field for exercise, but will be rewarded with knowledge which, while it is healthy to the soul, will prove invigorating to its own noblest powers.

But I will not enlarge on this point, farther than by stating the positions which I had in view under this head—viz. that the great principles of Unitarianism, (or, in other words, as I firmly believe, pure Christianity,) are easily understood: that they do not perplex and confound the understanding; that they are adapted to the intellectual wants of all, and especially of those for whom the Gospel was peculiarly designed, the poor and unlearned: that they relieve Christianity from those difficulties which erroneous views of it have caused, and which have led numbers ro relinquish it; and that they make Christian faith, where it has been founded on evidence, more firm and steady, by freeing it from the sources of doubt, and wavering, and perplexity. Such, I hesitate not in believing, have been the effects of Unitarianism in numerous instances. And I trust, under the blessings of God, such will be its effect, increasing in a rapid proportion.

II. Intimately connected with the foregoing remarks, is the important fact, that *Unitarian Christianity presents one object of religious worship, one object of the highest affections of the heart.*

The perplexities experienced by the thinking mind in connexion with this essential point, have often been the cause of the examination, and subsequent rejection, of the popular doctrines. If there are three persons, or intelligent agents, each infinite, each possessed of all the adorable perfections which belong to God—if, in short, there are three separate, distinct, infinite minds, of one substance, power, and glory, each subsisting separately, and capable of being made, separately, the object of thought, and of religious worship—(however much the mind may, by the aid of metaphysical subtilities, bring itself to believe that these three distinct infinite Minds or Persons are ONE GOD, and that by holding the existence of such three distinct Persons in the Godhead, the great principle of the divine unity is not violated,)—one thing is certain, that each being separately God, must be *the object of religious worship separately from the others.*

In accordance with this plain and necessary conclusion, prayers and other branches of religious worship, are offered up to each of the three Persons separately. The consistent Trinitarian, believing each Person to be truly God, and worshipping each separately, necessarily has three objects of worship. By what principle shall he regulate his devotions to each? If he rest satisfied with partial examination, still his mind is likely to be bewildered: but if he look into the Christian's directory, he there finds no precept directing the offering of religious worship to any other being but the Father; and, on the contrary, he finds numerous plain, direct declarations in the Law, and the Prophets, and the Gospel, confirmed most powerfully by the uniform example and instruction of our Saviour, all pointing to this great truth, that the FATHER is the *only* proper object of religious worship. If so, the conclusion necessarily follows, that HE is the only true GOD.

Through the embarrassment and perplexity with which, to the reflecting mind, Trinitarianism is often attended, respecting the direction of Christian worship, many have been led to consider the evidence of popular opinions, and to relinquish them for those plain fundamental truths which shine with clear and strong effulgence throughout the whole of revelation. And when they have embraced these, they have no longer any perplexity. Their devotions acquire a simplicity, which often adds to their fervency; and at least makes their devout affections steady and clear, and gives them the best prospect of shedding their influence over the whole tenor of life.

But, besides this consideration, there is another of great weight. Not merely are there, on popular doctrines, different objects of equal worship, but these have *different characters and offices assigned to them*. And it will generally be found, among those who hold the higher forms of what are called Evangelical doctrines, that he whom the Scriptures represent as the *effect* of God's love to mankind, is often thought of as the *cause, the procuring cause* of divine mercy; and thus that highest gratitude, which reason and revelation teach us is due to Jehovah, is diverted into a different channel. And can that commandment be then fulfilled, which our Saviour most solemnly sanctioned, when he said, 'The first of all the commandments is, Hear, O Israel, the Lord our God, the Lord is One, and thou shalt love the Lord thy God with all thy heart, and with all thy soul, and with all thy mind, and with all thy strength' [Deuteronomy 6: 4–5]?

I have indeed no doubt, that many who profess and believe Trinitarian sentiments, influenced by the plain principles, examples, and commands of the Gospel and of the Law, do, in practice, confine their worship, and the highest adoration of their hearts, to the Father, and love Jehovah as the supreme object of their best affections: but then they are so far (that is, practically) Unitarians; and we can only wish that they were so in avowed profession.

On this point Unitarianism is unrivalled. While it affords abundant grounds of love to him, who bore in his character so eminent a resemblance to the moral excellencies of the Supreme Being, and who was, under Him, the agent of communicating the richest gifts of divine mercy; while it warms the heart with gratitude to our Saviour, for his exertions and sufferings to insure and extend the blessed privileges of the Gospel; while it makes him the object of our faith and trust, as possessed of divine authority, sanctioned by the most signal marks of divine approbation; while it demands our reverence for him as the Son of God, as exalted to be the Lord of the dead and the living, and, under the appointment of God, to raise the dead and judge the world; it keeps clear and close to the great fundamental principle, 'Thou shalt worship Jehovah thy God, and to Him only shalt thou offer religious service' [Matthew 4:10]: it teaches us, (as the Scriptures teach us, and because the Scriptures teach us,) that HE is the only true GOD, that we ought to pay religious worship to Him alone, and that HE is LOVE; and His love the source of every blessing, temporal and spiritual;—that He therefore should be the object of the highest love, and gratitude, and trust, and reverence, and obedience.

III. It is a most important advantage of *Unitarianism, that it throws no impediment in the way of the great practical principles of the Gospel.*

Though it ascribes no merit to works, and represents all rewards of faith and obedience as solely the gifts of divine grace, yet it lays, as the Gospel does, the utmost stress upon good works, i. e. *Christian conduct springing from Christian principles,* such as love to God and to mankind, love to Christ, the desire of imitating his example and obeying his precepts, the precepts of his Gospel, the dictates of conscience enlightened by Christian duty, &c. From the necessity of a holy life and conversation to obtain the divine favour and final acceptance, Unitarianism presents nothing to draw off the mind: but, on the contrary, it lays the greatest, most steady, and most consistent stress upon this. It gives abundant hope to the broken and contrite heart; but it does not, through unhappy views of the work and merit of the Son of God, afford any room to delay the work of repentance, or to expect that strong and agonizing feelings, an appropriating faith in his merits, and inward assurance of pardon, will supply the place of a sober, righteous, and godly life. [...]

The present popular views of Christianity have a direct tendency to make religion greatly consist in frames and feelings; or at least to represent these as essential tests of the state of the soul. Now these very much depend upon the constitution of the individual, upon the state of his bodily system at the time, upon the strength of his imagination, and other causes utterly independent of Christian excellence. In proportion as this standard or test is adopted, the mind is led away from scriptural tests; and there is a great and natural leaning in the human mind to rest upon the former, which are obvious and easily applied, to the entire or partial exclusion of the latter. I do not think that this was so much the case with the Orthodox writers of past times (who seem to have had in view Christian principle, more than the peculiarities of Christian belief;) but if we are to judge by the publications, and discourses, and hymns of many belonging to what are termed the Evangelical classes at present, I think there is reason to believe that the test of Christian excellence, and grounds of the divine favour, are more now than formerly, a mysterious, inexplicable feeling, which they term faith, and the fervid emotions which are produced by the natural sympathy of the mind, and by excitements which may have a religious character, but which, as far at least as the individual is concerned, have nothing to do with religion.

'Religion,' as is excellently stated by one who knew its real power, but whose strong sensibilities and glowing ardour of expression may sometimes have contributed to propagate the very error of which I am speaking— 'Religion, in its most general view, is such a sense of God upon the soul, and such a conviction of our obligations to him, and of our dependence upon him, as shall engage us to make it our great care to conduct ourselves in a manner, which we have reason to believe will be pleasing to him'.[1] In such an account of it, I recognise the genuine spirit of the Christian: and to hinder this principle, in Unitarianism there is nothing; to excite it to action and give it influence, there is everything.

Unitarianism leads us to expect nothing from God without ourselves endeavouring to do his will. It places religion in the careful regulation of the heart and life by the spirit and precepts of Christ. It teaches us, most plainly and forcibly, that in the last great day 'every one shall bear his own burden' [Galations 6:5]; that we must be rewarded or punished 'according as our works have been' [Matthew 16:27]; and that our situation in a future state of retribution will be exactly proportioned to the character and conduct of the individual, appreciated with the most unerring precision, by him who will judge the world in righteousness, under the guidance and wisdom of Him who is all-wise. It encourages us to expect all needful aid and direction in the way of duty, in working out our salvation, in attending the sanctification of the heart; but it presents no encouragement unless we do strive, and watch, and pray. It leads us to attend to the *formation of habits*, because it encourages no presumptuous hopes of miraculous interference to make the Ethiopian change his skin, or the leopard his spots. It leads us, too, *to begin early;* and I cannot doubt, that the infinite importance of early attention to the religious and moral regulation of the character, is among none so strongly urged by their principles, as among the Unitarians. [...]

IV. *Unitarianism throws no impediment in the way of Christian liberality and affection.*

I do not see how it is possible to hold the doctrines of Unitarianism, and yet maintain that the favour of God and eternal salvation are confined to the narrow limits of sect and party. True it is, we are taught that there is 'no other name under heaven *given* among men, by which we must be saved' [Acts 4:12]—that God has seen fit to propose no other terms of salvation to mankind, than those of the Gospel, and to appoint no other Mediator to convey the blessings of the New Covenant; and therefore that no one can possess those inestimable blessings on the secure ground of *divine promise,* but through faith in Christ. But the Unitarian rejoices in the conviction that 'in every nation, he that feareth God and worketh righteousness will be accepted by him;' and that He who 'hath appointed to men the bounds of their habitation,' and given them their various talents, will accept them according to what they have, and not according to what they have not [Acts 10:35 and 17:26]. If the untaught Heathen, or the deluded Mahommedan, to whom the light of the Gospel has never been offered, do, according to the light they possess, faithfully obey the dictates of conscience, serving and loving the Deity as known to them, I cannot doubt that He who is the common Parent of all, will grant them here increasing light in the way of duty, and some portion of those present rewards which He has graciously connected with well-doing; and that in the future world He will make them partakers of blessings, of which millions of them have never heard, and unite them under him who must reign till all enemies are put under his feet. Too highly prizing the inestimable privileges, the sanctifying principles, the gracious hopes, the strengthening, healing consolations of the Gospel, to feel otherwise than an earnest desire that they may be diffused to all who share the gift of reason—feeling it his duty, (the debt of gratitude which he owes to the Author of all good, and to the friend and benefactor who shed his blood to communicate, assure, and extend, the blessings which he himself possesses, and the debt of love which he owes to all his brethren of mankind,) to contribute his efforts to the arrival of that period, when the name of God shall be universally hallowed, and His will done on earth as it is done in heaven, when all shall know the only true God, and Jesus Christ whom he hath sent—and rejoicing in all that is wisely done by others to promote the glory of God—the Unitarian has more honourable notions of the God of love, than to imagine that He will make hundreds and thousands of millions miserable for ever, solely because they do not receive him as their Saviour, whose name they have never heard.

But the worst influences of this tenet on the Christian character, are seen in the more limited relations and connexions of life. It is the parent of uncharitableness, and the foster-mother of persecution. To view ourselves as the exclusive objects of the divine favour, and all who do not entertain our views of the Christian faith as the objects of God's wrath and indignation, is not only injurious to his character, but has the direct tendency to generate spiritual pride, and to check the best affections of the heart toward those who differ from us. To account those our enemies who are, as we think, the enemies of GOD, is no part of Christianity; and those doctrines which lead to this estimation, lose the grand characteristic of the Gospel, while they destroy its delightful features as proceeding from the Father and Lord of all.

I rejoice in the belief, that multitudes of those who now, through the influence of human creeds, consign the Unitarian to eternal perdition, will hereafter stretch to him the right hand of Christian friendship, if we have the happiness to join them where, not for their unchristian errors, but for their Christian obedience, I doubt not they will gain admission. But the unhappy notion which they have of exclusive salvation, makes them here look upon him with unkind suspicion as to his motives and his conduct, prevents them from listening to his reasons, and induces them to place a barrier (too often insuperable) against the admission of the simple truths of the Gospel by those who are under their influence. [...]

Unitarianism does a vast service to the cause of Christian charity, by levelling those narrow fences within which modern Orthodoxy confines all that is truly good and excellent. It thus disposes us to give the right hand of fellowship to all, whose dispositions and conduct show they have sat at the feet of Jesus. It destroys all those narrowing views, which so often interfere with the great objects of benevolence; and it disposes us to co-operate with all who have them in view, and to think well of them, when they separate from us and we from them, to promote respectively our more limited opinions.

By the man who has drunk deeply into the spirit of that Saviour who loved all mankind without distinction of name or country—who has imbibed the principles of that religion which teaches us that love is the fulfilling of the law (of social duty), that without charity we are but as sounding brass or tinkling cymbals, and that the end of the commandments is 'charity out of a pure heart and faith unfeigned' [1 Timothy 1:5],—must it not be deemed a recommendation of any set of doctrines, and a presumption in favour of their being Christianity itself, that they promote these its grand essential qualities, and clear the way for their full exercise?

V. *Unitarianism shines forth resplendently, in respect to the character and dispensations of the great Father of all.*

The light of the Gospel hath not entirely dispelled the clouds and darkness, which human weakness and imperfection throw around the ways of God; and

Unitarianism cannot do more; but much that Unitarianism opposes, involves them in greater darkness, or, should I not say? in gloom. Gloomy indeed are those representations of the righteous Judge of the whole earth, which present him to us every revolving year allowing tens of millions of those, to whom His spirit hath given understanding, to go out of life, and fall into eternal misery, for want of that knowledge which His word could at once afford them, or of that grace which He who hath access to the heart could at once communicate. Terrific indeed are those doctrines, which teach us that His wrath could not be expiated, till its full vials had been emptied on the head of the merciful Redeemer of men; or that His justice could not be satisfied, till an innocent person had been punished in the place of the guilty. He who can dare to hope, that, among the millions and millions who for ever and ever must view their Creator only as the avenging Lawgiver and Judge, he stands secure from his awful indignation, may sing the hymn of gratitude for himself; but will not human weakness shrink back with horror at the prospect, that a time will come, when the ties which here bound him to all mankind, as the children of one common Father—the ties which bound him to those whom he saw doing good to men, and, as far as he could judge, obeying God, (ties which to feel was honourable,) the ties which bound him with closer affection to friend or relative, and even those which are formed by the nearest domestic relations—shall all be severed for ever, even where the only crime was unavoidable ignorance, or even where the friend or relative, the husband or the son, had in view, in the general tenor of his conduct, to live as in the sight of God, and with respect to the last great account? Will the expectation of individual happiness make the groans unheard, of misery unutterable, without alleviation, irremediable, and endless?

If this be Orthodoxy, no wonder that he, who sees written in the law of Moses, 'the Lord, the Lord God, merciful and gracious'—who sees in the Prophets that Jehovah 'desireth not the death of the sinner'—who hears the Apostles speaking of the kindness and grace of GOD—who hears his venerated Lord declare that 'HE is kind even to the unthankful and the evil'—who reads in the book of nature that 'the Lord is good to all, and his tender mercies are over all his works'—and who sees inscribed in unfading characters in the everlasting Gospel that 'GOD IS LOVE'—no wonder that he pronounces that it is not Christianity [Exodus 34:6, Luke 6:35, Psalm 145:9, 1 John 4:8].

I once asked a Unitarian friend, who, while among the Wesleyan Methodists had manifested the spirit of devotion, if she found her piety impeded, or its fervour lessened by her change of sentiments? Oh no! she replied; and she went on, with simple, serious feeling, to tell me with what unmingled delight, and unembarrassed love she now contemplated the perfections and dealings of her Heavenly Father, how much more she now possessed to feed the purest flame of devotion. And it must be so. Certainly the doctrines of Unitarianism bring home 'the terrors of the Lord.' They show that the holiness of God cannot look upon sin but with abhorrence; they show that His faithfulness and justice are concerned to punish the impenitent and disobedient; they teach us that His judgments will be administed with impartial equity, that everyone shall reap as he now sows, and that rewards or punishments shall be awarded according as our works have been: they impress the soul, therefore, with reverential awe of that great Being, who is Almighty, All-wise, All-holy, All-just, our Omniscient Witness, and our Final Judge: they will not allow of irreverence or familiarity towards the Infinite and adorable Majesty of heaven and earth. But at the same time, they present everything to enable us to offer to him the best affections of the heart. They teach us, in an especial manner, to view God as our Father; and in this, the most delightful and comprehensive appellation, (that in which our Saviour so continually represents the Great Being who sent him, and under which he teaches us to call upon Him), they include everything that can encourage, that can animate, that can console, that can prompt to submission, to reverence, to love, to gratitude, to trust, to the best tribute of prayer and praise, of adoration, resignation, and obedience: and by this endearing representation they give us, as the Scriptures do, from which they are derived, the pledge of parental love, of parental care, of parental guidance, of parental chastisements indeed, but also of parental mercy.

I well know that every Christian uses the appellation FATHER, and that he considers the Supreme Being as standing in this relation: but I ask, is it not at utter variance with those doctrines which make the *infinite satisfaction* of the Son of God the sole ground on which the sinner can rest his hopes; which represent the death of Christ as appeasing the wrath of God; which talk of God standing upon full satisfaction, and not remitting one sin without it; of the blood of Christ calming the Father's frowning face, of Jesus forcing Him to spare, &c? To my mind it is clear, that if the discourses of Jesus and his apostles have divine authority, those doctrines have not; and that he who, though in words adopting the latter, keeps close in thought and feeling to the former, is in reality a Unitarian at heart, even if he never heard the appellation.

Now Unitarianism presents nothing to interfere with these heart-inspiring representations of the paternal character of God. It teaches us, indeed, that our heavenly Father will, for the good of his large family, support his authority, and will punish the impenitent offender; it teaches us that in the future state he will exercise a righteous retribution, and that guilt and misery will never be separated: but it also teaches that in judgment he remembers mercy; that when he sees his paternal chastisements have done their work, and perceives the tokens of genuine and full repentance, he wants no satisfaction, no punishment; but receives his wandering child to duty and to himself; and if still he leaves him to feel the present consequences of his folly and disobedience, he cheers him with that hope which is an anchor of the soul, sure and steadfast. It teaches us, too, that in compassion to the weakness and necessities of his creatures, he has given us the assured promise and pledge of his pardoning grace: that he set forth a mercy-seat, where his gracious purposes might be fully made known; and, to strengthen the pledge, and to make it evident to all that the covenant was sure, by his all-wise appointment that mercy-seat was sprinkled with blood—the blood of the new covenant—the blood of Christ, 'as of a lamb without spot and blemish' [1 Peter 1:19]. In fine, it teaches us, in the words of inspired truth, that God is love; that because he is love, he sent his Son to save the world, and that since he spared him not, but 'freely delivered him up for us all,' we may rest assured of his readiness to give everything truly needful to his servants and children [Romans 8:32]. By thus representing the Lord of heaven and earth, the Unitarian doctrine, following its great teacher, displays a throne of grace with a merciful though righteous Sovereign seated on it, and that Sovereign our Father.

Note

1 [Philip] Doddridge's *[The] Rise and Progress of Religion in the Soul* [1745].

17

ANNA LAETITIA BARBAULD, 'THE NEW COMMANDMENT' (NO. 214)

In James Martineau (ed.), *Hymns for the Christian Church and Home* [1840] (London: Longmans, Green & Co., 1866), n.p.

Behold where, breathing love divine,
    Our dying Master stands!
His weeping followers, gathering round,
    Receive his last commands.

From that mild teacher's parting lips
    What tender accents fell!
The gentle precept which he gave
    Became its author well.

'Blest is the man whose softening heart
    Feels all another's pain!
To whom the supplicating eye
    Was never raised in vain.

He spreads his kind supporting arms
    To every child of grief;
His secret bounty largely flows,
    And brings unasked relief.

To gentle offices of love
    His feet are never slow;
He views through mercy's melting eye
    A brother in a foe.

Peace from the bosom of his God,
    My peace to him I give;
And when he kneels before the throne,
    His trembling soul shall live.'

5.4 Quakers

5.4 Quakers

Through the nineteenth century, the group known as Quakers or 'Friends' went through an internal revolution, from being an isolated sect in fear of its own survival to a thriving denominational alternative with a strong public presence. But '[t]his step from walled garden to the market-square was not taken without pains and blushes'.[1] While theologically orthodox, Quakers placed great emphasis on the divine spirit's direct communications to individuals, eschewing all external forms of worship and holding meetings that were silent unless members felt stirred to speak as divinely directed. Early nineteenth-century Quakers continued peculiarities of dress, language and lifestyle established in the seventeenth century, bearing the stigma attached to these as appointed sufferings. Ascetic in the extreme, they rejected many forms of culture – Mary Howitt wrote regretfully of her Quaker upbringing, 'It is impossible to give an adequate idea of the stillness and isolation of our lives as children.'[2] Yet paradoxically, many Quakers supported social causes (notably the abolition of slavery, penal reform, pacifism and temperance), although political quietism was also common. Between 1800 and 1859, membership had fallen from 20,000 to less than 15,000 and progressive members were glumly asking 'Has Quakerism a future?'[3] In the years to follow, Quakerism was transformed to conform more to the pattern of the world, abandoning its peculiarities and engaging more fully in civic life – a change which left some to mourn their loss of distinctiveness.

Perhaps because of their habits of doctrinal reserve, there are few early-century Quaker apologetic works. The extract below is from the view of a sympathetic outsider, Thomas Clarkson (1760–1846), a prominent Abolitionist who wrote a three-volume 'moral history' of Quakerism in homage to their sterling support. It is a sympathetic and respectful account of the religious logic behind the Friends' beliefs and habits, capturing the early-century Quaker ethos well enough to be reprinted in *The British Friend* journal through the 1850s under the series heading 'Friends: Their Origin, Distinguishing Principles, and Practices'. The extracts brought together here encompass Quaker attitudes to worship, culture and social issues. Clarkson first explains the key to Quaker practice as its utter reliance on the movements of the Holy Spirit, with religion understood as an entirely 'inward' phenomenon. He develops some of the repercussions of worship without forms, including its unusually egalitarian model of spirit-led ministry which included women as well as men (although see 5.1 Wesleyan Methodism). Clarkson then presents the benefits of silent worship as the soul's direct and wordless communion with the divine which can at best become 'sublime'. Clarkson normalises this practice by reference to works on the same subject by earlier (non-Quaker) divines such as John Hales's *Golden Remains* (1659) and George Monro's *Just Measures of the Pious Institutions of Youth* (1701).

The next section exemplifies the Friends' cultural asceticism in a diatribe on the effects of the novel, a scepticism shared to a lesser degree by many other dissenting groups but which was much eroded by the middle of the nineteenth century. This echoes exactly the anxieties that had dogged the new literary form in mainstream cultural debates through the previous half-century. Finally, Clarkson celebrates the Quaker social conscience, and what might be thought of as their noble contrariness, astutely arguing that their principled endeavours sprang from exactly the same root as their antisocial habits: a stubborn refusal to compromise with the world: 'few public evils would have arisen among mankind, if statesmen had adopted the system, upon which Quakers reason in political affairs [...] in condemning to detestation the memory of the man, who first made a distinction between expediency and moral right'. Quakers, he implies, when at their most world-rejecting, were the conscience of a compromised Christian society. (Note that a lengthy explanatory footnote has been omitted from the extract).

Notes

1 Owen Chadwick, *The Victorian Church*, 2 vols, 3rd edn (London: Adam and Charles Black, 1971), vol. 1, p. 426.
2 Mary Howitt, *Autobiography*, 2 vols (London: William Isbister Ltd, 1889), vol. 1, p. 45. See Elizabeth Isichei, *The Victorian Quakers* (London: Oxford University Press, 1970), pp. 144–147 and 152–154.
3 J. R. Rowntree, *Quakerism, Past and Present* (London: Smith, Elder and Co., 1859), p. 185.

18

THOMAS CLARKSON, *A PORTRAITURE OF QUAKERISM, AS TAKEN FROM A VIEW OF THE MORAL EDUCATION, DISCIPLINE, PECULIAR CUSTOMS, RELIGIOUS PRINCIPLES, POLITICAL AND CIVIL ECONOMY, AND CHARACTER, OF THE SOCIETY OF FRIENDS*

3 vols (London: Longman, Hurst, Rees and Orme, 1806), vol. 2, pp. 235–246 [abridged], 248–259 [abridged], 294, 295–300 [abridged]; vol. 1, pp. 123–129; vol 3, pp. 186–187, 199–205 [abridged].

[The Spirit]

The Quakers, then, believe that the spirit of God formed or created the world. They believe that it was given to men, after the formation of it, as a guide to them in their spiritual concerns. They believe that it was continued to them after the deluge, in the same manner, and for the same purposes, to the time of Christ. It was given, however, in this interval, to different persons in different degrees. Thus the prophets received a greater portion of it than ordinary persons in their own times. Thus Moses was more illuminated by it than his contemporaries, for it became through him the author of the law. In the time of Christ it continued the same office, but it was then given more diffusively than before, and also more diffusively to some than to others. Thus the Evangelists and Apostles received it in an extraordinary degree, and it became, through them and Jesus Christ their head, the author of the Gospel. But, besides its office of a spiritual light and guide to men in their spiritual concerns, during all the period now assigned, it became to them, as they attended to its influence, an inward redeemer, producing in them a new birth, and leading them to perfection. And as it was thus both a guide and an inward redeemer, so it has continued these offices to the present day.

From hence it will be apparent, that the acknowledgment of God's Holy Spirit, in its various operations, as given in different portions before and after the sacrifice of Christ, is the acknowledgment of a principle, which is the great corner stone of the religion of the Quakers. Without this there can be no knowledge, in their opinion, of spiritual things. Without this there can be no spiritual interpretation of the scriptures themselves. Without this there can be no redemption by inward, though there may be redemption by outward means. Without this there can be no enjoyment of the knowledge of divine things. Take therefore this principle away from them, and you take away their religion at once. Take away this spirit, and Christianity remains with them no more Christianity, than the dead carcass of a man, when the spirit is departed, remains a man. Whatsoever is excellent, whatsoever is noble, whatsoever is worthy, whatsoever is desirable in the Christian faith, they ascribe to this spirit, and they believe that true Christianity can no more subsist without it, than the outward world could go on without the vital influence of the sun. [...]

The Quakers have frequently said in their theological writings, that every man has a portion of the Holy Spirit within him; and this assertion has not been censured. But they have also said, that every man has a portion of Christ or of the light of Christ, within him. Now this assertion has been considered as extravagant and wild. The reader will therefore see, that if he admits the one, he cannot very consistently censure the other.

[Ministry]

It is a doctrine of the Quakers that none can spiritually exercise, and that none ought to be allowed to exercise, the office of ministers, but such as the spirit of God has worked upon and called forth to discharge it, as well as that the same Spirit will never fail to raise up persons in succession for this end.

Conformably with this idea, no person, in the opinion of the Quakers, ought to be designed by his parents in early youth for the priesthood: for as the wind bloweth where it listeth, so no one can say which is the vessel that is to be made to honour. Conformably with the same idea, no imposition of hands, or ordination, can avail any thing, in their opinion, in the formation of a minister of the Gospel; for no human power can communicate to the internal man the spiritual gifts of God.

Neither, in conformity with the same idea, can the acquisition of human learning, or the obtaining Academical degrees and honours, be essential qualifications for this office; for though the human intellect is so great, that it can dive as it were into the ocean and discover the laws of fluids, and rise again up to heaven, and measure the celestial motions, yet it is incapable of itself of penetrating into divine things, so as spiritually to know them; while, on the other hand, illiterate men appear often to have more knowledge on these subjects than the most learned.

Indeed the Quakers have no notion of a human qualification for a divine calling. They reject all school divinity, as necessarily connected with the ministry. They believe that if a knowledge of Christianity had been attainable by the acquisition of the Greek and Roman languages, and through the medium of the Greek and Roman philosophers, then the Greeks and Romans themselves had been the best proficients in it; whereas, the Gospel was only foolishness to many of these. They say with St. Paul to the Colossians, 'Beware lest any man spoil you through philosophy and vain deceit, after the tradition of men, after the rudiments of the world, and not after Christ' (Colossians 2:8). And they say with the same Apostle to Timothy, 'O Timothy! keep that which is committed to thy trust, avoid profane and vain babblings, and oppositions of science falsely so called, which some professing have erred concerning the faith' (1 Timothy 6: 20–21).

This notion of the Quakers, that human learning and academical honours are not necessary for the priesthood, is very ancient. Though George Fox introduced it into his new society, and this without any previous reading upon the subject, yet it had existed long before his time. In short, it was connected with the tenet, early disseminated in the church, that no person could know spiritual things but through the medium of the spirit of God, from whence it is not difficult to pass to the doctrine, that none could teach spiritually except they had been taught spiritually themselves.

[Women's ministry]

This qualification for the ministry being allowed to be the true one, it will follow, the Quakers believe, and it was Luther's belief also, that women may be equally qualified to become ministers of the Gospel, as the men. For they believe that God has given his Holy Spirit, without exception, to all. They dare not therefore limit its operations in the office of the ministry, more than in any other of the sacred offices which it may hold. They dare not again say, that women cannot mortify the deeds of the flesh, or that they cannot be regenerated, and walk in newness of life. If women therefore believe they have a call to the ministry, and undergo the purification necessarily connected with it, and preach in consequence, and preach effectively, they dare not, under these circumstances, refuse to accept their preaching, as the fruits of the spirit, merely because it comes through the medium of the female sex.

Against this doctrine of the Quakers, that a female ministry is allowable under the Gospel dispensation, an objection has been started from the following words of the Apostle Paul: 'Let your women keep silence in the churches, for it is not permitted unto them to speak' – 'and if they will learn any thing, let them ask their Husbands at home' (1 Corinthians 14:34–5). But the Quakers conceive, that this charge of the Apostle has no allusion to preaching. In these early times, when the Gospel doctrines were new, and people were eager to understand them, some of the women, in the warmth of their feelings, interrupted the service of the church, by asking such questions as occurred to them on the subject of this new religion. These are they whom the Apostle desires to be silent, and to reserve their questions till they should return home. And that this was the case is evident, they conceive, from the meaning of the words, which the Apostle uses upon this occasion. For the word in the Greek tongue, which is translated 'speak', does not mean to preach or to pray, but to speak as in common discourse. [...]

That the objection has no foundation, the Quakers believe again, from the consideration that the ministry of women, in the days of the Apostles, is recognised in the New Testament, and is recognised also, in some instances, as an acceptable service. Of the hundred-and-twenty persons who were assembled on the Day of Pentecost, it is said by St Luke, that some were women (Acts chap.1). That these received the Holy Spirit as well as the men; and that they received it also for the purpose of prophesying or preaching, is obvious from the same Evangelist: for first, he says, that 'all were filled with the Holy Ghost'. And, secondly, he says that Peter stood up, and observed, concerning the circumstance of inspiration having been given to the women upon this occasion, that Joel's prophecy was then fulfilled, in which were to be found these words: 'And it shall come to pass in the last days, that your sons and your daughters shall prophesy – and on my servants and handmaidens I will pour out in those days of my spirit; and they shall prophesy'. That women preached afterwards, or in times subsequent to the Day of Pentecost, they collect from the same evangelist.

[Silent worship]

Many people of other religious societies, if they were to visit the meetings of the Quakers while under their silent worship, would be apt to consider the congregation as little better than stocks or stones, or at any rate as destitute of that life and animation which constitute the essence of religion. They would have no idea that a people were worshipping God, whom they observed to deliver nothing from their lips. It does not follow, however, because nothing is said, that God is not worshipped. The Quakers, on the other hand, contend, that these silent meetings form the sublimest part of their worship. The soul, they say, can have intercourse with God. It can feel refreshment, joy, and comfort, in him. It can praise and adore him; and all this, without the intervention of a word. [...]

That worship may exist without the intervention of words, on account of this constitution of the soul, is a sentiment which has been espoused by many pious persons who were not Quakers. Thus, the ever memorable John Hales, in his *Golden Remains*, expresses himself: 'Nay, one thing I know more, that the prayer which is the most forcible, transcends, and far exceeds, all power of words. For St. Paul, speaking unto us of the most effectual kind of prayer, calls it sighs and groans, that cannot be expressed. Nothing cries so loud in the ears of God, as the sighing of a contrite and earnest heart. It requires not the voice, but the mind; not the stretching of the hands, but the intention of the heart; not any outward shape or carriage of the body, but the inward behaviour of the understanding.

How then can it slacken your worldly business and occasions, to mix them with sighs and groans, which are the most effectual prayer [?]'. [...]

Monro, before quoted, speaks to the same effect, in his *Just Measures of the Pious Institutions of Youth*. 'The breathings of a recollected soul are not noise or clamour. The language in which devotion loves to vent itself, is that of the inward man, which is secret and silent, but yet God hears it, and makes gracious returns unto it. Sometimes the pious ardours and sensations of good souls are such as they cannot clothe with words. They feel what they cannot express. [...] It was, I suppose, by some such method of devotion as I am now speaking of, that Enoch walked with God; that Moses saw him that is invisible; that the royal Psalmist set the Lord always before him; and that our Lord Jesus himself continued whole nights in prayer to God. No man, I believe, will imagine that his prayer, during all the space in which it is said to have continued, was altogether vocal. [...]'

These meetings then, which are usually denominated silent, and in which, though not a word be spoken, it appears from the testimony of others that God may be truly worshipped, the Quakers consider as an important and sublime part of their church service, and as possessing advantages which are not to be found in the worship which proceeds solely through the medium of the mouth. For in the first place it must be obvious that, in these silent meetings, men cannot become chargeable before God, either with hypocrisy or falsehood, by pretending to worship him with their lips, when their affections are far from him, or by uttering a language that is inconsistent with the feelings of the heart.

[Novels]

Some Quakers have been inclined to think, that novels ought to be rejected on account of the fictitious nature of their contents. But this consideration is, by no means, generally adopted by the society, as an argument against them. Nor would it be a sound argument, if it were. If novels contain no evil within themselves, or have no evil tendency, the mere circumstance of the subject, names or characters being feigned, will not stamp them as censurable. Such fiction will not be like the fiction of the drama, where men act and personate characters that are not their own. Different men, in different ages of the world, have had recourse to different modes of writing, for the promotion of virtue. Some have had recourse to allegories, others to fables. The fables of Aesop, though a fiction from the beginning to the end, have been useful to many. But we have a peculiar instance of the use and innocence of fictitious descriptions in the sacred writings. For the author of the Christian religion made use of parables on many and weighty occasions. We cannot therefore condemn fictitious biography, unless it condemn itself by becoming a destroyer of morals.

The arguments against novels, in which the Quakers agree as a body, are taken from the pernicious influence they have upon the minds of those, who read them.

The Quakers do not say, that all novels have this influence, but that they have it generally. The great demand for novels, inconsequence of the taste, which the world has shewn for this species of writing, has induced persons of all descriptions, and of course many who have been but ill qualified to write them. Hence, though some novels have appeared of considerable merit, the worthless have been greatly preponderant. The demand also has occasioned foreign novels, of a complexion by no means suited to the good sense and character of our country, to be translated into our language. Hence a fresh weight has only been thrown into the preponderating scale. From these two causes it has happened, that the contents of a great majority of our novels have been unfavourable to the improvement of the moral character. Now when we consider this circumstance, and when we consider likewise, that professed novel-readers generally read all the compositions of this sort that come into their way, that they wait for no selection, but that they devour the good, the bad, and the indifferent alike, we shall see the reasons, which have induced the Quakers to believe, that the effect of this species of writing upon the mind has been generally pernicious.

One of the effects, which the Quakers consider to be produced by novels upon those who read them, is an affectation of knowledge, which leads them to become forward and presumptuous. This effect is highly injurious, for while it raises them unduly in their own estimation, it lowers them in that of the world. Nothing can be more disgusting, in the opinion of the Quakers, than to see persons assuming the authoritative appearance of men and women before their age or their talents can have given them any pretensions to do it.

Another effect is the following. The Quakers conceive that there is among professed novel readers a peculiar cast of mind. They observe in them a romantic spirit, a sort of wonder-loving imagination, and a disposition towards enthusiastic flights of the fancy, which to sober persons has the appearance of a temporary derangement. As the former effect must become injurious by producing forwardness, so this must become so by producing unsteadiness, of character.

A third effect, which the Quakers find to be produced among this description of readers, is conspicuous in a perverted morality. They place almost every value in feeling, and in the affectation of benevolence. They consider these as the true and only sources of good. They make these equivalent to moral principle. And actions flowing from feeling, though feeling itself is not always well founded, and sometimes runs into compassion even against justice, they class as moral duties arising from moral principles. They consider also too frequently the laws of religion as barbarous restraints, and which their new notions of civilized refinement may relax at will. And they do not hesitate, in consequence, to give a colour to some fashionable vices, which no Christian painter would admit into any composition, which was his own.

To this it may be added, that, believing their own knowledge to be supreme, and their own system of morality to be the only enlightened one, they fall often into scepticism, and pass easily from thence to infidelity. Foreign novels, however, more than our own, have probably contributed to the production of this latter effect.

These then are frequently the evils, and those which the Quakers insist upon, where persons devote their spare-time to the reading of novels, but more particularly among females, who, on account of the greater delicacy of their constitutions, are the more susceptible of such impressions. These effects the Quakers consider as particularly frightful, when they fall upon this sex. For an affectation of knowledge, or a forwardness of character, seems to be much more disgusting among women than among men. It may be observed also, that an unsteady or romantic spirit or a wonder-loving or flighty imagination, can never qualify a woman for domestic duties, or make her a sedate and prudent wife. Nor can a relaxed morality qualify her for the discharge of her duty as a parent in the religious education of her children.

But, independently of these, there is another evil, which the Quakers attach to novel-reading, of a nature too serious to be omitted in this account. It is that those who are attached to this species of reading, become indisposed towards any other. This indisposition arises from the peculiar construction of novels. Their structure is similar to that of dramatic compositions. They exhibit characters to view. They have their heroes and heroines in the same manner. They lay open the checkered incidents in the lives of these. They interweave into their histories the powerful passion of love. By animated language, and descriptions which glow with sympathy, they rouse the sensibility of the reader, and fill his soul with interest in the tale. They fascinate therefore in the same manner as plays. They produce also the same kind of mental stimulus, or the same powerful excitement of the mind. Hence it is that this indisposition is generated. For if other books contain neither characters, nor incidents, nor any of the high seasoning, or gross stimulants, which belong to novels they become insipid.

[Purity of conscience]

It has been an established rule with the Quakers, from the formation of their society, not to temporise, or to violate their consciences; or, in other words, not to do that which as a body of Christians they believe to be wrong, though the usages of the world, or the government of the country under which they live, should require it; but rather to submit to the frowns and indignation of the one, and the legal penalties annexed to their disobedience by the other. This suffering in preference of the violation of their consciences, is what the Quakers call 'the bearing of their testimony', or a demonstration to the world, by the 'testimony of their own example', that they consider it to be the duty of Christians rather to suffer, than to have any concern with that which they conceive to be evil. The Quakers, in putting this principle into practice, stand, I believe, alone. For I know of no other Christians, who as a body pay this homage to their scruples, or who determine upon an ordeal of suffering in preference of a compromise with their ease and safety.

[Principle not pragmatism]

The next trait, which I shall lay open to the world as belonging to the Quaker character, is, that in all those cases, which may be called political, the Quakers generally reason upon principle, and but seldom upon consequences. I do not know of any trait, which ever impressed me more than this in all my intercourse with the members of this society. It was one of those which obtruded itself to my notice on my first acquaintance with them, and it has continued equally conspicuous to the present time.

If an impartial philosopher, from some unknown land, and to whom our manners, and opinions, and history, were unknown, were introduced suddenly into our metropolis, and were to converse with the Quakers there on a given political subject, and to be directly afterwards conveyed to the west end of the town, and there to converse with politicians, or men of fashion, or men of the world, upon the same, he could not fail to be greatly surprised. If he thought the former wise, or virtuous, or great, he would unavoidably consider the latter as foolish, or vicious, or little. Two such opposite conclusions, as he would hear deduced from the reasonings of each, would impress him with an idea, that he had been taken to a country inhabited by two different races of men. He would never conceive, that they had been educated in the same country, or under the same government. If left to himself, he would probably imagine, that they had embraced two different religions. But if he were told that they professed the same, he would then say, that the precepts of this religion had been expressed in such doubtful language, that they led to two sets of principles contradictory to one another. I need scarcely inform the reader, that I allude to the two opposite conclusions, which will almost always be drawn, where men reason from motives of policy or from moral right.

If it be true that the Quakers reason upon principle in political affairs, and not upon consequences, it will follow as a direct inference, that they will adopt the Christian maxim, that men ought not to do evil that good may come. And this is indeed the maxim, which you find them adopting in the course of their conversation on such subjects, and which I believe they would have uniformly adopted, if they had been placed in political situations in life. Had the Quakers been the legislators of the world, we should never have seen many of the public evils that have appeared in it. It was thought formerly, for example, a glorious thing to attempt to drive Paganism from the Holy Land, but Quakers would never have joined in any of the crusades for its expulsion. It has been long esteemed, again, a desideratum in politics, that among nations, differing in strength and resources, a kind of balance of power should be kept up, but Quakers would never have engaged in any one war to preserve it. It has been thought again, that it would contribute to the happiness of the natives of India, if the blessings of the British constitution could be given them instead of their own. But Quakers would never have taken possession of their territories for the accomplishment of such a good. It has been long thought again a matter of great political importance, that our West-Indian settlements should be cultivated by African labourers. But Quakers would never have allowed a slave-trade for such a purpose. It has been thought again, and it is still thought, a desirable thing, that our property should be secured from the petty depredations of individuals. But Quakers would never have consented to capital punishments for such an end. In short, few public evils would have arisen among mankind, if statesmen had adopted the system, upon which the Quakers reason in political affairs, or if they had concurred with an ancient Grecian philosopher in condemning to detestation the memory of the man, who first made a distinction between expediency and moral right. [...]

But this trait is nourished and supported again by other causes, and first by the influence, which the peculiar customs of the Quakers must occasionally have upon their minds. A Quaker cannot go out of doors, but he is reminded of his own singularity, or of his difference in a variety of respects from his fellow-citizens. Now every custom, in which he is singular, whether it be that of dress or of language, or of address, or any other, is founded, in his own mind, on moral principle, and in direct opposition to popular opinion and applause. He is therefore perpetually reminded, in almost all his daily habits, of the two opposite systems of reasoning, and is perpetually called upon as it were to refer to the principles, which originally made the difference between him and another citizen of the world.

Part 6

NEW NONCONFORMIST MOVEMENTS

6.1

Brethren

6.1 Brethren

What became known as the Plymouth Brethren, or simply Brethren, began as a movement of individuals who gathered to break bread and share ministry in private houses in the 1820s and 1830s. Their aim was to evade all aspects of Church organisation as a hindrance to pure spiritual fellowship. The dissenting principle that led Independents and Baptists to reject the national Church, Brethren took a step further and applied to dissenting Church organisations also. Holding fast to the notion of the priesthood of all believers, ministry was conducted in an egalitarian fashion not unlike the Quakers, and communion given a central role. The movement's collectivist, adventist and anti-clerical ethos produced 'a kind of Pentecostal communism' in imitation of the early New Testament Church.[1] The designation of the group was something of a misnomer, since the first meeting was in fact held in Dublin, soon followed by gatherings in Plymouth and Bristol, but in due course the movement grew into a recognised denomination with their own meeting rooms, and connections to similar movements across Europe and America.

The first extract from a pamphlet by J. N. Darby (1800–82) captures the early Brethren ethos, explaining why informal gatherings of believers better fulfil the biblical vision of the 'church' than any organisation did. Darby was a charismatic, forceful leader who headed the expansion of the movement in England, Ireland and Europe from 1830 to 1845. His fundamental premise is that the Bible left no instruction for the appointment of 'presidents and pastors', only Jesus's promise that 'where two or three are gathered together in my name, there am I in the midst of them' (Matthew 18:20), and the principle of the priesthood of *all* believers (1 Peter 2:9). The second part is a celebration of the spiritual liberty enjoyed by believers through knowing that simply meeting in fellowship is enough to fulfil their religious obligations and express their elect status.

The debate that resulted in a painful schism between 'open' and 'exclusive' branches of the movement in 1848 centred on whether God still worked within flawed ecclesiastical institutions, and whether fellowship could therefore be shared with members of these corrupt bodies. Those who thought not went on to be criticised for intolerance and bigotry, most famously in Edmond Gosse's depiction of his childhood in his tragi-comic *Father and Son* (1907). Darby led the exclusivist camp, but his stance of radical separatism provoked from others a more ecumenical defence that the spirit still worked in individuals despite the flaws of the institutions within which they worshipped: Brethren should not claim a monopoly on salvation.

The second extract was first sent as a corrective personal letter to Darby in 1836 by minister A.N. Groves (1795–1853), subsequently published under the heading 'On Departure from Catholic Christianity' within the pamphlet *Catholic Christianity; and Party Communion*. Groves regards Darby's exclusivism as a 'departure' from original Brethren principles, and itself as a setting up of humanly-constructed boundaries around the operations of grace. Groves's concern is that

Darby has begun to define the Brethren in terms of what they reject, not what they positively stand for, and he regrets the loss of their first humility when 'all our thoughts were conversant about how we might *ourselves* most effectually manifest forth that life we had received by Jesus [...] and where we might find that life in others'. While Groves clearly shares Darby's view that not all who worship in other churches are saved, he differs in assuming that at least some are. Pervading the letter is a fear of narrow-minded judgementalism overpowering loving fellowship, 'making *light* not *life* the measure of communion'. He eloquently summarises his non-exclusive philosophy: 'I would INFINITELY RATHER BEAR *with all their evils*, than SEPARATE from THEIR GOOD.' Both Darby's and Groves's writings demonstrate the paradoxical tension within Brethren thought between seeking to unify the elect through informal fellowship, and purist separation from the nominal Christian herd.

Note: 'Walkerites' and 'Glassites' were small Calvinist groups that broke away from the established churches respectively in Ireland in 1804, and Scotland in 1730. Lady Powerscourt, of Powerscourt House, County Wicklow, was an early supporter of the Brethren movement in Ireland.

Notes

1 W. B. Neatby, quoted in F. R. Coad, *A History of the Brethren Movement* (Exeter: Paternoster Press, 1968), p. 67.

19

J. N. DARBY, *REFLECTIONS ON THE RUINED CONDITION OF THE CHURCH; AND ON THE EFFORTS MAKING BY CHURCHMEN AND DISSENTERS TO RESTORE IT TO ITS PRIMITIVE ORDER*

(London: D. Walter, 1841), pp. 1–4, 20–24

CIRCUMSTANCES have latterly drawn the attention of many Christians to the question of the competency of believers, in our days, to form Churches after the model of the primitive Churches, and have led to the inquiry whether the forming of such bodies is at this time agreeable to the will of God. Some respected and beloved brethren insist that the forming and organizing of Churches is according to God's will, the only means of finding blessing in the midst of that confusion which is acknowledged to exist. Others consider that any such attempt is altogether man's effort, and as such is wanting in the very primary condition of lasting blessing, namely, the condition of entire dependance upon God; although it may be blessed by God up to a certain point on account of the sincerity of purpose and piety of those who take part in it.

The writer of these pages, bound by the strongest ties of affection and of love in Christ to many who belong to bodies assuming the title of *Church of God,* has studiously avoided all collision of judgment with his brethren on this subject, although he has often conversed with them concerning it. He has done no more than withdraw himself from the things he found among them, when those things appeared to him at variance with God's word, always endeavouring to "keep the unity of the spirit in the bond of peace," and remembering that word, "If thou take forth the precious from the vile, thou shalt be as my mouth," a direction of unspeakable value in the present confusion [Ephesians 4:3, Jeremiah 15:19]. His affection is not lessened—his attachment is neither interrupted nor impaired.

Two considerations especially constrain the writer to declare what to him appears the instruction of the Scriptures on this head—Duty to the Lord (and the welfare of his Church is the highest of all considerations)—and love to brethren—a love which must be guided by faithfulness to the Lord. He writes these pages because the project of making Churches is really the hindrance in the way of the accomplishment of what all desire, namely, the union of the saints in one body—first, because those who have attempted it, having gone beyond the power given them by the Spirit, the flesh has been fostered in them;—and secondly, because those who were wearied with the evil of national systems, thinking themselves under a necessity of choosing between such evil, and that which meets their view in the Dissenting Congregations, remain where they are standing, despairing of any thing better. In the actual condition of things it would be an extravagance to affirm that these Churches can realize the desired union; but I will not press that lest I should pain some of my readers. I shall rather endeavour to put in the foreground the points on which we are agreed, points which will at the same time assist us to form a right judgment on certain systems standing around us, systems which, if themselves incapable of yielding the good result desired by many brethren, leave to the partisans of each, as their only consolation and excuse, the thought that others can do no more than themselves—towards realizing the object in view.

The Lord's purpose in the gathering of the Saints on earth

It is the desire of our hearts, and as we believe God's will under this dispensation, that all the children of God should be gathered together as such, and, consequently, as *not of the world*—"The Lord hath given himself not for this nation only, but that he should gather together *in one* the children of God which are scattered abroad" [John 11:52].—This gathering together in one was then the immediate object of Christ's death. The salvation of the elect was as certain before his advent as afterwards. The Jewish dispensation which preceded his coming into the world, had for its object, not to gather the Church upon earth, but to exhibit the government of God by means of an elect nation. At this time the Lord's purpose is to *gather* as well as to *save,* to realise unity—not merely in the heavens, where the purposes of God shall surely be accomplished, but here upon earth by One Spirit sent down from heaven. By One Spirit we are all baptized into one body. This is undeniably the truth concerning the Church as it is set before us in the word. Men may go about proving that hypocrites and evil men had crept into the Church, but there is no resisting the inference that there was a Church into which they had crept. The gathering together of all the children of God in one body is plainly according to the mind of God in the word. [...]

The children of God have nothing to do but to meet together in the name of the Lord

With what design then am I writing?—Is it that Christians should do nothing?—No!—I have written from a desire that there should be less presumption and more diffidence in what we undertake to do:—and that we should feel more deeply the ruined condition to which we have reduced the Church.

If you say to me, "I have separated myself from the evil that my conscience disapproves, and which is at variance with the Word,"—it is well. If you urge that God's word requires the Saints to be one and united; that it tells us that there where two or three are gathered together, Jesus is in the midst of them, and that therefore you "assemble yourselves" together—I say again, it is well. But if you go on to tell me that you have organized a Church, or combined together with others to do so—that you have chosen a president or a pastor, and that, having done this, you are the *Church of God* of the place you inhabit:—I put this question.—My dear friends who has commissioned you to do all this?—Even according to your principle of imitation, (although to imitate *power* is an absurdity; and the kingdom of God is "in power"), where do you find all this in the word? I see no trace of the Churches having elected presidents or pastors.—You say that for the sake of order it must be so. My answer is, I cannot get off the ground of the word—"He that gathereth not *with me* scattereth" [Matthew 12:30]. To say that it is necessary that it should be so—is to reason after the manner of men—Your order being constituted by the will of man, will soon be seen to be disorder in the sight of God. If there are but two or three met together in the name of Jesus, he will be there. If God raises up pastors from amongst you or sends them among you, it is well;—it is a great blessing.—But ever since the day when the Holy Spirit formed the Church, we have no record in the word that the Church has chosen them.

What then, it will be asked, must we do?—That which Faith ever does . . . acknowledge its weakness and take the place of dependence upon God. God is sufficient in all ages for his Church. If you are but "two or three," meet together: you will find that Christ is with you. Call upon him. He can raise up whatever is needed for the blessing of the Saints, and doubt not He will do so. The blessing will not be ensured to us through a pretension on our part to be something when we are nothing. In how many places has not blessing to the Saints been hindered by this choosing of presidents and pastors. In how many places has not the practice led to the fall of those presidents themselves?—In how many places might not the Saints have assembled together with joy in the strength of that promise made by Christ to the "two or three" if they had not been scared by this pretended necessity for organization, and by charges of disorder, (just as if man were wiser than God), and if their fear of disorder had not persuaded them to continue a state of things which they confess to be wrong?—And often in these bodies constituted by man, has been seen either the domination of a single individual, or a struggle between several.

That which the Church specially needs is the deep feeling of her ruin and necessity, a feeling which turns for refuge to God—with *confession,* and keeps clear from all known evil—acknowledges the Spirit of Christ as the sole government of the Church, and by so doing acknowledges every one whom He sends, according to the gift such a one has received, and that with thanksgiving to Him, who by such gift constitutes such brother—a servant of all.

To acknowledge the World to be the Church, or to pretend to again set up the Church are two things equally condemned and unauthorised by the word.

If you say what then is to be done? I rejoin—Why are you ever thinking of *doing* a something?—To confess the sin which has brought us where we are, to humble ourselves low before the Lord, and separating from that which we know to be evil, to lean upon Him who is able to do all that is necessary for our blessing, without assuming to do more, ourselves, than the word authorises us to do;—such is the position, humble it is true—but proportionately blessed by God.

A point of the utmost importance, which they who wish to organize Churches, seem to have altogether lost sight of, is that there is such a thing as POWER, and that the Holy Spirit alone hath the *power* to gather and build up the Church. They seem to think that, as soon as they have certain passages of Scripture, they have nothing to do but to act them out—but, under the garb of faithfulness, there is in this a fatal error—it consists in leaving aside the presence and the power of the Holy Spirit.—We can only act out the word of God by the power of God.—But the constituting the Church was a direct effect of the *power* of the Holy Ghost. To leave aside that power, and still hold to the pretension of imitating the primitive Church is strangely to delude ourselves.

I know that those who esteem these little organized associations to be the Church of God, see nothing but mere meetings of men in every other gathering of God's children, There is a very simple answer on this matter. Such brethren have no promise authorizing them to again set up the Churches of God when they have fallen, whilst there is a positive promise that where two or three are gathered together in the *name of Jesus,* he is in their midst. Thus there is no promise in favour of the system which organizes Churches, whilst there is a promise for that "assembling together" which the children of God despise.

And what do we see to be the consequence of the pretensions of these bodies? Pride is nurtured in their presidents and their members, and those who contrast these pretensions with the reality, are disgusted and repelled: and thus the desired object is hindered, namely, the union of God's children.—Here and there the pastor's gifts may produce much effect, or it may happen that all who are Christians may be living in unity, and there will be much joy; but the same thing would have resulted though there should have been no pretension whatever to be the Church of God.

20

A. N. GROVES, 'ON DEPARTURE FROM CATHOLIC CHRISTIANITY'

In *Catholic Christianity and Party Communion* (London: Morgan & Chase, n.d.], pp. 10–16

Milford Haven, March 10*th,* 1836.

My Dear D——,

As the stormy weather threatens a little delay, I am not willing to leave England without a few words in reply to your notes, and a short explanation of some other points that interest me. I have ever regretted having had so few opportunities of seeing and conversing with you since my return to England, and thereby explaining many things that might have allowed us to depart on the whole more happily than now, yet I wish you to feel assured that nothing has estranged my heart from you, or lowered my confidence in your being still animated by the same enlarged and generous purposes that once so won and rivetted me; and though I feel you have departed from those principles by which you once hoped to have effected them, and are in principle returning to the city from whence you departed, still my soul so reposes in the truth of your heart to God that I feel it needs but a step or two more to advance, and you will see all the evils of the systems from which you profess to be separated, to spring up among yourselves. You will not discover this so much from the workings of your own soul, as by the spirit of those who have been nurtured up from the beginning in the system they are taught to feel the only tolerable one; that not having been led like you, and some of those earliest connected with you, through deep experimental suffering and sorrow, they are little acquainted with the real truth that may exist amidst inconceivable darkness: there will be little pity and little sympathy with such, and your union daily becoming one of doctrine and opinion more than life and love, your government will become—unseen, perhaps, and unexpressed, yet—one wherein, overwhelmingly, is felt the authority of *men;* you will be known more by what you witness *against* than what you witness for, and practically this will prove that you witness against all but yourselves, as certainly as the Walkerites or Glassites: your Shibboleth may be different, but it will be as *real*.

It has been asserted, as I found from your dear brother W—— and others, that I have changed my principles; all I can say is, that as far as I know what those principles were, in which I gloried on first discovering them in the word of God, I now glory in them ten times more since I have experienced their applicability to all the various and perplexing circumstances of the present state of the church; allowing you to give every individual, and collection of individuals, the standing *God* gives them, without identifying yourselves with any of their evils. I ever understood our principle of communion to be the possession of the common life or common blood of the family of God (for the life is in the blood); these were our early thoughts, and are my most matured ones. The transition your little bodies have undergone, in no longer standing forth the witnesses for the glorious and simple *truth,* so much as standing forth witnesses against all that they judge error, have lowered them in my apprehension from heaven to earth in their position of witnesses. What I mean is, that then, all our thoughts were conversant about how we might *ourselves* most effectually manifest forth that life we had received by Jesus, (knowing that that alone could be as the Shepherd's voice to the living children,) and where we might find that life in others; and when we were persuaded we had found it, bidding them, on the Divine claim of this common life, (whether their thoughts on other matters were narrow or enlarged,) to come and share with us in the fellowship of the common Spirit, in the worship of our common Head; and as Christ had received them, so would we to the glory of God the Father; and farther, that we were free, within the limits of the truth, to share with them in *part,* though we could not in *all,* their services. In fact, as we received them for the life, we would not *reject* them for their systems, or refuse to recognise any part of their systems, because we disallowed much. Trusting, that if this inter-communion could be established, to effect all we desire, by being upheld by God in walking in the light, as the Christ-like means of witnessing against any darkness that might be in them, according to the rule of the Lord; John iii. 19: 'This is the condemnation, that light is come into the world, and men loved darkness rather than light because their deeds were evil, neither will they come to the light lest their deeds should be reproved.' A more difficult ministry of witness, than a preaching one of words, or separating one of persons, yet possessing a *much more* mighty power over the hearts of others, and a much more influential one in blessing; and which, dear brother, I know no heart more ready to acknowledge than your own.

The moment the witnessing for the common life as our *bond* gives place to a witnessing *against* errors by separation of persons and preaching, (errors allowable compatible with the common life,) every individual, or society of individuals, first comes before the mind as those who might need witnessing against, and all their conduct and principles have first to be examined and approved before they can be received; and the position which this occupying the seat of judgment will place you in will be this: the most narrow-minded and bigoted will rule, because his conscience cannot and will not give way, and therefore the more enlarged heart must yield. It is into this position, dear D——, I feel some little flocks are fast tending, if they have not already attained it. Making *light* not *life* the measure of communion. But I am told by our beloved brethren, C. and H., that if I give up this position of witnessing *against evil* in this PECULIAR WAY OF SEPARATION from the systems in which any *measure* of it is mixed up, I make our position one of simple, unpardonable schism, because we might join some of the many other systems. I cannot be supposed, of course, to know fully *their* grounds of acting, but I thought I knew *yours,* at least your *original* ones. Was not the principle we laid down as to separation from all existing bodies at the outset, this: that we felt ourselves bound to separate from all individuals and systems, *so far* as they required us to do what our consciences would not allow, or retained us from doing what our consciences required, and no further? and were we not as free to join and act with any individual, or body of individuals, as they were free *not* to require us to do what our consciences did not allow, or prevent our doing what they did? and in this freedom did we not feel brethren should *not* force liberty on those who were bound, nor withhold freedom from those who were free?

Did we not feel constrained to follow the apostolic rule of *not judging other men's consciences,* as to liberty, by our own; remembering it is written, 'Let *not* him that eateth despise him that eateth not; and let not him which eateth not, judge him that eateth; seeing that God hath received' both the one and the other [Romans 14:3]? Now it is one of these two grounds; their preventing me from, or demanding from me, other than the Lord demands, that divides me in a *measure* from every system; as my *own proper* duty to God, rather than as witnessing against THEIR evils. As any system is in its provision narrower or wider than the truth, I either stop short, or go beyond its provisions, but I would INFINITELY RATHER BEAR *with all their evils,* than SEPARATE from THEIR GOOD. These were the *then* principles of our separation and intercommunion; we had resolved never to try to *get men to act* in UNIFORMITY *further than they* FELT in UNIFORMITY; neither by frowns, or smiles; and this for one simple reason, that we saw no authority given us from God thus to act; nor did our experience lead us to feel it the best means at all of promoting their blessing or our common aim of a *perfect spiritual uniformity* of judgment; whilst to ourselves it afforded a *ready* OUTLET to the PROPENSITIES of the FLESH, under the appearance of spiritual authority and zeal for the truth. But in all these matters, we desired that our way might be bright as the light, and our words drop noiselessly as the dew, and if, at the last, they remained 'otherwise minded,' we would seek of God, that even He should reveal it unto them. There is something at present so like building what you destroyed; as if when weak you can be liberal and large, but when holpen with a little strength, the *true* spirit of sectarianism begins to bud; that being *'one of us,'* has become a stronger bond than oneness in the power of the life of God in the soul.

I know it is said, (dear Lady Powerscourt told me so,) that so long as any terms were kept with the Church of England, by mixing up in *any* measure with their ministrations, when there was nothing to offend your conscience, they bore your testimony most patiently, but after your entire rejection of them, they pursued you with undeviating resentment, and this was brought to prove that the then position was wrong, and the present right. But all I see in this is, that whilst you occupied the place of only witnessing against those things which the divine life within themselves recognized as evil, and separating from them ONLY SO FAR as they separated from Christ, you established them as judges of themselves, and of themselves they were condemned; and at the same time you conciliated their heavenly affections, by allowing all that really was of the Lord, and sharing in it, though the system itself in which you found these golden grains, you could not away with. But the moment your position and your language implied a perfect separation, alike from the evil and the good, and a rejection of them, in consequence of their system, without discrimination, you no longer had their consciences with you, but they felt that though only a brother in a Father's house, you exercised more than a Father's power, without a Father's heart of mercy, and they, therefore, appealed from you to your common Head; both in behalf of themselves and their systems. There is no truth more established in my own mind than this; that to occupy the position of the maximum of power in witnessing to the consciences of others, you must stand before their unbiassed judgment as evidently *wishing* to allow in them *more* than their own consciences allow, rather than less; proving that your heart of love is more alive to find a covering for faults, than your eagle eye of light to discover them. I send you this letter as we were the first to act on these principles, rather than to H—— and C——, whose faith and love I do so truly desire to follow. They have written to me two very long and kind letters, which I purpose more effectually and fully to answer, by meeting the positions contained in them, in a little tract, which I hope to prepare on the voyage, and finally, to publish.

I particularly regret not meeting you at Bristol, as I had much to say to you relative to Rhenius, and other things connected with India, for my heart would naturally seek sympathy and fellowship with you and those dear brethren with whom I have no dividing thoughts relative to the great bearings of truth, or the truths themselves, in which lie the power and peace of the Gospel,—neither in the objects or principles of ministry do I differ;—my difference with you is only as to the manner in which you maintain your position of witnessing for the good against the evil. I feel no one ever expects me, when the acknowledged *visitor* in the house of another, to be answerable for the ordering of that house, or as thereby *approving* it—they would naturally come to the house in which I had control, and where the acts were looked upon as *mine,* to form such a judgment; and even in such a case, if I was but *one* among many in the government, no honest mind would make *me* responsible for faults, against which, in my place and according to my power, I protested; because I submitted to those acts in others, rather than forego a *greater* good, or incur a greater evil. If it is said man cannot discriminate, nor feel the *force* of my witness, unless I separate, not by heart and life, but by contiguity of person, altogether from all kinds of false systems; my answer is, that He, whose place it is to judge, and to whom we are called to approve our hearts, can; and to *Him,* in this matter, I am content to stand or fall.

Some will not have me hold communion with the Scotts, because their views are not satisfactory about the Lord's Supper; others with you, because of your views about baptism; others with the Church of England, because of her thoughts about ministry. On my principles, I receive them all; but on the principle of witnessing against evil, I should reject them all. I feel them all, in their several particulars, sinning against the mind and heart of Christ, and letting in, in principle, the most tremendous disorders, and it is not for me to measure the comparative sin of one kind of disobedience against another. I make use of my fellowship in the Spirit, to enjoy the common life together, and witness for that, as an opportunity to set before them those little particulars into which, notwithstanding all their grace and faithfulness, their godliness and honesty—they have fallen. Nor shall I ever feel separation from the good for the sake of the evil, to be my way of witnessing against it, till I see infinitely clearer than I now do, that it is *God's*. I naturally unite fixedly with those in whom I see and feel most of the life and power of God. But I am as free to visit other churches, where I see much of disorder, as to visit the houses of my friends, though they govern them not as I could wish; and, as I have said, I should feel it equally unreasonable and unkind, for any brother to judge me for it, though I leave him in perfect liberty to judge himself. You must not, however, dear brother, think, from anything I have said, that I shall not write freely and fully to you, relative to things in India, feeling assured in my own heart, that your enlarged and generous spirit, so richly taught of the Lord, will one day burst again those bands which narrower minds than yours have encircled you with, and come forth again, rather anxious to advance ALL the living members of the living Head into the stature of men, than to be encircled by any little bodies, however numerous, that own you for their founder. I honour, love, and respect your position in the church of God; but the deep conviction I have that your spiritual power was incalculably greater when you walked in the midst of the various congregations of the Lord's people, manifesting forth the life and the power of the gospel, than now, is such that I cannot but write the above as a proof of my love and confidence that your mind is above considering who these remarks came from, rather than what truth there may be in them.

Yours very affectionately in the gospel,

(Signed) A. N. GROVES.

6.2

The Church of Jesus Christ of Latter Day Saints

6.2 The Church of Jesus Christ of Latter Day Saints

As soon as the Church of Jesus Christ of Latter Day Saints, or Mormons as they quickly came to be known, was founded in North America by Joseph Smith in 1837, missions began in earnest to Britain which claimed many converts during the 1840s and 1850s. Growth focused on England's midlands and north-western counties, South Wales, and the west-central belt of Scotland, drawing in a mostly working-class and artisan membership. This was a supernaturalist, millennialist movement which believed in modern miracles and a living prophet, and avidly interpreted natural disasters as signs of divine judgement or warning. Converts were called to emigrate to the North American Western frontier to form a holy city in which the Messiah would in due course be manifest. While the movement was native to America, it had much in common with British popular millenarian movements, offering a new order with economic and social benefits. The 1851 census, taken when Mormonism was at its peak in Great Britain, showed 35,626 Mormons attending worship in England and Wales (considerably more than Quakers, for example), with several thousand having already emigrated, while Scotland boasted almost 10,000 converts by the end of the century.[1]

The Latter-Day Saints' Millennial Star was the voice of the church leadership to Britain's Latter Day Saints from 1840 to 1970. In the mid-century heyday of British Mormonism, it comprised news from the Zion community at Salt Lake City, stories of successful emigrations and of missions worldwide, a lengthy multi-part history of Joseph Smith who was acquiring the status of a martyr, defences of Mormon beliefs and morality (in the face of popular hostility and persecution), and eschatological analysis of natural disasters. Extracts are presented here from the 1853 journal, edited by Samuel W. Richards, which capture the condition of British Mormonism just before its numerical decline set in.

The first portion of a multi-part article 'Necessity of a Living Prophet' foregrounds the Mormon faith in ongoing direct divine action in history. The author John Jaques (1827–1900) became missionary, hymn writer and historian for the Latter Day Saints, emigrating in 1856. Jaques makes the case that a living religion needs a living prophet, characterising mainstream Christianity as fossilised by relying only on *dead* prophets' teachings, and little better than secularism in its denial of miracles in the present day. Jaques shows the kinship between latter-day prophets – such as Smith and his successor Brigham Young – and biblical models, having messages for their contemporaneous moment which are only incidentally relevant to posterity, and enduring discredit and persecution for discomforting the apathetic. Quoting from Jesus's diatribe against religious leaders who pay meticulous observance to religious externals but ignore the essence of the prophets' messages (Matthew ch. 23), Jaques similarly condemns those who reject latter-day prophets, harshly interpreting collective sufferings as divine judgement. With homely idiom and combative rhetoric, Mormonism is presented as a development, not denial of biblical faith, whose continued evolution is assumed: prophets will continue to supersede each other's teachings as Brigham superseded Smith.

The *Millennial Star* often called for converts to emigrate to the holy city in order to speed the Messiah's coming. By this point, the geographical focus had moved from Nauvoo to Salt Lake City in Utah, and the Perpetual Emigration Fund had been established to help finance the effort. 'Gathering' presents emigration as a religious duty whereby the righteous separate themselves from the unrighteous. The piece confronts some earthly realities – the personal cost of departure from familiar attachments, and the harsh aspects of the journey to the American West. The journey is paralleled with literary pilgrimages in Bunyan's *A Pilgrim's Progress* and Psalm 23, passage through the 'slough of despond' and 'the valley of the shadow of death' being the way to the land of blessing. But Zion is not purely a physical utopia for the dispossessed – it is also a spiritual state of community created among the saints en route as opportunities arise for mutual support and forbearance.

The poem 'Our Home at Great Salt Lake' by Elder William G. Mills emphasises the pains of departure from the familiar and fond. This is probably William Gill Mills (1822–95) from Ireland, a well-known hymn writer who became President of the Reading conference (the piece is signed off 'Newbury, Barks [Berkshire]').[2] He emigrated with his flock in 1855. The anticipated new spiritual home is celebrated for its international population, and its Old Testament-style plenitude of vines, figs and corn. The patriarchal order is affirmed in the role envisaged for 'the virtuous "fair"' to serve and soothe their 'lords' who are the expositors of truth. The use of general and collective nouns nicely evades the vexed issue of plural marriage which had recently been authorised by Church leaders. Homely comfort, material prosperity, social order and ecstatic spiritual experience make up this promised land.

Notes

1 Robert L. Lively, Jr, 'Some Sociological Reflections on the Nineteenth-Century British Mission', in Richard L. Jensen and Malcolm R. Thorp (eds), *Mormons in Early Victorian Britain* (Salt Lake City: University of Utah Press, 1989), pp. 16–30, on pp. 19–20; and Bernard Aspinwall, 'A Fertile Field: Scotland in the Days of the Early Missions', in Jensen and Thorp (eds), *Mormons in Early Victorian Britain*, pp. 104–117, on pp. 104 and 114–115.

2 See 'William Gills, Father of Mannie Pickett', in 'The Maria Louisa Pickett Family Website' at http://marialouisapickett.homestead.com/files/william_g._mills_history.htm [accessed 17 August 2020] and W. G. Mills, The History of the Chimburazo Emigrating Conference', in 'Saints by Sea: Latter-Day Saint Immigration to America' at https://saintsbysea.lib.byu.edu/mii/account/227?mii=on&netherlands=on&europe=on&scandinavia=on&keywords=William+g+mills&sweden=on [accessed 17 August 2020]

21

JOHN JAQUES, 'NECESSITY OF A LIVING PROPHET. PART 1'

The Latter-Day Saints' Millennial Star, 15:33 (13th August 1843), pp. 529–532

One of the distinguishing doctrines of the Church of Jesus Christ of Latter-day Saints, is, that a Prophet is necessary to stand at the head of the Church to lead and guide it. It is well known that this doctrine comes in contact with the teachings of the greater part of Christendom. The faith of modern Christians is not in Prophets or Apostles, that is, in living Prophets or Apostles. All Christians profess to reverence the Prophets and Apostles who lived in ages long since past. Abraham, Moses, Jesus, Peter, and Paul, are all believed in most faithfully. The most gifted divines of Christendom weekly and daily point the multitudes to the ancient Prophets, and enjoin their teachings upon the people. The Gospels, Epistles, and Prophecies, declared and written by the ancient Prophets, who spoke and wrote as they were moved upon by the Holy Ghost, are read and commented on with all diligence throughout Christian nations. The tombs of those Prophets are garnished, or they would be if known. Magnificent churches, chapels, and colleges are reared on every hand to the memory of those ancients who are renowned for having possessed the testimony of Jesus—the spirit of prophecy. It is a shame, in a Christian land, not to profess some kind of faith in the divine mission of the dead Prophets. It is scarcely considered respectable to throw discredit on those ancient worthies, or to speak irreverently of them. The man that does so is scouted from Christian society, branded as an infidel, shunned as a serpent, and piously consigned to those scorching regions where the thermometer rises to an unnameable height.

A common proverb says—"a bird in the hand is worth two in the bush." Scripture says—"a living dog is better than a dead lion" [Ecclesiastes 9:4]. And I would humbly ask—Does it ever occur to the pious, devoted Christians of modern times, that one Prophet living in our midst is worth two dead ancient Prophets? I apprehend the Christians of these times are far from applying proverb and Scripture after this fashion, for when one talks about God's having a living Prophet upon the earth, one is looked upon with a vacant, idiotic stare, then follow sneers, scoffs, and sage warnings of delusion, imposture, fanaticism. "A living Prophet in this enlightened Gospel age! Oh most horrible blasphemy, most awful presumption!"

and many kindred interjections burst from pious lips, just as though a Prophet never did live—never had a being—never walked upon God Almighty's earth—never existed anywhere, except in the mystical regions of imagination, like the redoubtable heroes of heathen mythology. A real live Prophet? Impossible! but if possible, and really so, a wonderful curiosity, (there was a wonder in heaven—that was nothing to the wonder of a living Prophet now upon the earth,) such a curiosity ought to be heralded through the world, by Barnum, then carefully stowed away in the British Museum, and secured by a lock that would keep Hobbs outside. Reader, pardon apparent levity, but such is the inconsistency of Christendom. Doubtless you can call to your recollection manifestations of this inconsistency, but, if you can not, just take the trouble to tell the nearest church or chapel minister that God has a Prophet now living on the earth—do this, and twenty to one but you will learn something of the matter.

If a man, for disbelieving in dead Prophets, is called an infidel, by what term shall we designate those who disbelieve in a living Prophet? Something worse than infidel, certainly. There is, generally, an air of mystery, more or less dense, surrounding the teachings of ancient writers, which forms a shadow of excuse for disbelief in ancient Prophets, but no such excuse can be urged on behalf of disbelief in a living Prophet. When a character or object is present with us, we can discern its features distinctly, but in proportion as it recedes from us, does that distinctiveness of feature vanish, therefore we are more able to appreciate an object when near than when distant. Again, should a misunderstanding occur, we can ask an explanation from a living Prophet, but from a dead Prophet we never think of asking explanations, therefore as a disbelief in Prophets is censurable, and displeasing to God, a disbelief in a living Prophet must be by far a greater sin than a disbelief in dead Prophets. And further, the man who disbelieves in dead Prophets does them no personal injury, for they are beyond his power, but the man who disbelieves in a living Prophet, very frequently does him considerable personal injury by misrepresentation, slander, and physical abuse, therefore the disbeliever in a living Prophet has the worst position in this particular. So the Christian should examine himself, and see whether he is in the faith of a living Prophet, before that Christian condemns, as an infidel, another man, for disbelieving in dead Prophets. Peradventure the Christian may find himself more of an infidel, than is the man whom he wishes to designate by that title.

It is no new thing for a living Prophet to be discredited, despised, and rejected of men, and most by those men who profess to reverence dead Prophets. Abraham, Moses, David, Jesus, Peter, Paul, and Joseph Smith, were successively disbelieved in while living, and Brigham Young is disbelieved in now, and principally by those who professed and profess to be the servants of God. Who disbelieved in Jesus while living? Those who professed the strictest faith in Moses and the old Prophets. "Have any of the rulers or the Pharisees believed on him?" asked the self-righteous Pharisees of the officers who were sent to secure the person of Jesus, but who were fascinated by the wisdom of his teaching. Said Jesus at one time—"O Jerusalem, which killest the Prophets, and stonest them that are sent unto thee," &c. Now, reader, you know, well enough, that in Jerusalem lived the most pious professors and doctors of the Jewish religion, and that these very professors and doctors were much more infidel in their opinions of the divine mission of Jesus, than the common people were. The character which Jesus gives of these learned and devoted rabbis, is by no means flattering, but very forcible, and may exactly suit certain characters in our day—"Woe unto you, scribes and Pharisees, hypocrites! because ye build the tombs of the Prophets, and garnish the sepulchres of the righteous, and say, If we had been in the days of our fathers, we would not have been partakers with them in the blood of the Prophets. Wherefore ye be witnesses unto yourselves, that ye are the children of them which killed the Prophets. Fill ye up then the measure of your fathers. Ye serpents, ye generation of vipers, how can ye escape the damnation of hell?" [Matthew 23: 27–33] Now it may appear strange to many, but it is manifest, from the above passages, that amongst the greatest and most determined enemies of God and His servants, are those who reverence dead Prophets, preach up their teachings, garnish the sepulchres of those Prophets, and build fine churches and chapels to their memory, yet deny that themselves have any need of a living Prophet. It has ever been the case, where Satan has had power amongst the children of men; and whilst man is subject to the influences of the evil one, it ever will be the case. It was the case with the Prophet Joseph Smith, and the religious professors of modern times. Joseph had no greater or more unrelenting persecutors than those who made a profession in dead Prophets. It is the case now with Brigham Young—he has no greater enemies than religious teachers, and among his greatest enemies may be named some who profess to revere the teachings of the dead Joseph. So ready is the human mind to dishonour a living Prophet, and at the same time to profess to honour dead Prophets.

Now there must be some cause for this apparent phenomenon. It appears strange, indeed, that men should honour certain characters who have long passed from this stage of action, and should, at the same time, despise and persecute a similar character who lives in their midst! What a marvellous perversity! How can the matter be explained? Very readily. It all springs from the truth of the proposition this article started with—the necessity of a living Prophet. Those teachings of dead Prophets which will apply to subsequent generations, should be prized and acted upon by subsequent generations. If this is not the case, a degree of condemnation will follow. But the greatest condemnation that can fall upon a people, *follows the rejection of living Prophets*. Why? Because those Prophets are commissioned by the Almighty to go directly to that people, with a particular revelation of His will to them—a revelation which, very likely, will only apply incidentally to future generations. Now, if those Prophets be rejected by the very people to whom they are sent, what will the most pious professions of faith in dead Prophets avail? Nothing. Those professions will be a solemn mockery before God. Such a course would add to the condemnation of any people. A living Prophet would be moved to rebuke them, as our Saviour rebuked the Scribes and Pharisees. Of what avail was it for the antediluvians to profess a faith in Adam, Abel, or Enoch, while, at the same time, the hiss of derision, and the finger of scorn, were directed towards

Noah, the living Prophet? Did faith in dead Prophets then avail? Not a jot. If the Ninevites had rejected Jonah, and professed faith in Noah, and Moses, what would have been the result? The destruction of Nineveh within the forty days. No people ever made greater professions of faith in dead Prophets, than the Jews did in the days of Jesus and the Apostles, yet did those very Jews reject living Prophets in the persons of our Lord and his disciples. What did the reverential professions of the Jews avail? Let the razing of the Temple of God, the destruction of Jerusalem, the dispersion of the Jews, their broken, cursed, and despised condition through a dreary night of seventeen centuries, be a sufficient answer. The ancient Lamanites and Nephites built up churches to themselves, and professed to follow Christ, while they rejected the teachings of the living Prophets Nephi and Mormon. What was the consequence? Let the filthy, degraded, wretched condition of the American Indians suffice for a reply. And in these days men—pious men—professed followers of the meek and lowly Jesus, have rejected the Prophet Joseph, have persecuted him unto the death—now his innocent blood crimsons the land that is foremost in professions of Christian liberty. Will these empty professions avert the wrath of an indignant God? Will not the people be visited by the Almighty for such things? Verily the most pious reverence for all the ancient Prophets will not atone for the innocent blood of one modern Prophet. Will those who reject the Prophet Brigham be justified in the sight of God, by solemn protestations of faith in Joseph? If they do, God will not prove Himself the same yesterday, to-day, and for ever. And should Brigham be taken away, will any one be accounted righteous before God, for rejecting future Prophets, though it is done under a profession of faith in Brigham? Let such beware, for the Almighty expects His living Prophet to be respected and listened to first. The Lord knows full well that if living Prophets are respected, dead ones will be. But if living Prophets are despised, how can true respect be paid to dead ones? Reverence for dead Prophets is a pious burlesque, when accompanied by contempt for living Prophets.

It is folly for any people to follow all the teachings of dead Prophets, for many of their teachings will not apply to generations who exist after those Prophets are dead. Many of the teachings of the Prophet of God, are local—only suited for a particular place and people, and particular circumstances, and not designed for universal application. For another people to apply to themselves such particular teachings, would be gross perversion, and evidence of great ignorance or wickedness. If any people were to build an ark because Noah did, what should we think of them? We should almost doubt their sanity. How foolish it would be for modern Egyptians to migrate to Palestine because the Israelites did! Equally unwise would it be for modern Christians to flee to the mountains of Judea, because Jesus instructed his disciples to do so at a certain time; or for Christians to sell all that they possess, and have all things common, because the primitive disciples did so. Who would now think of selling his garment, and buying a sword with the proceeds, because the Apostles were instructed so to do? Would it not be nonsense for a man who despises Brigham, and professes to regard the words of Joseph, to go to Kirtland or Nauvoo to build a Temple, because Joseph instructed the

Saints to gather there, and build Temples? Most certainly it would. Yet into such ludicrous dilemmas those persons who reject a living Prophet, and profess faith in dead ones, are unavoidably led. Men of this description reject the living Spirit that inspires a living Prophet, and gives life to all his teachings; and, instead thereof, follow the dead letter of those Prophets who have long bid adieu to their ministry on earth. Yet it is a well known Scripture maxim, that the letter killeth, but the Spirit giveth live.

22

ANON., 'GATHERING'

The Latter-Day Saints' Millennial Star, 15:3 (15th January 1853), pp. 33–35

The season of the year has now arrived when many of the British Saints will bid adieu to their friends, and kindred, and fatherland, to journey across the mighty deep to the land of Zion, that they may engage more fully in building up the Kingdom of God.

The spectacle of hundreds and thousands of persons readily sacrificing from religious motives the claims of country, relationship, and acquaintance, and emigrating to a land to them personally unknown—where they will be comparative strangers, must undoubtedly appear strange and unaccountable to the majority of mankind. But Saints, who have learned of the things of God in some small degree, whose minds have been opened to an understanding of the economy of salvation, know full well the righteousness and wisdom of the motives that induce them to forsake the land of their nativity, and gather themselves together on another land. They are able to give a reason for the hope that is within them in this respect. They know that wickedness can never be brought to an end until the wicked are destroyed from off the face of the earth, and that it is not the mind of God that the righteous should perish with the wicked. They know that if the righteous are ever to live peaceably upon the earth, and enjoy the blessings of the Kingdom of God, they must first be gathered out from the wicked, that the wicked may be taken from the earth, and so be prevented injuring and oppressing the righteous. They know that the revelations and laws of God are calculated to benefit men, socially, temporally, and spiritually; and they are also well aware that those laws cannot be fully kept, and consequently their benefits cannot be fully realized, by the people of God, until they be gathered from the midst of the nations, and become a people separate and distinct from all other people. These are some of the motives that induce the Latter-day Saints to emigrate in such startling numbers from the shores of Britain, and from all countries where they may be located.

Wickedness has long reigned in the palace and in the cottage; among all ranks and conditions of mankind: those who have practised it have spread themselves like a green bay tree, and luxuriated rankly in this lower world, at the expense of the honest, the sober, the industrious, the innocent, and the virtuous.

The purposes of the creation of this earth and mankind, have been little understood, and less cared for, by the majority of men. Virtue and integrity—pearls beyond all price, have been bought and sold for worse than filthy lucre, to be trampled underfoot of men, and accounted things of naught. The poor and the righteous have groaned under the iron hand of the oppressor, and longed for death, that they might be set free. The laws and ordinances and covenants of the God of Heaven, have been transgressed, and changed, and broken; and the earth is become defiled under the inhabitants thereof to such a degree, that nothing less than the consuming glory of the Lord will purify it from the abomination and defilement with which it is corrupted.

Notwithstanding the general dark and degraded state in which the majority of mankind are at the present time, there are still hundreds and thousands of men and women who ardently hope for better things, and earnestly seek for the truth as for a hidden treasure, and steadfastly pursue righteousness and equity as the pathway to eternal happiness. To such, the intelligence that the Almighty has once more looked down from the Heavens, and seen the low, fallen, corrupted state of the workmanship of His hands, and remembered His ancient covenant and promise to gather His people in one in the latter days, and establish His kingdom upon the earth, never more to be thrown down; that His will may be done upon the earth as it is done in the Heavens, that sin and suffering may cease, and righteousness, and truth, and peace, and everlasting joy and happiness prevail for evermore—to such this intelligence will prove more grateful than the haven of rest to the tempest-tossed mariner, or a green oasis to the weary traveller in a burning desert.

This the Almighty has done, and the gathering of the Latter-day Saints is to speed on this mighty and glorious work.

The above remarks may be more adapted to benefit those who are not as yet numbered amongst the people of God; but we wish to make a few observations for the benefit of the Saints, especially the emigrating ones.

No one having the name of a Saint should emigrate to the land of Zion, unless he do it with an eye single to the glory of God, and the building up of His Kingdom. When persons amongst the Latter-day Saints leave their native land with the intention of going right up to head quarters, and do it from unworthy motives, they generally get disappointed in the object of their ambition, and apostatize long before they reach the mountains, and often fall by the destroyer. Every one who emigrates for Zion, should see that his heart is right, and his actions pure before God, and set his face as a flint Zion-ward, determining not to heed the oily tales of apostates, nor the fears and falterings of weak brethren; but resolving to push onward with all faithfulness and diligence, turning neither to the right hand nor to the left, staying not on his way until he reach the mountains, where he can halt in peace and security, and look down in safety upon the turmoil, and strife, and desolation of an ungodly generation, who have sown to the wind and must reap the whirlwind.

Those who obey the great commandment to gather, must of course do it at a sacrifice, and in the face of many privations. Three or four hundred people from various parts of the country, and perhaps from various countries, differing in manners, habits, dispositions, and associations, suddenly lodged in the limited dimensions of a ship, cannot expect to be quite so comfortable, or have things so much their own way, as they may have been accustomed to in their own houses on the land. Still their comfort or discomfort will rest in a great measure with themselves. By watching and praying, and seeking the influence of the Holy Spirit, and exercising patience and forbearance, and cultivating a cheerful and obliging demeanour towards one another, the voyage to New Orleans may be converted into a pleasure-trip, and all privations and discomforts be forgotten in the peace and harmony which may prevail. A ship-load of gathering Saints, who are faithful in the observance of their duties, may exercise a control over winds, and waves, and untoward and uncomfortable circumstances, which they never before dreamt of. "The effectual fervent prayer of a righteous man availeth much" [James 5:16]. How much more then shall the faith and prayers of three hundred Saints have power to draw down the blessing of Heaven, seeing they have just made a sacrifice of their attachment to kin, and country, and worldly prospects, for the express purpose of fulfilling the Lord's commandment to gather, for it is a truth that "Sacrifice brings down the blessings of Heaven."

All good Saints have received of the one Spirit, which unites their hearts as one if they heed its gentle and peaceable whisperings, and leads them to bear with each others' infirmities and weaknesses, and exercise long-suffering, and kindly and charitable feelings towards each other, each esteeming his brother or his sister better than himself. These agreeable and unmistakeable traits of a Saint's character can be exhibited on a sea voyage, with the greatest benefit to all parties.

The valleys of the Mississippi and the Missouri may be likened to Bunyan's "slough of despond." Some of the Saints, when they arrive at this portion of their journey, having miscalculated their faith or their patience, through murmuring, or repining, or listening to the sophistical tales of wicked apostates, grow cold in the spirit of the work, and stay behind here, or are slothful and careless in pursuing their journey further; they ultimately lose the Spirit of the Lord entirely, and turn again to the beggarly elements, and become spiritually dead; and oftentimes temporal death follows; for the powers of darkness, the agents of both temporal and spiritual death, abound in those valleys; indeed the destroyer rides upon the face of the waters, and his influence prevails on the land to such an extent, that those valleys become to many, valleys of the "shadow of death."

It is indeed foretold that the time shall come when none but those who are upright in heart shall be able to go up to Zion; but the diligent, the faithful, and the upright, need be under no fear; for the promise of the Almighty is unto them, that He will still shield them as in the hollow of His hand, that they shall live to accomplish their work upon the earth, and though a thousand should fall at their side, and ten thousand be destroyed around them, yet they shall stand in holy places and not be moved. The great secrets of safety for the Saints are prayer and faithfulness, in performing their duties in the seasons thereof, in observing the ordinances and commandments and precepts of the Lord, and in a willing obedience to the counsels of those who may be set over them in the Holy Priesthood. By doing this, the emigrating Saints may live to accomplish the purest and best desires of their hearts—even to arrive at Zion in safety, and be instructed in the way of the Lord more perfectly; but those who neglect these things, will have themselves to reproach when they find their portion amongst degraded and abandoned apostates.

23

WILLIAM G. MILLS, 'OUR HOME AT GREAT SALT LAKE'

The Latter-Day Saints' Millennial Star,
15:22 (28th May 1853), pp. 351–352

Oh! where's the heart that wants to part
    From the early scenes of childhood's mirth!
And where's the soul that loves to stroll
    From the place that gave him birth!
We love them well, for like a spell,
Around our hearts they closely dwell,
And all our fond emotions tell—
    This is our native earth.
But we go away at God's command,
    And every scene forsake,
To dwell in a better, holier land—
    Our home at Great Salt Lake.

To that dear home, our brethren come
    From every land, o'er every sea;
There Truth displays her brightest rays,
    And makes us pure and free;
The loveliest flowers of nature's bowers,
The vine and fig-tree, will be ours,
And corn and wheat in ample stores,
    That all may happy be.
So we go away at God's command,
    And every scene forsake,
To dwell in a better, holier land—
    Our home at Great Salt Lake.

The virtuous "fair" are gathering there,
    As crowns of glory to their lords;
And with their smiles man's cares beguile,
    And cheer with loving words;

The noble sons of Holy Ones
Reveal the truth in firmest tones,
Which glows like fire within our bones,
    Or cuts like two-edged swords.
Then we'll go away at God's command,
    And every scene forsake,
To dwell in a better, holier land—
    Our home at Great Salt Lake.

Part 7

JUDAISM

7.1

Orthodox Judaism

7.1 Orthodox Judaism

The native population of Jews in England and Wales rose steadily from 25,000 in 1800 to 60,000 in 1880, and exponentially to 300,000 by 1914 through a wave of immigration from Eastern Europe.[1] While concentrated in London, there were Jewish communities and congregations in towns and industrial centres across the English midlands, South Wales, and also in Glasgow. Compared with communities in many parts of Europe, British Jews were relatively free from legal constraints, experiencing civil disabilities on the same terms as all other non-Anglicans. These were eroded piecemeal through the period 1829–71, during which the Jewish community was characterised by 'acculturation to middle-class English habits and values' and a self-conscious moderacy in ritual practice.[2]

Overseeing the completion of Jewish emancipation was Nathan Marcus HaKohen Adler [Natan ben Mordechai ha-Kohen] (1803–90) who was Chief Rabbi of the British Empire from 1845 to his death. His leadership brought in a new era of centralisation, forging greater unity and conformity among Jewish congregations in Britain and its colonies, and reducing local rabbinical authority. Adler's 1848 sermon delivered at London's Great Synagogue, which seeks to capture 'the substance of our holy faith, as we are *now* bound to believe and to practise it', can be seen as an act of consolidation, and containment of divisions that were arising within British Judaism. Alluding to the 'Thirteen Principles of Faith' written by medieval Sephardic Jewish philosopher Maimonides, which were long taken as the canonical creed of Judaism, Adler affirms God as creator and ordainer, and scriptural commandments as holistic rules for life aimed at individual wellbeing and social harmony ('all for our good'). His defence of the Oral Law against those who reject it as a 'disfigurement' of scriptural religion is clearly a rebuke to the Reform movement which had already set up a rival synagogue (see 7.2 Reform Judaism). Adler goes on to address the doctrine of future reward and punishment, but gives only brief attention to the soul's afterlife, preferring to emphasise the Zionist hope of an ideal future collective. He anticipates the Messiah event as the time when God's people are gathered from among the nations to return to their own land, heralding an era of peace, harmony and spiritual fulfilment which will include humanity at large: God's people are the means by which the world will be blessed. Adler's speech anticipates the growth of the Zionist movement in the second half of the century. Adler cites books from the Torah, the Talmud and other Rabbinic literature, and alludes to (presumably) Hillel the Elder, a Jewish scholar of the first century BCE. Of the many scriptural allusions that Adler references, only citations for direct quotations have been retained here.

While women's participation in the orthodox synagogue was limited, Jewish women's devotional writings took a more public turn in the nineteenth century to include materials for use in collective worship, and interpretations of the theological tradition (beginning in Britain with Grace Aguilar's *Spirit of Judaism*, 1842: see this series Vol. III, section 3). Nina Ruth Salaman (née Davis; 1877–1925) combined orthodox religious practice with radical views on women's status. She was an eminent Hebrew scholar, poet and translator, supported women's suffrage, and in 1919 became the first woman to preach in an Orthodox synagogue in Britain.[3]

'The Ark of the Covenant', published in the *Jewish Quarterly Review*, which featured many women writers during the 1890s, demonstrates Davis's distinctive orthodoxy in which women play a leading role. Inspired by a number of Talmudic sources, which Davis adds in an appendix in the original, the poem tells of a priest who mourns the loss of the Ark of the Covenant – the embodiment of the divine presence, or Shekinah – from the Temple: 'Surely the glory of the House is o'er, / Gone is the Presence, silent is the voice'. Experiencing a flash of prophetic insight, the priest has a vision of the Ark, and dies. It falls to a woman prophet '[w]ith God-lit eyes' to sense, and interpret, the vision for the people. She defines the Ark as an internal messianic event, whereby the Presence comes to dwell in the hearts of those with holy lives, fully realised after death. Hence, 'His Presence hath not gone before recall, / But bideth nigh'. Davis offers a spiritualised interpretation of the Shekinah, filled with hope and intense yearning.

Notes

1 David Englander, 'Anglicised not Anglican: Jews and Judaism in Victorian Britain', in Gerald Parsons (ed.), *Religion in Victorian Britain,* vol. 1: *Traditions* (Manchester: Manchester University Press, 1988), pp. 235–273, on pp. 240 and 253.
2 Todd Endelman, *The Jews of Britain, 1656 to 2000* (Berkeley, CA: University of California Press, 2002), p. 95.
3 Todd Endelman, 'Salaman, Nina Ruth', *Oxford Dictionary of National Biography*, 2018, https://doi.org/10.1093/ref:odnb/71436.

24

NATHAN MARCUS ADLER, *THE JEWISH FAITH: A SERMON DELIVERED IN THE GREAT SYNAGOGUE, DUKE'S PLACE, SABBATH, 24 SHEVAT, 5608 (29 JANUARY 1848)*

(London: Effingham Wilson, 5608–1848), pp. 1, 2–16

My dear Brethren,

AT this momentous time, when so much is spoken on subjects profoundly interesting to us, we not unfrequently observe how busy calumny is in plundering our holy faith of its godly character. [...]

Therefore, we think it our duty to try to bring the substance of our holy faith, as we are *now* bound to believe and to practise it, into the smallest possible compass; and though the topic is one not easily despatched, and is difficult to be condensed into one discourse, I could not but invite you to follow me on a subject which will require your concentrated and continued attention. Besides, when can such a task be more justifiable and more indispensable than this day, when we have just heard repeated the awful revelation on the mountain of Sinai. Therefore let us endeavour to give a sketch of our holy faith. We take our text from the book of Ecclesiastes (xii. 13, 14), running thus:—

סוף דבר הכל נשמע · את־האלהים ירא ואת־מצותיו
שמור כי־זה כל־האדם : כי את־כל־מעשה האלהים
יבא במשפט על כל־נעלם · אם־טוב ואם־רע:

"Let us hear the conclusion of the whole matter: Fear God and keep his commandments: for this is the whole of man. For God shall bring every work into judgment, with every secret thing, whether good or whether evil."

After the wisest of men had, in the book of Ecclesiastes, considered how man is so low and yet so high, so insignificant and yet of such great moment—after he had beheld his earthly possessions from a double point of view, in their importance and their vanity and vexation of spirit—after he had contemplated the various purposes and destinies for which man was created: he finally comes to that point which solves all the contradictions exhibited in that book: "Fear God, keep his commandments; for God shall bring every work into judgment." In these words are involved the three fundamental articles of our faith, into which the thirteen dogmas of Maimonides are condensed namely:—

I The Existence of God, מציאות השם.
II The Divine Revelation, תורה מן השמים.
III The Future Reward and Punishment, ועונש שכר.

May the Lord bless our humble words, that we may succeed in representing with dignity that which is most dignified!

I

To fear God means first to know God. While the fear of every other thing decreases in proportion as we approach to and are acquainted with it, the fear of God, on the contrary, increases the more we learn of Him, and the more our minds are filled with conceptions of His attributes. We tremble like our forefathers on the mountain of Sinai, when we perceive within and without us His thunderings and lightnings. True, it is difficult to comprehend those attributes: it is as if a child were to dig a hole in the ground for the purpose of exhausting the ocean. The study and labour of a life would not be sufficient to explore even one of the divine qualities. But to be convinced of His existence is not difficult. There is not a star that shines, not a plant that grows, not an insect that moves, but what is sufficient to confound the atheist. "Ask the fowls of the air, and they shall tell thee; the earth, and it shall teach thee; and the fishes of the sea, they shall declare unto thee that it is the hand of the Lord who has wrought them" (Job xii. 7). It cannot be by chance; for chance has neither order nor regularity. Blots of ink cast promiscuously on paper cannot form a well-written letter—but in the world there is the greatest order and regularity. Chance has no design or end; but the natural as well as the moral world affords the most conspicuous and striking proofs of profound design and wisdom. Whithersoever we look, the most minute and inconsiderable, as well as the most stupendous and illustrious, works of God bear equal marks of that exquisite wisdom.

To fear God signifies, in the second place, to know God rightly—not to fall into the hands of those rival enemies, superstition and unbelief, that is, to believe too much or too little. "Take ye good heed," said the Lord, "unto yourselves; for ye saw no manner of similitude on the day that the Lord spake unto you in Horeb out of the midst of the fire" (Deuteronomy iv. 15). The dogma, that the Supreme Being is a spirit—the highest spirit—incorporeal—and neither may nor can be represented by any likeness, is of the greatest moment. He is elevated above all the passions, free from all the foibles, exempt from all the frailties which degrade man. Let it not be objected, that we find in the Holy Bible many instances where corporeal attributes are imputed to God, where it speaks of God's anger, revenge, jealousy—of God's rising and moving; for bear in mind, that the Bible being written for men, the Lord descends therein to the level of human understanding, of human apprehension and human conception, and assumes human language— גדול נביאים שמדמים צורה ליוצרה "it is a great thing that the prophets were permitted to assign the image of man to the Creator who created man in his image" (Bereshith Rabba, 27; Moreh 1:46). But those expressions must be purged and purified in our minds from all gross associations; for "to whom will ye liken God? or what likeness will ye compare unto him?" (Isaiah xl. 18). There is none, either in the heaven or in the earth, who can be compared or likened unto him.

To fear God signifies, thirdly, to trust in and worship God. The fear of God also differs, in this respect, from the fear of any other power—that generally we cannot have confidence in him whom we fear; but the more we fear God the more our confidence in him must increase in strength. When we are convinced that with God is power which *can* give, and goodness which *will* give—that we owe to him alone all the benefits of our past and our present—that very often בנמו בעל הנם אינו מכיר "he who is the object of a miracle, at first does not perceive it" (Nidda 31, a),—such discovery of God's omnipresence, infinite goodness and kindness, must be a new ground of hope, of trust, and of cordial submission. We feel ourselves bound to worship him alone and none else; we feel it incumbent on us to lift up to him every day thanks הודה, praise תהלה, and supplication בקשה,—thanks for the past, praise for the present, and supplication for the future. It is true, that by uplifting our voice to heaven, we cannot convey to the Almighty any new knowledge; for he knows everything before we call, he hears before we cry. But though we cannot work a change in God, we can work a change in ourselves by making ourselves fit subjects for his benevolence, kindness and mercy, and qualifying us to receive his blessing.

II

But we must not only worship God at certain hours or periods; but our whole life must be one long spiritual service—we must *keep God's commandments* continually.

The Divine revelation is the next fundamental article of our faith. Observe, my brethren, they are HIS commandments. They are not the production of man, the offspring of mental contemplation, the fruit of human intellect: but, they are the superhuman communication from God, confirmed by miracles, and bestowed upon our forefathers in their own presence. Our holy religion is not a mystic revelation, a sealed book, a concealed communication; but it is founded on the fact, that six hundred thousand men saw and heard, and perceived it with all their senses:—פן־חשכח אח־הדברים אשר ראו עיניך רק השמר לך ושמר נפשך מאד, "Take heed to thyself, and keep thy soul diligently, lest thou forget the things which thine eyes have seen . . . especially the day that thou stoodest before the Lord thy God in Horeb . . . when the Lord spake unto you out of the midst of the fire" (Deuteronomy iv. 9–14). If the evidence of two witnesses is sufficient to prove the truth of a statement, even though the life of a man depend on that evidence, how much more has the strong testimony of such a multitude of individuals a claim upon our credence, confidence, and conviction. If the evidence of strangers, whose motives are unknown, is entitled to belief when affirming a common occurrence, how much more does the solemn fact testified by our ancestors, by our parents, who had a parental interest and desire not to mislead us, but to direct and to give us the best advice, the best inheritance, deserve our firm belief.

Besides, the commandments have their evidence, bear their godly character *in themselves*. Though we may not know the reason of each separate law and statute; yet, thus much is obvious, that they are all for our good. "Now, Israel, what doth the Lord thy God require of thee, but to fear the Lord thy God, to walk in all his ways, and to love him, and to keep the commandments of the Lord, and his statutes which I command thee this day (לטוב לך) *for thy good*" (Deuteronomy x. 12, 13). The commandments have for their aim and tendency, either duty towards God, or towards ourselves, or towards our fellow-creatures; but they have generally man, the *whole man* for their purpose, either his body or his intellect, his mind or his spirit. We ask you, my brethren, must not a law of which love towards God is the sun, the centre—as it were, the heart of its heart, the soul of its soul—a law which commands love towards our first benefactors, the representatives of God—our parents, love towards our wife, children, and family; love towards the stranger, orphan, and widow; love towards our country, whose air we breathe, whose language we speak, whose soil feeds us, and whose laws protect us, and finally, love towards *all* our fellowmen, so that Hillel considers the last as the basis of all commandments—must not such a law intend our good? Must not a law, which enjoins obedience consistent with the other laws of God, to the sovereign, to superiors, judges, to instructors and teachers, regard for the aged and experienced, the learned and the virtuous—must not such a law promote our temporal welfare? We ask further, a law which descends even to the feelings of the lower animals, and forbids to take the dam with her young, so that she may not feel how her young ones are bereft of their freedom—a law which takes care even of inanimate nature, when it bids us spare the trees in the hostile city,—must not such a law imbue us with kindness and affection?

But there are some who think that the *oral law* has altered and disfigured the *written* law, so that it is no longer the same. How erroneous, how false is such an opinion! Nothing but superficial reflection could have engendered it. You are aware it is an article of our belief, that the law given through Moses, (the greatest of prophets, who excelled all the sages that either preceded or succeeded him) has not been changed, nor ever will be changed; consequently, the oral law is not, and cannot be, a different code; but both the written and the oral law emanated from the same shepherd, the same legislator. "God hath spoken one, but I have heard two" (Psalm lxii. 11). For if even the text of a human law requires interpretation, and often admits of different constructions, how much more needful is interpretation to the profound word of God, which is like a fire, and a hammer that breaketh the rock in pieces, so that the sparks fly about. Now, my brethren, though Moses and the Prophets, inspired by the holy spirit, declared, explained, and unfolded the statutes, and handed them down to us, though our teachers derived decisions from the written law according to the exegetical canon, though our sages made ordinances and institutions to preserve the law, and established fences around it, so that the holy mountain might not be touched; yet they never deviated from, or counteracted the written law; on the contrary, they strove and laboured to explain every word, every letter, nay, every dot, to keep it as a sanctuary, as the greatest treasure of life.

III

But, besides the consciousness which accompanies obedience to God's commandments here, there is a higher and a greater recompense, which follows hereafter; for a *future reward and punishment*, is the *third* fundamental article of our faith. "God shall bring," concludes our text, "every secret thing into judgment." When we throw a glance upon the earth, we cannot deny that we meet with scenes which surprise us, and show that God hideth himself בעב הענן. We sometimes perceive that the virtuous are swept away and the worthless left to flourish; that merit languishes in neglected solitude, and vanity gains the admiration of the world. From the hand of violence, the righteous look up to God as the avenger, but they sometimes look up in vain. This Divine government conflicts with our notions of God's justice and wisdom, with the evident marks of order and righteousness which we discern within and without us. "Can iniquity," we ask with the Psalmist, "can iniquity be united with the throne of judgment? Can he who frameth the law, indulge in mischief?" (Psalm xciv. 20). Therefore, even the simplest intellect must admit that the righteous Lord will bring righteousness about; and if not here, then in the world which is to come. But that which reason only indistinctly conceives, our doctrine has clearly explained, and fully confirmed. The immortality of our soul is one of our holiest dogmas. God will judge the soul created in his image, which is light of his light, and spirit of his spirit. God in his revelation has promised by the lips of his prophets and saints, that the dust shall return to the dust, but the spirit shall return unto him who gave it, that he will not leave the soul in the grave, nor suffer his holy ones to see corruption, but he will shew them fulness of joy in his presence, and at his right hand pleasure for evermore. He has promised that our expectation shall not be cut off, but that we shall have places among the higher spirits, there where neither pain nor trouble, nor separation, nor death have any existence, but where light and glory dwell. He has vouchsafed that, though our flesh and our heart shall fail, still the Rock of our heart, our portion—God— is, and remaineth for ever.

And there is not only a futurity for the individual, but also for the people at large. The same God who bore us on eagles' wings above all impediment, and destined us to be ממלכת כהנים וגוי קדוש a kingdom of priests, and a holy nation, a pattern and a standard for all mankind; the same God, who, in consequence of our sins, has fulfilled every word of his threat, scattered us among the nations, and left us few in number, the same God who sifted the house of Israel as corn is sifted in a sieve—the same God will surely fulfil the other part of his revelation, that he will have compassion upon us, return and gather us from all the nations, and will bring us into the land which our fathers possessed. He will bring forth a root of David, which shall stand for an ensign of the people and re-establish the temple, the mountain of his house in the midst of Jerusalem, which shall be exalted above the hills, so that people shall flow unto it. But mind, my dear brethren, mankind at large has nothing to fear from the advent of the Messiah, has no reason to look upon it with an eye of envy or suspicion. How happy would the earth be if that great event would happen soon, very soon—that time not of sowing but of reaping, not of combat and labour, but of rest and enjoyment, not of hostility and discord, but of dove-like peace; that happy time which shall establish universal harmony in this world, when nation shall not lift up sword against nation, neither shall learn war any more, when every passion shall be tamed and appeased; when the earth shall be full of knowledge as the waters cover the sea; and what is still more, when all the inhabitants of the earth shall pay homage to the Lord; for in that day the Lord shall be one and his name One.

25

NINA DAVIS, 'THE ARK OF THE COVENANT'

Jewish Quarterly Review, 8:1 (October 1895), pp. 82–86

There is a legend full of joy and pain,
    An old tradition told of former years,
When Israel built the temple once again
    And stayed his tears.

'T was in the chamber where the Wood Pile lay,
    The logs wherewith the altar's flame was fed;
There hope recalled the Light of vanished day,
    The Light long fled.

A priest moved slowly o'er the marble floor,
    Sorting the fuel in the chamber stored;
Frail was his form, he ministered no more
    Before the Lord.

Wrapt in deep thought, with sad and mournful mien,
    Plying his axe with oft a troubled sigh,
Dreaming of glory that the House had seen
    In days gone by.

Mused of the time when in the Holy Place
    God's Presence dwelt betwixt the Cherubim,
And of the day he turned away his face,
    And light grew dim.

When the Shechinah from that erring throng,
    Alas, withdrew, yet tarried in the track,

As one who ling'reth on the threshold long
    And looketh back.

Then step by step in that reluctant flight
    Approached the shadow of the city wall,
And lingered yet upon the mountain height
    For hoped recall.

The Temple standeth, pride of Israel's race,
    Yet resteth there no sacred Ark of Gold,
God's Glory filleth not the Holy Place,
    Ah! loss untold.

Surely the glory of the House is o'er,
    Gone is the Presence, silent is the Voice;
They who remember that which is no more,
    Can they rejoice?

Convulsed, a sacred spasm seized his frame,
    The axe fell from his trembling hand's control,
A fire leapt upward, and the burning flame
    Consumed his soul.

His eyes were fixed upon the ground, he gazed
    Upon a stone of that smooth marble plain,
Which seemed as from its place it had been raised,
    And set again.

Into his heart there flashed prophetic light,
    With sudden force the secret was revealed;
Nought but one treasure sacred in his sight
    Lay there concealed.

As one of Heaven bid, who dare not wait,
    With step grown firm as with the strength of youth,
He hastened to his comrade to relate
    The wondrous truth.

His hand uplifted, and a light sublime
    Shot from his eyes and like a joy-beam shone;
He seemed a holy seer of olden time
    To look upon.

Yet from his parted lips no message came,
   In silence reached he his immortal goal,
And from its dwelling in the earthly frame
      Went forth his soul.

Soon o'er the house flew sad and strange reports,
   And men and women bristled at the sound,
And priests came swiftly from the sacred courts,
      And thronged around.

Piercing the crowd a woman made her way,
   Seeming to own a right which none gainsaid,
And neared the spot where that calm figure lay,
      The priestly dead.

And reverent to the prostrate form she passed:
   Pressing her lips upon the peaceful brow,
She whispered, "Thy desire hath come at last,
      'T is granted now."

Then spake the High Priest, "Wherefore dost thou thus?
   Is the dead thine that thou hast spoken so?
And knowest thou the secret hid from us,
      Which dealt the blow?"

"O priest, it is according to thy word,"
   She answered, "And I know that secret well,
He, as he breathed his last, the message heard
      And that did tell."

"Woman, thy tongue is false, thy word untrue,
   Yon priest divulged nought with his dying breath,
Nor uttered sound, ere to his heart there flew
      The shaft of death."

"My lord, thy servant lieth not," she said,
   "His soul departing did to mine unfold
A glorious light, and as his spirit fled
      The tale was told.

"Oft have I stood in prayer in yonder court,
   And marked that weak, wan figure, worn with care,

Transformed by heavenly light, and sacred thought,
        To beauty rare.

"On ye, O priests, his longing eyes were bent,
        While at the altar ye your charge have kept,
And oft a sigh so deep the silence rent,
        In prayer I wept.

"And I have read this day his life's fair dream,
        And in his death have seen that dream fulfilled,
The longing of his heart, the wish supreme,
        That faith instilled.

"Say ye, God's Ark is captive far away?
        And weep ye, Ichabod, the glory fled?
And mourn ye that the brightness of the day
        Is quenched and dead?

"Maybe 't is true that in a far-off land,
        The Ark of God in exile dwelleth still;
It resteth ever with the pure of hand
        Who do his will!

"Know then, ye priests and Levites, Israel, all,
        Hid in its place the Ark of God doth lie,
His Presence hath not gone beyond recall,
        But bideth nigh.

"Behold Thou comest as the dawn of day!
        Shechinah! changeless, to illume the night!
O thou, who art a lamp upon the way,
        Who art a light!

"Haste, brethren, let the gates asunder burst,
        Regain the Ark, the Covenant hold fast,
And by the glorious Second House, the First
        Shall be surpassed."

She ceased, and silence cast its shackles o'er
        The awe-struck crowd; her shadowy form moved on:
With God-lit eyes, she stood a moment more,
        And then was gone.

So was that death with life's quintessence crown'd;
    The truth illumined each inquiring face,
For all knew then God's Ark would yet be found
        Within its place.

7.2

Reform Judaism

7.2 Reform Judaism

Reform Judaism as it was practiced in Britain was a relatively minor development, in terms of its numbers and legacy, differing from Orthodoxy not in its essential theology, but in attitudes to scripture and ritual. Reform Jews recognised the divine authority only of the Written Law comprising the Law, the Prophets and the Writings, but not of the Oral Law, in accordance with the centuries-old Karaite tradition. Along with this narrower biblicism, and due in part to a desire to fit into mainstream patterns of work and social life, Reform Jews reduced the length of services and festivals, and their ministers gave more emphasis to preaching and pastoral work than to ritual.[1]

The first Reform congregation was formed in 1840 by a combination of Sephardi and Ashkenazi Jews departing other congregations. David Woolf Marks (1811–1909), a London-born Jew and scholar who had held roles in synagogues in Haymarket and Liverpool, and who had developed neo-Karaite views, became their minister in 1841. On his refusal to celebrate Second Days of religious festivals, he was excommunicated by Orthodox leaders, resulting in the formalisation of a new West London Synagogue of British Jews in 1842. Marks remained their leader until 1895, styling himself 'Reverend' rather than 'rabbi'. He wrote a new prayer book containing a liturgy with full English translation, curtailing repetitions, removing content deemed objectionable and omitting some rituals that had no basis in the Written Law.

Marks's consecration sermon for the new synagogue (extracted below) criticises the problems he sees in contemporary Jewish practice. He begins with a thinly veiled attack on the orthodox Chief Rabbi's assumption of authority over British Jews. Emphasising that ceremony is a means to religious life, not its end, and that much of Talmudic practice emerged from cultural contexts far different from the modern setting, he claims to return to the true spirit of Judaism as revealed in immutable divine law. Refuting the charge of 'Treason against Tradition', he claims to uphold an 'improved mode of worship'. He affirms written scripture as the 'unerring guide' to faith and practice, asks for prayer length to be curtailed, and emphasises religious instruction – especially for women as shapers of the next generation. Marks denounces a number of lively (and often noisy) communal practices that distracted worshippers from serious attention to the sermon and reading of the Torah. His stated aim to save the image of Judaism both to outsiders and to its own younger generation demonstrates an anxiety for Jewish practice to be compatible with social integration.

Reform Judaism did not flourish and grow in Britain as it did elsewhere, partly because Orthodox synagogues began to modify their ritual practices, and also because its liturgical and biblical conservatism did not go far enough for those with more liberal inclinations. (Reform congregations were subsequently established only in Manchester, Hull and Bradford.) Reform Judaism did not appeal to immigrant East End Jews for whom ritual was of primary importance, and who had less of a stake in cultural integration. Those for whom the authority of written scripture itself became an intellectual problem departed the West London synagogue to form the separate movement that came to be called Liberal Judaism (see 7.3).

Note

1 Michael A. Meyer, *Response to Modernity: A History of the Reform Movement in Judaism* (Detroit: Wayne State University Press, 1995), pp. 172–178, and David Englander, 'Anglicised not Anglican: Jews and Judaism in Victorian Britain', in Gerald Parsons (ed.), *Religion in Victorian Britain*, vol. 1: *Traditions* (Manchester: Manchester University Press, 1988), pp. 235–273, on pp. 256–259.

26

D. W. MARKS, *DISCOURSE DELIVERED AT THE CONSECRATION OF THE WEST LONDON SYNAGOGUE OF BRITISH JEWS, THURSDAY 16TH SEBAT A.M. 5602–27TH JANUARY 1842*

(London: Duncan & Malcolm, 5602–1842), pp. 6–9, 10–11, 12, 17–22

It may be well to offer here a word of explanation to those who, misguided by the insinuations of enemies to all improvement, will not take into account the value of changes by the benefits they confer, but who see treason in every attempt to reform the Ritual, and to found our religious practices on the basis of a sound and all-sufficient Exegesis of the Mosaic Code. Treason against the Tradition! is the watchword under whose influence the efforts of the best Israelitish hearts have for years been combated by men, whose exclusive fault has not always been that of the strictest adherence to existing institutions; and since we can scarcely hope that our efforts for the good of Israel, which we consider to be bound up with an improved mode of worship, will escape the enmity of those who are opposed to all change; and since there is a well-grounded fear that we shall be represented as entertaining opinions which are far from our minds; I will, in concise terms, state our impression on the Tradition, known by the name of Oral Law, and professedly contained in the Mishna and the Talmud.

The enemies of the Jews have never yet, since accusations against our people have appeared, omitted to preface their charges with the assertion, that the Jews consider the whole tenor of the Talmud as a work of divine inspiration: an assertion which has just as zealously been negatived by every defender of the Jewish system, as a condition, without which the defence of Judaism were impossible.

Now, let it not be supposed, that it is the intention of myself, or of any member of this congregation, whose humble organ I am, to vilify, in any way, the character of the traditional records. On the contrary, we recognize in them a valuable aid for the elucidation of many passages in Scripture; we feel proud of them as a monument of the zeal and mental activity of our ancestors; we hold it our duty to reverence the sayings of men, who, we are convinced, would have sacrificed their lives for the maintenance of that Law which God has vouchsafed to deliver unto us; but we must (as our conviction urges us) solemnly deny, that a belief in the *divinity* of those traditions written in the Mishna, and the Jerusalem and Babylonian Talmuds, is of equal obligation to the Israelite with the faith in the divinity of the Law of Moses. We know that these books are human compositions; and though we are content to accept with reverence from our post-biblical ancestors, advice and instruction, we cannot *unconditionally* accept their laws. For Israelites, there is but One immutable Law—the sacred volume of the Scriptures, commanded by God to be written down for the unerring guidance of his people until the end of time.

I have already stated, that in repelling attacks from without, the defenders of Judaism have invariably given up the point of considering the whole tenor of the Talmud as a work of divine character. But if this be a truth in controversy, how can the divine authority of the Talmud be upheld for the purpose of justifying ritual observances, at variance with the commands of God, and the spirit of our own age and feelings, which are clung to with a tenacity worthy of a better cause, merely because they can be traced to the Talmud? On all hands it is conceded that an absolute necessity exists for the modification of our worship; but no sooner is any important improvement proposed, than we are assured of the sad fact, that there is not at present any authority competent to judge in such matters for the whole House of Israel. Now, admitting this as a truth, (since the extinction of the right of ordination has rendered impossible the convocation of a Sanhedrin, whose authority shall extend over all Jewish congregations,) does it not follow, as a necessity, that every Hebrew congregation must be authorized to take such measures as shall bring the divine service into consonance with the will of the Almighty, as explained to us in the Law and in the Prophets?

Whilst the whole of Israel was under the guidance of legally constituted Sanhedrin, let us admit, that it was the duty of every Jew to pay implicit obedience in all practical matters to the heads of that body for the time being: but that tribunal has ceased—for fifteen hundred years we have been without a visible head, and therefore there exists not a shadow of reason for upholding the authority of human decisions, pronounced by men who are not "the judges in our days" (Deuteronomy, 17:9). The great principles of the Mosaic Law have been every-where held the same; but since those days, no absolute similitude of outward observances has been maintained in Israel. In spite of the horror with which beneficent measures of improvement are repulsed, under the plea of their disturbing the unity of Israel, it is a fact, that the customs of one portion of Israelites are distinct from those of another portion, in the same city, to a considerable extent. Important variations exist between the observances of the German and Portuguese synagogues, and greater differences still between those and the customs of the synagogue at Avignon; still, the unity of the people of Israel has never suffered from these discrepancies; although there has been no lack of malevolent designs, at different times and various places, to foment discord, and perhaps schism, between the various congregations of Israelites, on account of pretended deviations from prescribed practices. [...]

Not, then, to weaken, but to strengthen our faith; not to trespass against, but to consolidate the great principles of that law which our fathers tremblingly heard amidst the thunders of Sinai—this Synagogue has been established. Our unerring guide has been, and will continue to be, the sacred volume of the Scriptures; by that *alone* have we endeavoured to regulate our principles. In matters relating to public worship, we desire to reject nothing that bears the stamp of antiquity, when that stamp is genuine, and in accordance with the revealed will of God; nor to condemn any thing because it is new, provided the newness of the measure be consonant with the spirit of the religion given us by the Almighty through Moses; a religion so framed as to adapt itself to all our destinies, in all their various phases, whether politically glorious on the throne of David, or politically prostrate in the thraldom of dispersion. [...]

As Israelites, who have the glory of God at heart, we feel the importance of averting the evil blow, which ignorance and misconception cannot fail to strike at our hallowed institutions, especially in days, whose peculiar character it is, to submit every system to the severity of critical scrutiny. We feel that the time has arrived, when we must do our utmost to make our religion respected, not only in the sight of the world at large, but, which is of far greater concern, in the sight of our rising community, who will not rest satisfied with the insignificant assurance, that a practice must be revered because it has sprung into existence in countries, and under circumstances, totally different from those under the influence of which we live. That these grave and important considerations have alone moved us in the formation of our new congregation; אל אלהים ה׳· הוא יודע "THE GOD OF GODS, THE ETERNAL! HE KNOWETH" [Joshua 22:22]. [...]

Here, dear brethren, we perceive the sublime effects of divine worship, blending prayer with religious instruction. That these two great essentials were preserved in the Synagogue for centuries after Ezra and Nehemiah, cannot be doubted; and that they were productive of similar beneficial results, may be inferred from the piety which stamps the characters and writings of the men of those ages. Truly were their hearts rejoiced and their souls gladdened when they entered the house of God; here their hearts were purified by the sacred springs of religion; here they were inspired with the love of God and of their fellow-man; here their darkness was enlightened, their errors dissipated, their weakness sustained, their baneful passions controlled, their good desires strengthened; here religion gave a balm for every woe, and a remedy for every disease of the mind and of the heart.

Such, O dear brethren, were the sentiments which the Synagogue of olden days inspired; alas! for the change that has come over us! Where is the devotion that was wont to reign in the house of God? where the sacred fires that animated our fathers? where the pulpit that once taught the blessed truths of salvation and eternity? Does the service now impress us, do we leave our Synagogues better in mind or in spirit than we entered; do we feel as if we had been in converse with the most High; do we draw from it those benefits which it was intended and is calculated to effect?

Alas! my friends, that with a bitter heart and a mournful spirit, we are compelled to reply, "No!" to these important questions! To pray for protection, sustenance, health, life, salvation, and immortality, is to solicit blessings of the highest magnitude: and yet from the many abuses, which are permitted to distract the attention, and to banish devotion in most of the present Synagogues, can it be believed, that men are really impressed either with the nature or the import of the blessings which they ask of God? Who can reflect on the בית הכנסת ['beth knesset', house of meeting] of olden days, and not arrive at the painful conviction of the degeneracy of our modern houses of prayer—when we find the men's Synagogue but partially attended, the women's gallery almost solitary, the pulpit mute, and religious instruction totally exiled?

In endeavouring to trace the causes which have produced this painful contrast, we shall not discover them in the insufficiency of our holy religion, for that is eternal and immutable as its Almighty Founder; but in the abuses engendered by ages of darkness, superstition, and intolerance. Eastern customs totally at variance with the habits and dispositions of an enlightened people have been associated with our religious practices. Woman, created by God as a "help meet for man," and in every way his equal; woman, endowed by the same parental care, as man, with wondrous perceptions, that she might participate (as it may be inferred from holy Writ, that she was intended to participate) in the full discharge of every moral and religious obligation, has been degraded below her proper station. The power of exercising those exalted virtues that appertain to her sex, has been withheld from her; and since equality has been denied to her in other things, as a natural consequence, it has not been permitted to her in the duties and delights of religion. It is true that education has done much to remedy this injustice in other respects, yet does its memory live in the indifference manifested for the religious instruction of females.

It cannot be doubted, that this indifference is one of the fruitful sources of the laxity in the Jewish religion, which we so much deplore. The duties to be performed by women lie at the very foundation of human life; for as upon them depends the earliest education of the great body of mankind, and as the mind is ever powerfully influenced by the lessons received in infancy, it is as hopeless to expect a truly pious community, where proper religious instruction is withheld from females, as to look for effect without cause.

Another serious evil may be discovered in the extreme length of the prayers, and in the blending with them heterogeneous opinions and metaphysical disquisitions, that can have no affinity with prayer. This renders it impossible to command the unwearied attention of the congregation during the entire service, and defeats every effort to excite devotion.

An over-fondness for opinions of bye-gone times, and a veneration for every custom and observance that claims antiquity, have been equally detrimental to the interests of Judaism. To such lengths have these prejudices extended, that many institutions, which sheer necessity, and not choice, had led our fathers to adopt, have been rigidly adhered to in our times, although the causes that produced them have long ceased to exist. I may instance the several Chaldaic compositions, as scattered through the liturgy, and which could only have been introduced with the laudable intention of making the prayers intelligible to those uninformed in the sacred Hebrew; yet have these formulas been clung to with great tenacity, at a time, when it must be acknowledged, that the Chaldee has become obsolete, whilst the Hebrew is far better understood. Again, the observance of double festivals—a practice which originated before the astronomical calculation of the calendar was introduced—has, nevertheless, been rigorously upheld in days when our calculations are most minute, and when we are enabled to determine the months, even to a fraction of time. Thus, with directly contrary evidence before us, have we continued to pronounce in our Synagogues, אלה מועדי ה' מקראי קדש "These are the festivals of the Lord, holy convocations," both upon the days whereon God commanded their observance, and the days whereon He commanded it not [Leviticus 23:4].

If, in addition to these grave abuses, we consider the unseasonable hour at which the morning service commences, the levity occasioned by the מי שברך ['mi sheberach', blessings] during the reading of the Law, the sale and distribution of the מצות ['matzoth', unleavened bread], and the want of pulpit instruction, we shall have arrived at the principal causes that have depressed Judaism, and that have separated so many in Israel from their God.

It is, my friends, to remedy these glaring evils that this synagogue has been formed, and the improvements we have determined to introduce therein will, I trust in God, prove most effectual in restoring the house of worship to a state so pure, that the presence of God may abide there.

The time appointed for divine service is such as to enable the entire congregation, men, women, and children, to assemble prior to the commencement of prayer. The prayers will be read aloud by the minister only; appropriate psalms and hymns will be chaunted by the choir, and responses made by the congregation. The reading of the Law will not be interrupted by the עֲלִיָּה ['aliyoth', going up (to read from the Torah)], for, as that institution has long lost its primary aim, the necessity for it no longer exists. Free-will offerings, unaccompanied by personal compliments, will be permitted in the synagogue on the three festivals of Passover, Pentecost, and Tabernacles, as well as on such other days as occasions may require, after the book of the Law shall have been returned to the Ark. It will be incumbent upon children of both sexes, connected with this synagogue, to be publicly confirmed in their faith at the age of thirteen years; the catechetical exercises joined with this important ceremony will embrace the whole of the principles of the Jewish faith. As prayer will be offered up in Hebrew only, and as it is indispensable that every Israelite should perfectly understand the supplications he addresses to the Supreme Being, I confidently hope that the sacred language will be generally cultivated by both sexes of this congregation. The holy festivals will be celebrated on those days *only*, commanded by God through our legislator Moses. The days commemorative of the great events of Jewish history will be duly observed.

Thus have I, my friends, as amply as the limits of a discourse will permit, endeavoured to explain the motives that have prompted the present undertaking. I have considered the true objects of the synagogue, the sentiments it once inspired, and its present state of desolation. I have examined into the causes of the apathy to Judaism, existing among Israelites, and detailed our measures by which we hope to rekindle a love for our ancient faith, and to render our Synagogue a house of devotion and of religious instruction.

7.3

Liberal Judaism

7.3 Liberal Judaism

Liberal Judaism emerged in Britain at the end of the nineteenth century under the leadership of Claude Montefiore and Lily Montagu, the latter going on to become the movement's chief organiser and publicist in the early twentieth century. Montagu (1873–1963) was a pioneering social worker, suffragist and writer who became convinced that the orthodox Judaism in which she had grown up was not spiritually profound, and needed to evolve to meet the demands of new intellectual and social contexts: 'We cannot worship with our parents' hearts.'[1] She found a kindred spirit in Montefiore, a liberal interpreter of Judaism with universalist leanings, but continued to value Jewish religious forms as vehicles of ideal spirituality and promoted service to humanity as the true expression of faith.[2] Liberal Judaism differed from British Reform Judaism which was theologically conservative and biblicist (see 7.2).

In the face of what she saw as an existential crisis within Judaism, Montagu's article 'Spiritual Possibilities of Judaism Today' is her manifesto for a religious revival. Her categorisation of Jews into 'East End' and 'West End' alludes to the divisions that had arisen within British Jewry in the wake of large-scale immigration from Eastern Europe: between 1880 and 1914, 240,000 Jews (many fleeing persecution) moved to Britain.[3] The religious practices of this demographic were very different from those of the native Jewish population who emphasised acculturation and respectability; their ceremonies were elaborate and impassioned, conducted in their own synagogues in a spirit of separatism. To broadly anglicized middle-class British Jewry, the Eastern European influx was 'both an embarrassment and a rebuke', while to many of the immigrants British Judaism looked like a betrayal of religious distinction.[4]

Montagu de-emphasises geographical origins to consider 'East' and 'West' as differences of 'tone and temper', the first inclined to ceremonialism and uncritical adherence to tradition, the latter towards materialism and spiritual apathy. Montagu rejects both polarised alternatives, respecting 'East End' fervour as a challenge to native Judaism's 'spiritual lethargy', but insisting that theology must progress and that ritual serve as a means not an end in itself. For Montagu, this fusion of devotional spirit and critical intellect would form the foundation of a modern Judaism which was intellectually acceptable, spiritually satisfying, and socially engaged. Montagu's distinctive concern for children's spiritual welfare is evident: 'cheder' is an elementary school which teaches the basics of Judaism and Hebrew. At this stage, her aim was not to create a schismatic movement but, as she states, an inclusive association that would revitalise religious life. Montagu established the Jewish Religious Union in 1902, but opposition from Reform and Orthodox leaders forced a schism which led to the establishment of the Liberal Reform Synagogue in 1912. Montagu went on to preach, publish and lead in the cause of Liberal Judaism, and to support the formation of Liberal synagogues in Britain and worldwide.

Notes

1 Quoted by Ellen M. Umansky in 'Lily Montagu', *Jewish Women's Archive*, https://jwa.org/encyclopedia/article/montagu-lily [accessed 24 May 2019]
2 See Umansky, 'Lily Montagu', and Michael A. Meyer, *Response to Modernity: A History of the Reform Movement in Judaism* (Detroit: Wayne State University Press, 1995), pp. 212–221.
3 Figure from David Englander, 'Anglicised Not Anglican: Jews and Judaism in Victorian Britain', in Gerald Parsons (ed.), *Religion in Victorian Britain*, vol. 1: *Traditions* (Manchester: Manchester University Press, 1988), pp. 235–273, on p. 253.
4 David Feldman, *Englishmen and Jews: Social Relations and Political Culture 1840–1914* (Yale University Press, 1994), p. 7.

27

LILY MONTAGU, 'SPIRITUAL POSSIBILITIES OF JUDAISM TODAY'

Jewish Quarterly Review, 11:2 (January 1899), pp. 216–224, 225–226, 227–228, 229–230

The history of a community, like the history of an individual, is marked by the recurrence of periods of self-consciousness and self-analysis. At such times its members consider their aggregate achievements and failures, and mark the tendencies of their corporate life. Perhaps even, the sudden recognition of facts which have been unconsciously suppressed may lead to regeneration. For many years self-consciousness has been growing among English Jews, and they have expressed, in whispers to one another, dissatisfaction with their spiritual state. It requires, however, some stirring accident like the Conference on Religious Education held in June last, and the East End meetings resulting from it, to cause an effective diagnosis to be made. Until Jews are honest enough to recognize that the majority of them are either devoted to ceremonialism at the expense of religion, or indifferent both to ceremonialism and to religion; until they have energy to examine their religious needs and courage to formulate them, they are courting comfort at the expense of truth, and they must fail to restore to Judaism its life and the endless possibilities inherent in life.

It is not enough for us to give a frightened glance of recognition at our materialism and spiritual lethargy, and then seek to draw the veil in all speed, hoping impotently that grim facts will grow less grim if left alone. We have ultimately to confess that facts cannot be thus set aside by mere desire. Moreover, these facts prove on examination to be stimulating rather than terrifying, fraught with hope rather than with negation. If I appear dogmatic in my efforts to prove my contention that Judaism has been allowed by the timid and the indifferent to lose much of its inspiring force, I can only plead in excuse the sincerity of my convictions.

I take as the objects of my criticism the two most comprehensive types of English Jews, and for purposes of convenience call them "East End Jews" and "West End Jews" respectively. It must, however, be clearly understood that these two forms of religion do not prevail exclusively in any particular district of London. Representatives of both classes may sometimes live in the same house, and may, conceivably, belong to the same family. Again, a considerable district in West Central London is largely inhabited by "East End Jews," and many "West End Jews," with their vague ineffective aspirations, crowd the neighbourhood of Bishopsgate. But these epithets are intended to convey the idea of two sets of people, differing less in dogmatic belief than in the tone and temper of their minds, and especially in their view of the proper relations between religion and life. It will also be shown that, although these two classes are to-day quite unsympathetic to one another there are many signs of a better mutual understanding among members of the younger generation; and it is chiefly upon this reunion that I base my own belief in the possibilities of the reanimation of Judaism as a religious force. In my endeavour to rouse the lethargic I may perhaps have dwelt more fully on the defects of my two "types" than on their qualities, but I have little doubt that there will be many both able and willing to make the balance more even.

The "East End Jew," whose religion is vigorous in spite of its deformities, has no confidence in the shadowy faith of the "West End Jew," and refuses to be taught by "West End" methods. Examining this distrust, I find that it arises from the recognition of the dissimilarity in the two religions. The "East End Jew" is determined to follow the worship of his fathers, and spurns the flaccid religion of his "West End" brothers. To the pious "East End Jew" religion is obedience glorified into a cult; for him, God exists as a just Law-giver, ready to forgive and help those who obey the Law, delivered by him to his people through his servant Moses, and having misfortune and failure in reserve for the rebellious and indifferent. He is continuously conscious of the "God without," whom he seeks to approach at prescribed times and seasons. Every act of obedience tends to increase the sum of his righteousness; no evil can touch him while pursuing the divine mandate. He does not consciously strive to realize the "God within," and to develop it by communion with the divine Ideal of Truth and Love existing without, for the idea of an immanent divine presence does not seem to affect his creed. When he repeats the prayers ordered by his fathers, he is less stirred by the effort of the soul to hold communion with the Infinite than by a sense of righteousness resulting from unquestioning obedience. The glow which this obedience produces, suffuses his daily life, and encourages him to persevere in his rigid observances, and to face all earthly difficulties with courage and hope. Can we wonder that the "East End Jew" regards with half-scornful fear the man who, while still calling himself "Jew," ventures to neglect the ordinances prescribed of old, and makes no apparent sacrifice in the cause of his faith? For him, prosperity seems to authorize self-indulgence and laxity of conduct.

Admitting the possibility that prejudice and ignorance render the "East End" observer unappreciative in his criticism, can we substantiate for the "West End Jew" any claim to a deeply religious life? Can we deny that in many "West End" homes, callousness takes the place which religion should occupy? Having been born Jews, and believing it more respectable to be identified with some religion, the members of the class under consideration generally belong to some synagogue, and perhaps attend the services more or less regularly. But their religion is seldom interesting, never absorbing to them. They are far more concerned in the length of the service than in its adequacy to satisfy their spiritual needs. They make no demand on their Judaism; it has no real influence over them. They either sink into materialism or create a religion of their own, based on a vague belief in the existence of a higher law, and nourished by an exacting moral sense which requires self-restraint and self-development. This religion, without an historical past and admitting of no outward embodiment, is helpful only to those individuals whose moral strength is great enough to call it into existence. The vast majority of men and women need a more definite cult to draw them to their God. The strict system of religious discipline adopted in the "East End" has much definite and salutary influence. It awakens veneration and instigates self-sacrifice; it leads to morality, sobriety and strength of purpose. It encourages kindly intercourse between men, inducing often heroic acts of charity. I only venture to criticize it, because I see it worshipped as God alone should be worshipped; because true communion with God is being shut off from man by the observances which were intended to lead man to God. Even the recent remarkable gatherings of working Jews, bent on Sabbath observance, do not allay our apprehension for the future of Judaism. While admiring the earnestness which inspired these meetings, it is to be feared that the Sabbath, instead of being desired as a day for the renewal of spiritual life, or as a stimulus to moral progress, is now required for mere physical rest and idleness, and for the complete equipment of the ritual-god, which has been fashioned so curiously and is so generally worshipped. Indeed I tremble for the future of Judaism, as I recall the words that Isaiah addresses, in the name of the Lord, to the idolaters of all ages: "Your new moons and your appointed feasts my soul hateth: they are a trouble unto me; I am weary to bear them" (Isaiah i. 14).

Between the worship of ritual prevalent in the "East End," inspiring by its intense fervour, but repelling through the materialism and intolerance which it produces, and the vague religion of the "West End," existing apparently but to satisfy a convention, there seems indeed little affinity. Yet the children of both types of Jews are united by a common need which neither form of religion is able to satisfy. For the sons of the pious "East End Jew" are also beginning to question the meaning and value of the laws which bind their fathers' lives so closely. We see them shocked by their inconsistency, and disappointed by their inadequacy; we see them drifting away from the worship which, at least in its origin, was inspiring, and, for want of some better object, devoting themselves to "self." The daughters of the pious do not even attend the synagogue services, which have begun to weary their brothers. Through force of habit they cling to the domestic side of religion, but they do not attempt to ennoble the sordid elements in their lives by trying to introduce the ideal.

Similarly, when the children of the indifferent "West End Jews" have passed the period when the example of parents is followed without question, when they begin to think for themselves, they realize that they have no religion. The majority accept, after a period of uncertainty, the conventional pretences of their parents, and adhere to them until they become inconvenient, when they cast them off altogether. Many of the young men and women have periods of intense craving for some definite faith, and would even return to the Ghetto-worship if their minds could admit its principles. Perhaps they have glimpses, which fill them with extreme joy and hope, of a revived and ennobling Judaism, which might become the guiding inspiration of their lives. A few retain these visions, and are continually cheered by them; a very few seek to realize them more closely; the many prefer to banish disquieting dreams; and in choosing for the hour peace of mind, cut off for ever real happiness—spiritual joy, the best of the gifts which God offers to his children.

In what way does the community attempt to meet the needs of its younger members, in whom the hope of Judaism in the future rests, and to stay the current of indifference which, both in the "East End" and in the "West End," is threatening its foundations? Among some of the better educated parents who are conscious of their responsibilities, there is noticeable an ominous bewilderment, when they consider what form of religious instruction they are to give to their children. If they send them to religious classes at the synagogues, or if they arrange for masters to give private instruction, the success of their efforts depends generally on the personal force and influence of the teachers. The children are further required to attend the synagogue services, but these have no hold over their growing life. As a rule, they are inattentive; and if they pray at all, it is that the prayers may speedily end. The occasional introduction of a children's sermon does not for them materially relieve the tedium of the service. A preacher who speaks to a mixed congregation of adults and children is generally self-conscious, and his words are often addressed to unresponsive minds. The children are humiliated by the seeming publicity of their faults, and irritated by the silent or whispered delight of their elders, when some pulpit rebuke is especially applicable to them.

Yet children are naturally religious.

On the other hand, the "East End" parents are not satisfied that the instruction given by the Religious Education Board and the voluntary Sabbath-class teachers is adequate to satisfy the spiritual needs of their children, and at the educational conference the fact was generally deplored that these children were still further instructed out of school hours. It is still more deplorable that these very children, who have been subjected to this elaborate religious training, who have attended school and cheder, are found, when they have ceased to be students, and even during the period of their preparation, to be conscious of no anxiety to pray, of no sense that religion renders truthfulness and self-sacrifice obligatory. With some signal exceptions, the voluntary Sabbath-class teachers consider that they satisfy the claims of religion by insisting on extreme decorum in their class, and instructing it in the recital of prayers which are not felt or understood. The children are not awed by the grandeur of God, nor drawn to him by his love. They merely repeat a weekly lesson, which has become easy through iteration, and which can awaken no spiritual joy.

The members of the Religious Education Board are, doubtless, inspired by the highest motives. They would like to adopt the "East End" religion, and to teach it in an intelligent and enlightened manner, showing that the greater part of the observances are estimable only as methods, never as objects of worship. But the members of the Board belong to the leisured classes, and seem unable to carry out their scheme by personal effort; their own religion is not the "East End" religion, and they cannot impart a fervour for what they do not feel. They depute the work to others, who conscientiously teach religion as geography and history are taught. Consequently, although their pupils come to answer intelligently, the lessons they learn are not assimilated in a manner to influence their everyday life. Religion remains a subject to be noticed at certain specified times and seasons, but has no intimate connexion with life's joys and cares.

The conditions of modern Judaism, then, from every point of view, present a grievous aspect to honest observers. In vain we seek to gloss over facts; in vain we point triumphantly to our charity-lists, to our learning, to our position in the front of every rank and profession. We yet have to confess ourselves unable to impart to our children a strengthening faith. Are we not also becoming every year more self-indulgent, more ostentatious, less reverent? Why is there a growing tendency among all classes of Jewish youth to forget the serious purposes of life, and to set the pleasures of gain, of dress, of food, of dancing, and of acting, above all else that is desirable on earth? Why do we gamble so much? Why do we grudge personal service in combating the moral evils of our day? Why is complete personal sacrifice to the needs of our poor so rare among us? Why do our philanthropists, even our ministers, forbear to introduce religion into their visiting work, unless to or about those who are about to leave this world? Why cannot we suppress the lying and deceit which flourish in our midst? Why do our friends and relatives marry out of the faith, passing among the Gentiles as freethinkers, upon whom religion has no claim? Why are the old laws, which kept the minds of our fathers in pious subservience, still preserved, seeing that here and there they require a sermon to justify their existence, and a sacrifice of truth to facilitate their observance?

The answer to these questions must be, that the highest Jewish influences are for the time being dormant, and have ceased to inspire our lives; that our belief in a supernatural law is only a verbal one, and that in spite of our professions we are stirred by no desire to prepare ourselves for a better spiritual state. Indeed, without some strong spiritual awakening, how can we hope to arrest our degenerate tendencies?

Yet, in spite of all these depressing facts, in spite of our present callousness and inertia, there is every reason for hope—for hope, glorious and infinite. If we examine our Judaism with a trusting spirit, we find that it still contains the germs of life; we find that its abiding essence is simplicity and truth. At present our thinkers are oppressed by the religious lethargy from which our age is just emerging. Only now and again a true believer appears in our midst, one who clings to his religion, and derives from it spiritual joy and a stimulus to moral progress; who sacrifices his own pleasure constantly in order to serve his fellows; who draws inspiration at all times from God and from his creations, because *his* Judaism impels it. The problem before us is how to restore confidence to our thinkers, and to encourage them to free our religion from the earth which is clogging it, and to allow it to spread and to stimulate the lives of all generations. There is only one method by which we can hope to achieve these ends. *That method is association.* [...]

It is only by association that we can effectually enunciate the principle, that we are required to use in God's service all the gifts of mind and heart which he has granted to us, since it is a form of blasphemy to conceal or to pervert truth, in order to render our service of God acceptable to him. We, who are conscious of our great needs, must organize ourselves into an association to rediscover our Judaism, encouraging one another to reformulate our ideal. We shall be able to rally round us the discontented and weary, and together we may hope to lift Judaism from its desolate position and absorb it into our lives. Together we must sift with all reverence the pure from the impure in the laws which our ancestors formulated in order to satisfy the needs of their age, and refuse to resort to hair-splitting argument in order to reestablish a religion which was originally founded on a basis of truth, dignity and beauty. We must no longer grimly reiterate the fact that Judaism has ceased to appeal to us, and lack the energy to inquire into the cause of its degeneration. We must boldly follow Isaiah, Jeremiah and Ezekiel, and allow a place to progress in religious thought. Yet, at the outset of our search, we shall be persuaded that only the elect among us can worship at the "Fount of Inspiration" without some assistance in the form of a ritualistic system, and that the perpetuation of Judaism therefore requires the maintenance of certain ceremonial observances. For the essence of a religion cannot be transmitted in all its simplicity to a child, whose mind cannot conceive an abstraction, and a certain discipline of observance is essential to character-training. We can only combat our tendency to self-indulgence and to spiritual sloth by having fasts and holydays reserved for communion with God. Inspired by a natural desire to examine with all tenderness the possessions which our fathers preserved with so much courage and devotion, we shall probably find treasures of beauty and truth where we had expected deformity and deception. We shall then be able to assign to observances, which had been worshipped as the end, their proper place and function as means for the attainment of holiness. [...]

I have suggested the organization of an associated band of worshippers, bound together by the tenets of a living Judaism. It is possible to attempt a slight forecast of the lines on which such an association may work and its more immediate results. We may hope for the gradual abandonment of gambling and other vicious pleasures, the desire for a more simple life animated by love of truth and of piety, and an increase in the number and devotion of those who are ready to devote themselves to preventive rather than curative social work, and who would attempt relief by moral stimuli, as well as by material props. The present is the right hour, and England is the fit place for the initiation of this movement, which may restore to Judaism its glory.

In England Jews can freely develop all their powers, and follow, unquestioned, their ideals. If, then, the English Jews are better able than most of their continental brothers to recognize the potentiality of their spiritual inheritance, the obligation rests imperatively upon them to formulate its meaning and render it intelligible. By continuing to follow mechanically a religion which they have not the energy to revive, by maintaining tenets which jar on their sense of truth, they are neglecting their most urgent duties, and rendering themselves for ever unfit to serve their brothers. For we English Jews owe a duty to our less fortunate co-religionists, who are still suffering from the effects of persecution. In some countries we find Jews who have been denied the advantages of education, for whom persecution has tightened the spiritual bonds by causing them to build up a wall of observance effectually shutting out God's light. They are dimly conscious of a glorious inheritance transmitted to them by their fathers, and threatened by cruel and impious strangers. Too fearful to examine the nature of this inheritance, and to discover that its qualities defy the art of thieves, they fence it with rows of bulwarks constructed with pious ingenuity. Holy is the aim of the persecuted; there is no schism or rebellion in their midst; they do not understand that their service has been gradually diverted from the Giver of all good to the ritual gods, who were originally raised on high for the purpose of his defence. But when persecution ceases, and men are freed from its effects, they will examine the nature of the ritual gods they have served so conscientiously. A revulsion of feeling, a horror at their long idolatry may follow; tradition may lose its purifying hold over their minds, and they may yield themselves up to licence, and call it intellectual emancipation. It is possible for us in England to avert this catastrophe. At the moment when our persecuted brethren are in their greatest need, when they realize the hollowness of their worship, they may be saved from spiritual anarchy if they see among us a religion comprising all that was valuable and lovely in the ancient faith, embodied in forms acceptable to emancipated minds. [...]

Surely we English Jews can have no excuse for continued indifference and waiting. To us the call is clear and unmistakable. For our own sakes we must revive Judaism, and having reconciled its dogma with our highest conception of truth and beauty, allow it again to bind us to the God who cares for us. In order to answer the challenge of the "East End Jew," we must prove that our faith is no longer comatose, that we are truly striving after an ideal, and that we are ready to make any sacrifice that our religion may claim. For the sake of our foreign brothers, whose eyes are blinded by present misery from seeing the light which is within their reach, we English Jews must unite to strengthen our faith and proclaim the infinite hope contained within it.

There is everything to fear for the future of Judaism, until it can be accepted by the most enlightened among us. Better to have died in the Ghetto than to have outlived the possibilities of our religion. But surely there is no need for despair seeing that a broader and more beautiful worship, which will grow in intensity, as the needs of a more developed civilization become greater, can even now be dimly foreshadowed.

Part 8

RELIGIOUS TRADITIONS FROM ASIA

8.1

Hinduism

8.1 Hinduism

While there was no settled Hindu community in Britain during the nineteenth century, Hinduism influenced the religious landscape chiefly through the work of the pioneering Bengali intellectual and reformer, Rammohun Roy. Rammohun (1772–1833), who has been called the father of modern Hinduism, believed Hinduism to be at heart monotheistic, but corrupted in popular polytheistic and pagan practice. In Calcutta in 1823 Rammohun established a universalist theistic society which developed into the Brahmo Samaj, a monotheistic and socially progressive reform movement that had considerable impact on India's political elite, although it remained esoteric in relation to majority Hindu practice. Rammohun gained celebrity in Britain during the 1820s and 1830s, where he was feted on his three-year lecture tour especially by Unitarians with whom he had 'remarkable ideological kinship' in their shared commitment to rational religion and a social gospel.[1] After his unexpected death in 1833, Rammohun's tomb near Bristol became a site of pilgrimage for dozens of Brahmos throughout the remainder of the nineteenth century and well into the twentieth.[2]

Rammohun's *Abridgement of the Vedant* was his first publication in English (Calcutta, 1816 and London, 1817) and illustrates his claim that the earliest Hindu scriptures were monotheistic. In his introduction, he honours Byas (Vyasa), legendary author of some of the most important scriptures in Hindu tradition and 'divider' of the Veda. In his abridged translation, Rammohun concerns himself with the Vedant, the conclusion of the Veda and its most philosophical portion. The opening section extracted here establishes God as intelligent first cause, independent of all the objects and personages which scripture appears in a superficial sense to deify. But this sacralising language Rammohun interprets as a metaphorical expression of divine omnipresence, passionately opposing what he regards as vulgar 'corruptions' of pure Hinduism. Morality is presented as integral to worship, in terms of enlightened self-interest: righteous living brings its own rewards. Dramatically, the caste-inflected rules and rites which for many made it impossible to be a Hindu outside of India are declared entirely optional: 'Devotion to the Supreme Being is not limited to any holy place or sacred country.' In all this, Rammohun presents faith as a matter of reason rather than of intuition or cultural habit. As he notes in the preface, his aim was to reform ritualistic Hinduism, but also to deter Christian missionaries by showing that India had its own answer to local superstition. The work was well received in Britain and Germany where it fed the cause of religious universalism; this version is from a republication of Rammohun Roy's works edited by Jogendra Chunder Ghose, an Indian Hindu lawyer. (Note: a lengthy explanatory footnote is omitted).

The subsequent extracts demonstrate conflicting British and Indian responses to the heated issue of whether Rammohun was more Christian than Hindu. Many British Unitarians claimed him as one of their own, taking his unitarian exposition of the gospels (*Precepts of Jesus*, 1823) and his three 'Appeals' in response to opponents to prove his conversion. But there is no evidence to suggest that he abandoned all Hindu rites. His affinity with Unitarian Christians can be attributed to his skilful ability to 'localize' his core religious ideas 'by situating them within the linguistic and cultural horizons' of the audience with whom he was in dialogue.[3]

The poem by Miss Acland (unidentified) is one of several eulogies in Mary Carpenter's memorial volume by Unitarian women writers whose hero-worship was perhaps partly due to Rammohun's prominent support of women's rights in his native Bengal on matters including education, child marriage, and his influence in having the practice of *sati* banned in 1829. The poem celebrates Rammohun as an international prophet of religious universalism. However, a discourse of Christian superiority dominates the final three stanzas, which imply that while Rammohun was *for* India, he was not truly *of* it. Acland prophesies the completion of Rammohun's mission to lead India's 'children' out of their 'pagan night' by their future development of 'Christian sympathies' under the warmth and light shed by the 'Sun of Righteousness' (Malachi 4:2).

This Christian appropriation of Rammohun is explicitly challenged by the reviewer Kissory Chand Mittra (1822–1873), a Bengali author and journalist writing for the 1866 *Calcutta Review*. He insists that Rammohun's vision was 'pure monotheism', and that he judged all faith systems equally for their capacity to lead devotees to the divine absolute, working to remove the elements that obscured that ideal. The inclusion of this piece in the 1915 Calcutta edition of Carpenter's memoir suggests an agenda to decolonise Rammohun on the part of the Brahmo Samaj who were by then aligned with rising Indian nationalism.

Notes

1 David Kopf, *The Brahmo Samaj and the Shaping of the Modern Indian Mind* (Princeton: Princeton University Press, 1979), p. 11.
2 See appendix containing the list of visitors to Rammohun's tomb in Mary Carpenter (ed.), *The Last Days in England of Rajah Rammohun Roy*, revd edn (Calcutta: Rammohun Roy Library, 1915).
3 Lynn Zastoupil, 'Defining Christians, Making Britons: Rammohun Roy and the Unitarians', *Victorian Studies* (2002), pp. 215–243, on p. 222.

28

RAMMOHUN ROY, *TRANSLATION OF AN ABRIDGEMENT OF THE VEDANT, OR, A RESOLUTION OF ALL THE VEDS* [1817]

In *The English Works of Raja Ram Mohun Roy*, ed. Jogendra Chunder Ghose, 2 vols (Calcutta, 1885–1887), vol. 1, pp. 3–18 [abridged]

To
The Believers of the Only True God

The greater part of Brahmins, as well as of other sects of Hindoos, are quite incapable of justifying that idolatry which they continue to practise. When questioned on the subject, in place of adducing reasonable arguments in support of their conduct, they conceive it fully sufficient to quote their ancestors as positive authorities! And some of them are become very ill-disposed towards me, because I have forsaken idolatry for the worship of the true and eternal God! In order, therefore, to vindicate my own faith and that of our early forefathers, I have been endeavouring, for some time past, to convince my countrymen of the true meaning of our sacred books; and to prove, that my aberration deserves not the opprobrium which some unreflecting persons have been so ready to throw upon me.

    The whole body of the Hindoo Theology, Law, and Literature, is contained in the Veds, which are affirmed to be coeval with the creation! These works are extremely voluminous, and being written in the most elevated and metaphorical style are, as may be well supposed, in many passages seemingly confused and contradictory. Upwards of two thousand years ago, the great Byas, reflecting on the perpetual difficulty arising from these sources, composed with great discrimination a complete and compendious abstract of the whole, and also reconciled those texts which appeared to stand at variance. This work he termed *The Vedant*, which, compounded of two Sungscrit words, signifies *The Resolution of all the Veds*. It has continued to be most highly revered by all Hindoos, and in place of the more diffuse arguments of the Veds, is always referred to as equal authority. But from its being concealed within the dark curtain of the Sungscrit language, and the Brahmins permitting themselves alone to interpret, or even to touch any book of the kind, the Vedant, although perpetually quoted, is little known to the public: and the practice of few Hindoos indeed bears the least accordance with its precepts!

In pursuance of my vindication, I have to the best of my abilities translated this hitherto unknown work, as well as an abridgment thereof, into the Hindoostanee and Bengalee languages, and distributed them, free of cost, among my own countrymen, as widely as circumstances have possibly allowed. The present is an endeavour to render an abridgment of the same into English, by which I expect to prove to my European friends, that the superstitious practices which deform the Hindoo religion have nothing to do with the pure spirit of its dictates! [...]

My constant reflections on the inconvenient, or rather injurious rites, introduced by the peculiar practice of Hindoo idolatry, which, more than any other pagan worship, destroys the texture of society, together with compassion for my countrymen, have compelled me to use every possible effort to awaken them from their dream of error: and by making them acquainted with their scriptures, enable them to contemplate with true devotion the unity and omnipresence of Nature's God.

Abridgement of the Vedant

The illustrious Byas, in his celebrated work, the Vedant, insinuates in the first text, that it is absolutely necessary for mankind to acquire knowledge respecting the Supreme Being, who is the subject of discourse in all the Veds, and the Vedant, as well as in the other Systems of Theology. But he found, from the following passages of the Veds, that this inquiry is limited to very narrow bounds, *viz.* "The Supreme Being is not comprehensible by vision, or by any other of the organs of sense; nor can he be conceived by means of devotion, or virtuous practices!" (Munduc). "He sees every thing, though never seen; hears every thing, though never directly heard of! He is neither short, nor is he long; (Brih'darunnuc); inaccessible to the reasoning faculty; not to be compassed by description; beyond the limits of the explanation of the Ved, or of human conception!" (Cuthubulli). Byas, also, from the result of various arguments coinciding with the Ved, found that the accurate and positive knowledge of the Supreme Being is not within the boundary of comprehension; *i. e.* that *what,* and *how,* the Supreme Being is, cannot be definitely ascertained. He has therefore, in the second text, explained the Supreme Being by his effects and works, without attempting to define his essence; in like manner as we, not knowing the real nature of the sun, explain him to be the cause of the succession of days and epochs. He by whom the birth, "existence, and annihilation of the world is regulated, is the Supreme Being!" We see the multifarious, wonderful universe, as well as the birth, existence, and annihilation, of its different parts; hence, we naturally infer the existence of a being who regulates the whole, and call him the Supreme: in the same manner as from the sight of a pot, we conclude the existence of its artificer. The Ved, in like manner, declares the Supreme Being thus: "He from whom the universal world proceeds, who is the Lord of the Universe, and whose work is the universe, is the Supreme Being!" (Taittureeu).

The *Ved* is not supposed to be an eternal Being, though sometimes dignified with such an epithet; because its being created by the Supreme Being is declared in the same Ved thus: "All the texts and parts of the Ved were created:" and also in the third text of the Vedant, God is declared to be the cause of all the Veds.

The *void Space* is not conceived to be the independent cause of the world, notwithstanding the following declaration of the Ved, "The world proceeds from the void space" (Chhandoggu); for the Ved again declares, "By the Supreme Being the void space was produced." And the Vedant says: "As the Supreme Being is evidently declared in the Ved to be the cause of the void Space, Air, and Fire, neither of them can be supposed to be the independent cause of the universe" (14th text, 4th section, 1st chapter).

Neither is *Air* allowed to be the Lord of the Universe, although the Ved says in one instance, "In Air every existing creature is absorbed;" for the Ved again affirms, that "Breath, the intellectual power, all the internal and external senses, the void Space, Air, Light, Water, and the extensive Earth, proceeded from the Supreme Being!" The Vedant also says: "God is meant by the following text of the Ved, as a Being "more extensive than all the extension of Space" (8th, 3rd, 1st); *viz.* "*That* breath is greater than the extension of Space in all directions," as it occurs in the Ved, after the discourse concerning common breath is concluded.

Light, of whatever description, is not inferred to be the Lord of the Universe, from the following assertion of the Ved: "The pure Light of all Lights is the Lord of all creatures;" for the Ved again declares, that "The sun and all others imitate God, and borrow their light from him" (Moonduc); and the same declaration is found in the Vedant (22nd, 3rd, 1st).

Neither can *Nature* be construed by the following texts of the Ved, to be the independent cause of the world: *viz.* "Man having known *that* Nature which is an eternal being, without a beginning or an end, is delivered from the grasp of death!" and, "Nature operates herself!" because the Ved affirms that "No being is superior or equal to God!" (Cuthu) and the Ved commands, "Know God alone!" (Moonduc) and the Vedant thus declares: "Nature is not the Creator of the world, not being represented so by the Ved," for it expressly says, "God has by his sight created the Universe" (5th, 1st, 1st). Nature is an insensible Being, she is, therefore, void of sight or intention, and consequently unable to create the regular world (Cuthu).

Atoms are not supposed to be the cause of the world, notwithstanding the following declaration: "This (Creator) is the most minute Being." Because an atom is an insensible particle, and from the above authority it is proved, that no Being void of understanding can be the author of a system so skilfully arranged.

The *Soul* cannot be inferred from the following texts to be the Lord of the Universe, nor the independent Ruler of the intellectual powers; *viz.* "The Soul being joined to the resplendent Being, enjoys by itself," "God and the Soul enter the small void space of the heart;" because the Ved declares that "He (God) resides in the Soul as its Ruler," and that "The Soul being joined to the gracious Being, enjoys happiness" (20th, 2nd, 1st). The Vedant also says, "The sentient soul is not understood to reside as ruler in the Earth, because in both texts of the Ved it is differently declared from that Being who rules the Earth:" *viz.* "He (God) resides in the faculty of the understanding," and "He, who resides in the Soul, &c."

No *God* or *Goddess of the Earth* can be meant by the following text, as the ruler of the Earth, *viz.* "He who resides in the Earth, and is distinct from the Earth, and whom the Earth does not know," &c.: because the Ved affirms that, "This (God alone) is the ruler of internal sense, and is the eternal Being" (Brih'darunnuc); and the same is asserted in the Vedant (18th, 2nd, 1st).

By the text which begins with the following sentence: *viz.* "This is the Sun," and by several other texts testifying the dignity of the sun, he is not supposed to be the original cause of the universe, because the Ved declares, that "He who resides in the Sun (as his Lord) is distinct from the Sun" (Brih'darunnuc), and the Vedant declares the same (21st, 1st, 1st).

In like manner none of the celestial Gods can be inferred from the various assertions of the Ved, respecting their deities respectively, to be the independent cause of the Universe; because the Ved repeatedly affirms, that "All the Veds prove "nothing but the unity of the Supreme Being." By allowing the Divinity more than one Being, the following positive affirmations of the Ved, relative to the unity of God, become false and absurd: "God is indeed one and has no second" (Cuthu). "There is none but the Supreme Being possessed of universal knowledge" (Brih'darunnuc). "He who is without any figure, and beyond the limit of description, is the Supreme Being" (Chhandoggu). "Appellations and figures of all kinds are innovations." And from the authority of many other texts it is evident that any being that bears figure, and is subject to description, cannot be the eternal independent cause of the universe.

The Veds not only call the celestial representations Deities, but also in many instances give the divine epithet to the mind, diet, void space, quadruped animal, slaves, and flymen: [...] but [...] neither any of the celestial Gods, nor any existing creature, should be considered the Lord of the Universe, because the third chapter of the Vedant explains the reason for these secondary assertions thus: "By these appellations of the Ved which denote the diffusive spirit of the Supreme Being equally over all creatures by means of extension, his omnipresence is established" (Monduc): so the Ved says, "All that exists is indeed God," *i. e.* nothing bears true existence excepting God, "and whatever we smell or taste is the Supreme Being," *i. e.* the existence of whatever thing that appears to us relies on the existence of God (Chhandoggu). It is indisputably evident that none of these metaphorical representations, which arise from the elevated style in which all the Veds are written, were designed to be viewed in any other light than mere allegory. Should individuals be acknowledged to be separate deities, there would be a necessity for acknowledging many independent creators of the world, which is directly contrary to common sense, and to the repeated authority of the Ved. [...]

The fourteenth text of the second sect. of the third chapter of the Vedant declares, "It being directly represented by the Ved, that the Supreme Being bears no figure nor form;" and the following texts of the Ved assert the same, *viz*. "The true Being was before all" (Chhandoggu). "The Supreme Being has no feet, but extends everywhere; has no hands, yet holds every thing; has no eyes, yet sees all that is; has no ears, yet hears every thing that passes." "His existence had no cause." "He is the smallest of the small, and the greatest of the great: and yet is, in fact, neither small nor great!" [...]

Some celestial Gods have, in different instances, declared themselves to be independent deities, and also the object of worship; but these declarations were owing to their thoughts being abstracted from themselves and their being entirely absorbed in divine reflection. The Vedant declares: "This exhortation of Indru (or the god of atmosphere) respecting his divinity, to be indeed agreeable to the authorities of the Ved;" that is, "Every one, on having lost all self-consideration in consequence of being united with divine reflection, may speak as assuming to be the Supreme Being; like Bamdev (a celebrated Brahmun) who, in consequence of such self-forgetfulness, declared himself to have created the Sun, and Munoo the next person to Brahma" (30th, 1st, 1st). It is therefore optional with every one of the celestial Gods, as well as with every individual, to consider himself as God, under this state of self-forgetfulness and unity with the divine reflection, as the Ved says, "you are that true Being" (when you lose all self-consideration), and "O God I am nothing but you." The sacred commentators have made the same observation, *viz*. "I am nothing but true Being, and am pure Understanding, full of eternal happiness, and am by nature free from wordly effects." But in consequence of this reflection, none of them can be acknowledged to be the cause of the universe or the object of adoration. [...]

The Vedant shews that moral principle is a part of the adoration of God, *viz*. "A command over our passions and over the external senses of the body and good acts, are declared by the Ved to be indispensable in the mind's approximation to God, they should therefore be strictly taken care of, and attended to, both previously and subsequently to such approximation to the Supreme Being" (27th, 4th, 3rd); *i. e.* we should not indulge our evil propensities, but should endeavour to have entire control over them. Reliance on, and self-resignation to, the only true Being, with an aversion to worldly considerations, are included in the good acts above alluded to. The adoration of the Supreme Being produces eternal beatitude, as well as all desired advantages; as the Vedant declares: "It is the firm opinion of Byas that from devotion to God all the desired consequences proceed" (1st, 4th, 3rd); and it is thus often represented by the Ved, "He who is desirous of prospertity should worship the Supreme Being" (Monduc). [...]

It is optional to those who have faith in God alone, to observe and attend to the rules and rites prescribed by the Ved, applicable to the different classes of Hindoos, and to their different religious orders respectively. But in case of the true believers neglecting those rites, they are not liable to any blame whatever; as the Vedant says, "Before acquiring the true knowledge of God, it is proper for man to attend to the laws and rules laid down by the Ved for different classes, according to their different professions; because the Ved declares the performance of these rules to be the cause of the mind's purification, and its faith in God, and compares it with a saddle-horse, which helps a man to arrive at the wished-for goal" (36th, 4th, 3rd). And the Vedant also says, that "Man may acquire the true knowledge of God even without observing the rules and rites prescribed by the Ved for each class of Hindoos, as it is found in the Ved that many persons who had neglected the performance of the Brahminical rites and ceremonies, owing to their perpetual attention to the adoration of the Supreme Being, acquired the true knowledge respecting the Deity" (36th, 4th, 3rd). The Vedant again more clearly states that, "It is equally found in the Ved that some people, though they had their entire faith in God alone, yet performed both the worship of God and the ceremonies prescribed by the Ved; and that some others neglected them, and merely worshipped God" (9th, 4th, 3rd). [...]

Notwithstanding it is optional with those who have their faith in the only God, to attend to the prescribed ceremonies or to neglect them entirely, the Vedant prefers the former to the latter, because the Ved says that attendance to the religious ceremonies conduces to the attainment of the Supreme Being. [...]

Devotion to the Supreme Being is not limited to any holy place or sacred country, as the Vedant says, "In any place wherein the mind feels itself undisturbed, men should worship God; because no specific authority for the choice of any particular place of worship is found in the Ved," which declares, "In any place which renders the mind easy, man should adore God" (11th, 1st, 4th).

29

MISS ACLAND, 'THE RAJAH'S TOMB'

In Mary Carpenter (ed.), *The Last Days in England of Rajah Rammohun Roy* (London: Trubner & Co., 1866), pp. 176–177

THIS is the spot! There needs no sculptured line;
    No column marks the Rajah's lonely tomb;
But shadowing elms their drooping boughs incline,
    And shroud his cold remains in sacred gloom.

Yes; far from Ganges' consecrated wave,
    Beneath our pallid groves, and northern skies,
A stranger's hand hath laid thee in thy grave,
    And strangers' tears have wept thine obsequies.

A stranger? No; thy "caste" was human kind;
    Thy home—wherever Freedom's beacon shone;
And England's noblest hearts exulting shrined
    The turbaned offspring of a burning zone.

Pure generous mind! all that was just and true,—
    All that was lovely, holiest, brightest, best—
Kindled thy soul of eloquence anew,
    And woke responsive chords in every breast.

Sons of the western main around thee hung,
    While Indian lips unfolded Freedom's laws,
And grateful woman heard the Brahmin's tongue
    Proclaim her worth, and plead her widowed cause.

Ah! why did Fortune dash, with bitter doom,
    That cup of high communion from thine hand,
And scatter, darkly withering o'er the tomb,
    The blessings gathered for thy native land?

Be hushed our murmurs! He whose voice had won
    Thee, heav'n bound trav'ler, forth from Pagan night,
In mercy called the trusting spirit on,
    And bade it dwell with Uncreated Light.

Perchance when o'er thy loved paternal bower,
    The Sun of Righteousness shall healing rise,—
When India's children feel his noon-day power,
    And mingle all in Christian sympathies,—

Hither their pilgrim footsteps duly bound,
    With fervent zeal, these hallowed haunts shall trace,
And sweetly solemn tears bedew the ground
    Where sleeps the friend and prophet of their race!

30

KISSORY CHAND MITTRA, 'THE LAST DAYS IN ENGLAND OF RAJAH RAMMOHUN ROY' [1866]

In Mary Carpenter (ed.), *The Last Days in England of Rajah Rammohun Roy*, revd edn (Calcutta: Rammohun Roy Library, 1915), pp. 253–255

We are free to confess that from his attendance at their chapels, and his known bias to their doctrines, the Unitarian Christians of England had some sort of right to claim him as a co-religionist. In the same manner the special patronage, which he thought proper to bestow on Vedantism, made it more than probable that he was a Vedantist. The laudatory terms, in which he was accustomed to speak of the doctrines of Mahomet, were calculated to produce an impression that he was a believer in the Koran. But it would be waste of time to argue that he was not a Mahomedan. Neither was he a Unitarian Christian, as the testimony of Dr Carpenter himself already quoted, proves, that while in London, although he attended the Unitarian chapels, yet *it was his system to avoid so far identifying himself with any religious body as to make himself answerable for their acts and opinions.* We would go further and say, though it may startle and scarify the Brahmos of the old *régime*, that he was not a Vedantist. In truth, all speculation to his belief in any religion founded on his advocacy of certain doctrines inculcated by it, or his attendance at its place of worship are obviously futile. Rammohun Roy was essentially a Theist. He was, as we observed in the pages of this *Review* more than twenty years ago, a religious Benthamite, and estimated the different creeds existing in the world, not according to his notion of their truth, or falsehood, but by his notion of their utility; according to their tendency, in his view, to promote the maximization of human happiness, and the minimization of human misery. His patronage, therfere, of any system of creed cannot be construed into a profession of it. He endeavoured to refine all gross and idolatrous systems into a system of pure monotheism. Clear, subtle, daring and deep, he aimed at revolutionizing the religious world. Endowed with the faculty of generalization and animated by an earnest desire to sift and proclaim the truth, he had critically studied the Bible, the

Koran, and the Vedas. He had arrived at the conclusion that the Vedas inculcated pure monotheism, and the idolatry practised by his countrymen was a corruption of the ancient faith. He had publicly renounced that idolatry and declared it his mission to exterminate it, and to resuscitate the primitive and rational religion of the Vedas. He had learnt to appreciate the code of morality inculcated in the Bible, as the purest and loftiest; and he had done his best to expound and promulgate it to his countrymen. His three Appeals to the Christian Public, his Exposition of the Upanishads, and his Persian work *Tohufutal Mowahedeen* attest the consummate ability and unwearying zeal, with which he enforced monotheism as the substratum of the three principal religious systems of the world. His great object was to engraft a kind of universal Unitarianism on the prevailing religion of the country. But we have said that he was not a Unitarian, his Unitarianism was essentially different from that of the Channings and the Carpenters, the Priestleys and the Parkers. His was a sort of Catholic Unitarianism. It was philosophical theism. It was Natural Religion, which so many philosophers of ancient Greece and Rome followed. His advocacy and support of the cardinal doctrines inculcated by different religions, though it might apparently evince his vacillation, was in truth the result of Utilitarianism. But while he advocated the monotheistic principles of the Bible, the Vedas, and the Koran, he spared no system of idolatry. With a moral courage, rarely to be met with among Hindu reformers, he denounced the idolatrous prejudices of Hinduism, Mahomedanism, and Christianity with merciless, but impartial, severity.

This uncompromising and unsparing iconoclast while striving to eliminate superstition and hero-worship from the religious systems he had studied, failed not to extract from them the simple and saving truths of monotheism.

8.2

Zoroastrianism

8.2 Zoroastrianism

Zoroastrianism was brought to Britain by members of the Parsi ethnic group from India, perhaps as early as the eighteenth century, but arriving in larger numbers in the second half of the nineteenth century for business and educational purposes. By 1861 the Parsi community in London was sufficiently large and wealthy to establish the Zoroastrian Association, a House of Prayer and a cemetery. Dadabhai Naoroji (1825–1917) had two careers on his long stays in Britain, first in commerce and then politics, becoming the first Indian MP to serve in the British Parliament as Liberal representative for Central Finsbury, London, 1892–5. Naoroji encouraged the welfare of the Zoroastrian community in Britain, serving as President of the Zoroastrian Association from 1861 to 1907, and assiduously educating the British public about Parsi values and way of life.[1] The extract is taken from a lecture he gave to the Liverpool Literary and Philosophical Society when on business in the city in 1861.

Like Hinduism, Zoroastrianism in its traditional form was not easily isolable as a body of ideas separate from collective cultural practice, having a complex system of purity laws for domestic and communal life. The role of priests was largely ritualistic: it was only in the second half of the nineteenth century that attempts were made to codify Parsi theology as such, first by French and German orientalist scholars fascinated by the world's earliest religion, and subsequently by Parsis who themselves drew much on this European research. These works all tended to 'internalize the Protestant value-system' by diminishing the importance of ceremony and interpreting Zoroaster as a prophet of ethical monotheism.[2] This can be contrasted with Friedrich Nietzsche's celebration of Zoroaster's unsystematic pagan sensibility in *Thus Spake Zarathustra*, 1883–1885. For strategic reasons also, Parsi authors aspiring to public office were keen to engender an image of their faith as one suited to modern life.

Naoroji's work was written without the aid of European scholarship, and comprises a translation of a catechistic dialogue written in the early nineteenth century in order to counter (it seems) Christian mission, followed by some extracts from the Zend Avesta, the primary Zoroastrian scriptures, interlaced with commentary. Naoroji presents his theological inexpertise as a sign of the current state of Parsi religion, but positions himself as one of a reforming generation seeking to increase the faith's intellectual coherence and moral content. The lecture works to deconstruct several popular myths about Zoroastrianism: its excessive ritualism, priestcraft and pagan veneration of objects (above all, fire), and its dualism regarding the equality of good and evil with its consequent denial of original sin and of divine omnipotence – criticisms all made for example in John Wilson's 1843 *The Parsi Religion*.

After Naoroji's brief attack on priestly ignorance and empty ceremonialism, the catechism firmly distinguishes creator from creation by classifying venerated objects (such as the elements and celestial bodies) as representations, not embodiments, of the divine. Parenthetic insertions are either original to the catechism, or Naoroji's additions, and the asterisks imply his omissions. Naoroji later counters accusations of fire worship with some care. To reinforce the point, he points out that Zoroastrianism was a philosophical advance on the paganism which formerly prevailed in Persia, where Zoroastrianism originated. The summary of religious requirements emphasises the moral above the ritualistic, with superstition listed in the sins to avoid, and an insistence that judgement will be based on an individual's deeds and misdeeds – '[t]here is no saviour' to provide a get-out clause. This allusion to atonement doctrine suggests that the catechist is equipping the respondent to defend Zoroastrianism's ethical coherence as greater than Christianity's – an act of cultural self-preservation in the colonial context.

The extracts given from the Zend Avesta, accessed by Naoroji via a Gujerati translation, further emphasise Zoroastrianism as a form of ethical monotheism that was separable from its system of purity rites, although many Zoroastrians would certainly not have concurred with this view. The case is presented against dualism, Naoroji citing scripture's insistence on the final defeat of evil and triumph of good. His conclusion shows the tension between modernisers who want to place Zoroastrianism on a level with other world monotheisms, and traditionalists for whom faith was inseparable from a specific cultural environment and collective practice.

Notes

1 Rozina Visram, *Ayahs, Lascars and Princes: Indians in Britain 1700–1947* (London: Pluto Press, 1986), pp. 78–92.
2 John R. Hinnells, *Zoroastrians in Britain* (Oxford: Clarendon Press, 1996), pp. 69–70; Dosabhai Framji Karaka, *History of the Parsees including their Manners, Customs, Religion and Present Position*, 2 vols (London: Macmillan and Co., 1884), vol. 2, p. 209.

31

DADABHAI NAOROJI, *THE PARSEE RELIGION*

(Liverpool: [n.p.], 1861),
pp. 1–6, 7–9, 20–21, 23–26, 26–27

I will first give some account of the present state of the knowledge of the Parsees about their religion. The priests are a separate caste, and the priesthood is thus hereditary. As a body, the priests are not only ignorant of the duties and objects of their own profession, but are entirely uneducated, except that they are able to read and write, and that, also, often very imperfectly. To read and write they must learn, as they have to prepare by rote a large number of prayers and recitations, which, in the performance of their usual avocations, they are required to recite. Their work chiefly consists of reciting certain prescribed prayers on various religious occasions; to go to the fire-temple or sea-shore, and say a prayer for anybody that chooses to give a halfpenny; and to depend upon charities distributed on various joyous or mournful occasions. They do not understand a single word of these prayers or recitations, which are all in the old Zend language.

From the state of their education and knowledge, they are quite unfit for the pulpit; nor do they aspire to it, or seem to have any notion of the necessity of such teaching. The Parsees have, therefore, no pulpit at present. Far from being the teachers of the true doctrines and duties of their religion, the priests are generally the most bigoted and superstitious, and exercise much injurious influence over the women especially, who, until lately, received, no education at all.

The priests have, however, now begun to feel their degraded position. Many of them, if they can do so, bring up their sons in any other profession but their own. There are, perhaps, a dozen, among the whole body of professional priests, who lay claim to a knowledge of the Zend Avestá, the religious books of the Parsees; but the only respect in which they are superior to their brethren is, that they have learnt the meanings of words of the books as they are taught, without knowing the language, either philologically or grammatically. They have been taught certain meanings for certain words, and they stick to them as a matter of course. I doubt much whether any one of them has a clear notion of what grammar is, and as to a liberal education, they never had it, and do not, in consequence, understand the necessity of it.

Such being the state of knowledge of the religious guides and teachers among the Parsees, it may be easily conceived what could be expected from a layman.

The whole religious education of a Parsee's child consists in preparing by rote a certain number of prayers in Zend, without understanding a word of them; the knowledge of the doctrines of their religion being left to be picked up from casual conversation. Under these circumstances, a Parsee has not much opportunity of knowing what his creed really is; the translation, besides, of the Zend books, in the present vernacular of the Parsees, being of very recent date. But, unfortunately, this translation is a constant subject of dispute among the dozen would-be learned priests alluded to before. This shameful want of the means of religious education, and its slight extent among the Parsee children, have of late attracted the attention of the community, and efforts are being made to supply the deficiency.

In my ignorance of the Zend language, I cannot do more than depend upon this translation, though considered to be somewhat imperfect. But, for the purposes of a paper like this, the object of which is to give a general outline of the doctrines of the Parsee religion, I think these materials will suffice.

The traditional number of the books of the Zend Avestá is twenty-one, of which there are only three extant, and parts of two more, viz., the Yazashné, the Vandidád, and the Khordeh Avestá, and a part of the Visparad, and Vistásp Nusk.

There is a dialogue, in the vernacular, appended to the Khordeh Avestá (small Avestá), which, I think, gives a sufficiently accurate outline of the present belief of nearly the whole of the orthodox body. I do not know of a certainty who its author is. It has been composed more than a quarter of a century ago, when English ideas and education had not made much progress; and is, therefore, I think, the more valuable, as a faithful representation of the belief of the general mass.

The Khordeh Avestá is a collection of prayers addressed to God and several angels, and it is some of these prayers, the preparation of which by rote, forms the staple of the religious education of the Parsee child. At the end of this book is appended the dialogue, in the vernacular; and intelligent priests, masters, and parents, that could read, welcomed this aid, imperfect though it is, and a little irrelevant.

The subject of the dialogue is thus described:—

"A few questions and answers to acquaint the children of the holy Zarthosti community with the subject of the Mazdiashná religion (*i. e.*, of the worship of God). Dialogue between a Zarthosti master and pupil:—

Ques. Whom do we, of the Zarthosti community, believe in?

Ans. We believe in only one God, and do not believe in any besides him.

Ques. Who is that one God?

Ans. The God who created the heavens, the earth, the angels, the stars, the sun, the moon, the fire, the water, or all the four elements, and all things of the two worlds; that God we believe in—Him we worship, Him we invoke, and Him we adore.

Ques. Do we not believe in any other God?

Ans. Whoever believes in any other God but this is an infidel, and shall suffer the punishment of hell.

Ques. What is the form of our God?

Ans. Our God has neither face nor form, colour nor shape, nor fixed place. There is no other like Him; he is Himself singly such a glory that we cannot praise or describe Him; nor our mind comprehend Him.

Ques. Is there any such thing that God even cannot create?

Ans. Yes; there is one thing which God himself even cannot create.

Ques. What that thing is, must be explained to me.

Ans. God is the creator of all things, but if he wish to create another like Himself, he cannot do it. God cannot create another like Himself.

Ques. How many names are there for God?

Ans. It is said there are one thousand and one names; but of these one hundred and one are extant.

Ques. Why are there so many names of God?

Ans. God's names, expressive of his nature, are two, "Yazdan" (omnipotence), and "Páuk" (holy). He is also named "Hormuzd" (the highest of spirits), "Dádár (the distributor of justice), "Purvurdegár" (provider), "Purvurtar" (protector), by which names we praise him. There are many other names, also, descriptive of his good doings.

Ques. What is our religion?

Ans. Our religion is, "Worship of God."

Ques. Whence did we receive our religion?

Ans. God's true prophet—the true Zurthost [Zoroaster] Asphantamán Anoshirwán—brought the religion for us from God.

Ques. Where should I turn my face when worshipping the holy Hormuzd?

Ans. We should worship the holy, just Hormuzd with our face towards some of his creations of light, and glory, and brightness.

Ques. Which are those things?

Ans. Such as the sun, the moon, the stars, the fire, water, and other such things of glory. To such things we turn our face, and consider them our "kibleh" (literally, the thing opposite), because God has bestowed upon them a small spark of his pure glory, and they are, therefore, more exalted in the creation, and fit to be our "kibleh" (representing this power and glory).

Ques. Who was this true prophet, the true Zurthost?

Ans. The son of Porosaspé, who was the son of Pétéraspé, was the excellent Zurthost Ashphantamán Anoshirwane—chief of the wise, and the king of the learned—the worshipper of God. Him did God exalt over all mankind, admitted to his own presence; and by him did God send us his good Mazdiashná religion. *He* has been our prophet.

Ques. Have we had any other prophet after Zurthost?

Ans. No; we should remain attached with sincere faith to the religion brought by him.

Ques. Among the creation of Hormuzd in this world, which is the most exalted, and which the lowest?

Ans. The great prophet is the most exalted, and that prophet is the excellent Zurthost—none is higher than he; the height of dignity culminates in him, because he is the most beloved and honoured of God. The servant of all is iron.

Ques. What religion has our prophet brought us from God?

Ans. The disciples of our prophet have recorded in several books that religion. Many of these books were destroyed during the Alexandrian conquest, the remainder of the books were preserved with great care and respect by the Sassanian Kings. Of these again the greater portion were destroyed at the Mahommedan conquest by Khalif Omar, so that we have now very few books remaining, viz., the Vandidad, the Yazashné, the Visparad, the Khordeh Avestá, the Vistasp Nusk, and a few Pehlvi books. Resting our faith upon these few books, we now remain devoted to our good Mazdiashná religion. We consider these books as heavenly books, because God sent the tidings of these books to us through the holy Zurthost. [...]

Ques. What commands has God sent us through his prophet, the exalted Zurthost?

Ans. Many are those commands, but I give you the principal, which must always be remembered, and by which we must guide ourselves:—

To know God as one; to know the prophet, the exalted Zurthost, as his true prophet; to believe the religion and the Avestá brought by him, as true beyond all manner of doubt; to believe in the goodness of God; not to disobey any of the commands of the Mazdiashná religion; to avoid evil deeds; to exert for good deeds; to pray five times in the day; to believe in the reckoning and justice on the fourth morning after death; to hope for heaven and to fear hell; to consider doubtless the day of general destruction and resurrection; to remember always that God has done what he willed, and shall do what he wills; to face some luminous object while worshipping God.

Ques. If we commit any sin, will our prophet save us?

Ans. Never commit any sin under that faith, because our prophet, our guide to the right path, has distinctly commanded "you shall receive according to what you do." Your deeds will determine your return in the other world. If you do virtuous and pious actions, your reward shall be heaven. If you sin and do wicked things, you shall be punished in hell. There is none save God that could save you from the consequences of your sins. If any one commit a sin under the belief that he shall be saved by somebody, both the deceiver as well as the deceived shall be damned to the day of "Rastá Khez," (the day of the end of this world).* * *

Ques. Have any persons endeavoured to deceive the people by offering to intercede for them and to save them?

Ans. Some deceivers, with a view of acquiring exaltation in this world, have set themselves up as prophets, and going among the labouring and ignorant people, have persuaded them that, "if you commit sin, I shall intercede for you, I shall plead for you, I shall save you;" and thus deceive them, but the wise among those people know the deceit. They do not, however, dare to speak their mind for fear of the deluded multitude. Our prophet needed no exaltation here, he was exalted before God, and he told us the true command, "you shall receive according to your deeds." There is no saviour. In the other world you shall receive the return according to your actions. * * * Your saviour is your deeds, and God himself.

He is "Bakhsháyandé," (the pardoner), and "Bakhsháyazgar," (the giver). If you repent your sins and reform, and if the great judge consider you worthy of pardon, or would be merciful to you, He alone can and will save you.

Ques. Why are God and his prophet addressed in the rude singular "thou," instead of the polite plural "you?"

Ans. Because God is only *one*, and there is none like Him, and there is only *one* prophet.

Ques. What are those things by which man is blessed and benefitted?

Ans. To do virtuous deeds, to give in charity, to be kind, to be humble, to speak sweet words, to wish good to others, to have a clear heart, to acquire learning, to speak the truth, to suppress anger, to be patient and contented, to be friendly, to feel shame, to pay due respect to the old and young, to be pious, to respect our parents and teachers. All these are the friends of the good men and enemies of the bad men.

Ques. What are those things by which man is lost and degraded?

Ans. To tell untruths, to steal, to gamble, to look with wicked eye upon a woman, to commit treachery, to abuse, to be angry, to wish ill to another, to be proud, to mock, to be idle, to slander, to be avaricious, to be disrespectful, to be shameless, to be hot-tempered, to take what is another's property, to be revengeful, unclean, obstinate, envious, to do harm to any man, to be superstitious, and do any other wicked and iniquitous action. These are all the friends of the wicked, and the enemies of the virtuous."

Such is the religious knowledge which the Parsees of more than a quarter of a century ago endeavoured to communicate to their children, or at least wished them to be taught, but I do not think that even this dialogue had been, till very lately, made a necessary part of the child's religious education. From one question quoted, not quite bearing upon the Parsee religion, but evidently meant for a reason against Christianity, it may have struck the reader that this dialogue was perhaps written under the pressure of the efforts of Christian missionaries to convert Parsee youths.

It remains, however, to be seen how far the doctrines and injunctions taught in this dialogue are authorised by the Zend Avestá, and what other doctrines are taught in them. The best thing I can do, I think, is to give here a series of extracts from the translation of one of these Zend books, sufficient to give a faithful general notion of the doctrines and morality of the Zoroastrian religion. [...]

"1st Há.—The great judge, Hormuzd, of glory and brightness, the highest, the all-virtuous, the greatest, strictest, the all-wise, of the purest nature, the holiest, lover of gladness—invisible to the invisible, the increaser—He created our soul—He moulded our body—He gave us existence. Há 34.—I worship thee, O Hormuzd, above all others, I invoke thee above all others, all virtuous thoughts, all virtuous words, and all virtuous works, flow from thee. O Hormuzd, I invoke thy pure nature above all others. By my deeds may I exalt and honour thy name. Under the protection of thy great wisdom have I acquired wisdom. May I reach thee. May I always be firm in thy friendship and in holy deeds."

In Há 44 several extracts relate to this subject, especially God as the creator of all, ending in "Thou art the Creator of all Creation."

In a prayer to Hormuzd (Hormuzd Yasht) occurs this—"My name is the Creator of all."

Zurthost worships God not only in this world, but in the heavens also—Há 34, "O Hormuzd, I worship thee, and in the heavens, also, shall I worship thee much."

The Parsees believe in the existence of angels, created by God, with powers to aid and benefit mankind in various ways, and to be the superintending spirits of the various parts of creation. The chief among these are the angels of good conscience (Bahaman), and of high piety (Ardebehsht); the former is also the protecting angel of the harmless animals, and the latter the angel of fire.

"1st Há.—I invoke good conscience, high piety, love of excellence, high and perfect thought, Khordad and Amardad; all other angels that reach us; the angel 'Meher,' the lord and guardian of the forest, of thousand ears and ten thousand eyes of gladness and of comfort." Many other extracts can be made to deduce the above inference.

The various parts of creation are praised, or remembered, or considered holy, &c.

The first seven Hás contain many texts illustrative of this.

"The fire created by God, the time of day, the early dawn, the waters created by God, the year that is spent in holiness, the moon and the glorious sun, the ocean of light, the stars, the immeasurable light, the mountains and the trees, the forest, the sheep, and the harmless animals;" in short, nature, in her various parts and phenomena, is sometimes praised, sometimes remembered, sometimes described as holy.

As far as I have seen, there is no text in which any lifeless material object without intelligence or spirituality is invoked for assistance or benefit. Such prayers are always directed to intelligent spirits or angels, and to God above all, and as the Creator and Lord of all.

The Parsee believes in the immortality of the soul, and in rewards and punishments after death.

"Há 7.—O great and wise Lord, the reward that is due to the religious, may I and mine receive; that reward mayst thou give from thy stores of bounty in such a way, in this and the spiritual world, that I may be exalted, and may I live for ever and ever under thy all-holy leadership, and all-virtuous protection.

"Há 8.—May the aspirations of the holy be fulfilled, may the wicked and evil-doers be disappointed, and be swept away from the creation of the holy creator. The righteous are immortal."

Extracts from Há 31 bear on this point.

Notwithstanding the abhorrence of evil and evil-doers, the Parsee is made to wish that the wicked may be converted to virtue.

"Há 33.—The wicked are punished according to their thought, and words, and deeds. Better it be that they be introduced to a taste of learning. O Hormuzd, give them a desire for wisdom, that they may become promoters of holiness.

"Há 44.—O Hormuzd, why may not these sinners become virtuous?"

The Parsee rests his pardon on the mercy of God, and his reward on the bounty of God. [...]

The Parsee religion is for all, and not for any particular nation or people.

"Há 46.—May all men and women of the world become my followers, and become acquainted with thy exalted religion. Whoever accepts Zurthost's religion, praises it, and meditates on it, and studies it much, to him God gives a place in the other world; and in this world Bahaman (good conscience) gives him exaltation."

The Parsee religion contains no propitiating of the devil. There is not a single reference to the thoughts, or words, or deeds of evil spirits, without wishing destruction or reformation to them.

"Há 1.—I learn the Zurthosti religion, the worship of God, which is different to that of the Dews (the evil spirits), and is like the Justice of God.

Há 8.—May the wicked and the evil-doers be disappointed, and be swept away from the creation of the holy Creator.

Há 12.—I am of the religion of the worship of God, I praise that religion and declare it before the wicked, and praise it with good conscience, and virtuous words, and virtuous deeds.

Há 44.—O Hormuzd, why may not these sinners become virtuous?

Há 33.—The wicked are punished according to their thoughts, words, and deeds. Better it be that they be introduced to a taste of learning. O Hormuzd, give them a desire for wisdom, that they may become promoters of holiness."

The Parsees are called by others, "Fire Worshippers," and they defend themselves by saying that they do not worship the fire, but regard it and other great natural phenomena and objects as emblems of the divine power. To me it appears that the imputation, on the one hand, is wrong, and the defence, on the other hand, a little overshot. Though the Parsee "remembers, praises, loves, or regards holy," whatever is beautiful, or wonderful, or harmless, or useful in nature, he never asks from an unintelligent material object, assistance or benefit; he is, therefore, no idolater, or worshipper of matter. On the other hand, when the Parsee addresses his prayers to Hormuzd, or God, he never thinks it at all necessary that he should turn his face to any particular object. He would say, and does say, his "Hormuzd yasht" (prayer to Hormuzd) anywhere whatever without the slightest misgiving. Again, when he addresses the angel of water, or any other but that of fire, he does not stand before the fire. It is only when he addresses the angel of fire that he turns his face to the fire. In short, in addressing any particular angel, he turns his face to the object of that angel's guardianship as his emblem. But, in his prayers to Hormuzd, he recognises, or uses, or turns his face to no emblems whatever. Since fire only could be brought within the limits of a temple—any of the grand objects of nature (as the sea, the sun, &c.) being unavailable for this purpose—the temples naturally became the sanctuaries of fire alone, and hence has arisen the mistake of the Parsees being regarded as "Fire Worshippers."

This much is clear in Há 30—"He who knows God through his works reaches him;" but I do not recollect meeting with any text enjoining a Parsee to turn his face to any particular object as an emblem of God; though he is directed, as in the above text, to rise from Nature to Nature's God.

I do not recollect meeting with a text, that "the Evil Spirit is cöeval with God." In one place Há 19, all wicked spirits are spoken of as having come into existence after a certain event—"Tell me, O great invisible God, the creator and promoter of all creation, what were thy words before the existence of the heavens, before the waters, * * before the wicked spirits of dull reason, before all creation," &c. Whether these wicked spirits include or not the well-known Harimàn among them, I cannot tell. It is generally supposed that Hormuzd and Harimàn are good and evil principles. I do not think that I have met with any text that supports this theory, as far as Hormuzd is concerned, or in which the good principle is personified. Hormuzd is distinctly "The intelligent living Creator," as far as I can gather, and not a mere personification of the principle of good—a Creator distinct from his creation, either material, moral, intellectual, or spiritual.

In the Yazashné, scarcely once even is Harimàn mentioned. Harimàn, not by this very name, but by the name of Angare Meniús is mentioned in the Vandidad as having, to thwart Hormuzd's good works, produced several evils. This Angare Meniús is rendered in the Gujarati translation, Gana Minó, which, I think, means the "sinning angel," though I am not quite sure of it. I am not at present able to say more about the age, or nature, or meaning of Harimàn; but one thing is clear, that evil will have an end.

"Há 31.—On the day of reckoning all the wicked shall be annihilated." [...]

These extracts are, I think, sufficient to give a general idea of the character and doctrines of the Parsee religion; but it must be remembered that I am not well qualified to speak with any authority on the subject. I have received at third hand the extracts I have given. The original Zend is translated into Pehlvi, from the Gujarati translation of which I have given in English. This Gujarati translation is considered rather imperfect, and in several places it is so confused that I have omitted giving some more extracts, simply because they are ambiguous or unintelligible.

I have avoided giving any opinion on, or discussing any of the doctrines. I give the extracts as faithfully as my hurried reading has permitted, leaving it to the reader to draw his own conclusions.

Besides the Yazashné, from which the preceding extracts are given, there are only three or four other books considered by the Parsees as a portion of their original religious books.

But priestcraft acting upon ignorance has not failed to do its usual work, and has left a legacy of a few books which the Parsee has no reason to be thankful for. Many ceremonies and notions have thus been introduced, and the reformers of the day contend that all those ceremonies and notions that have no authority in the original Zend Avestá ought to be abolished and disavowed. Of course the old orthodox Parsees and the Priests do not like this at all.

8.3

Islam

8.3 Islam

The earliest mosque in Britain was recorded as being in Cardiff in 1860, but it was in the last decade or so of the century that a vocal Muslim community emerged, led by British converts. These had typically spent time in colonial territories where Islam was dominant, and were struck by the faith's apparent reasonableness when compared with the mysterious doctrines of Christianity. The first purpose-built mosque opened in Woking in 1889 (still in use today), while a Muslim Institute thrived in Liverpool in the 1890s under the leadership of the charismatic Abdullah [born William] Quilliam, Sheikh-ul-Islam of the British Isles (see this series Vol. III, section 4). Attending these were individuals born into Islam who formed an increasing, if small, presence in the national population from 1870 onwards. These included visiting Indian nobility and their households, Indian academics, university students (also from Africa), doctors, barristers, entrepreneurs, chefs and entertainers; plus a wave of mostly Yemeni immigrants following the opening of the Suez Canal. Perhaps the best-known native Muslim living in Britain from 1887 was Abdul Karim, one of the Queen's Indian servants, who is known to have attended the Woking mosque on at least a few occasions.[1]

Syed Ameer Ali (1849–1928) was an Indian-born Muslim who divided his time between his homeland and Britain. A prominent figure in Indian law and politics, he set up the National Mohammedan Association in India and in Britain was appointed to the Judicial Committee of the Privy Council. For years he was Chairman of the Committee of the Woking Mosque, and in 1910 he set up a fund to build the first mosque in London.[2] His book, called *The Spirit of Islam* in later editions, was written with a dual audience and purpose in mind – to shape the development of Islam in India, but also to help 'the diffusion of Islamic ideas in the West' (Preface, p. ix). With universalist tendencies, the author regards ethical theism as the root idea in all world faiths, but claims Islam's superiority to Christianity in realising this ideal.

The extract emphasises Islam's abstraction of the divine and resistance to anthropomorphisms which lead to idolatry, a weakness seen to contaminate both Judaism and Christianity: the culmination of this failing is the worship of Christ as man-god. Assuming a historical-critical perspective on the New Testament, the author attributes Jesus's purported divine nature to a mythological layer added by gospel-writers to the historical reality of Jesus the preacher. Mohammed's mission was to call humanity back to pure theism.

In capturing the spirit of Islam as a lived ethos, Syed Ameer Ali presents a rigorously social religion: charity is written into the primary demands of the faith, while the absence of a priesthood, and the universal requirement for pilgrimage, confirm an egalitarian and self-directed faith. Drawing attention to Mohammed's reverence for animals as fellow-creatures has particular resonance in the context of the developing animal rights movement in Britain. Fasting is advocated not in a spirit of asceticism or penitence, but as an education in habits of self-restraint.

The Spirit of Islam answers two orientalist stereotypes of Islam, still common at the time if slightly less virulent than earlier in the century. The contrast of Muslim cultures as static to the West's progressiveness is undermined by the argument that Islam, through its simple focus on reason and conscience and its relative lack of rite or dogma, has a built-in flexibility to adapt to humanity's advancing moral sensibility. Secondly, the work counters accusations of Islam's inherent oppression of women, epitomised in the image of the harem and Mohammed's polygamy. Syed Ameer Ali presents women's legal status in Islamic law to be superior to that enjoyed by many women of Christendom, alluding to rights (financial, maternal, sexual) recently won, or still being fought for, in Britain. The author alludes to his earlier published discussion of Muslim women's superior legal condition to that of her English sisters, which occupies several chapters of *The Personal Law of the Muhammedans* (1880). Overall, Islam is presented in its ideal form as the religion most in tune with advanced intellectual and social developments, less trammelled than Christianity by a fossilised belief system and a limited mandate for charity. While the author's theological erudition is shown in his extensive reference to Christian and Islamic scholarship, only references for direct quotations have been retained.

Notes

1 See G. Beckerlegge, 'Followers of "Mohammed, Kalee and Dada Nanuk": The Presence of Islam and South Asian Religions in Victorian Britain', in John Wolffe (ed.), *Religion in Victorian Britain*, vol. 5: *Culture and Empire* (Manchester: Manchester University Press, 1997), pp. 221–267, on pp. 243–65.
2 Rozina Visram, *Ayahs, Lascars and Princes: Indians in Britain 1700–1947* (London: Pluto Press, 1986), pp. 97–102.

32

SYED AMEER ALI, *THE LIFE AND TEACHINGS OF MOHAMMED: OR, THE SPIRIT OF ISLAM*

(London: W.H. Allen & Co., 1891),
pp. 226–231, 233–234, 254–255, 262, 266–267,
268–270, 271–272, 274–275, 362–365

The Ideal of Islam

The principal basis on which the Islamic system is founded are (1) a belief in the unity, immateriality, power, mercy, and supreme love of the Creator; (2) charity and brotherhood among mankind; (3) subjugation of the passions; (4) the outpouring of a grateful heart to the Giver of all good; and (5) accountability for human actions in another existence. The grand and noble conceptions expressed in the Koran of the power and love of the Deity surpass everything of their kind in any other language. The unity of God, His immateriality, His majesty, His mercy, form the constant and never-ending theme of the most eloquent and soul-stirring passages. The flow of life, light, and spirituality never ceases. But throughout there is no trace of dogmatism. Appeal is made to the inner consciousness of man, to his intuitive reason alone.

Let us now take a brief retrospect of the religious conceptions of the peoples of the world when the Prophet of Islâm commenced his preachings. Among the heathen Arabs the idea of Godhead varied according to the culture of the individual or of the clan. With some it rose, comparatively speaking, to the "divinisation" or deification of nature; among others it fell to simple fetichism, the adoration of a piece of dough, a stick, or a stone. Some believed in a future life; others had no idea of it whatever. The pre-Islâmite Arabs had their groves, their oracle-trees, their priestesses, like the Syro-Phœnicians. Phallic worship was not unknown to them; and the generative powers received adoration, like the hosts of heaven, under monuments of stone and wood. The wild denizens of the desert, then as now, could not be impervious to the idea of some unseen hand driving the blasts which swept over whole tracts, or forming the beautiful visions which rose before the traveller to lure him to destruction. And thus there floated in the Arab world an intangible, unrealised conception of a superior Deity, the Lord of all.

The Jews, those great conservators of the monotheistic idea, as they have been generally regarded in history, probably might have assisted in the formation of this conception. But they themselves showed what strange metamorphoses can take place in the thoughts of a nation when not aided by a historical and rationalistic element in their religious code.

The Jews had entered Arabia at various times, and under the pressure of various circumstances. Naturally the ideas of the different bodies of emigrants, refugees, or colonists would vary much. The ideas of the men driven out by the Assyrians or Babylonians would be more anthropomorphic, more anthropopathic, than of those who fled before Vespasian, Trajan, or Hadrian. The characteristics which had led the Israelites repeatedly to lapse into idolatry in their original homes, when seers were in their midst to denounce their backslidings, would hardly preserve them from the heathenism of their Arab brothers. With an idea of "the God of Abraham" they would naturally combine a materialistic conception of the Deity, and hence we find them rearing "a statue representing Abraham, with the ram beside him ready for sacrifice," in the interior of the Kaaba.

Amongst the later comers the Shammaites and the Zealots formed by far the largest proportion. Among them the worship of the law verged upon idolatry, and the Scribes and Rabbins claimed a respect almost approaching adoration. They believed themselves to be the guardians of the people, the preservers of law and tradition, "living exemplars and mirrors, in which the true mode of life, according to the law, was preserved."[1] They looked upon themselves as the "flower of the nation," and they were considered, through their intercourse with God, to possess the gift of prophecy. In fact, by their people as well as by themselves they were regarded as the prime favourites of God.[2] The veneration of the Jews for Moses went so far, says Josephus, that they reverenced his name next to that of God; and this veneration they transferred to Ezra, the restorer of national life and law under the Kyânian dynasty (Ezra 7:10 et seq.).

Besides, the mass of the Jews had never, probably, thoroughly abandoned the worship of the Teraphim, a sort of household god made in the shape of human beings, and consulted on all occasions as domestic oracles, or regarded perhaps more as guardian penates (Judges 18:14). This worship must have been strengthened by contact with the heathen Arabs.

When Jesus made his appearance in Judæa, the doctrine of divine unity and of a supreme Personal Will, overshadowing the universe with its might and grace, received acceptance only among one race—the worshippers of Jehovah. And even among them, despite all efforts to the contrary, the conception of the Divinity had either deteriorated by contact with heathen nations, or become modified by the influence of pagan philosophies. On the one hand, Chaldæomagian philosophy had left its finger mark indelibly impressed on the Jewish traditions; on the other, their best minds, whilst introducing among the Greek and Roman philosophers the conception of a great Primal Cause, had imbibed, in the schools of Alexandria, notions hardly reconcilable with their monotheistic creed.

The Hindoos, with their multitudinous hordes of gods and goddesses; the Mago-Zoroastrians, with their two divinities struggling for mastery; the Greeks, Romans, and Egyptians, with their pantheons full of deities whose morality was below that of the worshippers,—such was the condition of the civilised world when Jesus commenced his preachings. With all his dreams and aspirations, his mind was absolutely exempt from those pretensions which have been fixed on him by his over-zealous followers. He never claimed to be a "complement of God," to be a "hypostasis of the Divinity."

Even modern idealistic Christianity has not been able yet to shake itself free from the old legacy bequeathed by the anthropomorphism of bygone ages. Age after age everything human has been eliminated from the history of the great Teacher, until his personality is lost in a mass of legends. The New Testament itself, with "its incubation of a century," leaves the revered figure clothed in a mist. And each day the old idea of "an Æon born in the bosom of eternity," gathers force until the Council of Nice gives it a shape and consistency, and formulates it into a dogma.

Many minds, bewildered by the far-offness of the universal Father, seek a resting-place midway in a human personality which they call divine. It is this need of a nearer object of adoration which leads modern Christianity to give a name to an ideal, clothe it with flesh and blood, and worship it as a man-God. [...]

In the long night of superstition the Christians had wandered far away from the simplicity of the Nazarene teachings. The worship of images, saints, and relics had become inseparably blended with the religion of Jesus. The practices which he had denounced, the evils which he had reprehended, were, one by one, incorporated with his faith. The holy ground where the revered Teacher had lived and walked was involved in a cloud of miracles and visions, and "the nerves of the mind were benumbed by the habits of obedience and belief."[3]

Against all the absurdities we have described above, the life-aim of Mohammed was directed. Addressing with the voice of truth, inspired by deep communion with the God of the universe, the fetich worshippers of the Arabian tribes on one side and the followers of degraded Christianity and Judaism on the other, Mohammed, that "master of speech," as he has been so truly called, never travelled out of the province of reason, and made them all blush at the monstrousness of their beliefs. Mohammed, the grand apostle of the unity of God, thus stands forth in history in noble conflict with the retrogressive tendency of man to associate other beings with the Creator of the universe. [...]

Do the preachings of this desert-born prophet, addressing a larger world and a more advanced humanity, in the nobility of their love, in their strivings and yearnings for the true, the pure, and the holy, fall short of the warnings of Isaiah or "the tender appeals of Jesus"?

The poor and the orphan, the humble dweller of the earth "with his mouth in the dust," the unfortunate being bereft in early life of parental care, are ever the objects of his tenderest solicitude. Ever and again he announces that the path which leads to God is the helping of the orphan, the relieving of the poor, and the ransoming of the captive. His pity and love were not confined to his fellow-beings, the brute creation shared with them his sympathy and tenderness. [...]

In the Koran animal life stands on the same footing as human life in the sight of the Creator. "There is no beast on earth," says the Koran, "nor bird which flieth with its wings, but the same is a people like unto you – unto the Lord they shall return" [Al-Ana'am, 'Livestock', 6:38]. It rook centuries for Christendom to awaken to a sense of duty towards the animal creation. Long before the Christian nations ever dreamt of extending towards animals tenderness and humanity, Mohammed proclaimed in impressive words the duty of mankind towards their dumb and humble servitors. These precepts of tenderness so lovingly embalmed in the creed are faithfully rendered into a common duty of everyday life in the world of Islam. [...]

The Religious Spirit of Islâm

[...] The Islâm of Mohammed recognises no cast of priesthood, allows no monopoly of spiritual knowledge or special holiness to intervene between man and his God. Each soul rises to its Creator without the intervention of priest or hierophant. No sacrifice, no ceremonial, invented by vested interests, is needed to bring the anxious heart nearer to its Comforter. Each human being is his own priest; in the Islâm of Mohammed no one man is higher than the other. [...]

The institution of fasting has existed more or less among all nations. [...] The example of Jesus consecrated the custom in the Church. But the predominating idea in Christianity with respect to fasts generally, is one of penitence or expiation; and, partially, of precedent. Voluntary corporal mortifications have been as frequent in the Christian Church as in other Churches; but the tendency of such mortifications has invariably been the destruction of mental and bodily energies, and the fostering of a morbid asceticism. The institution of fasting in Islâm, on the contrary, has the legitimate object of restraining the passions, by diurnal abstinence for a limited and definite period, from all the gratifications of the senses, and directing the overflow of the animal spirits into a healthy channel. Useless and unnecessary mortification of the flesh is discountenanced, nay, condemned. Fasting is prescribed to the able-bodied and the strong, as a means of chastening the spirit by imposing a restraint on the body. For the weak, the sickly, the traveller, the student (who is engaged in the pursuit of knowledge – the *Jihâd-i-Akbar*), the soldier doing God's battle against the assailants of the faithful, and women in their ailments, it is disallowed. Those who bear in mind the gluttony of the Greeks, the Romans, the Persians, and the pre-Islamite Arabs, their excesses in their pleasures as well as their vices, will appreciate the value of the regulation, and comprehend how wonderfully adapted it is for keeping in check the animal propensities of man, especially among the semi-civilised races. [...]

No religion of the world prior to Islâm had consecrated charity, the support of the widow, the orphan, and the helpless poor, by enrolling its principles among the positive enactments of the system.

The *agapae*, or feasts of charity among the early Christians, depended on the will of individuals; their influence, therefore, could only be irregular and spasmodic. It is a matter of history that this very irregularity led to the suppression of the "feasts of charity or love-feasts" only a short time after their introduction.[4]

By the laws of Islâm every individual is bound to contribute a certain part of his substance towards the help and assistance of his poorer neighbours. This portion is usually one part in forty, or 2 ½ per cent. on the value of all goods, chattels, emblements, on profits of trade, mercantile business etc. But alms are due only when the property amounts to a certain value, and has been in the possession of a person for one whole year; nor are any due from cattle employed in agriculture or in the carrying of burdens. Besides at the end of the month of Ramazân (the month of fasting), and on the day of the Eed-ul-Fitr, the festival which celebrates the close of the Moslem Lent, each head of a family has to give away in alms, for himself and for every member of his household, and for each guest who breaks his fast and sleeps in his house during the month, a measure of wheat, barley, dates, raisins, rice, or any other grain, or the value of the same.

The rightful recipients of the alms, as pointed out by the practice of Mohammed and his disciples, are (1) the poor and the indigent; (2) those who help in the collection and distribution of the obligatory alms; (3) slaves, who wish to buy their freedom and have not the means for so doing; (4) debtors, who cannot pay their debts; (5) travellers and strangers. General charity is inculcated by the Koran in the most forcible terms. But the glory of Islâm consists in having embodied the beautiful sentiment of Jesus into definite laws.

The wisdom which incorporated into Islâm the time-honoured custom of annual pilgrimage to Mecca and to the shrine of the Kaaba, has breathed into Mohammed's religion a freemasonry and brotherhood of faith in spite of sectarian divisions. The eyes of the whole Moslem world fixed on that central spot, keep alive in the bosom of each some spark of the celestial fire which lighted up the earth in that century of darkness. Here, again, the wisdom of the inspired lawgiver shines forth in the negative part of the enactment, in the conditions necessary to make the injunction obligatory: – (1) The ripeness of intelligence and discernment; (2) perfect freedom and liberty; (3) possession of the means of transport and subsistence during the journey; (4) possession of means sufficient to support the pilgrim's family during his absence; (5) the possibility and practicability of the voyage. [...]

Nothing can be simpler or more in accord with the advance of the human intellect than the teachings of the Arabian Prophet. The few rules for religious ceremonial which he prescribed were chiefly with the object of maintaining discipline and uniformity, so necessary in certain stages of society; but they were by no means of an inflexible character. He allowed them to be broken in cases of illness or other causes. "God wishes to make things easy for you, for", says the Koran, "man was created weak" [An-Nisa, 'Women', 4:28]. The legal principles which he enunciated were either delivered as answers to questions put to him as the chief magistrate of Medîna, or to remove or correct patent evils. The Prophet's Islâm recognised no ritual likely to distract the mind from the thought of the one God; no law to keep enchained the conscience of advancing humanity. [...]

Religion ought to mean the rule of life; its chief object ought to be the elevation of humanity towards that perfection which is the end of our existence. The religion, therefore, which places on a systematic basis the fundamental principles of morality, regulating social obligations and human duties, which brings us nearer and nearer, by its compatibility with the highest development of the intellect, to the All-Perfect – that religion, we say, has the greatest claim to our consideration and respect. It is the distinctive characteristic of Islam, as taught by Mohammed, that it combines within itself the grandest and the most prominent features in all ethnic and catholic religions compatible with the reason and moral intuition of man. It is not merely a system of positive moral rules, based on a true conception of human progress, but it is also "the establishment of certain principles, the enforcement of certain dispositions, the cultivation of a certain temper of mind, which the conscience is to apply to the ever-varying exigencies of time and place".[5] The Teacher of Islam preached, in a thousand varied ways, universal love and brotherhood as the emblem of the love borne towards God. "How do you think God will know you when you are in His presence – by your love of your children, or your kin, of your neighbours, of your fellow-ceatures!"[6] "Do you love your Creator? love your fellow-beings first." "Do you wish to approach the Lord? love his creatures, love for them what you love yourself, reject for them what you reject for yourself, do unto them what you wish to be done unto you." He condemned in scathing language the foulness of impurity, the meanness of hypocrisy, and the ungodliness of self-deceit. He proclaimed, in unmistakable terms, the preciousness of truth, charity, and brotherly love.

The wonderful adaptability of the Islamic precepts to all ages and nations; their entire concordance with the light of reason; the absence of all mysterious doctrines to cast a shade of sentimental ignorance round the primal truths planted in the human breast, – all prove that Islâm represents the latest development of the religious faculties of our being.

The Status of Women in Islâm

The improvement effected in the position of women by the Prophet of Arabia has been acknowledged by all unprejudiced writers, though it is still the fashion with bigoted controversialists to say the Islâmic system lowered the status of women. No falser calumny has been levelled at the great Prophet. Nineteen centuries of progressive development working with the legacy of a prior civilisation, under the most favourable racial and climatic conditions, have tended to place women in most countries in Christendom, on a higher social level than the men, – have given birth to a code of etiquette which, at least ostensibly, recognises the right of women to higher social respect. But what is their legal position even in the most advanced communities of Christendom? Until very recently, even in England, a married woman possessed no rights independently of her husband. If the Moslem woman does not attain, in another hundred years, the social position of her Christian sister, there will be time enough to disclaim against Islâm as a system and a dispensation. But the Teacher who in an age when no country, no system, no community gave any right to woman, maiden or married, mother or wife, who in a country where the birth of a daughter was considered a calamity, secured to the sex rights which are only unwillingly and under pressure being conceded to them by the civilised nations in the nineteenth century, deserves the gratitude of humanity. If Mohammed had done nothing more, his claim to be a benefactor of mankind would have been indisputable. Even under the laws as they stand at present in the pages of the legists the legal position of Moslem females may be said to compare favourably with that of European women. We have dealt in another place at length with this subject. We shall do no more here than glance at the provisions of the Moslem codes relating to women. As long as she is unmarried she remains under the parental roof, and until she attains her majority she is to some extent under the control of the father or his representative. As soon, however, as she is of age, the law vests in her all the rights which belong to her as an independent human being. She is entitled to share in the inheritance of her parents along with her brothers, and though the proportion is different, the distinction is founded on the relative position of bother and sister. A woman who is *sui juris* can under no circumstances be married without her own express consent, "not even by the sultan." On her marriage she does not lose her individuality. She does not cease to be a separate member of society.

An antenuptial settlement by the husband in favour of the wife is a necessary condition, and on his failure to make a settlement the law presumes one in accordance with the social position of the wife. A Moslem marriage is a civil act, needing no priest, requiring no ceremonial. The contract of marriage gives the man no power over the woman's person, beyond what the law defines, and none whatever upon her goods and property. Her rights as a mother do not depend for their recognition upon the idiosyncracies of individual judges. Her earnings acquired by her own exertions cannot be wasted by a prodigal husband, nor can she be ill-treated with impunity by one who is brutal. She acts, if *sui juris*, in all matters which relate to herself and her property in her own individual right, without the intervention of husband or father. She can sue her debtors in the open courts, without the necessity of joining a next friend, or under cover of her husband's name. She continues to exercise, after she has passed from her father's house into her husband's home, all the rights which the law gives to men. All the privileges which belong to her as a woman and a wife are secured to her, not by the courtesies which "come and go", but by the actual text in the book of the law. Taken as a whole, her status is not more unfavourable that that of many European women, whilst in many respects she occupies a decidedly better position. Her comparatively backward condition is the result of a want of culture among the community generally, rather than of any special feature in the laws of the fathers.

Notes

1 [Johann von] Döllinger, *The Gentile and the Jew* [*in the Courts of the Temple of Christ*, trans. N. Darnell (1862)], vol. ii, p.308.
2 Josephus, [*Jewish*] *Antiquities*, xvii, 24. They were, so to speak, the Brahmins of Judaism.
3 [Johann Lorenz von] Mosheim, [*An*] *Ecclesiastical History* [*Ancient and Modern*, trans. Archibald Maclaine 1819], vol. i, p. 432.
4 [August] Neander, [*General History of the Christian Religion and Church*, 6 vols (1825–52)], vol. I, p. 450 et seq.; Mosheim, vol. II, p. 56.
5 [Henry Hart Milman, *The History of Christianity from the Birth of Christ to the Abolition of Paganism in the Roman Empire*, 3 vols (London: John Murray, 1840), vol. I, p. 206].
6 Mishkât [*The Book of Hadith: Sayings of the Prophet Muhammed from the Mishkat Al-Masabih*], bks xxii–xxiii, chaps xv and xvi.

Part 9

INTERPRETIVE TRADITIONS

9.1

Radical Christianity

9.1 Radical Christianity

Radical Christianity has a long history among individuals and groups who read the Bible from the viewpoint of the poor and marginalised, and have interpreted sin and salvation in material as well as spiritual terms. In this tradition, the gospel is understood as a mandate for liberation of the oppressed, a conviction that has empowered the dispossessed over centuries sometimes to challenge the status quo, and to criticise religious leaders for neglecting the divine call for social justice.[1] Chartist Christianity was a manifestation of this tradition, whose writers interpreted their tradition in the light of their experience of economic deprivation and political disenfranchisement. Gerald Parsons makes the case for 'the existence of a widespread working-class version of Christianity, at variance with the official versions on offer from the churches' which was uninterested in dogma and focused on the practical ethics of the Bible.[2] It was firmly 'this-worldly' in outlook.

Reverend Joseph Rayner Stephens (1805–79) seceded from the Wesleyans to form the Stephensite Methodists, which had their own circuit of preachers. He delivered the sermon below just a few days after being arrested and charged with seditious conspiracy. Stephens first defends the political preacher on the grounds that the gospel is inevitably political because it makes prescriptions for social relations. He preaches the liberation principle that the laws of heaven apply on earth, not merely in the afterlife. Stephens attacks particular institutions that were common targets in Chartist writing for their utilitarian usage of the poor – the factory system, Malthusian philosophy, and the 1834 Poor Law. (The alarming proposal, which he takes as a serious threat, to gas children of the poor in order to relieve overpopulation was in fact issued satirically in an anti-Poor Law pamphlet, *The Book of Murder!*) Stephens was no socialist or even democrat.[3] His ideal political model here is conscientious paternalism. His tone reaches moral infuriation as he recalls the Old Testament Prophets who poured the wrath of God upon religious leaders for their neglect of justice. He refers to the judgment of King Balshazzar who receives a condemnatory message direct from God (Daniel 5), while the pamphlet's title page quotes the prophet's divine condemnation of injustice (Ezekiel 22:29–30). Stephens's aim is the political awakening of the clergy.

Chartism produced many radical hymns to be sung to popular hymn tunes at Chartist camp meetings and on marches. The anonymously authored 'Hymn Thirteenth' from the *National Chartist Hymn Book* treats the resurrection of Christ as a symbol of 'perfect liberty' which is realised in the six-point Charter: redemption equates to political emancipation. The gospel event blurs with the mythical image of the rising phoenix, in fiery and explosive language evocative of Shelley's 'The Mask of Anarchy'. 'Britannia's Sons' was a well-known hymn written by John Bramwich (1803–46), a Leicester framework knitter (a trade that endured infamous hardship) and a Mormon convert. Crucial to his radical theology is Bramwich's denial that the status quo is divinely intended, but is rather a sinful human distortion of God's universal provision. Bramwich's assertion of fellowship between Britain's working poor and slaves with African roots was a common Chartist trope and might seem a rather careless parallel, but his ten years of army service in the West Indies suggests perhaps a more responsible analysis of capitalist exploitation as an international structure. The hymn provided the title *God Made Man, Man Made the Slave* to the autobiography of George Teamoh, a former slave who became a Virginian senator in 1869.[4]

The revolting disparity between divine provision and social reality is the theme of Thomas Cooper's 'God of the Earth, And Sea, And Sky'. Cooper (1805–92) was a Chartist writer of national renown, a shoemaker, Wesleyan preacher and journalist, often in trouble with the authorities for seditious activities; his best-known work, *The Purgatory of Suicides* (1845), was written during a two-year stint in Stafford jail. Cooper evokes the biblical exodus of the Israelites as a paradigm for the modern 'wretched and poor', although the hope of liberation is only tentative. The poem conveys poignantly the sense of spiritual alienation felt by those suffering permanent hardship. Such a work presents a very different aspect of Victorian doubt to the intellectual angst of the comfortable classes: deprived of the experience of divine care by human agency, Cooper does not seem to doubt that God exists, but that he exists for such as him.

Notes

1 See Christopher Rowland, *Radical Christianity: A Reading of Recovery* (Cambridge: Polity, 1988), p. 9.
2 Gerald Parsons, 'A Question of Meaning: Religion and Working-Class Life', in Gerald Parsons (ed.), *Religion in Victorian Britain*, vol. 2: *Controversies* (Manchester: Manchester University Press, 1988), pp. 63–87, on p. 77.
3 Eileen Yeo, 'Chartist Religious Belief and the Theology of Liberation', in Jim Obelkevich, Lyndal Roper and Raphael Samuel (eds), *Disciplines of Faith: Studies in Religion, Politics and Patriarchy* (London: Routledge & Kegan Paul, 1987), pp. 410–421, on p. 417.
4 See Ned Newitt (ed.), *The Anthology of Leicester Chartist Song, Poetry and Verse* (Leicester: Leicester Pioneer Press, 2006), p. vi.

33

JOSEPH RAYNER STEPHENS, *THE POLITICAL PREACHER: AN APPEAL FROM THE PULPIT ON BEHALF OF THE POOR*

(London: [n.p.], 1839),
pp. 14–17, 18–20, 22–23, 26–28, 31–32

I am well aware, my brethren, that I have been charged with a deviation, a positive departure from the line of duty prescribed to the profession, of which I am an unworthy member, though I trust an upright, a sincere and a devoted one. It is said that I have dishonoured and desecrated the holy office, by neglecting the purely religious and spiritual claims, which the church has made upon the time, the talents and the influence of her ministers; by postponing the discussion of abstract doctrines, the tenets of a metaphysically reasoned system of theology, or the admitted articles of a settled and established orthodoxy; and instead of this, or before this, or along with this, insisting on the obligation the whole christian world is under to carry into actual, visible, immediate practice the plain precepts of that religion, whose first and last and only law on earth is that we should love our neighbour as ourself; doing unto others as we would they should do unto us. It has been my practice, and has been charged upon me as a crime, to apply the rules of God's commandments to various institutions of the social system, in my own immediate neighbourhood, and in the country at large; to bring the principles and operations of the manufactures, the commerce and the legislation of this professedly christian land to the standard of God's holy word, the law of the Creator, the witness-bearer of his mind and will to man. I have asked whether merchants, senators and statesmen are amenable to any authority higher than their own will, or whether they are free to do what their own thirst for gold and lust of power may lead them to attempt to execute upon the poor, the weak, the unfriended and defenceless portions of the community. I have asked whether all rights are not reciprocal, all duties relative, all privileges mutual, held together by all in the holy bonds of righteousness and love; whether there be not some given, acknowledged and universally admitted standard of truth and untruth, right and wrong, good and evil; whether that standard be not the written word of God, whether that God, by whom that word was written, be not the One law-giver, the King of kings, the Lord of lords, the only Ruler of princes? If it be so, and that it is so none will gainsay, I have gone on to enquire, whether the practices of the factory system, for instance, are in accordance with the precepts of our most holy religion; whether Christian mill-owners are justified in pursuing a system of manufacture, which has done more to injure the health, impair the constitution, demoralize the character of a vast mass of our population, than any other recorded in history; which has made such a fearful waste of the natural, the social and the moral life of our industrious countrymen, that it has become a question, not only whether the silken chord that should bind society in love, can any longer hold her various members within its soft and peaceful circle; but whether the race itself, the human breed be not so far degenerate as to threaten imbecility, idiotcy or actual extinction to a most extensive and alarming degree? I have asked, especially, whether the principles of our modem political economy can be made to quadrate with the statements of divine revelation; whether it be indeed true that the earth is too small for its inhabitants; whether the beings born into the world are indeed too many, and multiply too fast for its harvests, the production of its husbandry, and the supplies that lie hidden in the mysterious, inexhaustible storehouses of the great Creator of heaven and earth; whether to keep down the population of a christian country be in accordance with the commandments of that Father in heaven, who made man at first in his own likeness, a being of knowledge and righteousness; who loved him from the beginning, and sent his Son to seek the lost and raise the fallen; to whose eye all the springs of action in man were opened and uncovered; and who had not to learn from another what man was and what he was not, what he knew and what he did not know, what he could do and what he could not do, where and how he would settle in his wanderings through this wilderness, where and how he would have to live and move and have his being here upon earth during his progress through the world of men and things seen to the world of beings and of things as yet unseen. [...]

With the book in my hands, in which these lovely laws are laid down by the Maker of the world, for the guidance of his children in their dealings with each other, I have gone to the anti-christian statute of professedly christian senators, called the "poor law amendment act," and have asked whether we are to believe God, when he says that he has filled the whole earth with plenteousness, or are to believe the framers of that "act," who tell us that for myriads of her children nature has furnished no provision, no place at her niggard board; whether God is true and to be trusted, when he bids man and woman leave father and mother, for the sake of the nearer and holier love they bear to one another and be no longer twain, but become one, one flesh, one body, one in being and in blood; when he blesses them, thus made one, and bids them be fruitful and multiply and fill up the earth, which he made to yield them sustenance in their youth, support in their manhood and succour in their old age: or whether they are true and to be trusted, who philosophise love into wayward lust, make a mockery of marriage, call the purest and profoundest of our affections the prejudices of education, and ridicule our belief in the religious sanction of those affections as the stupid superstition of an ignorant and barbarous age, that knew nothing of the application of "steam" to factory machinery, or of "gas" to the humane project of "painless extinction" for every child born to us above two in a family; who prove to us by figures and calculations and tables that God was altogether under mistake when he made so small a world for so numerous a population; who insist upon it, that, unless we hasten to rescue Deity from the fatal errors of his original scheme, the earth will become a dreary wilderness, and men be driven to devour one another; that the best way of restoring the equipoise between mouths and meat is at once to cut away the right of the poor to be fed from their parent soil, to degrade, starve, imprison and separate them; and thence proceed to sever every virtuous tie, and encourage the wildest libertinism and the most promiscuous concubinage, as a means of thinning the too thickly rising shoots on the human field; and finally, as the grand climax of the new science of morals and religion, apply the "gas" to every third new-born babe, and consign the bodies of the little innocents to the "paradise of infants" called up by the genius of the "New poor law," whose magic wand has swept away the paradise of Eden, and left us in its stead the garden of the ghosts of our little ones, scientifically slaughtered by the high priests of Moloch, the blood-thirsty monster, whom they would impiously install in the holy seat of the Eternal.

To the principles of this "Act" I have applied every test, which as man, a subject, and a christian I have been taught by nature, by the English constitution and by divine revelation to apply to every thing, that comes within the range of the instincts, the liberties and the religion of man. It has been weighed in these balances and has been found wanting. [...]

It is thus, and thus only, that I have wandered away to what have hitherto been considered the forbidden paths of politics, by the introduction into my discourses of subjects, which, I am sorry to say, for so many years, if not ages, have been looked upon as foreign from the pulpit; and, as it may happen that the bonds, by which you and I have been held together, now, for some years, in love and brotherly kindness, may be broken asunder; as it may happen, and before very long, that you and I may have to bid one another farewell, it is only right to you and to myself and to the truth, whose interpreter I am; to the book, whose expounder I have endeavoured to be; to the service and master, whose minister I am, it is only right that I should, this day, in the opening service of the new year, again repeat, what I have so often asserted, that unless a priest, minister, clergyman, religious teacher, call him what you may, unless a priest of the living God be, in this sense of the word, a politician in the pulpit, he has no business there at all. I contend that law and religion can never be separated. If you attempt to dissociate or disunite them, it is like attempting to dissociate and disunite the soul from the body, expecting after you have done so, to find a living man before you. The body without the spirit is dead; faith without works is dead; religion without politics is dead; the one is the body, the other is the soul. Read this book, the Bible, from the beginning to the end, and tell me whether in its code of laws, you find one of them all, that does not apply to this world, and to this world only? These are the laws of God. For whom? For angels, for archangels, for devils, for archdevils? No! but for man. They are the laws of God; to be kept, where? In heaven, in hell? No! but upon earth. "Thy will be done on earth as it is in heaven" [Matt 6:10]. The laws here given are given to man for him to keep on earth; that by so keeping the law, and doing the will of God here, he may liken himself to the angels, that are in heaven, and thus, in this probationary state, prepare himself, by a life of holiness, for that place "at God's right hand where there are pleasures for evermore" [Psalm 16:11]. Nothing can be clearer than this; and to talk about religion, the application and practice of divine truth, having no connection with politics is at one blow to break up and sweep away the whole building of God. As well might it be said that the pulpit and the preacher have nothing to do with the inculcation of parental and filial privilege and obligation, as that they have nothing to do with the connection of law and freedom, of right and happiness, of the mutual claims, duties, and relations of rich and poor, high and low, the governer and the governed. [...]

I have not time this afternoon to particularise. If begun at all, it would lead me to an enumeration of every single precept, almost every single passage I have found recorded in the word of God, from Genesis to Revelation, where the Almighty has communicated his general will or entrusted his special messages to his servants the priests. How often do you read in this book, of God telling his prophets to go the poor, the low, the vile, the wretched, the helpless and the defenceless, the filth, the scum and off-scouring of mankind, to pour out upon their heads the phial of his indignation: I say, how often do you find God's message to his priests to that effect? Assuredly not often. But how often do you find God bidding his priests go to the princes, to the elders and to the rulers; how often do you read of God saying, go now to this king and to that court; go now to this council and that confederacy; whether of high priests, or of rulers, or of the elders, or of the shepherds, or of the priests of the people; and prophecy against them, the princes of Sodom, the rulers of Gomorrah, priests perjured by their perversion of the word of God, and rulers abandoned through their usurpation of the power of God; a corrupt priesthood joining hands with a tyrannical power, and thus hand in hand, arm in arm and foot to foot, marching onward, committing devastation, and making ravages of the chosen heritage of God?

How are these men to be met? How are these wicked rulers to be met? How are these priests and elders to be met? If they are to be met by force, I cannot help it. If they are to be met by force, from whence is that force to come? If they are to be slain by the sword, who is to wield it? These are solemn questions, my brethren. I pray you ask one another, ask the wisest and meekest and most submissive of your fellow countrymen for an answer to them. Is all this oppression and cruelty to continue? Are the Lord's poor to be trodden down, the lambs of his fold to the prey of the ravening wolf? Are the very men, who ought to guard and shelter, to feed and nourish the flock, to become its ravagers and destroyers? Is law, intended for the defence of the good and the punishment of the wicked, to be made itself an engine and instrument of evil? Are the magistrate and the minister, whose authority to reward the righteous and chastise the misdoer is of God and comes from heaven, to forget whence and for what that awful power has been given them? Are "the kings of the earth" to "set themselves," and "the rulers" to "take counsel together against the Lord and against his anointed?" [Psalm 2:2] No! not with impunity, not without visitation. Whenever they thus conspire, their end is at hand. Vengeance awakes, and destruction draws near. Reason and revelation alike tell us that they are to be met; that is clear. They must be met; that is certain, or God is to allow oppression and deceit and robbery, fraud and rapine, cruelty and murder, and every species of tyranny to ride and lord it over his heritage; which would be a libel on religion. It would be blasphemy against the attributes of God. But he will not allow it to continue. The wickedness of the wicked is to be brought to an end. It must therefore be withstood that it may be overthrown. But by whom, and in what way? The only way that a good man would wish, that a good man would choose, that a good man would advise and recommend, so long as there was any chance, any hope of its being effectual, is for the priests of the most high God to come forward and discharge the duties of their office, and on the floor of the Senate, in the camp of our armed hosts, in the court of Royalty, in the midst of the rulers, and the elders, at the gate of the Temple, yea, at the very foot of our national altar, to say to the spiritual and political shepherds of the people "the mouth of the Lord hath spoken it" [Isaiah 1:20]. The handwriting is even now to be seen upon the wall, in letters of living fire; it glares upon the awe-struck faces of the British Belshazzar and his thousand lords, who drink the blood of the poor out of the golden cups they have sacrilegiously taken from the sanctuary of that jealous God, whose anger is hot to follow and swift to overtake and destroy all them, no matter how high and mighty, that build and uphold their houses by oppression, that feast upon the spoil of unrighteousness, and make sport of the sufferings of those, whose wretchedness has been occasioned by their unhallowed and ruthless violence. God himself has come out of his place, and by a thousand tokens, stranger and far more terrible than the "fingers of a man's hand," that wrote upon the wall of the king's palace, MENE, MENE, TEKEL, UPHARSIN, has made known to us our sin and his displeasure, our national transgressions and his awakened indignation [Daniel 5:5 and 25]. [...]

It is the imperative duty of every man to do all he can to restore his country to moral health and social soundness again, by the love be bears to his brethren, by the reverence he bears to the ashes of his fathers, and by the oath that binds him in cheerful allegiance to the God of all his mercies. But most of all are the clergy called to this solemn service. The ministers of religion are the ambassadors of the Most High, the representatives of Jesus. They stand amongst their fellow men in the room and stead of him, "whom no man hath seen or can see," save in the person of his appointed messengers [1 Timothy 6:16]. As he, therefore, is emphatically the father of the fatherless, the husband of the widow, the friend, helper, deliverer and avenger of the lonely, the forlorn, the weak and the oppressed, so ought they, in his name, to plead for those, who cannot speak for themselves; to undertake the cause of those, who cannot act on their own behalf; and, heedless of all risks, fearless of all consequences, hurl the thunders and shoot the lightnings of heaven at the strong and daring rebels against God, who, by oppressing the poor, reproach their offended Maker. The christian ministry was designed to stand for ever as a moral breakwater against the swelling surge of pride and oppression.

34

[ANON.,] 'HYMN THIRTEENTH'

National Chartist Hymn Book (Rochdale: [1845]), p. 12

Hail, glorious morn! when Christ arose,
    And burst the fetters of the tomb,
And triumphed o'er his cruel foes
    Who stood amazed, – confounded, – dumb.

While time, and tide, and planets roll,
    Tho' kings, and priests, and tyrants join
To crush the burstings of the soul,
    Inspir'd with *truth – pure truth shall shine*!

Nor fear, nor sword, nor dungeons vile,
    Shall quench the ever-burning spark;
Although its path may be awhile
    Sunless and cheerless, – dreary, – dark.

It burns, and shall for ever burn,
    The fire of perfect liberty;
All men its principles shall learn,
    And then we shall, we must be free.

But Christ has risen from the dead
    And gained a glorious victory;
Then follow him – the Truth – your Head,
    Demand your Charter, and be free.

35

JOHN HENRY BRAMWICH, 'A HYMN'

Northern Star, 4 April 1846, 1st edn, p. 3

Britannia's sons, though slaves ye be,
God your Creator made you free;
He, life to all, and being, gave –
But never, never made a slave!

His works are wonderful to see –
All, all proclaim the Deity; –
He made the earth and formed the wave –
But never, never made a slave!

He made the sky, with spangles bright –
The moon to shine by silent night –
The sun, – and spread the vast concave –
But never, never made a slave!

The verdant earth on which we tread
Was, by His hand, all carpeted;
Enough for all He freely gave –
But never, never made the slave!

All men are equal in His sight, –
The bond, the free, the black, the white; –
He made them all, – them freedom gave –
He made the man, – *Man made the Slave!*

36

THOMAS COOPER, 'GOD OF THE EARTH, AND SEA, AND SKY'

English Chartist Circular 2:74 (1842), p. 88

God of the earth, and sea, and sky,
To thee thy mournful children cry!
Didst though the blue that bends o'er all
Spread for a general funeral pall?

Sadness and gloom pervade the land;
Death, – famine, – glare, on either hand! –
Didst thou plant earth upon the wave
Only to form one general grave?

Father! why didst thou form the flowers?
They blossom not for us, or ours!
Why didst thou clothe the fields with corn?
Robbers from us our share have torn.

The ancients of our wretched race
Told of thy sovereign power and grace
That in the sea their foes o'erthrew –
Great Father! is the record true?

Art thou the same who, from all time,
O'er every sea, through every clime; –
The stained oppressor's guilty head
Hath visited with vengeance dread?

To us, – the wretched and the poor,
Whom rich men drive from door to door, –
To us, then, make thy goodness known
And we thy lofty name will own.

Father! our frames are sinking fast! –
Hast thou our names behind thee cast?
Our sinless babes with hunger die!
Our hearts are hardening! – hear our cry!

Appear as in the ancient days;
Deliver us from our foes! – and praise
Shall from our hearts to thee ascend –
To God, our FATHER and our friend!

9.2

Feminist Religion

9.2 Feminist Religion

The priorities of nineteenth-century religious feminists were to free faith from its patriarchal constraints in order to find spiritual sources of empowerment for women and for the values associated with female character, and to recognise a neglected female aspect in the deity. These aspirations were first manifest in radical socialist feminist sects of the 1830s and 1840s, which venerated embodiments of 'the Woman Doctrine' or 'Woman Power' in order to usher in a millennium based on love and social harmony. Their legacy is felt among later feminist reformers and writers from a wide political and doctrinal spectrum, including those with relatively orthodox beliefs and others invested in new religious movements like Theism and Theosophy. These are significant precursors to the modern transatlantic school of feminist theology.

The figure of the Madonna was adopted as a symbol of the divine feminine by a number of women with Protestant backgrounds, especially in the wake of Mary's Immaculate Conception being formalised as doctrine in 1850, which raised her closer to divine status. Frances Power Cobbe (1822–1904) reflects on this phenomenon in the account of her travels in Italy where she witnessed the Marian cult as everyday social practice. Believing that religion should evolve to embody humanity's ever-advancing moral sensibilities, Cobbe interprets the intensified veneration of Mary as a revolution in modern Christianity which emphasises divine love and compassion over the cruder virtues of strength and authority. Crucially, this includes abolishing the doctrine of hell. Prevailing stereotypes of women as innately sympathetic, and maternal love unconditional, lead Cobbe to characterise this new divine characterisation as inevitably 'Feminine' and 'Motherly'.

But Cobbe is no sentimentalist, going on to identify problems in considering Mary (as doctrinally defined) as a divine image. First, she is subordinate to, and separate from, the masculine deity: a higher concept is that God per se 'is our father and mother both': here Cobbe paraphrases Unitarian Transcendentalist Theodore Parker, whose works she admired immensely.[1] Secondly, she objects to the 'vile ethics of asceticism' which sacralise a *virgin* mother and thereby denigrate female sexuality. Only when the image is removed from the context of doctrine – be that Catholic or Protestant – and treated as an autonomous spiritual symbol does the Madonna provide a satisfactory image of the divine feminine, for Cobbe and for contemporaries such as Anna Jameson and Harriet Beecher Stowe.[2]

While Cobbe turned to European Catholic iconography for feminist religious sources, Evangelical campaigner Josephine Butler (1828–1906) found them in the Bible and took this as her subject in the introduction to her edited collection of feminist essays. Earlier women Bible exegetes had tended to focus on female Bible characters in their quest for empowering exemplars,[3] but Butler goes straight to the central protagonist: she claims Jesus as Liberator and model of a feminist gospel. As in John Seeley's 1865 *Ecce Homo*, his role as atoning saviour is set aside in her focus on his social actions and philosophy – specifically regarding women. She constructs a montage of incidents from the gospels where Jesus respects, heals and comforts women, often defending them against prejudicial attacks from the populace and even from his own disciples; she also claims women's privileged status as Jesus's confidants, implying that women better understood his mission than did his more vocal male peers (see Luke 7, 8, 24; Mark 5, 16; John 8).

It was not unusual among more liberal biblicists to distinguish between Jesus's timeless messages and Paul's time-bound interpretations, and Butler makes a case for Paul's misogynistic betrayal of Jesus's feminism. She presents Paul as the head of a tradition of androcentric interpreters from whom the gospel must now be liberated, commissioning women to speak in this cause while – in a subversion of Paul's infamous injunction – *men* remain silent in the churches (see 1 Corinthians 13:34–5). Butler identifies herself as pioneer of a new feminist hermeneutic tradition, but also locates this in a wider nineteenth-century movement of liberation theology, citing enslaved African-Americans who found radical messages in the Bible which their masters were unable, or unwilling, to perceive.

Notes

1 See Cobbe's 'Introduction' to her edition of Theodore Parker's *Collected Works*, 12 vols (London: Trubner & Co., 1863), vol. 1, pp. v–xxxvi, on p. xviii.
2 See Kimberley VanEsveld Adams, *Our Lady of Victorian Feminism: The Madonna in the Work of Anna Jameson, Margaret Fuller and George Eliot* (Athens: Ohio University Press, 2001), pp. 1–4.
3 Rebecca Styler, 'A Scripture of Their Own: Nineteenth-Century Bible Biography and Feminist Bible Criticism', *Christianity and Literature* 57:1 (Fall 2007), pp. 65–85.

37

FRANCES POWER COBBE, 'MADONNA IMMACOLATA'

In *Italics: Brief Notes on People, Politics and Places in Italy in 1864* (London: Trubner & Co., 1864), pp. 321–334

Man needs for his God just so many attributes as at the stage of his progress he perceives to be Divine. First, Retributive Justice and Power; then Wisdom; then Clemency and Mercy; at last, perfect Love. The epoch at which a new conception is to be added to the old must always be one of religious excitement proportioned to the religious earnestness of the nation which receives it and of its advance towards monotheism. A fresh Ganesa or Avatur of Vishnu was doubtless added to Braminism, a Minerva or Prometheus to Greek mythology, without disturbance or difficulty. But when the Jews added to their conceptions of Jehovah the idea of the Father of *All* men—when the Arabs took in the thought of the absolute Sovereignty of Allah—there were the stupendous revolutions of Christianity and Islam. Probably, if we could discern their sources, we should find that, at bottom, all the stirrings of religious change, the enthusiastic devotion to new found Gods (such as Mithras and Serapis), by the old heathens, and the rise of the great Orders of Catholicism and Sects of Protestantism, pointed to some modification of, or rather accretion to, the prior idea of God.

    Not to press this thought too far, we may at least admit, that a Theology which does not make place for all the great Attributes which the human consciousness and Reason announce to us as belonging to our Maker, must remain a Theology liable to disturbance and modification whenever its deficiency becomes sensible. If it be a dogmatic Theology, professing to contain the whole scheme of Divine things, then it must either perish or submit to the scandal of adding a new Dogma to its canon. Only a Theology which professes itself incomplete, and leaves room for fresh truths, can admit of *constitutional* Progress without such Revolutions. At this hour the Church of England heaves in the struggle to admit the modern idea of Divine Goodness, that is, of a Goodness which must exclude the existence of Hell. The heart of the nation presses for the reception of the new idea. The clergy vehemently refuse it entrance, and thereby do their uttermost to make the Reform a Revolution. The Church of Rome, a few years ago, was disturbed by the popular outcry for the authorisation of a doctrine which, in fact, amounted to the apotheosis of a Feminine Divinity. The Pope took up the cause, and stopped all further struggle by proclaiming to astonished Catholics that a New Dogma had been *defined*—the Virgin was born Immaculate. Very absurd, and very pitiful, in some respects, was this great Romish movement; but under the guise of a tenet only fit for the diseased imaginations of mediæval monks to have invented, it is possible we may find there lurked some Idea whose development marked a real step in the progress of Catholic Christendom. "The world never apostatizes." Designing priests, politic Popes, fanatic monks and nuns have not *made* Mariolatry, only fostered it. Mariolatry means something beyond a scheme for the aggrandisement of any Church or Order. It were worth a great deal if we could find out what that meaning really is. A modification of creed, which has been going on in an ever increasing ratio for a thousand years throughout half Christendom, till it has fairly made a new Trinity, and directed all the freshest and most enthusiastic devotion to a new Divinity, is surely a phenomenon worthy of profoundest study. Its cause—could we ascertain it—might avail not a little to throw light on the mysteries of the religious nature of man and the Divine truths towards which (albeit, dimly, and in many a misleading myth and fable) his aspirations must point.

The clue which may, perhaps, guide us some steps in this inquiry, must be the answer to the question, "What is it which Catholics worship in the Madonna?" It is quite clear, as we have already remarked, that they have idealised her out of all identity with the historical wife of the Nazarene carpenter. The "Blessed Mother of God," "Queen of Heaven," "Star of the Sea," is quite another personage from any recorded by Biblical historians or even Patristic traditionalists. What is this idealised Madonna? If we had found her in Greek, Hindoo, or Egyptian pantheon, how should we have described her? Which Divine Attribute does she represent? There can be little doubt, I think, that the Madonna personifies Goodness, Mildness, Pity,—in a word, Motherly *Tenderness*. She is the representative of all the feminine virtues and perfections, Purity, Simplicity, Humility; but, above these and in pre-eminent degree, of Maternal *Love*. Men worship in the Madonna idealised Motherhood endowed with the blooming beauty and dignity of one of the old Immortal gods, and made mysteriously sacred by the added halo of virginity. She is Ceres and Minerva and Isis and Saraswati in one, and something more than all, as the imagination of modern Europe is more profound and tender than that of ancient Greece or Egypt or India. In worshipping the Madonna, the Catholic then worships a divinity who stands in his soul's temple for the purest and most tender Love. Power, Wisdom, Sanctity are attributed to her in so far as they are needful to make up the conception of deity, but she is not adored primarily as Powerful, Wise, or Holy,—but as tenderly Loving. She is neither the Creating, Redeeming, nor Sanctifying God. Men do not look on her with awe as Omnipotent, nor with gratitude as a self-sacrificing Saviour, nor does it seem they often pray to her for spiritual Sanctification. They look to her with adoring affection as the most loveable being they conceive in the universe, and they implore her to comfort their sorrows and fulfil their desires, with precisely the same confiding freedom with which they rested their heads on their mother's lap in childhood, or asked of her indulgence the toys they coveted.

The relation of the devotee to the Madonna is simply a repetition of the sweet and tender drama of infancy, acted in after life with a mother crowned with stars and able to grant all entreaties. Mary is addressed as "Parent of God," but she is felt rather to be the Universal Mother of Mankind. I have noticed in museums, where considerable numbers of images of Penates have been collected, that most of them were evidently miniature portraits of women; doubtless of the deceased female ancestors of the family, or occasionally, perhaps, of some special benefactresses. The sort of *dulia* paid to these Penates was perfectly human Mother Worship—death alone had effected such Apotheosis, or rather, Canonisation, as there was. Among the Chinese, as we all know, the worship of deceased parents, male and female, is the most vivid part of the national religion. A different phase of the sentiment is the adoration for a being not the mother of the individual worshipper, but contemplated abstractedly as a representative of Motherhood. The Ephesian Diana, Ceres, and Isis seem to have belonged to this order among the heathens. The Catholic Olympus, beside several canonised human Mothers (among whom St. Monica is most noticeable), gives a supreme place to a Divine Mother in whom,—as all Manhood was incarnated in her Son,—so all Womanhood might be personified. The process by which the historical Mary of Nazareth was transformed into such an ideal of Womanhood is not difficult to understand. If *any* one were to be so transformed in the Catholic theology it could only be the Virgin. As her Son was the new Adam, so must she have been the new Eve. The mystery of her Virgin Motherhood lifted her at once into a region wherein no dignity, however stupendous, could seem altogether out of place. Admitting Christ to be the God-Man, if there were to be a God-woman, it could only be his mother, whom St. Athanasius himself had recognised as "Parent of God". The Child, as in the Chinese custom, ennobled the Parent; nor was there any other human relative to dispute her claims—wife, or daughter, or even sister— specified by the history. The Incarnate Deity *had* a mortal Mother; but for other human ties, they were either non-existent, or explained away by the story. Thus the only candidate for apotheosis in the Catholic theology was Mary of Nazareth. No marvel was it, then, that when the sentiment of the Church demanded the elevation of a new Divinity who should personate the Feminine Attributes, it was on the head of the Virgin it placed the heavenly crown bestowed by the Father and the Son, and made with "Madonna Incoronata" the new Trinity of Southern Christianity.

What does this wide-spread sentiment, requiring this new divinity, indicate? It can surely only point to the fact that there was something lacking in the elder creed, which, as time went on, became a more and more sensible deficiency, till at last the instinct of the multitude (acting under essentially polytheistic conceptions) filled it up in this amazing manner. Other Divine attributes had been personified before, but Maternal Tenderness had been left out, and after long pressure was thus admitted at last. The position of the highest canonised saint was not sufficient for its representative. She has become, in strictest sense, "the Divine Mother."

There is a great truth and a great error in this wonderful act of Catholic Christendom. The Protestant, who looks on it as mere stupid dereliction and idolatry, is exceedingly mistaken. The Reformed Churches have rather to ask themselves whether, in abjuring Mariolatry, they have not also abjured somewhat with which their creed can ill dispense. Had the old Egyptians reformed themselves, by abandoning the altars of Osiris (the Divine Goodness), and confining themselves to Ra and Thoth, the representatives of Power and Wisdom, should we have said they gained much by the change while the Goodness of God remained forgotten? The Catholic world has found a great truth—that Love,—motherly tenderness and pity, is a divine and holy thing, worthy of adoration. They have fallen into a great error, by conceiving of it, not as it is, in truth, the character of the One blessed "Parent of Good, Almighty," but as the attribute of another and inferior being. The truth is one the world should learn. The error is an inevitable result of the whole system of Catholic theology; in fact, is the original error of all Polytheism—the attribution to secondary objects of worship of the honour due to the One God alone. How is the truth to be learned—the error to be foresworn? Only in one way. When mankind, at large, receives the blessed faith that *all* goodness and tenderness, as well as justice, and power, and holiness, are absolutely impersonated in God—that *He* is "our Father and our Mother both," and that we have no need to multiply deities, and invent new gods, since every adorable attribute exists in its plenitude in HIM.

To purify our creed, by simply rejecting any Divine Person, without taking up, at the same time, every Divine idea that Person conveyed to the mind of his worshipper, is impossible. We do not thus attain to more truth, but to less truth. Monotheism is not the *analysis* of Deity, with the reservation of one or more attributes. It is the *synthesis* of all the true conceptions of God ever vouchsafed to man.

How much the world wants this truth, which Catholic Christendom has revealed in its myth of the Virgin's Coronation, there is small need to tell. The heart of humanity longs to rest itself on the compassion of its Creator. We have had enough of hell and "terrors of the Lord." The cry which has come from ten thousand voices of our English clergy in behalf of the dreadful doctrine, does but testify to their sense that its power is passing—nay, has actually passed away. We are sick of such night-mare horrors, and turn away with disgust from the religious systems in which they lie embedded. We crave, one and all of us, for a God whom we can perfectly, spontaneously, absolutely adore. *That* God is He, and He alone, who unites in one the Father's justice and the Mother's love.

But if we need to adopt the truth, shadowed out by Mariolatry, we cannot blind ourselves to the evils resulting from the errors mixed up therewith. In adding—as it has practically done—a new deity to its Pantheon, the Romish Church has not only gone one step further in Polytheism; it has gone a great way towards severing, even further than hitherto, the bond between morality and religion. Though the belief that the *One* great Judge is *also* our tender Parent, can only serve to help us to better obedience,—the belief that the Judge is a separate God, and our beloved and chosen Deity quite another—is no harmless delusion. Devotion to Mary does not mean at all, necessarily, a seeking for *spiritual* benefits of any kind. Mary may be most ardently worshipped, and her votary, in fact, live in complete adoration of her (*i.e.*, in what he believes to be a highly religious state) with exceedingly little of moral training whatever. Nor is this all. The vile ethics of asceticism are visible through the whole myth of the Madonna. Albeit a mother, and worshipped precisely because she is a mother, it is so managed, that natural, human motherhood, such as God has made it, should receive, not honour, but insult through her. She is a *Virgin;* herself "immaculately conceived." Her pictures must present, not glorious embodiments of maternity, like the old marble Niobe, but impossible combinations, after which the painter toils in vain—the Maiden and the Mother in one. The laws which God has given to our nature, beautiful and sacred as they are; the relations He has made so inexpressibly dear and sweet, are all vilified by this degrading conception. He who would naturally feel that a human mother, pure and good, was the holiest thing in all the world, is bade by every image of the Madonna to believe she is *not* the holiest, *not* the most Divine. She would be holier if God's laws had been set aside, had she been a Virgin-mother. To be Divine she must have escaped—not the weaknesses and frailties of our nature, for of them there is no question, but—the beneficent material laws under which we exist. Is it any marvel that when such ideas are taught by every symbol of religion which meets the worshipper's eye, his sense of the sanctity of natural purity should be completely perverted? The deification of virginity can never be otherwise than the desecration of marriage.

38

JOSEPHINE E. BUTLER, 'INTRODUCTION'

In Josephine E. Butler (ed.), *Woman's Work and Woman's Culture: A Series of Essays* (London: Macmillan & Co., 1869), pp. liii–lx

Once more I venture to say I appeal to Christ, and to Him alone, as the fountain-head of those essential and eternal truths which it is our duty and our wisdom to apply to all the changing circumstances of human society. Believing as I do that He is Very God, and that He was in human form the Exponent of the mind of God to the world, I hold that His authority must be higher than that of any man or society of men by whom the Truth which we receive from them, so far as we receive Truth from them at all, can only be transmitted. I believe all His acts to have had a supreme and everlasting significance. The teaching of His great typical acts is not less profound than that of His words. His teaching was for all time; much of St. Paul's was for a given time. There has been at all times a silent minority who have held this belief, and gone back to this standard. In the darkest ages of the Church there have been women whose whole lives were a protest against the capricious and various teachings of the Church concerning women, and who consequently endured a life-long martyrdom. In the days of Luther and of the Puritans this silent minority maintained a similar protest against errors of a somewhat different tendency. I know not myself to what rightly to apply the name of Church, if it be not to such a company of faithful men and women who throughout all the ages have reflected the teaching of Christ himself in its integrity. These all asserted the equality of all men and women, and asserted it on Christ's teaching. I am not speaking here of any intellectual equality, about which more than enough has been said on both sides, and respecting which it seems to me that men are more anxious to retain a theory undisturbed, than to bring that theory to the test, which not the past, but a hoped-for future alone can supply. Of these subtle subdivisions, physical, intellectual, and moral, in which the inferiority or equality of women is so jealously defined and guarded in theory, I find no hint whatever in Christ's teaching. The equality He proclaimed is on a wider and deeper basis, and until the truth of *that* equality is felt and admitted by Christendom, and recognised in our laws, our customs, and our religion, there will continue to be the uncertainty

330

and unhappiness which now exist, and the reiterated attack and defence on the subject of those intellectual and moral ranks which, when truly known, and then only, will incline us to praise the excellence of God's creation, instead of taunting each other. Among the dullest of the poor slaves, before their emancipation, there were some whose intellects were so quickened by the agony of the iron of slavery which had entered their souls, that they discovered for themselves that principle so dreaded by those who would maintain for themselves the monopoly of privileges. Crouching among the sugar-canes, they secretly searched throughout the Bible for arguments against slavery, and so keen, and so dangerous to the minds of their masters, were the arguments which those poor negroes drew from the Scriptures, (in spite of the sanction which on the surface and at first sight many parts of the Bible seem to give to slavery,) that the masters found it convenient to forbid the reading of the Bible to their slaves. I need scarcely say that it was through a steady gaze fixed on Christ himself, not on Moses or St. Paul, that these slaves discovered the truth that liberty and equality are the law of Christ for the world. Similarly, the same intense gaze, quickened by suffering and solitary questioning on a state of things that seems to us unjust, has led a silent minority of women in all times, and a greater number in these latter times, to conclusions which, had they been earlier expressed, would have been stamped as revolutionary.

The limits of this Essay are far too short to admit of more than the very slightest indication of Christ's teaching about women. In those beautiful pages of "Ecce Homo," which speak of Christ's dealings with certain women, and in which His acts are allowed to have a significance of which all ages should have availed themselves for guidance, the writer is nevertheless deficient and one-sided. How could he but be so? for he is a man; and to bring the fulness of the reflected light of intelligent consciences to bear upon the principles announced by Christ's acts and words towards women, would need the combined thoughtfulness and wisdom of a man and a woman; and the writer is a man and not a woman, nor does he thoroughly know women. There are few men who can thoroughly know the minds of women in a state of society in which the reality of woman's nature is repressed, and it is especially difficult for those who are in a position of life which confines their intercourse to women of their own class, which is only one class among many. The author of "Ecce Homo" has set the example to those to whom it did not occur to do so for themselves, of venturing straight into the presence of Christ for an answer to every question, and of silencing the voice of all theologians from St. Paul to this day, until we have heard what the Master says. It may be that God will give grace to some woman in the time to come to discern more clearly, and to reveal to others, some truth which theologians have hitherto failed to see in its fulness; for from the intimacy into which our Divine Master admitted women with Himself it would seem that His communications of the deepest nature were not confined to male recipients; and what took place during His life on earth may, through His Holy Spirit, be continued now. It is instructive to recall the fact that the most stupendous announcement ever made to the world—the announcement of an event concerning which the whole world is divided to this day, and which more than all others is bound up with our hopes of immortality—the resurrection of Christ—was first made to women; nor can we wonder,—looking back over the ages since then, and seeing how any truths asserted by women, not at once palpable to the outward sense or proveable by logic, have been accounted as idle tales—that of the first apostles it should have been said, "the words of the women seemed unto them as idle tales," when they declared that Christ was risen. Among the great typical acts of Christ which were evidently and intentionally for the announcement of a principle for the guidance of society, none were more markedly so than His acts towards women; and I appeal to the open Book and to the intelligence of every candid student of Gospel history for the justification of my assertion, that, in all important instances of His dealings with women, His dismissal of each case was accompanied by a distinct act of *Liberation*. In one case He emancipated a woman from legal thraldom: His act no doubt appeared to those who witnessed it as that of a dangerous leveller; for while He granted to the woman a completeness of freedom from the tyranny of law which must have electrified the bystanders, he imposed upon the men present, and upon all men by implication, the higher obligation which they had made a miserable attempt to enforce upon one half of society only, and the breach of which their cruel laws visited with terrible severity on women alone; they all went out convicted by conscience, while the woman alone remained free; but, be it observed (for this is sometimes perversely overlooked by persons who claim an immunity which is licentiousness, and who strike at the very root of equality, by separating self-restraint from the liberty which ought to be common to all), free in a double sense, free alike from the inward moral slavery and from the harsh, humanly-imposed judgment. The emancipation granted to another in the matter of hereditary disabilities was signal. In a moment he struck off chains which had been riveted by the traditions of centuries, and raised her from the position, accepted even by herself, of a "Gentile dog" to one higher than the highest of the commonwealth of Israel. In another case His "Go in peace," and words of tender and respectful commendation to one who had been exiled from society, contrasted solemnly with His rebuke to His self-satisfied host, who, while firmly holding his place among the honoured of this world, marvelled that Christ should not seem to be aware "what manner of woman" it was who touched Him. To another, before ever she had spoken a word, He cried, "Woman, thou art loosed!" and to objectors He replied, "Shall not this woman, being a daughter of Abraham, whom Satan hath bound these eighteen years, be loosed from this bond on the Sabbath day?" The tyrannies and infirmities from which He freed these persons severally, were various and manifold, and this does but increase the significance of his whole proceeding towards them. Search throughout the Gospel history, and observe his conduct in regard to women, and it will be found that the word liberation expresses, above all others, the act which changed the whole life and character and position of the women dealt with, and which ought to have changed the character of men's treatment of women from that time forward. While in His example of submission to parents, of filial duty and affection, in His inculcation of the sacredness of marriage, and of the duty of obedience to laws which *ought* to be obeyed, His righteousness far exceeded the righteousness of the Pharisees of His own or of the present day, it seems to me impossible for anyone candidly to study Christ's whole life and words without seeing that the principle of the perfect equality of all human beings was announced by Him as the basis of social philosophy. To some extent this has been practically acknowledged in the relations of men to men; only in one case has it been consistently ignored, and that is in the case of that half of the human race, in regard to which His doctrine of equality was more markedly enforced than in any other. It is no wonder that there should be some women whose love for *this Saviour* exceeds the love which it is possible for any man to feel for Him, and that, retiring from the encounter with prejudices which are apt to lurk even in the minds of the most just and most generous of men, they should be driven to cast themselves in a great solitude of heart before *Him,*—for He only is just—He only is holy—He only is infinitely tender.

9.3

Poetic and Aesthetic Religion

9.3 Poetic and Aesthetic Religion

A Victorian legacy of Romanticism was the increased identification of the spiritual with the aesthetic. While many came to regard the Bible as a book of symbols, literature (and especially poetry) was credited with scriptural qualities.[1] The metaphorical status of religious language was recognised in all liberal religious developments, while a new openness emerged towards non-scriptural imagery of the divine. Through the Romantic impulse, the poet claimed vatic capacities, and in a more modest sense many novelists believed their fiction to be a form of preaching. This poeticisation of religion was not purely focused on the spiritual power of the word – the ritualist sensibility valued aesthetic objects as channels of divine grace, appealing to emotion and imagination as well as the intellect. The extracts from Howitt and Jameson demonstrate literary and visual aspects of the Victorian aesthetic-religious sensibility.

Rejecting the asceticism of her Quaker background (see 5.4), Mary Howitt (1799–1888) embraced a life of literary activity, co-producing with her husband *Howitt's Journal of Literature and Popular Progress* which offered entertaining and improving reading for the lower and middle classes, and authoring many tales, poems, essays and translations. Her poem identifies with the Romantic vatic ideal of 'Poetry' as a spiritual capacity to perceive the infinite through finite forms, and to identify with the progressive cause of humanity. She presents an encounter with the 'spirit of poetry' as inspiration and authority for her authorial vocation, alluding to grove and mountain top, the classical and scriptural loci for such epiphanies. Her terms are evocative of the Holy Spirit, left as a post-lapsarian consolation to encourage and teach the inhabitants of a world bereft of God's direct presence. It is likely that Howitt was influenced by the Quaker idea of the 'inner light' by which God was thought to commune directly with a worshipper's spirit; her literary partner William Howitt characterised Wordsworth's philosophy as 'poetic Quakerism'.[2] Following a tribute to poet-heroes including Milton ('the blind old man') and Goethe, Howitt presents herself as a humbler acolyte who accepts her calling with the reluctance of Moses. (The 'poor peasant' may be Robert Burns, although the significance of speaking 'in Mary's voice' remains obscure). Although at first Howitt associates poetry with ecstatic vision, she shifts the emphasis to scenes of humble life and the writer's humanist task to feel and generate expansive human sympathy. Her softening of the mighty force into a 'friend' may also be a vestige of her Quaker heritage, as is perhaps her confidence to claim for herself a spiritual capacity that was widely assumed to be uniquely masculine.

Anna Jameson (1794–1860) was a popular and influential art critic with Broad Church leanings and feminist credentials. Her four-volume series *Sacred and Legendary Art* (1848–1852) was a sympathetic and respectful analysis of an essentially Roman Catholic iconographical tradition across several centuries, which she presents as a 'Poetry' of the sacred suited to the 'state of feeling' in which they were produced.[3] More than this, she interprets these images as a visual folk theology that arose from the repressed yearnings of a populace alienated from the church, whom she accuses of veiling the compassionate gospel through its authoritarianism and theological obfuscation. She credits the spiritual perceptions of the laity with keeping alive the idea of an inclusive gospel based on pacific social values, giving special place to women and the poor, a theme she sees in the paintings discussed. Referencing 'the poet', she paraphrases Wordsworth's defence of the products of imagination in the context of his argument in *The Excursion* that popular spiritual metaphors preceded, and would supersede, formal religious systems (*The Excursion*, book IV, lines 760–1 in the 1814 edition).

Jameson connects her argument to other scholarship that similarly applied a respectful cultural relativism to popular beliefs of the past and their embodiments. She alludes to Francois Guizot's idea of folk literature as a 'national poetry' in his highly acclaimed *History of Civilisation in Europe* (1828), and Henry Hart Milman's discussion in *The History of Christianity* (1840) of a 'polytheistic' phase in medieval Christianity which incorporated saint iconography. But, although ostensibly speaking as a historian, Jameson indirectly addresses her own era's movement to liberalise and humanise dogma, most evidently when contrasting the Church's 'God of Vengeance' with the paintings' suggestions of a deity in sympathy with human suffering, and the divine potential in human beings themselves. The narrative voice slips between that of historical distance – '[w]e are critical, not credulous' – and enthusiastic championing of popular religious metaphor over the repressive dicta of the Church.

Notes

1 Charles LaPorte, *Victorian Poets and the Changing Bible* (Charlottesville: University of Virginia Press, 2011), pp. 1–2. See also T. R. Wright, *Theology and Literature* (Oxford: Basil Blackwell, 1988), pp. 146–149.
2 *Homes and Haunts of the Most Eminent British Poets* [1847] (London: George Routledge & Sons Ltd, 1894), p. 542.
3 Anna B. Jameson, 'Preface to First Edition', *Sacred and Legendary Art*, 2 vols [1848], new edn (London: Longman, Green & Co., 1890), vol. 1, pp. vii–ix, on p. vii.

39

MARY HOWITT, 'THE SPIRIT OF POETRY'

In *Ballads and Poems* (London: Longman, Brown, Green and Longmans, 1847), pp. 265–269

Men build to thee no shrine,
Yet every holy place is filled with thee;
Dim groves and mountain-tops alike are thine,
Spirit of Poetry!
Island and ocean-peak;
Seas where the keel of ships shall never go;
Cots, palaces, and graves; whate'er can speak
Of human love or woe;

All are the shrines where thou
Broodest with power, not visible, yet strong;
Like odour from the rose, we know not how
Borne to the sense along.
Oh! spirit, which art pure,
Mighty and holy, and of God art sprung;
Which teachest to aspire and to endure,
As ne'er taught human tongue;

What art thou? A glad spirit,
Sent down, like Hope, when Eden was no more,
From the high heavenly place thou didst inherit,
An Eden to restore;
Sent down to teach as never
Taught worldly wisdom; to make known the right;
And the strong armour of sublime endeavour
To gird on for the fight.

I see whom thou hast called;
The mighty men, the chosen of the earth,
Strong minds invincible, and disenthralled,

Made freemen at their birth.
I see, on spirit-wings,
How thou hast set them high, each like a star,
More royal than the loftiest names of kings,
Mightier than conquerors are;

How hast thou cast a glory
Over the dust of him, sublimely wise,
The blind old man, with his immortal story
Of a lost Paradise;
How thou, by mountain-streams,
Met'st the poor peasant, and from passion's leaven
Refined his soul, wooing with holy themes
In Mary's voice from heaven.

'Twas thou didst give the key
Of human hearts to Goethe, to unlock
Their sealed-up depths, like that old mystery
Of the wand-stricken rock.
All these I see, and more;
All crowned with glory, loftier than their race;
And, trembling, I shrink back, abashed and poor,
Unworthy of thy grace.

For what am I, that thou
Shouldst visit me in love, and give me might
To touch, like these, man's heart, his pride to bow;
Or, erring, lead him right?
Oh! dost thou visit me?
Is it thy spirit that I feel in all;
Thy light, yet brighter than the sun's, I see?
Is thine this spiritual call?

It is! it is! Though weak
And poor my spirit, thou dost condescend
Thy beauty to unveil, and with me speak
As gentle friend with friend.
With thee I walk the ways
Of daily life; and, human tears and sighs
Interpreting, so learn to love my race.
And with them sympathise.

Hence is it that all tears
Which human sorrow sheds are dear to me;

That the soul struggling with its mortal fears
    Moveth me mightily.
    Hence is it that the hearts
Of little children and unpractised youth
So gladden me with their unworldly arts,
    Their kindness and their truth.

    Hence is it that the eye
And sunken cheek of poverty so move,
Seen only by a glimpse in passing by,
    My soul, to human love.
    Spirit, I will not say
Thou dost not visit me; nor yet repine,
Less mighty though I be, less great than they
    Whom thou hast made divine.

40

ANNA B. JAMESON, 'INTRODUCTION'

In *Sacred and Legendary Art*, 2 vols [1848], new edition (London: Longmans, Green & Co., 1890), vol. 1, pp. 1–7

We cannot look round a picture gallery—we cannot turn over a portfolio of prints after the old masters, nor even the modern engravings which pour upon us daily, from Paris, Munich, or Berlin—without perceiving how many of the most celebrated productions of Art, more particularly those which have descended to us from the early Italian and German schools, represent incidents and characters taken from the once popular legends of the Catholic Church. This form of '*Hero-Worship*' has become, since the Reformation, strange to us—as far removed from our sympathies and associations as if it were antecedent to the fall of Babylon and related to the religion of Zoroaster, instead of being left but two or three centuries behind us, and closely connected with the faith of our forefathers and the history of civilisation and Christianity. Of late years, with a growing passion for the works of Art of the Middle Ages, there has arisen among us a desire to comprehend the state of feeling which produced them, and the legends and traditions on which they are founded;—a desire to understand, and to bring to some surer critical test, representations which have become familiar without being intelligible. To enable us to do this, we must pause for a moment at the outset; and, before we plunge into the midst of things, ascend to higher ground, and command a far wider range of illustration than has yet been attempted, in order to take cognizance of principles and results which, if not new, must be contemplated in a new relation to each other.

The Legendary Art of the Middle Ages sprang out of the legendary literature of the preceding ages. For three centuries at least, this literature, the only literature which existed at the time, formed the sole mental and moral nourishment of the *people* of Europe. The romances of Chivalry, which long afterwards succeeded, were confined to particular classes, and left no impress on Art, beyond the miniature illuminations of a few manuscripts. This legendary literature, on the contrary, which had worked itself into the life of the people, became, like the antique mythology, as a living soul diffused through the loveliest forms of Art, still vivid and vivifying, even when the old faith in its mystical significance was lost or forgotten. And it is a mistake to suppose that these legends had their sole origin in the brains of dreaming monks. The wildest of them had some basis of truth to rest on, and the forms which they gradually assumed were but the necessary result of the age which produced them. They became the intense expression of that inner life, which revolted against the desolation and emptiness of the outward existence; of those crushed and outraged sympathies which cried aloud for rest, and refuge, and solace, and could nowhere find them. It will be said, 'In the purer doctrine of the GOSPEL.' But where was that to be found? The Gospel was not then the heritage of the poor: Christ, as a comforter, walked not among men. His own blessed teaching was inaccessible except to the learned: it was shut up in rare manuscripts; it was perverted and sophisticated by the passions and the blindness of those few to whom it *was* accessible. The bitter disputes in the early Church relative to the nature of the Godhead, the subtle distinctions and incomprehensible arguments of the theologians, the dread entertained by the predominant Church of any heterodox opinions concerning the divinity of the Redeemer, had all conspired to remove *Him*, in His personal character of Teacher and Saviour, far away from the hearts of the benighted and miserable people—far, far away into regions speculative, mysterious, spiritual, whither they could not, dared not follow Him. In this state of things, as it has been remarked by a distinguished writer, 'Christ became the object of a remoter, a more awful adoration. The mind began, therefore, to seek out, or eagerly to seize, some other more material beings in closer alliance with human sympathies.' And the same author, after tracing in vivid and beautiful language the dangerous but natural consequences of this feeling, thus sums up the result: 'During the perilous and gloomy days of persecution, the reverence for those who endured martyrdom for the religion of Christ had grown up out of the best feelings of man's improved nature. Reverence gradually grew into veneration, worship, adoration: and although the more rigid theology maintained a marked distinction between the honour shown to the martyrs, and that addressed to the Redeemer and the Supreme Being, the line was too fine and invisible not to be transgressed by excited popular feeling.'[1]

'We live,' says the poet, 'through admiration, hope, and love.' Out of these vital aspirations—not indeed always 'well or wisely placed,' but never, as in the heathen mythology, degraded to vicious and contemptible objects—arose and spread the universal passion for the traditional histories of the saints and martyrs,—personages endeared and sanctified in all hearts, partly as examples of the loftiest virtue, partly as benign intercessors between suffering humanity and that Deity who, in every other light than as a God of Vengeance, had been veiled from their eyes by the perversities of schoolmen and fanatics, till He had receded beyond their reach, almost beyond their comprehension. Of the prevalence and of the incalculable influence of this legendary literature from the seventh to the tenth century, that is, just about the period when Modern Art was struggling into existence, we have a most striking picture in Guizot's 'Histoire de la Civilisation.' 'As after the siege of Troy (says this philosophical and eloquent writer) there were found, in every city of Greece, men who collected the traditions and adventures of heroes, and sung them for the recreation of the people, till these recitals became a national passion, a national poetry; so, at the time of which we speak, the traditions of what may be called the heroic ages of Christianity had the same interest for the nations of Europe. There were men who made it their business to collect them, to transcribe them, to read or recite them aloud, for the edification and delight of the people. And this was the only literature, properly so called, of that time.'

Now, if we go back to the *authentic* histories of the sufferings and heroism of the early martyrs, we shall find enough there, both of the wonderful and the affecting, to justify the credulity and enthusiasm of the unlettered people, who saw no reason why they should not believe in one miracle as well as in another. In these universally diffused legends, we may recognise the means, at least one of the means, by which a merciful Providence, working through its own immutable laws, had provided against the utter depravation, almost extinction, of society. Of the 'Dark Ages,' emphatically so called, the period to which I allude was perhaps the darkest; it was 'of Night's black arch the key-stone.' At a time when men were given over to the direst evils that can afflict humanity,—ignorance, idleness, wickedness, misery; at a time when the everyday incidents of life were a violation of all the moral instincts of mankind; at a time when all things seemed abandoned to a blind chance, or the brutal law of force; when there was no repose, no refuge, no safety anywhere; when the powerful inflicted, and the weak endured, whatever we can conceive of most revolting and intolerable; when slavery was recognised by law throughout Europe; when men fled to cloisters, to shut themselves from oppression, and women to shield themselves from outrage; when the manners were harsh, the language gross; when all the softer social sentiments, as pity, reverence, tenderness, found no resting-place in the actual relations of life; when for the higher ranks there was only the fierce excitement of war, and on the humbler classes lay the weary, dreary monotony of a stagnant existence, poor in pleasures of every kind, without aim, without hope; *then*—wondrous reaction of the ineffaceable instincts of good implanted within us!—arose a literature which reversed the outward order of things, which asserted and kept alive in the hearts of men those pure principles of Christianity which were outraged in their daily actions; a literature in which peace was represented as better than war, and sufferance more dignified than resistance: which exhibited poverty and toil as honourable, and charity as the first of virtues; which held up to imitation and emulation self-sacrifice in the cause of good, and contempt of death for conscience' sake; a literature in which the tenderness, the chastity, the heroism of woman, played a conspicuous part; which distinctly protested against slavery, against violence, against impurity in word and deed; which refreshed the fevered and darkened spirit with images of moral beauty and truth; revealed bright glimpses of a better land, where 'the wicked cease from troubling,' and brought down the angels of God with shining wings and bearing crowns of glory, to do battle with the demons of darkness, to catch the fleeting soul of the triumphant martyr, and carry it at once into a paradise of eternal blessedness and peace!

Now the Legendary Art of the three centuries which comprise the revival of learning, was, as I have said, the reflection of this literature, of this teaching. Considered in this point of view, can we easily overrate its interest and importance?

When, after the long period of darkness which followed upon the decline of the Roman Empire, the Fine Arts began to revive, the first, and for several ages the only, impress they received was that of the religious spirit of the time. Painting, Sculpture, Music, and Architecture, as they emerged one after another from the 'formless void,' were pressed into the service of the Church. But it is a mistake to suppose, that in adroitly adapting the reviving Arts to her purposes, in that magnificent spirit of calculation which at all times characterised her, the Church from the beginning selected the subjects, or dictated the use that was to be made of them. We find, on the contrary, edicts and councils *repressing* the popular extravagances in this respect, and denouncing those apocryphal versions of sacred events and traditions which had become the delight of the people. But vain were councils and edicts; the tide was too strong to be so checked. The Church found herself obliged to accept and mould to her own objects the exotic elements she could not eradicate. She *absorbed*, so to speak, the evils and errors she could not expel. There seems to have been at this time a sort of compromise between the popular legends, with all their wild mixture of northern and classical superstitions, and the Church legends properly so called. The first great object to which reviving Art was destined, was to render the Christian places of worship a theatre of instruction and improvement for the people, to attract and to interest them by representations of scenes, events, and personages, already so familiar as to require no explanation, appealing at once to their intelligence and their sympathies; embodying in beautiful shapes (beautiful at least in their eyes) associations and feelings and memories deep-rooted in their very hearts, and which had influenced, in no slight degree, the progress of civilisation, the development of mind. Upon these creations of ancient Art we cannot look as *those* did for whom they were created; we cannot annihilate the centuries which lie between us and them; we cannot, in simplicity of heart, forget the artist in the image he has placed before us, nor supply what may be deficient in his work, through a reverentially excited fancy. We are critical, not credulous. We no longer accept this polytheistic form of Christianity; and there is little danger, I suppose, of our falling again into the strange excesses of superstition to which it led. But if we have not much sympathy with modern imitations of Mediæval Art, still less should we sympathise with that narrow puritanical jealousy which holds the monuments of a real and earnest faith in contempt. All that God has permitted once to exist in the past should be considered as the possession of the present; sacred for example or warning, and held as the foundation on which to build up what is better and purer. It should seem an established fact, that all revolutions in religion, in government, and in art, which begin in the spirit of scorn, and in a sweeping destruction of the antecedent condition, only tend to a reaction. Our puritanical ancestors chopped off the heads of Madonnas and Saints, and paid vagabonds to smash the storied windows of our cathedrals;—*now*, are these rejected and outraged shapes of beauty coming back to us, or are we not rather going back to them? As a Protestant, I might fear lest in doing so we confound the eternal spirit of Christianity with the mutable forms in which it has deigned to speak to the hearts of men, forms which must of necessity vary with the degree of social civilisation, and bear the impress of the feelings and fashions of the age which produce them; but I must also feel that we ought to comprehend, and to hold in due reverence, that which has once been consecrated to holiest aims, which has shown us what a magnificent use has been made of Art, and how it may still be adapted to good and glorious purposes, if, while we respect these time-consecrated images and types, we do not allow them to fetter us, but trust in the progressive spirit of Christianity to furnish us with new impersonations of the good—new combinations of the beautiful. I hate the destructive as I revere the progressive spirit. We must laugh if any one were to try and persuade us that the sun was guided along his blazing path by 'a fair-haired god who touched a golden lyre;' but shall we therefore cease to adore in the Apollo Belvedere the majestic symbol of light, the most divine impersonation of intellectual power and beauty? So of the corresponding Christian symbols:—may that time never come, when we shall look up to the effigy of the winged and radiant angel trampling down the brute-fiend, without a glow of faith in the perpetual supremacy and final triumph of good over evil!

Note

1 [Henry Hart] Milman, Hist. of Christianity [*The History of Christianity from the Birth of Christ to the Abolition of Paganism in the Roman Empire*, 3 vols (London: John Murray, 1840)], vol. iii. 540.

9.4

Natural Religion

9.4 Natural Religion

Many nineteenth-century religious movements sought to re-emphasise divine immanence, a theme felt to have been diminished by the transcendent emphasis in Calvinism and Deist rationalism. Liberal theological developments spoke of the divine indwelling of the human and non-human natural world, and in the second half of the century orthodox Christians broadly shifted their emphasis from atonement to incarnation, finding greater affinity between the earthly and divine.[1] Personal and social salvation were increasingly interpreted in terms of natural processes rather than miraculous interventions. The extracts given here make the case for God's habitation in nature, the first from the viewpoint of a Unitarian Transcendentalist who saw himself in continuity with the Romantic poets, and the second from a High Church Anglican, for whom the incarnation had always been the pre-eminent spiritual event and archetype.

Theodore Parker (1810–60) influenced liberal religious thinkers on both sides of the Atlantic in locating the evidences for God within the natural order and the human mind, rather than in external sources such as scripture or history. This lecture was first published in his 1842 *Discourse of Matters Pertaining to Religion*. He presents an ecstatic perception of the world in which the divine is 'wholly, vitally, essentially present'. Rejecting the mechanistic image of the clockmaker God, he claims the world is perpetually activated by supernatural energy. He gathers together a montage of Bible episodes describing exceptional divine visitations via natural phenomena to Abraham, Moses, Jesus, Elijah, and in the act of creation itself, from which Parker draws the implication of nature's permanently inspired condition: 'A voice cries to him from the thicket, "God will provide." The bushes burn with deity. Angels minister to him. [...] God's fair voice [...] whispers, in nature, still and small, [...] moving on the face of the deep, and bringing light out of darkness' (cf. Genesis 22:11–13, Exodus 3:2–4, Matthew 4:11, 1 Kings 19:12, Genesis 1:2–3). The infinite is ever-present and ever-sensible, so that nature becomes a continuous revelation and epiphany. Parker clarifies that this is not paganism – God is immanent in matter, yet simultaneously 'transcends the world' – but he nonetheless acknowledges some continuity with the nature worship that constituted the earliest religion. He is also keen to show his philosophy is not anti-scientific: natural law is affirmed as the mode by which God consistently operates. In this sense, Parker supernaturalises nature while naturalising the divine.

Parker recognises his roots in the work of British Romantic poets, quoting from line 31 of Coleridge's 'Hymn before Sun-Rise in the Vale of Chamouni', an adoration of the deity written at the foot of Mont Blanc. A phrase from Wordsworth's 'Intimations Ode' is quoted to celebrate the vestigial pre-lapsarian sensibility within human beings that enables this enchanted perception. Parker then briefly extends his logic to affirm human nature as also home of the divine, although it is the non-human natural world that evokes his full poetic energy. Parker's extensive footnote references to other scholars have been removed from the extract as given here, as is also the case for Illingworth's.

While Parker's thinking might be described as post-Christian, John Richardson Illingworth (1848–1915) offers an emphatically Christian perspective on the naturalness of the divine. A liberal High Anglican cleric, his contribution to the seminal collection of essays on incarnational theology, *Lux Mundi* (1889), titled 'The Incarnation in Relation to Development', took from Darwinism the implication that the world was a unitary organism inhabited by a progressive divine intelligence. His later book, of which part of chapter 3 is given here, reflects in more detail on the exact nature of this relationship between spirit and matter in a firmly Trinitarian context. He applies the analogy of human personality to show the simultaneous truth of immanence and transcendence, on the grounds that we are materially constituted, yet our transcendent dimension is evident in thought, will and moral choice. This capacity, though, is only realisable in our bodily actions and creations, and the impact we have on other material objects and beings in our environment. While we are more than just matter, matter is the only vehicle for our spirits' communication with others.

By this logic, Illingworth rejects forms of religion that are too reductively materialist, namely pantheism, which he terms 'materialism grown sentimental', and modern forms of monism which deny the possibility of self-consciousness and by extension moral choice. Yet he also rejects an excessive emphasis on the separation of spirit from matter, such as he sees in Enlightenment deism that sets creator apart from the created world in the mechanistic 'watch-maker' model of the deity. He settles on Trinitarian theology as the best available image of divine immanence and transcendence in one, picturing Christ as the incarnation of God (as both the father's creation and habitation), and as a type of what the earth is, and what humans are also to be. Illingworth suggests therefore that religious orthodoxy is an intensification of, not departure from, a natural truth written through the universe, making dogma more acceptable in a sceptical era. As with Parker, the starting point for contemplating the nature of God is not scripture or Church teaching, but ourselves, and the phenomena available to our senses.

Note

1 Linda Woodhead, 'Introduction', in Linda Woodhead (ed.), *Reinventing Christianity: Nineteenth-Century Contexts* (Aldershot: Ashgate, 2001), pp. 1–21, on pp. 2–3; and Boyd Hilton, *The Age of Atonement: The Influence of Evangelicalism on Social and Economic Thought 1795–1865* (Oxford: Clarendon Press, 1988), p. 5.

41

THEODORE PARKER, 'THE RELATION OF THE RELIGIOUS SENTIMENT TO GOD, OR A DISCOURSE OF INSPIRATION' [1842]

In Frances Power Cobbe (ed.), *Collected Works*, 12 vols (London: Trubner & Co., 1863), vol. 1, book 2 pp. 110–117

The relation of Nature to God

To determine the relation of Man to God it is well to determine first the relation of God to Nature—the material world—that we may have the force of the analogy of that relation to aid us. Conscious man may be very dissimilar to unconscious matter, but yet their relations to God are analogous. Both depend on him. To make out the point and decide the relation of God to Nature we must start from the Idea of God, which was laid down above, a Being of Infinite Power, Wisdom, Justice, Love, and Holiness. Now to make the matter clear as noonday, God is either present in all space, or not present in all space. If infinite, he must be present everywhere in general, and not limited to any particular spot, as an old writer so beautifully says: "Even Heaven and the Heaven of Heavens cannot contain Him" [1 Kings 8:27]. Heathen writers are full of such expressions. God, then, is universally present in the world of matter. He is the substantiality of matter. The circle of his being in space has an infinite radius. We cannot say, Lo here, or Lo there—for he is everywhere. He fills all Nature with his overflowing currents; without him it were not. His Presence gives it existence; his Will its law and force; his Wisdom its order; his Goodness its beauty.

It follows unavoidably, from the Idea of God, that he is present everywhere in space; not transiently present, now and then, but immanently present, always; his centre here; his circumference nowhere; just as present in the eye of an emmet as in the Jewish holy of holies, or the sun itself. We may call common what God has cleansed with his presence; but there is no corner of space so small, no atom of matter so despised and little, but God, the Infinite, is there.

Now, to push the inquiry nearer the point. The Nature or Substance of God, as represented by our Idea of him, is divisible or not divisible. If infinite he must be indivisible, a part of God cannot be in this point of space, and another in that; his Power in the sun, his Wisdom in the moon, and his Justice in the earth. He must be wholly, vitally, essentially present, as much in one point as in another point, or all points; as essentially present in each point at any one moment of time as at any other or all moments of time. He is there not idly present but actively, as much now as at creation. Divine omnipotence can neither slumber nor sleep. Was God but transiently active in Matter at creation, his action now passed away? From the Idea of him it follows that He is immanent in the world, however much he also transcends the world. "Our Father worketh hitherto," and for this reason Nature works, and so has done since its creation [John 5:17]. There is no spot the foot of hoary Time has trod on, but it is instinct with God's activity. He is the ground of Nature; what is permanent in the passing; what is real in the apparent. All Nature then is but an exhibition of God to the senses; the veil of smoke on which his shadow falls; the dew-drop in which the heaven of his magnificence is poorly imaged. The Sun is but a sparkle of his splendour. Endless and without beginning flows forth the stream of divine influence that encircles and possesses the all of things. From God it comes, to God it goes. The material world is perpetual growth; a continual transfiguration, renewal that never ceases. Is this without God? Is it not because God, who is ever the same, flows into it without end? It is the fulness of God that flows into the crystal of the rock, the juices of the plant, the life of the emmet and the elephant. He penetrates and pervades the World. All things are full of Him, who surrounds the sun, the stars, the universe itself; "goes through all lands, the expanse of oceans, and the profound Heaven" (Virgil, Georgic IV. 222).

Inanimate matter, by itself, is dependent; incapable of life, motion, or even existence. To assert the opposite is to make it a God. In its present state it has no will. Yet there is in it existence, motion, life. The smallest molecule in a ray of polarized light and the largest planet in the system exist and move as if possessed of a Will, powerful, regular, irresistible. The powers of Nature, then, that of Gravitation, Electricity, Growth, what are they but modes of God's action? If we look deep into the heart of this mystery, such must be the conclusion. Nature is moved by the first Mover; beautified by him who is the Sum of Beauty; animated by him who is of all the Creator, Defence, and Life.

Such, then, is the relation of God to Matter up to this point. He is immanent therein and perpetually active. Now, to go further, if this be true, it would seem that the various objects and things in Nature were fitted to express and reveal different degrees and measures of the divine influence, so to say; that this degree of manifestation in each depends on the capacity which God has primarily bestowed upon it; that the material but inorganic, the vegetable but inanimate, and the animal but irrational world, received each as high a mode of divine influence as its several nature would allow.

Then, to sum up all in brief, the Material World with its objects sublimely great, or meanly little, as we judge them; its atoms of dust, its orbs of fire; the rock that stands by the sea-shore, the water that wears it away; the worm, a birth of yesterday, which we trample underfoot; the streets of constellations that gleam perennial overhead; the aspiring palm tree, fixed to one spot, and the lions that are sent out free, these incarnate and make visible all of God their several natures will admit. If Man were not spiritual, and could yet conceive of the aggregate of invisible things, he might call it God, for he could go no further.

Now, as God is Infinite, imperfection is not to be spoken of Him. His Will therefore—if we may so use that term—is always the same. As Nature has of itself no power, and God is present and active therein, it must obey and represent his unalterable will. Hence, seeing the uniformity of operation, that things preserve their identity, we say they are governed by a Law that never changes. It is so. But this Law—what is it but the Will of God? a mode of divine action? It is this in the last analysis. The apparent secondary causes do not prevent this conclusion.

The things of Nature, having no will, obey this law from necessity. They thus reflect God's image and make real his conception—if we may use such language with this application. They are tools, not Artists. We never in Nature see the smallest departure from Nature's law. The granite, the grass, keep their law; none go astray from the flock of stars; fire does not refuse to burn, nor water to be wet. We look backwards and forwards, but the same law records everywhere the obedience that is paid it. Our confidence in the uniformity of Nature's law is complete, in other words, in the fact that God is always the same; his modes of action always the same. This is true of the inorganic, the vegetable, the animal world. Each thing keeps its law with no attempt at violation of it. From this obedience comes the regularity and order apparent in Nature. Obeying the law of God, his omnipotence is on its side. To oppose a law of Nature, therefore, is to oppose the Deity. It is sure to redress itself.

But these created things have no consciousness, so far as we know, at least, nothing which is the same with our self-consciousness. They have no moral will; no power in general to do otherwise than as they do. Their action is not the result of forethought, reflection, judgment, voluntary obedience to an acknowledged law. No one supposes the Bison, the Rosebush, and the Moon, reflect in themselves; make up their mind and say, "Go to, now, let us bring up our young, or put forth our blossoms, or give light at nightfall, because it is right to do so, and God's law." Their obedience is unavoidable. They do what they cannot help doing. Their obedience, therefore, is not their merit, but their necessity. It is power they passively yield to; not a duty they voluntarily and consciously perform. All the action, therefore, of the material, inorganic, vegetable, and animal world is mechanical, vital, or, at the utmost, instinctive; not self-conscious, the result of private will. There is, therefore, no room for caprice in this department. The Crystal must form itself after a prescribed pattern; the Leaf presume a given shape; the Bee build her cell with six angles. The mantle of Destiny is girt about these things. To study the laws of Nature, therefore, is to study the modes of God's action. Science becomes sacred, and passes into a sort of devotion. Well says the old sage, "Geometry is the praise of God." It reveals the perfections of the Divine Mind, for

God manifests himself in every object of science, in the half-living Molecules of powdered wood; in the Comet with its orbit which imagination cannot surround; in the Cones and Cycloids of the Mathematician, that exist nowhere in the world of concrete things, but which the conscious mind carries thither.

Since all these objects represent, more or less, the divine mind, and are in perfect harmony with it, and so always at one with God, they express, it may be, all of deity which Matter in these three modes can contain, and thus exhibit all of God that can be made manifest to the eye, the ear, and the other senses of man. Since these things are so, Nature is not only strong and beautiful, but has likewise a religious aspect. This fact was noticed in the very earliest times; appears in the rudest worship, which is an adoration of God in Nature. It will move man's heart to the latest day, and exert an influence on souls that are deepest and most holy. Who that looks on the ocean, in its anger or its play; who that walks at twilight under a mountain's brow, listens to the sighing of the pines, touched by the indolent wind of summer, and hears the light tinkle of the brook, murmuring its quiet tune,—who is there but feels the deep Religion of the scene? In the heart of a city we are called away from God. The dust of man's foot and the sooty print of his fingers are on all we see. The very earth is unnatural, and the Heaven scarce seen. In a crowd of busy men which set through its streets, or flow together of a holiday; in the dust and jar, the bustle and strife of business, there is little to remind us of God. Men must build a cathedral for that. But everywhere in nature we are carried straightway back to Him. The fern, green and growing amid the frost, each little grass and lichen, is a silent memento. The first bird of spring, and the last rose of summer; the grandeur or the dulness of evening and morning; the rain, the dew; the sunshine; the stars that come out to watch over the farmer's rising corn; the birds that nestle contentedly, brooding over their young, quietly tending the little strugglers with their beak,—all these have a religious significance to a thinking soul. Every violet blooms of God, each lily is fragrant with the presence of deity. The awful scenes, of storm, and lightning and thunder, seem but the sterner sounds of the great concert, wherewith God speaks to man. Is this an accident? Ay, earth is full of such "accidents." When the seer rests from religious thought, or when the world's temptations make his soul tremble, and though the spirit be willing the flesh is weak; when the perishable body weighs down the mind, musing on many things; when he wishes to draw near to God, he goes, not to the city—there conscious men obstruct him with their works—but to the meadow, spangled all over with flowers, and sung to by every bird; to the mountain, "visited all night by troops of stars;" to the ocean, the undying type of shifting phenomena and unchanging law; to the forest, stretching out motherly arms, with its mighty growth and awful shade, and there, in the obedience these things pay, in their order, strength, beauty, he is encountered front to front with the awful presence of Almighty power. A voice cries to him from the thicket, "God will provide." The bushes burn with deity. Angels minister to him. There is no mortal pang, but it is allayed by God's fair voice as it whispers, in nature, still and small, it may be, but moving on the face of the deep, and bringing light out of darkness.

> Oh Joy that in our embers
> Is something that doth live,
> That Nature yet remembers
> What was so fugitive.

Now to sum up the result. It seems from the very Idea of God that he must be infinitely present in each point of space. This immanence of God in Matter is the basis of his influence; this is modified by the capacities of the objects in Nature; all of its action is God's action; its laws modes of that action. The imposition of a law, then, which is perfect, and is also perfectly obeyed, though blindly and without self-consciousness, seems to be the measure of God's relation to Matter. Its action therefore is only mechanical, vital or instinctive, not voluntary and self-conscious. From the nature of these things, it must be so.

Statement of the analogy drawn from God's relation to Nature

Now if God be present in Matter, the analogy is that he is also present in Man. But to examine this point more closely, let us set out as before from the Idea of God. If he have not the limitations of matter, but is Infinite, as the Idea declares, then he pervades Spirit as well as Space; is in Man as well as out of him. If it follows from the Idea that he is immanent in the Material World—in a moss; it follows also that he must be immanent in the Spiritual world—in a man. If he is immanently active, and thus totally and essentially present, in each corner of Space, and each Atom of creation, then is he as universally present in all Spirit. If the reverse be true, then he is not omnipresent, therefore not Infinite, and of course not God. The Infinite God must fill each point of Spirit as of Space. Here then, in God's presence in the soul, is a basis laid for his direct influence on men; as his presence in Nature is the basis of his direct influence there.

As in Nature his influence was modified only by the capacities of material things, so here must it be modified only by the capabilities of spiritual things; there is assumed the forms of mechanical, vital, and instinctive action; here it must ascend to the form of voluntary and self-conscious action. This conclusion follows undeniably from the analogy of God's presence and activity in Matter. It follows as necessarily from the Idea of God, for as he is the materiality of Matter, so is he the spirituality of Spirit.

42

J. R. ILLINGWORTH, 'DIVINE IMMANENCE IN NATURE'

In *Divine Immanence: An Essay on the Spiritual Significance of Matter* (London: Macmillan, 1898), pp. 64–73

What is the relation of the material universe to that Spirit of which it so persistently seems to speak? The experience with which we are dealing has, as we have seen, been historically compatible with theories of every description; but those theories are not all equally tenable on other grounds.

Polytheism and dualism, for instance, are no longer possible interpretations; for the universe is obviously one. Its unity of structure and development, though often maintained in other ages, has been placed by modern science in an entirely new light; and that unity leaves no place for the thought of contradictory beings at its helm. If the system of things be guided by spiritual power, that power must be ultimately one. And if we are to form any further conjecture of the way in which this Spirit is related to the material order, we must recur to the starting-point of all our knowledge, namely, ourselves. Human personality, however little we may comprehend it, is yet the thing that we know best, as being the only thing that we know at first hand, and from within. And further, human personality exhibits spirit and matter in combination; such intimate combination that, as we have seen above, they do not admit of being completely sundered. It is in human personality alone, therefore, that we must look for light upon our subject; the limited light indeed of a lantern carried in our own uncertain hand, but still the only light that we can possibly possess.

Now we find on reflection that what we call our spirit transcends, or is, in a sense, independent of the bodily organism on which otherwise it so entirely depends. Metaphysically speaking this is seen in our self-consciousness, or power of separating our self as subject from our self as object, a thing wholly inconceivable as the result of any material process, and relating us at once to an order of being which we are obliged to call immaterial. But as metaphysical analysis is 'caviare to the general,' while the metaphysically-minded will find this point amply illustrated by most modern philosophers, it will be sufficient for our purpose to appeal to the more familiar field of morals.

Morally speaking, we are responsible for our actions. That is a fact which no sane man doubts. It is the assumption on which the whole course of our political and social life is carried on; and if a man takes leave to deny it, except in theory, law soon interferes for his correction. There is no fact in the world that, in their misery, men would more gladly have denied; yet they are agreed to treat its denial as a manifest absurdity. Surely, then, it is as strong a conviction as any that can be conceived. And this conviction is amply sufficient for our purpose; for it implies that we are self-identical and free, the same personal unit to-day that we were when born—whereas all the matter of our bodies has changed—and capable of determining ourselves from within, whereas all matter is determined by something else, and from without. Our present object is not to argue these points, which have been argued abundantly elsewhere, but simply to refer to them, as results of past argument, in illustration of the fact that, with all our dependence upon matter, we yet transcend it; we move in a plane above it, and are, though in a limited degree, its masters and not its slaves. This, then, is one aspect of the relation between spirit and matter, as known within the circle of our own personality. And when we pass beyond that circle to mould the external world to our use, through various forms of scientific invention, and artistic creation, it becomes still more apparent that spirit has a dominant and transcendent relation to matter.

But from another point of view our spirit may be described as 'immanent' in matter. It not only works through the brain and nervous system, but, as a result, pervades the entire organism, animating and inspiring it with its own 'peculiar difference'; so that we recognize a man's character in the expression of his eye, the tone of his voice, the touch of his hand; his unconscious and instinctive postures, and gestures, and gait. Nor is this 'immanence' confined to the bodily organism. It extends, in what may be called a secondary degree, to the inanimate objects of the external world. For a man imprints his spiritual character upon all the things with which he deals, his house, his clothes, his furniture, the various products of his hand or head. And when we speak of a man's spirit surviving in his works, the expression is no mere metaphor; for through those works, even though dead and gone, he continues to influence his fellowmen. And when we look at the pictures of Raffaelle, or listen to the music of Beethoven, or read the poetry of Dante, or the philosophy of Plato, the spirit of the great Masters is affecting us as really as if we saw them face to face: it is immanent in the painted canvas and the printed page.

Spirit then, as we know it in our own personal experience, has two different relations to matter, that of transcendence, and that of immanence. But though logically distinct, these two relations are not actually separate; they are two aspects of one fact; two points of view from which the single action of our one personality may be regarded. As self-conscious, self-identical, self-determined, we possess qualities which transcend or rise above the laws of matter; but we can only realize these qualities, and so become aware of them, by acting in the material world; while conversely material objects—our bodies, and our works of art—could never possibly be regarded as expressions of spirit, if spirit were not at the same time recognized as distinct from its medium of manifestation.

If then we are to raise the question, 'what is the relation of the supreme Spirit to the material universe?' this is the analogy upon which we must proceed; for we have no other. We may indeed decline the problem as wholly insoluble; but if we attempt its solution at all, it must of necessity be upon the lines of the only experience which we possess—this experience in which transcendence and immanence are combined.

This at once excludes pantheism, the belief that God is merely immanent in matter; for attractive as this creed has often seemed to worshippers of nature, it cannot really be construed into thought. Spirit which is merely immanent in matter, without also transcending it, cannot be spirit at all; it is only another aspect of matter, having neither self-identity nor freedom. Pantheism is thus really indistinguishable from materialism; it is merely materialism grown sentimental, but no more tenable for its change of name.

The logical opposite of pantheism is deism, in the sense of belief in a merely transcendent God; and this is equally inconsistent with our analogy; for as we have no experience whatever of spirit or matter as existing apart, we cannot conceive either term of the deistic universe. But deism of this kind, though it has occupied an important place in history, is scarcely a form of thought with which at the present day we need to reckon. It belongs to a metaphysical rather than a scientific atmosphere and age.

Yet another view of the question has been suggested under the name of monism; the view that 'matter in motion is substantially identical with mind,' that they are two aspects of one thing, which from the outside we call matter, and from the inside mind. At first sight this seems only another name for materialism; and, in fact, the word monism is expressly used by Haeckel as synonymous with scientific materialism. But its use has also been advocated in a theistic sense; the mental aspect being regarded as prior in importance, though not in existence to the material,—a position very much akin to Spinozism. Now the supposed advantage of this theory is, that it abolishes all the difficulties of dualism. But it is obviously no more than an imaginative conjecture, and upon what does it rest? 'We have only to suppose that the antithesis between mind and motion—subject and object—is itself phenomenal or apparent, not absolute or real' (G. R. Romanes, *Mind and Matter; and Monism [Mind and Motion; and Monism]*, 1895). That is to say that, when we are confronted in our personal experience with a dualism, whose mystery we cannot solve, we may at once attain intellectual satisfaction, by the simple expedient of assuming it to be an illusion. But this is precisely what the materialist does, and is condemned for doing; and we are no more justified in discrediting the primary facts of consciousness in the interests of spirit, than in the interests of matter. Monism, in short, whether material or spiritual, is not based upon what we know in ourselves, and what is, to that extent, solid fact; but upon distrust of what we think we know in ourselves—a sceptical foundation, which cannot possibly support a positive conclusion. It should further be noticed that, in the above quotation, mind and matter are treated as synonymous with subject and object. This in itself is a mistake, but a mistake essential to the theory. For it is only by considering mind as a mere series of subjective or mental states, that we can plausibly consider motion as its parallel concomitant. But the characteristic of mind, as we know it in our personal spirit, is that it is both subject and object at once; it is capable of becoming its own object, and saying I am I. It is through this power of self-consciousness or self-diremption, that spirit transcends matter, as we have already had occasion to point out; and it is precisely this power which we are unable to conceive as having any material equivalent. Monism, in fact, started from the physical side, from analysis of the cerebral conditions of thought; it rests on physical analogies, and is coloured by physical modes of thought; and the attempt to make it metaphysically tenable seems an impossible *tour de force*.

It remains then that we confine ourselves to the analogy of our personal experience, and conceive of God as at once transcending and immanent in nature; for however incomprehensible this relationship may be, we know it in our own case to be a fact, and may legitimately infer its analogue outside ourselves.

On this analogy then, the divine presence which we recognize in nature will be the presence of a Spirit, which infinitely transcends the material order, yet sustains and indwells it the while. We cannot indeed explain the method, either of the transcendence, or of the indwelling; but we come no nearer to an explanation, by attempting, with any of the above-mentioned theories, to obtain simplicity by suppressing either aspect of the only analogy that we possess. But it will be remembered that in our own case we noticed two degrees of immanence; our essential immanence in our body, which is consequently often called our person; and our contingent immanence in the works which we are free to create or not at will. The question therefore inevitably arises, under which of these analogies are we to think of God's relation to the world. Is the universe His body, or His work? Different answers have been given to this question by different thinkers; and it is obvious that no answer can be more than conjectural or hypothetical.

Under these circumstances we are entitled to urge, that the Trinitarian conception of God, which we Christians have independent reasons for believing to be true, is intellectually the most satisfactory; since it embraces both the kinds of immanence in question, and therefore harmonizes with the entire analogy of our personal experience. For according to this doctrine, the Second Person of the Trinity is the essential, adequate, eternal manifestation of the First, 'the express image of His person,' 'in whom dwelleth the fulness of the Godhead bodily,' while 'by Him all things were made.' Here then we have our two degrees of immanence; the complete immanence of the Father in the Son, of which our own relation to our body is an inadequate type; and, as a result of this, His immanence in creation, analogous to our presence in our works; with the obvious difference, of course, that we finite beings who die and pass away, can only be impersonally present in our works; whereas He must be conceived as ever present to sustain and animate the universe, which thus becomes a living manifestation of Himself;—no mere machine, or book, or picture, but a perpetually sounding voice.